New Directions in Ethics

Series editors: Marcia Baron, Indiana University, and Michael Slote, University of Miami

This series seeks to take advantage of and promote the richness and diversity that have characterized recent work in ethics. It construes the ethical in a broad way that includes moral theory, legal philosophy, political philosophy, applied ethics, moral psychology, and the history of ethics; and it will include ambitious new work within the major traditions as well as contributions that don't necessarily fit within familiar categories. Books appearing in the series will be non-technical and accessible in a way that invites broader readership; they will include work not only by established scholars but also by promising newcomers.

The Virtue Ethics of Hume and Nietzsche

Christine Swanton

WILEY Blackwell

This edition first published 2015
© 2015 John Wiley & Sons, Ltd.

Registered Office
John Wiley & Sons Ltd, The Atrium, Southern Gate, Chichester, West Sussex,
PO19 8SQ, UK

Editorial Offices
350 Main Street, Malden, MA 02148-5020, USA
9600 Garsington Road, Oxford, OX4 2DQ, UK
The Atrium, Southern Gate, Chichester, West Sussex, PO19 8SQ, UK

For details of our global editorial offices, for customer services, and for information about how
to apply for permission to reuse the copyright material in this book please see our website at
www.wiley.com/wiley-blackwell.

Library of Congress Cataloging-in-Publication Data
Swanton, Christine, 1947–
    The virtue ethics of Hume and Nietzsche / Christine Swanton.
        pages   cm
    Includes bibliographical references and index.
    ISBN 978-1-118-93939-0 (cloth)
1. Hume, David, 1711–1776.   2. Nietzsche, Friedrich Wilhelm, 1844–1900.   3. Ethics.
4. Virtue.   I. Title.
    B1499.E8S93 2015
    171′.30922–dc23
                                                    2014049534
A catalogue record for this book is available from the British Library.

Cover image: L: Engraved portrait of David Hume © Biblioteca de Catalunya, Barcelona / iberfoto /
Superstock. R: Portrait of Friedrich Nietzsche c. 1905 © Nicku / Shutterstock

Set in 10/12pt Minion by SPi Publisher Services, Pondicherry, India
Printed and bound in Singapore by Markono Print Media Pte Ltd

1   2015

To the memory of Bob Solomon

Contents

Preface

This book is dedicated to the late Robert Solomon whose regular visits to the University of Auckland Philosophy Department over a period of many years caused, by a process of osmosis, an increasing appreciation of the resources for ethics of the Continental tradition and particularly Nietzsche. Both he and Kathy Higgins, to whom I am also indebted, helped me to see how the area of virtue ethics could be enriched by attention to not only Continental philosophy but also psychology including psychoanalysis, important for a study of Nietzsche.

In the case of Hume, my interest was also triggered by people, devotees of Hume, and in particular those attending a Hume Society dinner at an APA Pacific Meeting whose attendees displayed all the Humean virtues of charm, cheerfulness, and friendliness, not to mention wit. They encouraged me to attend the International Hume Society Conference in Utah which featured many great papers on Hume's ethics, and I was hooked. My thanks in particular to Jackie Taylor, and Rachel Cohon. I owe thanks also to Anne Jacobson for encouraging me to write a paper for her edited collection *Feminist Interpretations of Hume*.

I am indebted to Julian Young, a former colleague, for many conversations on Nietzsche (and Heidegger) and for inviting me to present at a conference on communitarian aspects of Nietzsche's thought at Wake Forest. My thoughts on Nietzsche and altruism were also developed in an invited paper at the University of Southampton at a conference on Nietzsche.

I would like to thank Garrett Cullity for comments on response dependence, and many conversations and comments on the thick concepts. I am grateful too to my PhD student Nicholas Smith who provided comments on all chapters of my penultimate draft, and who had an unerring eye for weaknesses and obscurities. Thanks Nick.

A great debt of gratitude is due also to the series editors Marcia Baron and Michael Slote who made comments on all chapters of earlier drafts, which resulted in considerable improvements.

Acknowledgments to previously published work are as follows:

Chapter 3 is a modified and extended form of "Can Hume Be Read as a Virtue Ethicist?" *Hume Studies* 33 (2007), 91–113. Reprinted with permission.

Chapter 6 contains some material from "Nietzsche and the Collective Individual" in *Individual and Community in Nietzsche's Philosophy*, ed. Julian Young (Cambridge: Cambridge University Press, 2014), 302–335. © Cambridge University Press 2014, reprinted with permission.

Chapter 7 contains material from "Can Nietzsche Be Both an Existentialist and a Virtue Ethicist" in *Values and Virtues*, ed. Timothy Chappell (Oxford: Oxford University Press, 2006), 171–188. © Oxford University Press 2006, reprinted with permission.

Chapter 8 contains material from "Robert Solomon's Aristotelian Nietzsche" in *Passion, Death and Spirituality: The Philosophy of Robert C. Solomon*, ed. Kathleen Higgins and David Sherman (Dordrecht: Springer, 2012), 113–126. © Springer 2012, reprinted with permission.

In this work I use the Selby-Bigge, Nidditch, and Miller editions of Hume's *A Treatise of Human Nature*; the *Enquiries Concerning the Principles of Morals*; and the *Essays Moral, Literary and Political*, respectively. I also made an effort to include the Norton and Norton paragraph citations to the *Treatise* in the first citation of a passage. Abbreviations used for these purposes are:

E = *Enquiries Concerning Human Understanding and Concerning the Principles of Morals*, 3rd edition, ed. P.H. Nidditch (Oxford: Clarendon Press, 1975)

Miller = *Essays, Moral, Political, and Literary*, ed. Eugene F. Miller (Indianapolis: Liberty Fund, 1987)

T = *A Treatise of Human Nature*, ed. L.A. Selby-Bigge (Oxford: Clarendon Press, 1968), preceded where applicable by the paragraph numbering of David and Mary Norton's edition (Oxford: Clarendon Press, 2000)

Christine Swanton
Auckland, New Zealand
August, 2014

Introduction

As is well known by now, virtue ethics is a vibrant development in modern substantive moral theorizing, no longer in its infancy. What is relatively new in that development is the deployment of texts other than those of the ancient Greek moral theorists, for contemporary virtue ethics has to date been dominated by the eudaimonist tradition of the ancients, notably Aristotle. Yet other philosophers can also be seen as having an ethics of character, and as rich sources for the future development of virtue ethics. For Hume and Nietzsche to be included within this category, a virtue ethical interpretation of their texts is needed, just as attention to Aristotle's texts has underpinned neo-Aristotelian virtue ethics. The task of this book is to provide just such an interpretation.

Hume and Nietzsche are among the great philosophers in the field of ethics. Yet it is still a matter of controversy how their moral philosophy should be read. Are they skeptics or immoralists, relativists or subjectivists, of perhaps an existentialist kind (in the case of Nietzsche) or sentimentalist kind (in the case of Hume). If their moral theory is to be read as objectivist and substantive should they be read as consequentialists, or perhaps virtue ethicists? This book rejects readings which are neither realist nor objectivist, offering instead a virtue ethical map of their moral philosophy.

Yet their moral theorizing has been understood as starkly different from each other, so much so that it may seem odd to think of them both as virtue ethicists. Hume and his predecessors such as Francis Hutcheson have been described as "warm" while Nietzsche is "cool" (if not downright cold and ruthless).[1] Nietzsche is popularly thought of as an immoralist egoist, while Hume on recent interpretations is seen as a forerunner of an ethics of care.[2] On my view this contrast should not be overstated. Hume has a central role for self-love in his moral philosophy as well as for benevolence, while Nietzsche is not an egoist in a crude sense, making room for altruistic virtue properly understood. For Hume, lack of self-love contaminates character; not only is a person so afflicted "abject" but her self-contempt underlies vices such as tendencies to insolence (to inferiors) and servility (to superiors). Nietzsche traces the role of self-contempt in vice more extensively. By contrast with Nietzsche, Hume focuses more on other-regarding aspects of virtue and vice. However in a "Wide Reflective Equilibrium" of the "Grand Unified Virtue Ethics" the thoughts of these thinkers and others would be integrated, but that mammoth task is not attempted here.

In a work which purports to offer virtue ethical interpretations of philosophers who have not traditionally been read in this way, four basic questions need to be addressed.

(1)   Given that my interpretation presupposes that virtue ethics is not defined in terms of the eudaimonist tradition of the ancients, how should we understand virtue ethics, and a virtue ethical interpretation?

(2)   Why should the ethical writings of Hume and Nietzsche be understood as fitting naturally into the virtue ethical fold?

(3)   Granted that there are features of Hume and Nietzsche which might appear to provide insuperable obstacles to a virtue ethical interpretation, how can these features be seen as compatible with a virtue ethical map of their thought?

(4)   Given that the virtue ethics of Hume and Nietzsche differs from that of Aristotle, what aspects of their ethical writings add to the virtue ethical tradition broadly conceived?

The first two problems are the topics of Part I. Chapter 1 discusses the idea of interpretation as a map, and argues that virtue ethics should be seen as a genus (or more accurately a family) of moral theory. More particularly virtue ethics as such is a family; Aristotelian (or neo-Aristotelian) virtue ethics is a genus of virtue ethics; while Aristotle's virtue ethics is a species of virtue ethics. This understanding, which I argue mirrors deontology as a family, Kantian ethics as a genus, and Kant as a species of deontology, allows for the possibility of Nietzsche and Hume being read as virtue ethicists.

Can Hume and Nietzsche be seen as natural candidates for interpretation as virtue ethicists? It would seem so, for the normative ethical concepts under scrutiny in both Nietzsche and Hume are qualities of persons and actions as described by the so-called thick concepts, such as truthful, honest, just, benevolent, as well as charming, witty, hasty, attentive, complaining, craving solitude, joyful, and a host of others. This feature of Nietzsche's and Hume's works makes their ethical writings extremely rich and subtle. Furthermore their focus on the thick concepts allows for no natural place to drive an important distinction between the moral and the non-moral. A vast number of virtues are all important to varying degrees, in varying circumstances, to leading a good life proper to human beings. Leading such a life is the overarching organizing concept in their moral theorizing, as it is for Aristotle, and indeed for virtue ethics in general.

Not only are Nietzsche's and Hume's writings notable for the prevalence of thick concepts, the excellences of character (virtues) are central in their moral theorizing.

It is not unusual now for Hume to be read as part of a virtue ethical tradition. Jacqueline Taylor claims that "Hume's moral philosophy may plausibly be construed as a version of virtue ethics [for] among the *central* concepts of his theory are character, virtue and vice, rather than rules, duty, and obligation."[3] This reason for classing Hume as a virtue ethicist conforms to my basic definition of virtue ethics in *Virtue Ethics: A Pluralistic View*,[4] and elaborated in my article "The Definition of Virtue Ethics"[5] according to which virtue ethical theories are those in which virtue concepts are central. Nietzsche too has been seen as a fitting subject for a virtue ethical reading. In his *Living With Nietzsche*,[6] Robert C. Solomon maps Nietzsche onto Aristotle in a fundamental respect. Agreeing with Julius Moravscik's claim that Aristotle and Nietzsche were "two of a kind … both functionalists, both naturalists, both 'teleologists,' standing very much opposed to the utilitarians and Kantians," Solomon claims: "Nietzsche's ethics, like Aristotle's can best be classified in introductory ethics readers as an ethics of 'self realization.' "[7] Accordingly, for him, "what is essential to this view of ethics … an ethics of virtue, aretaic ethics – is that the emphasis is wholly on excellence, a teleological conception."[8] Chapters 6 and 7 elaborate the way in which excellence features centrally in Nietzsche within a self-realizationist understanding of the doctrine of will to power. Essential to this understanding is taking seriously Nietzsche's claim that psychology is the "queen of the sciences," for it is through his psychology, in particular the psychology that goes beyond the surfaces of human motivation to its "depths," that we can understand the way in which "will to power" is distorted or otherwise. This qualitative evaluation of will to power is the key to understanding the difference between virtue and vice in Nietzsche.

Despite the apparent naturalness of embracing Hume and Nietzsche within the virtue ethical fold, serious obstacles to such a reading exist. The third basic question above thus needs to be addressed: in Part II I consider problems raised by Hume's sentimentalism and notion of justice, and in Part III problems raised by Nietzsche's apparent egoism, immoralism, and existentialism. Consider first Hume, the subject of Part II. To be clear about the task ahead, let me summarize how you *cannot* read Hume if he is to be part of the virtue ethical tradition. All of the following common readings of Hume have to be rejected.

(A) *A "non-sensible" subjectivist.* Wiggins's "sensible subjectivism" I do not regard as incompatible with virtue ethics. Discussion of this issue is a topic of Chapter 3. There I argue for an (emotional) response dependence interpretation of Hume which allows for a realist and objectivist interpretation of virtue, according to which properties of persons can be properly understood as "naturally fitted" to be called virtues. This view is the essence of Hume's sentimentalism; hence I argue that a virtue ethical map is compatible with Hume's sentimentalism.

(B) *A non-rationalist.* In standard virtue ethics, ethics is at least in part a reason giving and reason responsive enterprise. In Chapter 3 I show how Hume can be understood as conceiving ethics as a rational enterprise of a kind compatible with virtue ethics. Central to this view is the idea that the "Reason" proper to the operations of what Hume calls the faculty of understanding does not exhaust the space of rationality, and indeed the view of ethics as a reason responsive enterprise.

(C) *A hedonist.* To show that Hume can be read as a virtue ethicist one also needs to show that he has an aretaic conception of many important values such as pleasure. This is a complex but vital issue for a virtue ethical reading, so in this Introduction I shall say a little about it. According to virtue ethics, many so-called values are not truly values or goods unless they are, as we may say, infused with virtue. Pleasure, on this view, is not, as Aristotle would put it, good without qualification unless it exhibits virtue. As I have argued elsewhere, virtue ethics rejects "list theories" of the good or "values" which subscribe to what I have called "The Thesis of Non-Aretaic Value": "Virtues and vices are understood derivatively as forms of responsiveness to, or as instrumental in the promotion of (or minimization of respectively) 'base-level' goods or evils, or intrinsic values or disvalues, understood non-aretaically."[9]

Can Hume be seen as rejecting such a thesis? Although he does not actively address the issue, his writings, by comparison with modern theories, are shot through with aretaic notions, such as decency, admirability, good breeding, and politeness, which inform the value notions. For example one may think that cheerfulness is a virtue simply because it spreads pleasure. But not so for Hume; his view is more sophisticated than that. What merits approbation is cheerfulness which diffuses pleasure having a certain aretaic quality, dependent on the status of those spreading cheer, and on the nature of the pleasure as temperate and decent: "In all polite nations and ages, a relish for pleasure, if accompanied with temperance and decency, is esteemed a considerable merit, even in the greatest men; and becomes still more requisite in those of inferior rank and character" (E para. 203, 251).

The passage suggests that the status of cheerfulness as a virtue is dependent on the aretaic *sources* of the pleasure diffused, as well as on the aretaic *nature* of that pleasure. Pleasure can be indecent, crude, impolite, and intemperate, and if it possesses these qualities it is no longer valuable or good.

Another problem lies in the fact that Hume says in the *Treatise* that "the very essence of virtue ... is to produce pleasure and that of vice to give pain" (T 2.1.7.4 / 296). This may suggest a hedonistic reading of the *criteria* of virtue. However as I argue in Chapters 2 and 3, Hume's remark concerns meta-ethics and not the criteria of virtue. The claim about essence refers to Hume's response dependent view of virtue: one might say that just as it is the "essence" of redness to produce red sensations, so it is the "essence" of virtue to produce pleasure (more specifically that kind of pleasure which constitutes the *moral* sense). In fact, directly after the quoted passage, Hume claims that "the virtue and vice must be part of our character in order to excite pride and humility." He is referring to the definition of virtue as a power to elicit certain sentiments. In short, as I shall argue, to read the claim about essence as endorsing a hedonistic understanding of the criteria of virtue is to confuse the definition of virtue and the moral sense, with the criteria of virtue.

(D) *A consequentialist.* Virtue ethics is a type of non-consequentialist normative ethical theory, because not all virtues have as their point or rationale the promotion of good, or value. Some are virtues because they are expressive of flourishing states (e.g., joyfulness), some are closely connected to respect and status (e.g., justice and honesty), some are centrally concerned with the manifestation of love, affection, or other bonds between individuals or between individuals and institutions or projects (e.g., friendship, loyalty, perseverance). Responsiveness expressive of bonds in, for example, grief is not and need not be proportional to degree or strength of value. Consequences then are not the only things that matter morally for the virtue ethicist.

In Chapter 5 (and also in Chapter 4 in relation to justice) I argue in detail that Hume should be read in this manner, as a pluralistic non-consequentialist about virtue. Though we may admire and take delight in some, indeed most, virtues because they are effective in promoting some end – the good of mankind – some may be delighted in and admired for other reasons. Hume's system allows for the possibility that judgments about what traits are virtues may be correctly grounded in features other than consequences, features that also make a trait "naturally fitting" for possession by human beings. Charm, tenderness, enthusiasm for dazzling qualities may be fitting or not, for all kinds of reasons. For example, charm that is fitting is engaging, as opposed to sleazy or insincere; the right sort of honesty is honorable as opposed to weak divulgence of what should not be divulged; proper deference, opposed to servile deference, is well bred; attentiveness can be delicate, as opposed to invasive; tenderness can be cloying or fittingly expressive of affection. One of the marks of an authoritative judge is that she is discriminating, and is able to distinguish between the excessive joyfulness of a mind "disordered by the frenzies of enthusiasm" ("Of Refinement in the Arts," Miller 299) and healthy joyfulness. Charm that is employed in a manipulative way to get a job, is unnaturally excessive, or is expressive of a narcissistic personality, will not give immediate pleasure to an authoritative judge. It will not be registered as engaging. This permits considerable latitude allowed by difference in social custom: what might count as excessive politeness or charm in Australasia may not be regarded as such elsewhere. There is not here however a recipe for relativism: much scope for social critique exists.

It is unquestionable that virtue and vice are the central objects of moral evaluation for Hume, but if any of the above types of interpretation are correct he can be read as a theorist of virtue but not as a virtue ethicist.

Second, let me summarize common understandings of Nietzsche which also have to be rejected if he is to be understood as a virtue ethicist.

(A) *An egoist (of an "immoralist" kind).* In Chapter 6 I argue that the sense in which Nietzsche is an egoist is compatible with a virtuous altruism. Nietzsche subscribes to what may be called "virtuous egoism" and attacks what may be called non-virtuous altruism. Central to virtuous egoism is affirmation of one's *own* life, and central to non-virtuous altruism is that it is self-sacrificing in a deplorable way. Virtuous egoism for Nietzsche, I argue, is compatible with having a stake in one's society and other people, and is to be contrasted with the egoism of the immature.

(B) *A perfectionist-consequentialist.* According to this view, life affirmation is not for all; the point of many lives is to be mere instruments for the production of the highest good, whether understood as the highest form of culture or the highest types of human being. In Chapter 6 I argue against this view, distinguishing it from the much more benign view that even if the above are the highest values, the majority are not to be seen as mere instruments for its production. Rather the failure of the "herd" to affirm their *own* lives in ways proper to *them* (e.g., such failures as being lazy, excessively imitative, hedonistic, complacent, resentment-filled) creates an environment completely inimical to the development of "man's lucky hits": the higher types.

(C) *A consequentialist about power.* According to this type of consequentialism the highest value is power, a value to be maximized, either within an egoist or non-egoist consequentialist moral framework. From the perspective of a virtue ethical interpretation the problem here is structurally similar to the problem of reading Hume as a hedonist. To be a virtue ethicist, Nietzsche has to have an aretaic conception of power, or the "will to power." According to this conception, at the core of virtue is undistorted will to power, whereas vice is marked by distorted kinds. Taking seriously the importance Nietzsche places on depth psychology, I argue in Chapters 6 and 7 for an evaluation of will to power as qualitative, showing how vice is characteristically marked by distorted forms of will to power as forms of escape from self. A number of distortions are discussed through understanding Nietzsche via the psychological dissection of Freudian and Adlerian conceptions of neurosis and perversion characterizing self-sacrifice, resentment, forms of punitive rigoristic "justice" unleavened by grace, cruelty, bad conscience, and forms of the ascetic ideal.

(D) *A moral relativist.* Nietzsche's apparent relativization of virtue to types of human beings, as well as his perspectivism about knowledge, have led to understandings of Nietzsche as a moral relativist. I argue against this view in Chapter 8, showing how a universalism in Nietzsche's conception of many important virtues such as generosity, justice, consideration (respect), wisdom, is compatible with a sophisticated relativization of virtue to such factors as one's talents, strength, and the narrative particularities of one's life. This relativization occurs within a dynamic "virtue ethics of becoming," described further in Chapter 10.

Consider now the fourth question posed earlier. It is not enough to show how Nietzsche and Hume can be read as virtue ethicists; we want to know how they in their different ways take virtue ethics further than does Aristotle. What new insights would virtue ethicists do well to examine? Consider first Hume. Book II of the *Treatise*, "The Passions," provides an insightful and remarkably detailed account of various emotions and feelings ranging from love and pride, hope and joy, esteem and contempt, compassion and benevolence. This discussion is of immense value for accounts of the virtues, and what makes traits virtues. What I call "virtue clusters" are associated with these various "passions." We can speak accordingly of the joy-based cluster, the pride-based cluster, the esteem-based cluster, and so on. Of particular importance is the fact that attention to the nature of these clusters allows for an understanding that the features which make traits virtues are quite varied. For example, passions such as grief and love in the form of tenderness, affection, friendship speak to the bonds we have between individuals, and as Hume makes clear, in for example his discussion of grief, the strength and virtuousness of bonds does not necessarily track the value of those to whom we are bonded. Again, Hume speaks of virtuous modes of deference, at the core of which is the passion of esteem, according to status properties. The variety of features which make traits virtues demonstrate, as I argue in Chapter 5, that Hume should be read as a pluralist about virtue of a non-consequentialist kind.

It is unquestionable in my view that the great contribution made by Nietzsche to virtue ethics is his depth psychological account of the nature of virtue and vice. Unlike traditional virtue ethics Nietzsche focuses on motivational failings of great concern to the existentialist tradition, forms of escape from self, which are the topics of Chapters 6 and 7. Chapter 6 is specifically occupied with one such form, escape from self into otherness manifested by the self-sacrificing individual. Nietzsche is especially concerned too with escape from one's individuality, creativity, and "genius" manifested by the "herd" personality in his hedonism, laziness, imitativeness, and complacency. Resentment as externalized self-contempt is also a "danger of dangers" for Nietzsche, for its powerful cultural contagion results finally in an overturning of values into those which suit the weak, values which provide a hostile environment for the development of "higher" human beings.

In keeping with the name of the series to which this book is a contribution, Part IV "New Directions" addresses another aspect of the fourth question above: Can we see Hume and Nietzsche heralding new types of virtue ethics? In Chapter 9 I outline a virtue ethics of love which is inspired by Hume's notion of love discussed in Chapter 5. In Chapter 10 I explore a Nietzschean virtue ethics of creativity inspired by the dynamic features of Nietzsche's notion of overcoming, and his elusive phrase "Become who you are."

Notes

1 See Michael Slote, "Agent-Based Virtue Ethics," *Midwest Studies in Philosophy*, 20 (1995), 83–101.
2 See, e.g., Anne Jaap Jacobson, *Feminist Interpretations of David Hume* (University Park: Pennsylvania State University Press, 2000); Michael Slote, *Morals from Motives* (Oxford: Oxford University Press, 2001), viii–ix.
3 "Virtue and the Evaluation of Character," in *The Blackwell Guide to Hume's Treatise*, ed. Saul Traiger (Oxford: Blackwell, 2005), 276–295. My italics.
4 *Virtue Ethics: A Pluralistic View* (Oxford: Oxford University Press, 2003), 4–5.
5 "The Definition of Virtue Ethics," in *The Cambridge Companion to Virtue Ethics*, ed. Daniel Russell (Cambridge: Cambridge University Press, 2013), 315–338.
6 *Living With Nietzsche: What the Great "Immoralist" Has to Teach Us* (Oxford: Oxford University Press, 2003).
7 Ibid., 129.
8 Ibid., 131.
9 *Virtue Ethics: A Pluralistic View*, 34.

Part I
A Virtue Ethical Map

Chapter 1

Interpretation as a Map

1.1 The Notion of an Interpretative Map

In recent times there has been a broadening and enrichment of the church of virtue ethics: Aristotle and neo-Aristotelianism are no longer seen as the sole inspiration for modern developments of a virtue ethical tradition.[1] Hume and Nietzsche are now important figures in this trend, but to fully justify this view we need to see how their philosophies can reasonably be seen as species of virtue ethics.

Placing philosophers within certain philosophical traditions is a fraught business, which requires some justification. To situate Hume and Nietzsche within a virtue ethical tradition in particular may raise eyebrows. Marcia Baron puts the problem this way:

> The history of ethics is not generally well served by asking whether Kant, or Rousseau or Hume counts as a –ist, where the relevant "ism" was developed in an entirely different era, responding to very different concerns from those that animated the work of the person in question.[2]

To classify Hume as a sentimentalist or as a moral sense theorist is acceptable. To classify him as a virtue ethicist, however, may fall foul of the worry: it may unhelpfully employ a category whose home in a modern context is a protagonist in modern debates about, for example, consequentialism versus deontology, conducted in books such as *Three Methods of Ethics*.[3] In Hume's day the central debates were between moral sense theorists and the Rationalists. In Nietzsche's times cultural critique within a historicist *Volkisch* tradition emphasizing concepts such as heritage and decadence held sway.

The Virtue Ethics of Hume and Nietzsche, First Edition. Christine Swanton.
© 2015 John Wiley & Sons, Ltd. Published 2015 by John Wiley & Sons, Ltd.

As the hermeneutic tradition has taught us, however, interpreting texts is an ongoing process, characterized not only by a sensitivity to the historical conditions of the writer but also by a critique of patterns of interpretation that themselves have been conditioned by the then prevailing theoretical preconceptions and concerns. Such critique may transform earlier interpretation in the light of new possibilities opened up by new ways of understanding. For as Ricoeur argues, the process of interpretation is "ill represented by a personification of the text as a conversational partner," for with writing, the conditions of dialogue are no longer fulfilled.[4] So how can we conceptualize more precisely the requirements of both historical sensitivity and meaning relative to the world of the interpreter?

I address this problem by employing David Schmidtz's helpful notion of moral theory as a map.[5] A map offers an interpretation of a terrain or subject matter that is "stylized," "abstract," and "simplified."[6] A virtue ethical reading of Hume then, as a map of the terrain of Hume's texts, is a somewhat abstract simplified reading of that terrain. In essence, the idea of a map enables us to conceive of interpretation as satisfying the twin desiderata of accuracy, understood in terms of sensitivity to historical context and authorial intent, and meaningfulness within the world of the interpreter. For Schmidtz such meaningfulness is essentially helpfulness: indeed for a map to be a good map it must be, according to Schmidtz, both accurate and helpful.

How can the notion of moral theory as a map resolve the problems posed above? In response to any charge that a virtue ethical map is historically insensitive it may be claimed that not only is virtue ethics a well established and indeed ancient tradition, or set of traditions, but that it need not be constrained by the modern debates, which are even now developing an "old fashioned" feel. Virtue ethics has moved on from debates about virtue versus duty and rules for example. Nonetheless, the objection goes, even where use of a virtue ethical framework is not distorted by modern concerns of little relevance to Hume and Nietzsche, reading Nietzsche and Hume as virtue ethicists is untimely, for virtue ethics was not a category salient in their philosophical context. However that does not imply that the category is not applicable: the accuracy of that claim depends on one's conception of virtue ethics, discussed in the next chapter.

Whether or not the application of the category is appropriate depends on the second desideratum of interpretation: meaningfulness relative to the world of the interpreter. Interpretation is not only a creative critique of past patterns of interpretation of the text by deploying possibly new or neglected understandings and theoretical media (such as virtue ethics). It is also contextualized by implicit criticism of the manner in which those very media are currently understood. In particular I shall open up new understandings and developments of virtue ethics which are arguably more suitable for interpreting Nietzsche and Hume.

We have seen that for Schmidtz a good map is (a) accurate and (b) helpful. Let us consider each of these requirements in more detail. The requirement of accuracy implies that there is a definite terrain or subject matter of a map, and that it is therefore possible for maps to be inaccurate. In arguing against subjectivist or irrationalist interpretations of Hume's ethics, then, one argues that these readings are inaccurate and should be discarded. However the requirement of accuracy allows for the possibility that several different maps may be good maps of the same terrain. For example I argue in Chapter 2 and Chapter 3 that a virtue ethical map of Hume is not incompatible with a map that reads him as a sentimentalist or as a moral sense theorist. I shall also argue in Chapter 7 that a virtue ethical reading of Nietzsche is not incompatible with an existentialist reading. Indeed requirement (a) is the more satisfied *ceteris paribus* the richer and less simplified is the map. Integrating several different maps within the overall category of one map (such as virtue ethics) is *ceteris paribus* the way to make the overarching map more accurate. However requirement (a) is constrained by requirement (b): to maintain helpfulness a map must remain simplified and abstract. There will then be a creative tension between accuracy and helpfulness, precluding an extreme reading of the requirement of accuracy where there is a refusal to categorize at all.

The requirement of helpfulness addresses the worry that only categories current at the time of Hume and Nietzsche be applied to those figures. Helpfulness is a contextual notion. An extremely important context is the need to bring into salience features of Hume and Nietzsche which have been systematically ignored, neglected, or distorted as a result of interpretations reflecting previous (or indeed current) moral theoretic tendencies, such as forms of moral skepticism, emotivism, or subjectivism. The provision of objectivist moral theoretic maps of these thinkers has proved difficult in a climate where virtue ethics was relatively invisible as a moral tradition, but where non-objectivist readings have continued.

Another aspect of helpfulness is the ability of a map to provide a sufficiently rich understanding. As suggested, richer understanding is gained by showing how various maps (e.g., the sentimentalist and virtue ethical maps of Hume) can be seen as compatible with each other. This feature harmonizes with the requirement of accuracy, but as already noted, at some point going for richness may come into tension with the requirement of helpfulness. As Schmidtz says, maps are not comprehensive, and in two ways. They do not map everything: "they do not say how to reach all destinations."[7] Nor do they show all the fine details. A virtue ethical map for example makes virtue and vice salient, and in so doing will fail to highlight other aspects of thought which are of concern in other maps. For example, my virtue ethical map does not emphasize Nietzsche's relationship with Jonathan Ree and the progression of his thought from the "positivist" influence of Ree's thought and Darwinism, to the rejection of this thought in later writings.[8] Furthermore my virtue ethical map will concentrate on Nietzsche's mature ethical writings which are of greatest importance for elucidation of the virtue ethical nature of Nietzsche's ethics. Nor will my virtue ethical map emphasize or attempt to map in detail ongoing debates about differences between Hume's *Treatise* and *Enquiries* except insofar as aspects of that debate impinge on interesting features in a virtue ethical interpretation.

1.2   A Metaphysical Map

A complete map of Nietzsche and Hume, whether or not it involves a virtue ethical map of their ethics, ideally requires a thoroughly explicated conception of their metaphysical perspective. Alas the issues surrounding both philosophers would take us so far afield that it would be too cumbersome to provide this. In this section therefore I will offer instead a very abstract map of the main issues and my general position.

Nietzsche and Hume are remarkably similar in their debunking of traditional systematizing metaphysics that offer conceptions of absolute human independent perspectives on the world, an ego or self that is a "neutral" or "indifferent" "substratum" (Nietzsche), a conception of moral truth or obligation as "eternal" and "immutable" (Hume), a conception of free will that is a mental entity separated from the "deed" understood sufficiently richly to include motive and passion or emotion. For Nietzsche as for Hume, the drive to a pure, absolute, human perspective-free metaphysical view of the world is sourced in a theological ahistorical conception of purity, a failure to appreciate the limitations of scientific reason in fields such as ethics, and a basic fear of naturalistic messiness and plurality. Says Nietzsche:

> Against this theologians' instinct I wage war: I have found its traces everywhere … This faulty perspective on all things is elevated into a morality, a virtue, a holiness: … and no *other* perspective is conceded any further value once one's own has been made sacrosanct with the names of "God," "redemption," and "eternity." I have dug up the theologians' instinct everywhere: it is the most widespread, really *subterranean*, form of falsehood found on earth.[9]

Hume's attack on the "theological instincts" of the moral rationalists, notably Samuel Clarke, in Book III of the *Treatise*, can be seen in the same light. According to Paul Russell, the "riddle of the *Treatise*" which is the riddle of combining Hume's skepticism with his naturalism, can be resolved if we appreciate that "the direction and structure of Hume's thought in the *Treatise* is shaped on one side by his attack on the Christian metaphysics and morals and on the other by his efforts to construct in its place a secular, scientific account of morality."[10] We can read both Hume and Nietzsche as rescuing "morals" or conceptions of a good life from an underpinning in religious morality and associated theological doctrines, rather than as skeptics about morality. Such a reading requires new, possibly radical, theoretical orientations rather than wholesale rejection of morality. The foundation for such an account is the destruction of metaphysical postulates underlying natural religion such as certain conceptions of free will, "priestly dogmas" "invented on purpose to tame and subdue the rebellious reason of mankind" (E 156) such as the infinite divisibility of matter and "secret" cause; and in general an "overall skeptical objective to show the weakness and limits of human understanding as it relates to all arguments that aim to prove the existence of God."[11]

Controversy surrounds the issue of what exactly replaces false metaphysics for Hume and Nietzsche. Again at a highly abstract level we can speak of two broad options. We can read both Hume and Nietzsche as offering a commonsense metaphysics where the notion of a Cartesian self is replaced with a commonsense view of a human being conceived as a persisting but changing entity with more or less robust character traits,[12] but less robust than conceived by Aristotle. We can replace the Kantian noumenal "thing in itself" with a commonsense idea of a thing. We can replace the metaphysical notion of free will with commonsense conceptions of virtues of being responsible and taking responsibility. Alternatively we can conceive of both philosophers as rejecting a commonsense "thing-based" metaphysics, replacing it with various forms of "no-self" views, a metaphysics of "forces" (Nietzsche) where things are reduced to quanta of forces, and events replace things as metaphysically fundamental.

However, even if these thinkers are interpreted as offering revisionary metaphysics, there is an issue about the implications of such metaphysics for their ethics. Consider for example Steven D. Hales and Rex Welshon's controversial account of Nietzsche's "ontological perspectivism" based centrally on texts not always taken seriously: Nietzsche's *Nachlass* and *Will to Power*.[13] Assume that their use of these texts is justified, and that they are correct in interpreting them as claiming that "the world is ephemeral, energetic, transient, and in motion, that it is composed of events, and that each member of the set of events is nothing more than 'a determination of degrees and relations of force' (WP 552) such that at the fundamental levels, there are nothing but logically atomic events of power, referred to by the terms 'quanta of power' and 'dynamic quanta.'"[14] It does not follow from this claim about "fundamental level" ontology that normal understandings of individuals, virtue, and vice are undermined. For just as particle physics does not undermine our understanding of tables as solid objects with flat surfaces suitable for working at and eating off, so "quanta of power" metaphysics does not necessarily vitiate our normal understating of virtue and vice as traits that last over time.

It is not my plan in this book to argue that at a theoretical level the debunking of traditional "theological" metaphysics is replaced by commonsense metaphysical views as opposed to revisionary metaphysics. What is clear is that from a practical perspective both philosophers have a deflationary view friendly to the evident virtue-centeredness of their moral philosophy. For Nietzsche metaphysics is "that science ... which deals with the basic errors of man – but as if they were basic truths."[15] Rather, a "higher culture" values "the little, humble truths, those discovered by a strict method, rather than the gladdening and dazzling errors that originate in metaphysical and artistic ages and men."[16] Hume's "science" of morality and his experimental method generally can be seen in the same light. I shall show that Hume's and Nietzsche's attacks on "traditional" metaphysics, Nietzsche's perspectivism, and Hume's sentimentalism, are consistent both with kinds of pluralism whose parameters will be explicated, and with the kind of objectivity and non-relativism in ethics which is necessary for a virtue ethical interpretation.

1.3   A Naturalistic Map

For Nietzsche and Hume virtue is somehow sensitive to the nature of human beings as *human* beings. Most importantly human beings are creatures that grow, develop, and mature from a state of childhood dependency through to maturity and old age, having characteristic needs studied by biological, psychological, and social sciences, characteristic kinds of projects and relations that make their lives meaningful for them, and needing education and enculturation through which those needs and projects are understood and articulated. Virtues as *human* excellences reflect this nature of humans.

Accordingly I believe that both Hume and Nietzsche accept what I call *The Constraint on Virtue*:

> What counts as a virtue is constrained by an adequate theory of human growth and development.

The Constraint on Virtue is offered here at a very high level of abstraction, since it features in Hume and Nietzsche in different ways. For Hume, what counts as an "adequate theory" is interpreted through a "moral sense" itself expressive of a fundamental humanity and benevolence. The deliverances of such an outlook yield criteria of virtue discussed in Chapter 5. Nietzsche accepts the constraint because, as I shall argue in Chapter 6, what Nietzsche calls "the *development-theory of the will to power*" is for him the appropriate and non-superficial psychology through which human beings are to be understood,[17] and which uncovers the nature of their virtues and vices. Traits violating the constraint would exhibit distorted "will to power" (in various types of individual) and as such would not be virtues.

There is then a sense in which both Nietzsche and Hume are naturalists. To understand which sense we need to make a crucial distinction between what McDowell calls "bald naturalism" and "scientistic naturalism":

(1) *Bald Naturalism*: "Conceptualizations of things as natural" in the sense of being subsumable "under the laws of natural science" "exhaust the conceptualizations of things that stand a chance of truth."

(2) *Scientistic Naturalism*: Domains such as the ethical do "stand a chance of truth" since they are natural, where the natural is to be understood as subsumable under the laws of natural science.[18]

McDowell argues in *Mind and World*[19] that one can be a naturalist while rejecting both bald naturalism and scientistic naturalism. Bald naturalism is rejected because things standing a chance of truth, such as the ethical, are not to be conceptualized as subsumable under the laws of natural science. In that case scientistic naturalism is rejected because naturalism should not be understood in the scientific way.

I wish to affirm that like McDowell, Hume and Nietzsche should be understood as naturalists but as neither bald nor scientistic naturalists. The question remains: what is their kind of naturalism? The Constraint on Virtue implies that they are naturalists in the "spare" sense defined by Huw Price:

(3)   *Spare Naturalism*: "the view that natural science constrains philosophy ... and that philosophy properly defers to science, where the concerns of the two disciplines coincide." [20]

This sense of naturalism Brian Leiter describes as "Results Continuity." Results Continuity "requires that philosophical theories ... be supported or justified by the results of the sciences: philosophical theories that do not enjoy the support of our best science are simply *bad* theories." [21] That Hume believes that ethics is naturalistic in this sense is clear in the following passage: "the most abstruse speculations concerning human nature, however cold and uninteresting, become subservient to *practical morality*; and may render this latter science more correct in its precepts, and more persuasive in its exhortations" (T 3.3.6.6/621).

Where an ethical view is naturalistic in the "spare" sense, it is not necessarily the case that it is naturalistic in the scientistic sense. Nor need it be naturalistic in a sense which I call scientific naturalism.

(4)   *Scientific Naturalism*: The claims of ethics can be *derived* from the findings of science alone.

Here science is not necessarily understood as the natural sciences in McDowell's sense of the paradigmatic natural sciences, where things are understood as subsumable under law-like generalizations. Results continuity does not entail scientific naturalism even where "science" is understood as disunified in the sense that there is no unitary scientific method, and/or there is no fundamental unity of content. [22] The German tradition recognized this with the distinction between two types of *Wissenschaften* (forms of knowledge): the *Geisteswissenschaften* and the *Naturwissenschaften*. Bruno Bettelheim, in a critique of the "scientistic" bad translations of Freud, describes the former (sciences of the spirit) as "idiographic" because they "seek to understand the objects of their study not as instances of universal laws but as singular events: their method is that of history" since they "deal with events that never recur in the same form – that can be neither replicated nor predicted." [23] The latter by contrast are "nomothetic" since they seek to explain and verify through the medium of universal law discovered through the method of experimental replication.

Admittedly with this distinction what counts as science becomes vague. However even if history counts as a "science of the spirit" the scientific stance alone is not sufficient for Hume to uncover the world of ethics, even though he makes plain (as we see in the next chapter) that ethics is beholden to the results of science. He is not a scientific naturalist. Spare naturalism can be non-reductivist, exhibiting "results continuity" without it being reduced to the concepts and results of science.

But as we all know Hume is an "empiricist." How can Hume not be a scientific naturalist and yet be an empiricist? The challenge in understanding Hume's naturalism is to square his non-reductivist spare naturalism with his empiricism.

What is empiricism? Empiricism in "its most general sense ... designates a philosophical emphasis on the relative importance of experience and processes grounded in experience, in contrast to reasoning and theorizing a priori."[24] In line with this general sense of empiricism, Don Garrett distinguishes no less than five kinds of empiricism, of which the most important for our purposes is Conceptual Empiricism:[25]

(5) *Conceptual Empiricism*: The content of all concepts can be traced to experience.

Conceptual Empiricism involves a "rejection of the Rationalists' common distinction between intellect and imagination as two distinct representational faculties of the mind," thus rejecting the idea that "nonimagistic ideas of intellect can serve as a fertile source of nonexperiential cognitive content."[26] Hume is not only a spare naturalist, he is a conceptual empiricist: as we shall see, metaphysical and religious postulates violating this form of empiricism are rejected. Hume then is not only a spare naturalist but a naturalist as opposed to a supernaturalist. We should note that even if a form of virtue ethics is naturalistic in Price's "spare" sense, it need not be naturalistic as opposed to "supernaturalistic"[27] in its metaphysics.[28]

Thus we have to reconcile the following features of Hume's philosophy:

(a) Spare naturalism
(b) Conceptual empiricism
(c) Rejection of scientific reductivism
(d) Rejection of supernaturalism.

He cannot reconcile (a) and (b) by affirming scientific reductivism, and he cannot reconcile (a) and (c) by affirming supernaturalism. So how can Hume hold all of (a)–(d)?

The key is to understand the nature of Hume's ethical empiricism. Chapters 2 and 3 will explicate Hume's ethical naturalism via his *ethical* empiricism. That empiricism is revealed by his response dependence virtue ethics, according to which the "experience" grounding ethical concepts is constituted by the passions, and that the imagination, central to the construction of all concepts for Hume including those of ethics, can be assessed as reasonable (or otherwise) by standards different from those applicable to what Hume calls "Reason" or intellect in a narrow sense.

It may be surprising to find that Hume subscribes to conceptual empiricism in ethics. For (conceptual) empiricism is normally thought to be the view that genuine concepts are derived from observation; observation is normally thought to involve the five senses alone (as opposed to dubious forms of "perception" such as a "moral sense" understood as a special form of perception), and therefore moral concepts are derivable from those very types of observations that constitute the world of natural science. Thus according to Quine "the difference between science and ethics is that scientific claims, unlike moral claims are responsive to observation," hence a coherence theory is "evidently the lot of ethics."[29]

The way to reconcile Hume's non-reductivist spare naturalism and his empiricism is to claim that for Hume there is a form of genuine observation which is not reducible to the perception of the five senses. This form is yielded by those passions (emotions and feelings) constituting and conditioning the "moral sense." It is important to realize that the moral sense is not a special sense involving a "moral sense organ."[30] In line with Bernard Williams's claim that the materials of ethics should not be seen as constituted from "special" materials, Hume understands the "moral sense" as a complex but ordinary, characteristic, emotional capacity based on benevolence and sympathy, and constrained by self-love, as we explore in the next two chapters.

What about Nietzsche? Leiter believes that Nietzsche too is a naturalist in the sense of "Results Continuity", citing Nietzsche's claim that we must "translate man back into nature ... hardened in the discipline of science" where man is understood as "*homo natura*."[31] However Janaway questions this, claiming that what scientific results justify or support in Nietzsche is obscure, citing as an example Nietzsche's claim that the origin of bad conscience is "instincts whose outward expression against others is blocked turn themselves inwards and give rise to the infliction of pain on the self."[32] He ascribes to Nietzsche a weaker "Results Continuity" which requires simply that "explanations in philosophy be compatible with our best science, or not be falsified by appeal to our best science."[33] However on my view this is too weak. It is true that the will to power hypothesis for example is not meant to be "results continuous" with the scientific biology of the time believed by Ree, and the "English psychologists," a target of attack in the *Genealogy of Morals*. But that does not invalidate results continuity in Leiter's sense: one just has to pick the right domain. That domain is the depth psychology which *explains* the passage cited by Janaway as "obscure," and which I discuss in Chapter 7 (see section 7.4). That domain in turn arguably requires the sensitivities proper to understanding psychology as a discipline essentially involving (but not wholly involving) the *Geisteswissenschaften* – the particular idiographic, intuitive, and indeed empathetic methods of the "sciences of the spirit."

On my view then the ethics of both Nietzsche and Hume conform to "spare naturalism", rejects bald naturalism, and both scientistic and scientific naturalism. Their spare naturalism is empirical, in the broad sense of an approach based on experience as opposed to theological dogma or doctrine. It essentially includes emotional experience of meanings which may be theorized through what might be broadly called the *Geisteswissenschaften* including history and psychology. This feature allows them to be naturalist without being scientific or scientistic naturalists. As we see in the next chapter I interpret both as response dependent virtue ethicists, according to which certain responses, interpretations, or perspectives are nonetheless necessary for a world of ethics to exist.

1.4   A Psychological Map

Of great importance for a virtue ethical map of Hume and Nietzsche is their emphasis on psychology. There are two major uses of Hume's psychology in my virtue ethical interpretation of him. The first concerns the metaphysics of ethics. For Hume, what John McDowell calls the *logos* of the practical world[34] is furnished by a certain emotional orientation to it. The world of ethics does not exist as such a world if we do not possess in human nature a passion of benevolence and some sympathy based on that passion. This is made clear in many passages in Hume, including the discussion of the "fancied monster" in the *Enquiries*:

> Let us suppose, if the prosperity of nations were laid on the one hand, and their ruin on the other, and he were desired to choose; that he would stand like the schoolman's ass, irresolute and undetermined, between equal motives … (E 235)

For such a being the world of ethics is unintelligible, whereas a selfish person possessing a modicum of benevolence has at least a glimmer of an emotional orientation that allows him to make a distinction between "what is useful and what is pernicious"(E 235). As a result, Hume on my view is opposed not to the existence of moral facts, propositions about which are made true by factors outside the agent (as well as within the agent), but only to a certain construal of moral facts. In particular Hume's targets are the following beliefs:

(a)   Moral facts are facts about the "eternal immutable fitnesses" of things.
(b)   Recognition of such facts by the reason of the understanding putatively capable of ascertaining truths about such fitnesses, is sufficient to motivate.
(c)   Moral facts (construed as above) can even directly motivate without the intermediary of belief or other psychological states of the agent.[35]

On my account of Hume, he holds the following:

(a)   There are moral facts which are constituted not by eternal immutable fitnesses but by "natural fitnesses."
(b)   Such facts cannot be recognized by theoretical reason as such, by the understanding, but they can be recognized by an emotionally constituted "moral sense."
(c)   Given this, such recognition can motivate, since the moral sense is inherently practical, and as such makes the world of ethics as a practical orientation to the world, intelligible.

Indeed to possess a virtue is not simply to possess a faculty or skill in knowing moral facts, but to be disposed to be motivated by such knowledge.

The second important feature of Hume's psychology is basic to his understanding of the criteria of virtue. Hume's discussion of the passions in Book II of the *Treatise* lays the foundations of my pluralistic, non-consequentialist, and non-hedonistic account of Hume's criteria of virtue. Consequently my view of Hume is opposed to Kemp Smith's view that in Book II of the *Treatise*, the passions "play ... no really distinctive part in his system."[36] In Chapter 5 I show on my virtue ethical interpretation just how central are the passions to Hume's conception of virtue.

In Hume passions are a species of "impressions" which, unlike "ideas," do not "represent" the world. Impressions are divided into impressions of sensation and impressions of reflection. The former are divided into sense impressions such as color or sound, and pleasure and pain. The latter are divided into the passions and sentiments. Though they do not represent, they may or may not be "naturally fitted" to the world. Anger may be excessive, joy may exhibit "disordered enthusiasm," hope may be misplaced, pride overweening, and so on. At the core of virtue are the passions: indeed as we shall explore in Chapter 4, one of Hume's theses about virtue (which gives him problems in relation to the artificial virtues) is that virtue proper involves a characteristic natural passion, such as affection. Given that passions are at the heart of virtue, and that Hume's account of the various passions, such as love and pride, is complex and varied, a rich virtue-pluralism characterizes his moral philosophy. Or so I shall argue in Chapter 5.

Turn now to Nietzsche. It is well known that Nietzsche considered himself a psychologist, indeed "one without equal" or even the "first." Yet Jacob Golomb complains that despite the passing of a century most Nietzsche interpreters "have failed to come to grips with the *essential* psychological aspects of his thought."[37] A virtue ethical interpretation of Nietzsche is in a good position to redress this deficiency. Since virtues as character traits constitute motivational and emotional dispositions, theorizing about virtue is considerably enriched if background psychological theory is provided. Indeed in my own interpretation of Nietzsche "the *essential* psychological aspects of his thought" are central.

Golomb distinguishes two aspects of Nietzsche's psychology. First, his "unique psychological genealogical method" "freezes our will to believe life-nihilating values."[38] In this process, Nietzsche recognizes the important psychological fact that entrenched, fundamental, and emotionally laden beliefs are not done away with simply by a putatively decisive refutation through argument. There is too much resistance:

> Do not deride and befoul that which you want to do away with for good but respectfully *lay it on ice*, and, in as much as ideas are very tenacious of life, do so again and again. Here it is necessary to act according to the maxim: "One refutation is no refutation."[39]

Rather for Nietzsche such beliefs need to be unmasked and their dubious cultural heritage displayed and exposed. They can then be seen as less enticing, less like "sacred cows."

Second, intertwined with and reinforcing the therapeutic process of psychological genealogy is Nietzsche's positive psychology which so influenced the psychoanalytic movement in Germany and thereby depth psychology in general. Included here, is at least Freud himself[40] and those who deployed Nietzsche's rejection of hedonistic principles in justifying their schisms with Freud over libido theory. Prominent among these are Alfred Adler who used Nietzsche's notion of will to power as a developmental concept (Nietzsche himself described his psychology as "the developmental theory of will to power"),[41] and Otto Rank who was influenced from earliest days by Nietzsche in his emphasis on the will to creativity and strivings to affirm one's difference and individuality.[42]

Several features common to particularly Freudian/Adlerian analysis and Nietzsche influence my own interpretation of the latter, and are summarized here. All will occupy a place in my virtue ethical reading.

(1) For Nietzsche, psychology should be reinstated as the "Queen of the Sciences"[43] if moral philosophy is to "venture into the depths" and escape the superficial "timidities" of traditional moral theorizing.

(2) According to Nietzsche "man is more sick, more uncertain, more mutable, less defined, than any other animal ... he is *the* sick animal"; he "is the most chronically and deeply sick of all sick animals."[44] Because of this, insights into human nature (as with Freud) are best achieved for Nietzsche through investigation into a variety of sicknesses, rather than by a detailed account of a perfected human being with a definite *telos*. A detailed account of human perfection is replaced by a philosophy for the "convalescent," with emphasis on "overcoming." It is not suggested that sickness is the only thing to be overcome: various human weaknesses are perpetual issues for us. As Nietzsche claims in *Zarathustra*, "And life itself confided this secret to me: ... I am *that which must always overcome itself*." "I must be struggle and a becoming and an end and an opposition of ends – ah, whoever guesses what is my will should also guess on what *crooked* paths it must proceed."[45] The nature of the "crooked paths" is explored in Chapter 10, where I outline Nietzsche's "virtue ethics of becoming."

(3) Conscious psychological states are only a fraction of our psychological states in general. Like the proverbial iceberg, most are below the water line: unconscious. "For the longest time, conscious thought was considered thought itself. Only now does the truth dawn on us that by far the greatest part of our spirit's activity remains unconscious and unfelt."[46]

(4) Furthermore these "unthought" and "unfelt" states can be causally efficacious: "instincts which are here contending against one another" can cause "hurt" to self and other, "violent exhaustion" in thinkers.[47]

(5) Hence, in order to investigate "surface" phenomena, the results of the "contending instincts," we have to venture into the depths: the unconscious phenomena. Once we do venture into the depths we will find that a large number of our conscious states are pathological (sourced as they are in pathological depth states). Citing an insight of Leibniz, Nietzsche claims "what we call consciousness constitutes

only one state of our spiritual and psychic world (*perhaps a pathological state*) and *not by any means the whole of it.*"[48] This insight is by now acknowledged by neuro-science in its discussion of for example what has been called "dark energy"; the brain's default mode network (DMN), whose role in preparing the brain for conscious activity is under study:

> As most neuroscientists acknowledge, our conscious interactions with the world are just a small part of the brain's activity. What goes on below the level of awareness – the brain's dark energy for one – is critical in providing the context for what we experience in the small window of conscious awareness.[49]

Furthermore it is now believed that depression (where "patients exhibit decreased connections between one area of the DMN and regions involving emotion")[50] and other disorders are caused by damage to the DMN.

(6) Hence for Nietzsche venturing into the depths is central to a normative analysis of depth psychological states as they feature in virtue and vice. For Nietzsche what has "decisive value" in action lies in its depths rather than in its surface intention,[51] as we shall explore in Chapters 6 and 7. Indeed a section in *The Gay Science* is headed "Unconscious Virtues." These are virtues described by Nietzsche as qualities "which we know either badly or not at all and which also conceal themselves by means of their subtlety even from very subtle observers."[52]

(7) Amongst the pathological states are regression to more primitive states (as in "noble" morality), repression (as in "slave" morality and the "ascetic ideal"), resigna-tion (the classic philosophers' pathology), and the controlling, self-controlled, pseudo-ideal of autonomy in an extreme form (represented on my view by the "sovereign individual"). All of these pathologies are discussed below.

(8) Like Freud's dynamic theory of human psychology, Nietzsche's psychological theory is one that postulates drives as energetic psychological forces which conflict with each other: "every single one of them [drives] would be only too pleased to present *itself* as the ultimate goal of existence and as the legitimate *master* of all the other drives. For every drive is tyrannical."[53]

(9) Hence psychological conflict ("the contending instincts") is endemic to the human condition: what creates neurosis however is not psychic conflict as such but certain problematic "resolutions" of that conflict.

(10) In a psychoanalytic understanding of Nietzsche, the libido theory of Freud must be rejected in favor of Adler's emphasis on power and the inferiority com-plex. This is anticipated by Nietzsche's attack on "the pleasure principle," and his notion of will to power and its distortions in forms of self-contempt and escape from self.[54]

(11) As in Freud, individual psychology is interpreted through cultural analysis and critique, since the specific manifestations of individuals' sickness are in large part, at least, a product of cultural sickness. This claim is of paramount importance

for Nietzsche. Psychological interpretation must not be confused with an "individualistic" interpretation, according to which persons are viewed as if they were not shaped by their cultures. Indeed Nietzsche frequently draws our attention to the virtues of different ages which may be embryonic in earlier ages.[55]

By the same token, for Nietzsche cultural sickness causes individual sickness, which in turn reinforces cultural sickness. As Christopher Janaway rightly points out, for Nietzsche "the natural and cultural realms seem to interpenetrate."[56] Our expressions of a need to "vent our strength," expand, incorporate, and so on, are interpreted through, and have meaning within, our cultural practices and language.

The need for interpretation within psychology and culture is of cardinal importance for Nietzsche's understanding of a human being as "*homo natura*," though we need to have a critical perspective on those interpretations which are "varnish" and expressive of human vanity.[57] In his *Nietzsche on Morality*, Brian Leiter makes a sharp contrast between the naturalism of Freud and Hume and the postmodernism of Foucault, claiming that Nietzsche belongs in the company of the former. In this I completely agree. However we must be careful to note that the contrast Leiter draws between the ideas that there are deep facts about human nature and that "all such putative facts are *mere* interpretations"[58] may mislead. As is well known Nietzsche claims that there are no moral facts, only interpretations of such facts.[59] What Nietzsche means by this claim is that there are no *facta bruta*, and we cannot escape interpretation. Challenging situations for example do not simply *cause* drives to "overcome"; they are *interpreted* as challenging in various sorts of ways, and the interpretations of the weak will differ from those of the strong. This is compatible not only with the view that some interpretations are "varnish," but also with the view that some are serious misinterpretations. As we have already seen, he claims for example that the "theological instinct" is a form of interpretation (a "perspective") that is faulty and distorted; indeed the most "widespread falsehood" on earth. Moral facts *properly* interpreted are deep, and free from fundamental distortions. We need to have a critical perspective on those interpretations which are shallow, expressive of human vanity, or are downright pernicious.[60]

This chapter has provided background for a virtue ethical map of Hume and Nietzsche. Describing the basic nature of that map is the task of the next chapter. Parts II and III provide the map itself.

Notes

1   A recent collection focused on this theme is *Aristotelian Ethics in Contemporary Perspective*, ed. Julia Peters (New York: Routledge, 2013).

2   Marcia Baron, "Virtue Ethics in Relation to Kantian Ethics: An Opinionated Overview and Commentary," in *Perfecting Virtue: New Essays on Kantian Ethics and Virtue Ethics*, ed. L. Jost and J. Wuerth (Cambridge: Cambridge University Press, 2011), 8–37, 33.

3   Marcia W. Baron, Philip Pettit, and Michael Slote (Oxford: Blackwell, 1997).

4 James J. DiCenso, *Hermeneutics and the Disclosure of Truth: A Study in the Work of Heidegger, Gadamer, and Ricoeur* (Charlottesville: University Press of Virginia, 1990), 114. See Paul Ricoeur, *Hermeneutics and the Human Sciences*, ed. and trans. John B. Thomson (Cambridge: Cambridge University Press, 1981), 45.

5 See his *Elements of Justice* (Cambridge: Cambridge University Press, 2006).

6 Schmidtz, 21.

7 Schmidtz, 22.

8 Nonetheless this is interesting: see Robin Small, *Nietzsche and Ree: A Star Friendship* (Oxford: Clarendon Press, 2005).

9 *The Antichrist*, in *The Portable Nietzsche*, ed. and trans. Walter Kaufmann (New York: Penguin, 1976), sect. 9, 575–576.

10 Paul Russell, *The Riddle of Hume's Treatise: Skepticism, Naturalism, and Irreligion* (Oxford: Oxford University Press, 2008), viii.

11 Russell, 185.

12 On this issue, see Annette C. Baier, *Death and Character: Further Reflections on Hume* (Cambridge, MA: Harvard University Press, 2008).

13 Hales and Welshon, *Nietzsche's Perspectivism* (Urbana: University of Illinois Press, 2000).

14 Hales and Welshon, 63.

15 "On First and Last Things," in *Human, All Too Human: A Book for Free Spirits*, trans. Marion Faber with Stephen Lehmann (Lincoln: University of Nebraska Press, 1984), sect. 18, 26.

16 "On First and Last Things," sect. 3, 15.

17 "On the Prejudices of Philosophers," in *Beyond Good and Evil: Prelude to a Philosophy of the Future*, trans. R.J. Hollingdale (London: Penguin, 1973), sect. 23, 53.

18 "Response to J.M. Bernstein," in *Reading McDowell: On* Mind and World, ed. Nicholas H. Smith (London: Routledge, 2002), 297–300, 297.

19 Cambridge, MA: Harvard University Press, 1994.

20 "Naturalism Without Representationalism," in *Naturalism in Question*, ed. Mario De Caro and David MacArthur (Cambridge, MA: Harvard University Press, 2004), 71–88, 71.

21 *Nietzsche on Morality* (London: Routledge, 2002), 4. Leiter's italics.

22 See further John Dupré, *The Disorder of Things: Metaphysical Foundations of the Disunity of Science* (Cambridge, MA: Harvard University Press, 1993).

23 *Freud and Man's Soul* (London: Fontana, 1985), 41–42.

24 *Encyclopaedia of Empiricism*, ed. Don Garrett and Edward Barbanell (London: Fitzroy Dearborn, 1997).

25 Don Garrett, *Cognition and Commitment in Hume's Philosophy* (Oxford: Oxford University Press, 1997).

26 *Encyclopaedia of Empiricism*.

27 This is a term of Barry Stroud. By "supernaturalism" he means "the invocation of an agent or force that somehow stands outside the familiar natural world and whose doings cannot be understood as part of it": "The Charm of Naturalism," *Naturalism in Question*, 21–35, 23.

28 This point is made by Julia Annas in her "Virtue Ethics: What Kind of Naturalism," in *Virtue Ethics, Old and New*, ed. Stephen M. Gardiner (Ithaca, NY: Cornell University Press, 2005), 11–29.

29 "On the Nature of Moral Values," in *Theories and Things* (Cambridge, MA: Harvard University Press, 1981), 55–66, 63. For an examination of this argument, see Folke Tersman, "Quine on Ethics," *Theoria* 64 (1998), 84–98.

30 Christopher Hookway, "Fallibilism and Objectivity: Science and Ethics," in *World, Mind and Ethics: Essays on the Ethical Philosophy of Bernard Williams*, ed. J.E.J. Altham and Ross Harrison (Cambridge: Cambridge University Press, 1995), 46–67, 66.

31 *Beyond Good and Evil*, sect. 230, cited in Brian Leiter, *Nietzsche on Morality*, 6.

32 Christopher Janaway, *Beyond Selflessness: Reading Nietzsche's Genealogy* (Oxford: Oxford University Press, 2007), 37.

33 Ibid.

34 See his "Two Sorts of Naturalism," in *Virtues and Reasons*, ed. Rosalind Hursthouse, Gavin Lawrence, and Warren Quinn (Oxford: Oxford University Press, 1998), 149–179.

35   See further Sophie Botros, *Hume, Reason and Morality: A Legacy of Contradiction* (Abingdon: Routledge, 2006), 69.

36   Norman Kemp Smith, *The Philosophy of David Hume* [1941] (Basingstoke: Palgrave Macmillan, 2005), 160.

37   "Introductory Essay: Nietzsche's New Psychology," in *Nietzsche and Depth Psychology*, ed. Jacob Golomb, Weaver Santaniello, and Ronald Lehrer (Albany, NY: State University of New York Press, 1999), 1–19, 1. See also Graham Parkes, *Composing the Soul: Reaches of Nietzsche's Psychology* (Chicago: University of Chicago Press, 1994).

38   "Introductory Essay," 1.

39   Friedrich Nietzsche, "The Wanderer and His Shadow," in *Human, All too Human*, trans. R.J. Hollingdale (Cambridge: Cambridge University Press, 1986), 311.

40   See Ronald Lehrer, "Freud and Nietzsche, 1892–1895," in *Nietzsche and Depth Psychology*, 181–203. Freudian ideas anticipated by Nietzsche according to Lehrer include dynamic unconscious mental functioning, catharsis, repression in relation to incompatible ideas/desires.

41   See Ronald Lehrer, "Adler and Nietzsche," in *Nietzsche and Depth Psychology*, 229–245.

42   See Claude Barbre, "Reversing the Crease: Nietzsche's Influence on Otto Rank's Concept of Creative Will and the Birth of Individuality," in *Nietzsche and Depth Psychology*, 247–267.

43   *Beyond Good and Evil*, sect. 23.

44   *On the Genealogy of Morals*, trans. Douglas Smith (Oxford: Oxford University Press, 1996), Third Essay, 13, 100.

45   *Thus Spoke Zarathustra*, in *The Portable Nietzsche*, ed. and trans. Walter Kaufmann (New York: Penguin, 1976), Part II, "On Self Overcoming," 227.

46   *The Gay Science*, trans. Walter Kaufmann (New York: Vintage Books, 1974), Book 4, sect. 333, 262.

47   Ibid.

48   *Gay Science*, Book 5, sect. 357, 305. My italics.

49   Marcus E. Raichle, "The Brain's Dark Energy," *Scientific American* 302.3, 44–49, 49.

50   Ibid., 49

51   "The Free Spirit," *Beyond Good and Evil*, sect. 32, 63.

52   Book 1, sect. 8, 82–83.

53   "On the Prejudices of Philosophers," *Beyond Good and Evil*, sect. 6, 37.

54   I agree however with those commentators, notably Bernard Reginster in *The Affirmation of Life: Nietzsche on Overcoming Nihilism* (Cambridge, MA: Harvard University Press, 2006), who place the doctrine of will to power historically "in the context of a response to Schopenhauerian pessimism" and as a "substitute for the Schopenhauerian concept of the will to live" (105–106).

55   See *Gay Science*, Book 1, sect. 9, 83; *Zarathustra*, Part II, "On the Tarantulas."

56   Janaway, *Beyond Selflessness*, 149.

57   "Our Virtues," *Beyond Good and Evil*, sect. 230, 162.

58   *Nietzsche on Morality*, 2. Note that Leiter reports here that Freud claims to have stopped reading Nietzsche for fear that he had anticipated too many of his ideas about human nature and the unconscious forces. Indeed I show how Nietzsche anticipates Freud in Chapter 8, especially in connection with Nietzsche's views on cruelty.

59   To make this point he claims: "There are no moral phenomena at all, only a moral interpretation of phenomena." "Maxims and Interludes," *Beyond Good and Evil*, sect. 108, 96.

60   "Our Virtues," *Beyond Good and Evil*, sect. 230, 162.

Chapter 2

Hume and Nietzsche as Response Dependence Virtue Ethicists

2.1 Introduction

The task of this chapter is to describe in broad outline the kind of virtue ethics I attribute to Hume and Nietzsche. Any work purporting to bring Nietzsche and Hume into the virtue ethical fold has to deal both with the alleged vagueness of the notion of virtue ethics itself, and the understanding of virtue ethics via one tradition, particularly the Aristotelian. In my *Virtue Ethics: A Pluralistic View*, I offered a relatively simple and basic definition of virtue ethics as a type of theory in which "the notion of virtue is central in the sense that conceptions of rightness, conceptions of the good life, conceptions of 'the moral point of view' and the appropriate demandingness of morality, cannot be understood without a conception of relevant virtues."[1] This does not imply that "character is primary" in the sense that the evaluation of action is entirely derivable from the evaluation of agents' character. Rather as I argue in "The Definition of Virtue Ethics," virtue ethics should be regarded as virtue notion-centered, and virtue notions include the notions of virtuous character, virtuous motives, virtue rules, virtue notions as applied to acts, and the targets or aims of virtues.

Clearly, if virtue ethics is *defined* via its main traditional source, ancient eudaimonistic virtue ethics, it will become controversial at the very least to class Hume and Nietzsche as belonging to virtue ethical traditions. However, understanding virtue ethics through the centrality of virtue notions will allow us to have a broader conception of virtue ethics, without losing our grip on the idea of virtue ethics as a distinctive kind of moral theory. Virtue ethics could then be seen as a family of different kinds of virtue ethical theories. It is useful to make a comparison between virtue ethics seen as a family with conceptions of other types of moral theory, such as deontology, understood in a broad way as a duty-centered type of theory. In a

The Virtue Ethics of Hume and Nietzsche, First Edition. Christine Swanton.
© 2015 John Wiley & Sons, Ltd. Published 2015 by John Wiley & Sons, Ltd.

comparison between virtue ethics and other moral theories it is really important that like is compared with like.

(1)   Virtue ethics as a family is properly compared with, for example, deontology.
(2)   Aristotelian virtue ethics as a genus of virtue ethics is properly compared with, for example, Kantian ethics as a genus of deontology.
(3)   Actual Aristotle as a virtue ethicist is properly compared with actual Kant.

If these comparative structures are not adhered to, two problems arise. First virtue ethics as a genre of moral theory is seen as conceptually tied to just one progenitor such as Aristotle. This is equivalent to forging a conceptual tie between deontology and Kant, or consequentialism and Bentham. However, deontology is represented historically by at least Kant and W.D. Ross. (It is not suggested that Ross is Kantian; only that his theory comes within the family of theory that is duty-centered.) Similarly, seeing virtue ethics as a family of theories allows us to represent virtue ethics historically (more or less controversially) by (at least) Aristotle, Confucius and Neo-Confucians, Nietzsche, and Hume. Of course Kant and Ross, like Aristotle and Hume, are very different. What unifies them at an abstract version of a map is that for the former pair of thinkers, the notion of duty is central, whereas for the latter pair virtue notions are deemed central. Such an understanding of virtue ethics and deontology would reveal fundamental differences between these two families of theory without overly narrowing virtue ethics to Aristotle's or Aristotelian eudaimonism.

Second, if the above comparative structures are not properly recognized unfair demands for neat and tidy definitions of virtue ethics can be made. If virtue ethics in general is seen as comparable with Kantianism, or even Kant, rather than deontology in general, we could then understand virtue ethics simply by reference to the one thinker, just as Kantianism could be understood with reference to the real Kant, as opposed to the variety of positions represented by Korsgaard, Baron, Hill, Cummiskey, and so on. However, the multi-headed beast that is virtue ethics is not like this: it is more like deontology in being represented historically by several figures. Hence no single thinker or even tradition can be seen as the one anchor point for a definitional understanding of virtue ethics.

There are two major differences between Aristotelian eudaimonistic virtue ethics and that of Hume and Nietzsche, discussed in this chapter. First, though character plays an important, even central role in their theories, the notions of ideal character and character as a highly robust set of dispositions are not evident. This is not to say that the important aspirational feature of virtue ethics is absent: rather their aspirational standards do not terminate in ideals of perfection.[2] Improving, "self-overcoming," and "convalescing" where aspirations are "all too human" (in Nietzsche's language) or are relative to what is "common and usual" in human nature (Hume) are the aspirational goals, rather than the god-like idealizations of the Greek tradition.

Second, I understand the virtue ethics of Nietzsche and Hume in an empiricist naturalistic manner explicated in the last chapter. That understanding is here elaborated through a characterization of their virtue ethics as response dependent (sections 2.3–2.4).

2.2   Character in Hume and Nietzsche

Nietzsche in particular places common conceptions of character into question. Indeed he seems skeptical about the existence of traits of character, a feature incompatible with virtue ethics in orthodox forms. On closer examination we see this is not so. First his views are motivated by a keen eye for the complexity of ethics and a hatred of oversimplification and excessive abstraction, including overly abstract characterizations of virtue. For him, virtue is highly differentiated or contoured according to "ages, peoples ... great and small individuals"[3] and roles (necessitating the study of the "manners of scholars, of businessmen, artists, or artisans").[4] A second motivation is his objection to "character" as construed by a society "still dominated by the herd instinct." Here character is understood in terms of a "firm reputation" and as "dependable" to the point that "all change, all re-learning, all self-transformation" is brought into "*ill repute*."[5] None of this is opposed to virtue ethics as such, especially a reforming virtue ethics which may emphasize the "burdened" character of virtue,[6] the "aspirational" and even transformational character of virtue,[7] and the "differentiated" character of virtue (see further Chapter 8).

For Hume, character rather than action is the central object of moral appraisal, for the following reason:

> Actions are by their very nature temporary and perishing; and where they proceed not from some cause in the characters and disposition of the person, who perform'd them, they infix not themselves upon him, and can neither redound to his honour, if good, nor infamy, if evil. (T 2.3.2.6/411)

Again, Hume claims, "Actions themselves, not proceeding from any constant principle, have no influence on love or hatred, pride or humility; and consequently are never consider'd in morality" (T 3.3.1.4/575). Actions may be "blamable," says Hume, if they are contrary to "rules of morality and religion" (and can thus be assessed as wrong *qua* "bare" actions), but unless proceeding from something "durable or constant" in the person (i.e., character), they cannot "redound to infamy" or merit punishment (T 2.3.2.6/411). Nor should character be seen merely as tendencies to action for Hume. What is required for redounding to honor or infamy is quality of motive ("when we praise any actions, we regard only the motives which produced them" (T 3.2.1.2/477)). Indeed as T 411 claims, what is required is stable or constant motive.

Hume and Nietzsche are alike in downgrading the importance of a distinction bet-ween moral and non-moral virtues.[8] What makes a character trait a virtue is for Nietzsche and Hume the same in a fundamental respect: they are simply excellent or admirable mental qualities characterized most importantly by motivational and passional disposi-tions. Both philosophers countenance a large number of such traits. Nonetheless Hume in particular has been criticized for failure to demarcate the moral from the non-moral, even though there is no agreement on how this distinction is to be drawn. Christine Korsgaard notes that Hume has a "notorious" doctrine "that there is no important dis-tinction between moral virtues and natural abilities."[9] However, there is for Hume a distinction between virtues and "bodily endowments" such as basic athleticism (since the latter is not a "mental quality"). Furthermore he claims that one should not exag-gerate differences between natural abilities *that are also mental qualities* (of which his examples are being good natured, having sense, knowledge, and judgment) and "moral virtue." Indeed Hume says that such "natural abilities" should not be excluded from the catalog of virtues. At the very least, "they give a new lustre to the other virtues" (T 3.3.4.2/607). Certainly on Aristotle's own view of virtue, virtue proper or "full" virtue *requires* practical wisdom ("sense," "knowledge," and "judgment"), unlike "natural virtue." The latter is being good natured without (much) wisdom, which is for Aristotle an inferior form of "virtue." Hume by contrast seems to allow Aristotle's natural virtue to be virtue proper, although he does not always appear to be comfortable with this, citing with approval the lines of the "elegant and judicious poet": "Virtue (for mere good-nature is a fool) / Is sense and spirit with humanity" (E App. IV, para. 265, 317).

Hume claims in short that good sense gives luster to a virtue such as generosity; that is, good sense improves the generosity that Aristotle would call a "natural virtue." By the same token, being good natured gives luster to wise generosity that would otherwise be forced or grudging; indeed for virtue in its best form, being good natured is a basic emotional orientation.

In reply one might argue the following. Granted that at T 606–607 Hume refuses to exclude qualities like good sense from the catalog of virtues, but if virtues are not dis-tinguished from realized talents such as excellence at rugby playing (which requires mental qualities), what is to stop such a sporting excellence being classed as a virtue?[10] A fuller account of Hume's position is given in Appendix IV of the *Enquiries*, "Of Some Verbal Disputes." Here he claims not that there is *no* distinction between virtues and realized talents, but that there is no sharp distinction between them:

> I do not find that in the English or any other modern tongue, the boundaries are exactly fixed between virtues and talents, vices and defects, or that a precise definition can be given of the one as contradistinguished from the other. (E App. IV, para. 262, 313)

Furthermore, he claims, the problem of where to draw the line is of no great moment, since different contexts, personalities, cultures, and even personal preferences about what virtues one prefers to have oneself and what virtues one would "rather pass with the world" (para. 264, 316) will govern the way the line is drawn. Certainly Hume himself is quite happy to class many "intellectual" virtues such as "prudence, penetration, discernment, discretion" as genuine virtues for they, like the so-called "moral" virtues, "have a considerable influence on conduct" (para. 262, 313), and it would be very odd to describe a person as a "man of great virtue, but an egregious blockhead" (para. 262, 314). Again qualities of the "head" as opposed to the "heart," such as "industry, frugality, temperance, secrecy, perseverance" (para. 262, 313) are "genuine" virtues for Hume.

2.3   Hume and Nietzsche's Virtue Ethics as Response Dependent

Here we address the question: What type of virtue ethics best suits Hume's and Nietzsche's views? I believe that on a virtue ethical map of their moral philosophy Hume and Nietzsche can be read as offering an under-explored option for virtue ethics – what may be called response dependent virtue ethics.[11]

According to Charles Pigden, "Hume was regarded both in his own day and for the next 200 years (roughly 1740–1940) as a dissident disciple of Francis Hutcheson and Hutcheson was a moral realist," in the following sense: "moral judgments are 'truth-apt,' true or false, and … some such judgments are (literally) true; and true … with respect to their distinctively moral contents."[12] In particular, "in today's jargon" Hume should be read as following Hutcheson in being a response dependence theorist. I shall concur with this interpretation, elaborating the details in Chapter 3. A response dependence reading of Nietzsche will also be offered. In Chapter 6 I show how such a reading makes sense of his idea of "will to power" as a key interpretative notion: "will to power" in human beings is the generic attitude to the world within which normative interpretations are made meaningful through central concepts such as strength, health, life affirmation.

On a response dependent virtue ethics, properties such as being virtuous are, in a sense, genuine properties of objects and not mere modifications or projections of our sensibilities. Nonetheless, on a response dependent view, we need a distinctive kind of human response or interpretation as a background within which such properties can be intelligibly admired, praised, and considered excellences in people. In the words of John McDowell, moral properties are not "brutely there – not there wholly independent of our sensibilities – any more than colours are."[13]

The core idea of the response dependence view I attribute to Hume and Nietzsche is this: certain sensibilities to ethical properties such as being virtuous or valuable are essential to the very intelligibility and thereby the existence of those properties as ethical properties. That idea can be expressed as:

(RD)   An ethical property is response dependent if and only if the property is open to certain responses or construals in responders having appropriate sensibilities, and these responses or construals are what make the property intelligible as an ethical property. Without that mode of intelligibility, the property (such as being courageous, being generous, being amiable, or being patient), could not exist as an *ethical* property (namely a virtuous trait), though it could exist as a property determined by other modes of intelligibility.[14]

(RD) is a thesis about the very intelligibility of ethical properties. As such it is a thesis about the existence of ethical properties as *ethical* properties. A similar thesis applied to redness is a thesis about the existence of redness as a phenomenological "secondary quality": it is not a thesis about the existence of redness as a "microscopic textural property" of the surface of an object.[15]

For the sake of brevity let us (following the terminology of McDowell) call the "mode of intelligibility" of ethics the "*logos*" of ethics, though I do not want to commit myself to the thesis that this consists of (or consists entirely of) the "space of reasons" given much contemporary understandings of the notion of a reason. More to our purposes we need to ask this: In what specific kind of way are ethical properties such as virtue response dependent in the manner specified by (RD) for Hume and Nietzsche? They have rather different views on the nature of the responses necessary for the intelligibility of a world containing virtue and vice properties. For Hume, such responses involve a basic "moral sense" for which at least minimal benevolence combined with empathic capacity is necessary, and which is constituted by the sentiment of approval or disapproval of virtue and vice respectively. The "passion" of benevolence is "internal to our frame and constitution," though notice that for him it is (in its mature form) a desire for another's happiness or good, and happiness and good are both highly sophisticated ethical concepts.

Hume's view that benevolence is inherent to our constitution anticipates modern findings in developmental psychology. According to Michael Shermer, citing Paul Bloom's experiments on babies: "Bloom provides experimental evidence that our 'natural endowments' include a moral sense – some capacity to distinguish between kind and cruel actions; empathy and compassion – suffering at the pain of those around us and the wish to make the pain go away."[16] This moral sense is possessed even by babies from three months old, "far too early to attribute to learning and culture."[17] Bloom himself cites the Sentimentalist thinkers as the philosophical precursors of these findings, frequently citing Adam Smith's *The Theory of the Moral Sentiments*.

Notice that the "moral sense" of babies is not a *logos*, or for McDowell even experience, but for our purposes this does not matter: the rudiments of an ethical sensibility are in place, and this rudimentary sensibility becomes more sophisticated over time. Without that sensibility, as Bloom claims, mere preference for helping behaviors manifested even in babyhood, and a learned knowledge of the rules of morality will not be tantamount to a moral sense, for psychopaths may manifest such preferences and have knowledge of moral rules, but fail to possess the moral emotions constituting the moral sense.[18] Assuming the basic emotional rudiments are in place, that sensibility develops through social induction into a framework of intelligibility of the ethical constituted by thick concepts such as (for Hume) justice being honorable and injustice dishonorable (see Chapter 4). Our competence with these concepts is informed not only by basic emotional orientations but also by cultural understandings of their point and function in the practical realm; cultural understandings themselves interpreted through tradition, as particularly Nietzsche emphasizes. McDowell refers to this induction by the German term *Bildung*[19] while Hume describes the "artifices" of "public praise and blame," "private education," "custom," and "any artifice of politicians" (T 3.2.2.25–26/500). For both Hume and Nietzsche thick virtue and vice concepts are at the centre of the *logos* of the ethical and the practical generally. Unfortunately the development of sensibility can become more distorted in the process of sophistication. Neither Hume nor Nietzsche take current understandings of the thick concepts for granted; Nietzsche indeed argues that our culture and the tradition which spawns it have so distorted our understandings of thick concepts that those understandings should be turned on their head. While Hume thinks nonetheless that exemplars of virtue are in our midst, Nietzsche awaits "the man of the future."

For Nietzsche responses at the basis of the *logos* of the practical/ethical involve forms of "will to power" manifesting a variety of will-oriented phenomena ranging from aggression to creativity to generosity. Again we should distinguish between rudimentary and increasingly sophisticated responses where what Nietzsche calls "drives" become interpretations deploying understandings of thick concepts. Indeed the other-regarding "moral sense" of babies is held to contain an aggressive element of rudimentary justice. In some of Bloom's experiments babies exhibited aggressive smacking of "naughty puppets" in contexts suggesting that the "moral sense" includes a "rudimentary sense of justice – a desire to see good actions rewarded and bad actions punished."[20] This aspect of the "moral sense" Nietzsche would include under the general rubric "will to power" which in distorted though sophisticated forms yields punitive or resentment-filled distortions of justice (see Chapter 8).

What Hume's moral sense and Nietzsche's orientations of (aspects of) will to power permit for Hume and Nietzsche respectively then, is making the world of ethics open to us as an ethical world: an openness whose basic materials in early sensibility are refined from the preconceptual phase of babyhood through to old age. Just as morality for Hume is beyond the reach of the understanding of him who has no benevolence nor any "relish" for virtue, in short no moral sense, so for Nietzsche genuine virtue is unintelligible to individuals who are will-less, who have no sense of who they are or what is to their advantage, and who have not a shred of productivity or creativity in their nature.[21] Nietzsche's "Last Man" of *Zarathustra* who is a will-less passive individual only concerned with his comfort is the equivalent in "moral blindness" to Hume's "fancied monster," whose lack of benevolence makes him totally unable to discriminate on grounds of moral importance between trivial inconveniences from large-scale human suffering.

However as already indicated openness to the world of ethics is a far cry from competence. It is important to appreciate that the sensibilities characterizing Hume's moral sense, and Nietzsche's basic "life affirming" will to power, theoretically permit ethical competence, at least with time, but do not constitute it. They enable us to constitute our world as having an ethical dimension: they do not comprise the whole of our ethical competence or provide an epistemology of ethics. There are several reasons for this. First as we have seen both the moral sense and will to power may be rudimentary or even distorted. As I understand both Nietzsche and Hume, ethics may be intelligible to those with quite distorted sensibilities such as the griping miser (Hume) or even to those suffering from the "Christian neurosis" (Nietzsche). Those with distorted sensibilities may be wrong, even seriously so, but if they are sufficiently sophisticated ethics is at least intelligible to them. Hume's *Essays* are particularly informative about a wide range of distortions. In "Of Superstition and Enthusiasm" Hume speaks of two kinds of emotional distortion pertaining particularly to religious belief: "Weakness, fear, melancholy" and "raptures, transports and surprising flights of fancy" (Miller 74). In his "Dignity or Meanness in Human Nature" Hume claims that even though a person may possess "a delicate sense of morals," this sense, when "attended with a splenetic temper," "is apt to give a man a disgust of the world" (Miller 81). His essay "Of Refinement in the Arts" speaks of love of luxury, and conditions under which approvals of luxury can be distorted: "men of libertine principles bestow praises even on vicious luxury, and represent it as highly advantageous to society" while "men of severe morals blame even the most innocent luxury" (Miller 269).

What counts as so distorted that there is no moral sense or creative take on the world, is something inherently vague. Even the will-less individual has some "will to power": after all as Nietzsche says, "Life itself is will to power."[22] He claims that even those suffering from the Christian neurosis are creative: they have after all revalued values but in a highly distorted way. The chronically callous and unjust are likely to have some benevolence even if minimal. Hume's "sensible knave" is capable of approving justice as a virtue; he through selfishness does not want to apply its precepts to himself. Our understandings of thick concepts may be wrong and distorted but on one thing Hume is clear: without a moral sense informed by "the original instinct" of benevolence ethics does not exist as an intelligible realm. This issue is discussed in the next chapter.

Second, even those with relatively healthy undistorted sensibilities may not be refined, judicious, or expert. Even a highly life affirming will to power may not go hand in hand with the expertise for which Nietzsche takes credit as the "first" psychologist. Consider too this example from MacIntyre's *After Virtue*:

> She [Jane Austen] praises the virtue of being socially agreeable, as Aristotle does, although she values more highly – in her letters as well as in her novels – the virtue of amiability, which requires a genuine loving regard of other people as such, and not only the impression of such a regard embodied in manners. She is, after all, a Christian, and therefore deeply suspicious of an agreeableness that conceals a lack of true amiability.[23]

To distinguish between amiability and social agreeableness as virtues in a subtle way may require an Austen; to distinguish between helpfulness as a "life affirming" virtue of strength and helpfulness as expressive of "life denying" self-contempt, may require a Nietzsche. At any rate such distinctions require a competence that far outstrips what constitute the intelligibility conditions for ethics: the basic orientations which allow for openness to an ethical dimension of reality.

Third, as we discuss further below, even expert and authoritative sensibilities may not accurately represent virtue. Even the world's foremost psychologist and cultural commentator may not have access to the best science (not yet available) which helps us understand the nature of virtue and vice.

What for Hume and Nietzsche respectively is the function of the moral sense or will to power as intelligibility conditions for ethics? It is to make available to us a basic distinction between the polarities of virtue and vice. The response dependent character of *specific* virtues and vices constituted by appropriate or fitting patterns of motives, emotions, and behavior involving resentment or its absence, joy, love, boredom, hope, pride in objects connected to self, ambition, are not as such part of those sensibilities, but enable ethical competence in general. In Hume, the large array of passions which provides the richness of the moral landscape is not reducible to the moral sense itself, a sensibility which makes intelligible the fundamental moral distinction between virtue and vice; traits to be approved and disapproved respectively. In beings such as us that sense could hardly function in the practical world without a competent grasp of concepts such as contemptible, lovable, (genuinely) humorous, which ground our judgments of virtue and vice. In Nietzsche there is a similar richness constituted by the many and varied manifestations and expressions of "will to power" in relation to such things as compassion and pity, punishment and discipline.

This realization resolves an important problem in the understanding of both Hume's and Nietzsche's response dependence. It might be thought that for Hume and Nietzsche respectively there are only two ethical responses or "wills": the approvals or disapprovals of the moral sense, or life affirming or life denying will to power, where these are appropriate to the polar opposites, virtue and vice respectively. However in a section of her book *Divine Motivation Theory* entitled "The Myth of Value Polarity"[24] Linda Zagzebski argues persuasively that this is an inaccurate and grossly oversimplified view of ethics. Ethical competence requires viewing the world of ethics as multifaceted, where the facets are conceptualized through notions such as contemptible, pitiable, enviable, unjust, lovable, humorous. Although passions, unlike belief, do not for Hume represent the world, ethical competence requires understanding how they are fitting or unfitting to their objects, how they may be expressed in fitting or unfitting ways, at fitting or unfitting times and so on. For example grief may seem excessive but be appropriate for one's intimates and thus fitting and virtuous; pride may be overweening and thus unfitting and vicious; wit, a virtue for Hume, may descend into non-virtuous forms such as sarcastic and cruel quips, or buffoonery; cheerfulness, also a virtue for Hume, may take the non-virtuous form of a tendency toward dissolute mirth. As he says: "Cheerfulness could scarce admit of blame from its excess, were it not that dissolute mirth, without a proper cause or subject, is a sure symptom and characteristic of folly, and on that account disgustful" (E para. 208, 258 n. 1).

On Hume's view then, properties such as being lovable, contemptible, pitiable are response dependent properties whose force as ethical is reliant on the moral sense, but whose passional base provides the richness and substance of our ethical lives as expressed in corresponding virtue. For example being lovable is a property which has the power to excite a certain passion in us, namely for Hume the "indefinable" passion of love which is expressible in the various virtues of love. All these notions (such as being lovable) pass the empiricist test of being grounded in "observation": in this case emotional observation. Emotion is thus seen as something that "reveals reality and part of the reality it reveals is evaluative"[25] and virtuous emotion reveals it in a non-distorting way.

Similarly it would be a mistake to think that for Nietzsche "will to power" is just a single drive such that ethics simply consists of maximal expression or promotion of "will to power" or even "life affirming" will to power. Ethics for Nietzsche is vastly more complex than the simple "value polarity" of will to power or will-lessness (or even of life affirming or life denying will to power). As we shall explore particularly in Chapters 6 and 7, the world of ethics for Nietzsche is hugely multifaceted, for "will to power" itself has a great variety of forms such as the "will to truth," the "will to a system," the "unconditional will to justice," and the "will to memory." It also has many aspects, even healthy strong aspects: for example in his metaphor of the "metamorphoses of the spirit" in *Zarathustra*, Nietzsche speaks of a strong form of endurance, for example "stepping into filthy waters when they are the waters of truth," making friends with those who do not listen (the camel); an aggressive creation of space for the "freedom to create" by saying "a sacred 'No' even to duty" (the lion); and the will to say "a sacred 'Yes'" by creating new values for which a "letting go" will to return to the receptivity and innocence of the child is necessary: "the child is innocence and forgetting, a new beginning" necessary for "the game of creation."[26] The ethical status of these "wills" is cashed out through a sophisticated, normative interpretation of types of will to power. This normative interpretation essentially comprises a discussion of virtues and vices constituted by the complex, multifarious types of weak and strong, life affirming or life denying, dispositions expressing these "wills."

There is one further important feature of Hume's and Nietzsche's response dependence which needs to be highlighted and further emphasized. Their response dependence is at bottom emotional response dependence. For Hume the pleasurable love of virtue constituting the approval of the moral sense is a pleasure that speaks to the fundamental condition of the moral sense – our basic benevolence – desire for another's good. For Nietzsche the nature of the ethics-constituting response is inherently creative. The value properties of the world are dependent on our creative emotional take on that world: "we who think and feel at the same time are those who really continually fashion something that had not been there before: the whole eternally growing world of valuations, colors, accents, perspectives, scales, affirmations, and negations."[27] A more generally applicable response dependent view, then, allows for both relatively passive and relatively active forms of engagement or modifications of our sensibilities and wills.

It is important to notice then that though both Hume's and Nietzsche's response dependence views of ethics are emotional response dependence views, they take different forms. A response dependence view need not take the form of a "spectator" sentiment (the moral sense) as in Hume. For Nietzsche it is a will or drive that constitutes the fundamental ethics-constituting response. For him certain situations can then be understood as having a power to arouse or bring to expression desires or drives to overcome, resist, or change things, in those who have "will to power" (in properly human form). Situations or objects are seen as challenging, resistances to overcome, exploitable for our creative purposes, inspirational (for creative purposes), to be improved upon, or, even to be "incorporated" or destroyed. Such ethically significant properties can thus receive a response dependent analysis, dependent on the generic or schematic concept of "will to power." Nietzsche's response dependence is thus not best described in the traditional way of situations or objects having powers to *modify* our sensibilities,[28] for that sounds altogether too passive. Rather situations and objects are seen as having powers to engage our productive or creative "wills." In *The Gay Science* Nietzsche claims:

> Whatever has value in our world now does not have value in itself; according to its nature – nature is always value-less but has been given value at some time as a present – and it is we who gave and bestowed it.[29]

This passage and others are generally given an anti-realist and/or a non-cognitivist reading,[30] but a response dependent reading is a natural one, and in keeping with a virtue ethical interpretation. On my view, the claims in *Gay Science* 301 and 299 can be seen as analogous to Hume's discussion of the disenchanted scientific properties of a circle by comparison with its beauty (see further Chapter 3). Just like Hume, Nietzsche denies that there are moral or value properties of objects in the sense that they exist entirely independent of emotional response, perspective, or interpretation. In particular what Nietzsche and indeed Hume would deny is that the "scientific" viewpoint gives you *the* real properties of things which are thus (in reality) valueless. Like John McDowell they would deny that the one and only objective viewpoint is a scientific one; a viewpoint that is perspective-free, emotion-free, and interpretation-free, while all other viewpoints are merely projection. On my interpretation then, when Nietzsche says that nature is valueless he is making the same point as Hume: nature is not inherently full of value independent of interpretation and sensibility; value is rather a response dependent property. Though Hume and Nietzsche are spare naturalists and not supernaturalists, they both reject scientific naturalism.

Understanding Hume's and Nietzsche's response dependence as broadly speaking emotional response dependence accounts for the fact that, as Hume and Nietzsche believed, "morality" (whether sound or otherwise) engages our will and passions, and drives action. For example as Hume puts it:

> Extinguish all the warm feelings and prepossessions in favour of virtue, and all disgust or aversion to vice: render men totally indifferent towards these distinctions; and morality is no longer a practical study, nor has any tendency to regulate our lives. (E para. 136, 172)

Notice however that it does follow from this that the moral sense, as an appreciative sentiment, itself motivates. Indeed as argued in the next chapter this is not the case: rather the moral sense brings forth the world of ethics, which as a whole has motivational force. Notice too, that this basic motivational feature of "morality" is not to be confused with the meta-ethical position known today as "internalism," the view that anyone who (sincerely) judges that she is morally required to do something will be motivated at least defeasibly to do that thing. What we may call Hume's practicality thesis quoted above does not entail internalism which applies to each and every moral judgment, as opposed to the "tendency" of morality as a whole. Indeed I shall not attribute internalism to Hume: he claims after all "Tis one thing to know virtue, and another to conform one's will to it" (T 3.1.1.22/465–456).[31]

Let us now summarize the core features of the response dependent virtue ethics ascribed to Hume and Nietzsche. The "moral sense" and "will to power" are for Hume and Nietzsche respectively, the fundamental responses (Hume) or motivational drives (Nietzsche) which constitute the world of ethics as an intelligible world. For Hume, what is enabled by the moral sense (a pleasurable love of virtue and a displeasurable hatred of vice, constituting sentiments of approval of virtue and disapproval of vice), is making intelligible the fundamental moral distinction between virtue and vice. Virtues are "powers" to give rise to love in the form of approbation and so forth in creatures such as us, namely those capable of benevolence, which I shall argue (Chapter 3) is for Hume a condition of possessing a moral sense. For Nietzsche the fundamental distinction between virtue and vice is intelligible only to those possessing a sufficiently creative orientation to the world. In short for both, virtue and vice are genuine properties of persons but are intelligible as such only through certain emotional sensibilities.

2.4   Response Dependence in Virtue Ethics: A Problem

The previous section outlined the basic nature of the differing sensibilities which for Hume and Nietzsche bring the world of ethics as a world of normativity into being. But how can that world be understood, in an appropriate way, as a normative world? How in particular does a response dependent account preserve the notions that we do not simply perceive moral properties as we perceive redness, but that we reason about such questions as: What merits a trait being called a virtue? How can we improve our character? How do we reason about ethical matters in order to resolve disagreement in a rational way? For example if a character trait such as benevolence is to merit the ascription "virtue" such benevolence must be characteristically well motivated and well directed; if we engage in a situation calling it an "improvement" the situation must merit such engagement; if we are warranted in "exploiting" a resource such exploitation cannot be vicious. As McDowell put it, not all situations causing fear *merit* being called dangerous; similarly not all situations exciting benevolent or compassionate feelings warrant certain kinds of (what is regarded as) helpful response. Cowards have the wrong view of what is genuinely dangerous or to be avoided, callous and overly sentimental people do not possess benevolence as a virtue. Similarly we may give the wrong values to the world "as a present" (as Nietzsche puts it in the quotation above from *The Gay Science*): indeed, as Nietzsche argued persistently, the prevalent attitudes about virtue are wrong and damaging.

This issue is brought into sharp relief by McDowell in his "Values and Secondary Properties," a discussion which highlights some problematic features in the presentation of response dependence in ethics. The root of the problem is the association of the secondary property analysis with the idea of perceptual appearance, and the association of response dependence in ethics with that analysis. Conceiving ethical properties as secondary properties has resulted in conceiving them in terms of *perceptual* appearance. Here for example is McDowell's notion of a secondary property:

A secondary quality is a property the ascription of which to an object is not adequately understood except as true, if it is true, in virtue of the object's disposition to present a certain sort of perceptual appearance: specifically, an appearance characterizable by using a word for the property itself to say how the object perceptually appears.[32]

The "perceptual appearance" account of secondary properties is reinforced by McDowell's gloss of Locke. McDowell claims that his account of secondary qualities "is faithful to one key Lockean doctrine, namely the identification of secondary qualities with 'powers to produce various sensations in us.'"[33] However McDowell glosses Locke's "sensations" as "perceptual appearance," claiming that this is harmless.[34] Unfortunately it is not harmless, for it removes from view an interpretation of "sensation" (or some related notion) in terms of for example Hume's notion of "impression" which includes pleasure and pain, desire and aversion, the passions (emotions), and even the will (which for Hume is not strictly comprehended among the passions, and is indefinable (T 2.3.1.2/399)). It also renders invisible Nietzsche's conception of ethics (properly conceived) as being (on my view) essentially connected with "will to power" through the ideas of strong, healthy productivity and creativity.

Most seriously, a tendency to deploy perceptual analogies to the ethical case makes it hard to see how responses can be justified in a reason giving or reason responsive way. As McDowell claims, there is a disanalogy between values and colors:

> The disanalogy now, is that a virtue (say) is conceived to be not merely such as to elicit the appropriate "attitude" (as a colour is merely such as to cause the appropriate experiences), but rather such as to *merit* it.[35]

On my reading of Nietzsche and Hume as response dependence theorists, the problem is resolved by clarifying the kind of response dependence I ascribe to them. Once this is done we can see how the disanalogy can be recognized within a response dependence analysis. To recall: the core idea expressed by (RD) is that sensibilities to ethical properties such as being virtuous or valuable are essential to the intelligibility and thereby the existence of those properties as *ethical* properties. In order to gain a clearer understanding of how traits *merit* ascription as virtues we need a clearer understanding of what (RD) entails. (RD) has generally been construed as a claim that ethical properties are relational, rather than monadic. Thus we have a principle such as:

(R)   A person's being virtuous consists in her virtuousness evoking some relevant response.

However as Wiggins notes "redness is an external, monadic property of a [British] postbox."[36] That view is compatible with (RD) and a rejection of what Williams calls the "absolute conception" by contrast with "peculiar" conceptions, "ones available only to a more or less restricted set of subjects, who share a contingent sensory apparatus, or culture or history."[37] The point is that though being red is a monadic property of things, its intelligibility as a color property depends on the "peculiarities" of our sensory apparatus. We also tend to think that having a virtuous trait is a monadic property of an agent,[38] though its intelligibility as an ethical property depends on the "peculiarities" of our emotional/volitional apparatus. (RD) does not entail (R). Once the mode of intelligibility of normative properties as normative is in place they may be construed as monadic within that mode of intelligibility.

We have not yet solved our problem, for understanding normative properties as response dependent in the sense of (RD) is not sufficient for understanding them as normative. As we have seen, we want to say for example that a trait V is a virtue if and only if V merits the relevant response (and does not just cause it). A standard solution to this problem is to claim that the merit conferring properties are determined by the sensibilities and capacities of competent, qualified agents. So we have for example:

(Q)   V is a virtue if and only if competent, qualified agents judge or experience V as a virtue (for example they have sentiments of approbation upon contemplating the trait).

Is (Q) the right way of construing what constitutes for Hume and for Nietzsche the normativity of properties such as virtue? There is a problem if we understand the response dependent nature of virtue as a normative property in terms of (Q). What *makes* it the case that a trait merits status as a virtue does not seem to depend on the responses of an agent, even a qualified one, but on certain facts, such as the trait systematically producing good consequences (important for both Hume and Nietzsche).[39] Given this feature of virtue, there is the possibility of a lack of connection between the judgments of virtuous agents and status of traits as virtues or vices. Competent agents, even practically wise agents,[40] may be wrong about key facts such as consequences. Competence is not the same as omniscience or infallibility. Competent agents have access to relevant background theories of human nature and wise, relatively informed views about long-term consequences, but some of these theories and beliefs may be false. Furthermore, as we explore more fully in Chapter 8, virtuous agents have limited perspectives. For Nietzsche even agents with superior perspectives cannot be objective: for objectivity many perspectives have to be brought to bear on a subject.

These are serious objections to (Q) but I read neither Hume nor Nietzsche as espousing (Q). Virtue for them is response dependent in that (RD) is satisfied, but whether or not some trait actually is a virtue (merits the relevant responses) depends on the obtaining of facts which may not be known to the most competent agents in a society, including those deemed most virtuous. For Hume such agents may be historically situated in such a way that key facts are not known or systematically misinterpreted (see for example the discussion of homosexuality in Chapter 5); for Nietzsche an entire culture may be so benighted, that dominant conceptions of virtue and vice need to be overturned. It will be claimed that in these cases exemplars of virtue in a society are not *genuine* exemplars, but in that case (Q) would not be able to connect responses to virtue. At any rate the core objection that key facts may be out of reach of the genuinely virtuous who have but limited perspective, remains.

It may be replied that (Q) should be read as applying to agents with ideal or idealized virtue,[41] but it is unclear how "human" those possessing idealized virtue are intended to be. Are they for example omniscient? Do they have no psychological conflicts whatsoever? Such a conception of virtue is alien to both Hume and Nietzsche.[42] Nietzsche speaks extremely vaguely of "the man of the future" at the end of Essay 2 of *The Genealogy of Morals* and in *Beyond Good and Evil* but notoriously (though sensibly on my view) says virtually nothing about the properties of such a type.[43]

The idea that "moral response-dependent meta-ethical theories characterize moral properties in terms of the reactions of certain classes of individuals"[44] is not strictly accurate on the above view. Certain general sensibilities (not necessarily qualified) are certainly required if we are to have what McDowell calls "unmediated openness" to a world of ethics.[45] We have called what is required for unmediated openness to ethical properties the intelligibility conditions or *logos* required for a grasp of ethical properties as ethical. But conditions for unmediated openness are not tantamount to an epistemology. *Accurate representation* of such properties is not constituted by, fully determined by, such general sensibilities, not even qualified ones. Once the world of ethics is intelligible as such a world, we can speak intelligently about how to accurately represent virtues as monadic properties of agents, their qualities as dispositions, and their targets for action and feeling. That is we can talk intelligently about what makes traits of character virtues and what virtue demands of us, but the deliverances of even qualified sensibilities are not the truth makers of claims that V is a virtue, or demands thus and so.

Accurate representation of for example the consequences of traits then may outrun the epistemic capacities of the virtuous and the wise. Once the world of ethics is made intelligible, science becomes its handmaiden. As Hume claims in the *Enquiries Concerning the Principles of Morals*:

> Men are now cured of their passion for hypotheses and systems in natural philosophy, and will hearken to no arguments but those which are derived from experience. It is full time that they should attempt a like reformation in all moral disquisitions; and reject every system of ethics, however subtle or ingenious, which is not founded on fact and observation. (E para. 138, 174–175)

Both Hume and Nietzsche appeal to "fact and observation" on countless occasions when making judgments about virtue and vice. In short both are naturalists in Leiter's sense of Results Continuity (see Chapter 1). However, without the requisite sensibilities, the import of properties for the normative world of virtue and vice, properties such as consequences for harm and the possession and exercise of talents, will be absent, and there will be no such world.

The question now arises: what then is the relation between virtuous agents and fittingness in the sense of accurate representation? Could it be that the responses of such agents are a necessary condition of accurate representation of virtue and vice? As McDowell argues, the emotional construals of virtuous agents are at least characteristically necessary for such representation, and this I think is the view of both Hume and Nietzsche. For Hume (as we saw above) the joyless individuals of monkish virtue, the miser, she of overheated imagination, the "severe moralist," the sensible knave, all have distorted emotional takes on the world due to their greed, selfishness, asceticism, punitive severity. For Nietzsche, she of life denying nature, whose will to power is distorted by resentment or self-hating asceticism, may have access to facts, but her construal of those facts in the normative domain will be selective and distorted. More than virtuous emotional construal, however, may be required for accurate representation: even the most sagacious, even the most life affirming of us, may be relevantly limited and not accurately fix on the fitting.

In general what determines accurate representation of virtues as traits of agents, what determines their meriting esteem as virtues, is that they are in Hume's words "naturally fitted" to be so esteemed. This book explores the multifaceted, pluralistic, ways traits are fitted to be called virtues and vices in both Hume and Nietzsche.

Here though we need to clear up a meta-ethical issue concerning talk of fittingness. Hume's talk of natural fittingness may suggest that we should supplement the basic response dependence thesis (RD) with what has been called the "fitting attitude" thesis of value which analyzes "value or some limited range of values, in terms of evaluative attitudes endorsed as fitting – or, alternatively, as appropriate, correct, merited, proper, rational, or warranted."[46] Fitting attitude forms of response dependence theory are distinguished from dispositionalism according to which funniness for example is simply "whatever amuses normal humans in standard conditions."[47] Hume is not a dispositionalist about virtue – he does not affirm simply that virtue is whatever causes sentiments of approbation in normal humans under normal conditions. What makes it naturally fitting that certain traits be virtues on Hume's view is specified by the criteria of virtue, for example, that they tend to the good of mankind (see further Chapters 3 and 5), and as already suggested, normal humans under normal conditions may be wrong about key facts, such as consequences. I doubt that Nietzsche would subscribe to dispositionalism either, since our "normal" condition and that of our culture is one of sickness.

Should we ascribe fitting attitude analyses to Hume or Nietzsche? In standard forms, fitting attitude analyses of value "reduce values to a fundamentally different sort of notion, involving what one ought, or has reason to feel."[48] The reason for this is that fittingness is seen, indeed necessarily seen, as "distinct from other forms of endorsement of an attitude, for instance as prudent or morally obligatory."[49] However, natural fittingness for Hume just is the generic thin evaluative notion whose cash value in specific areas of evaluation is spelled out in terms of virtue, where the various virtues are themselves understood in a response dependent way. Any distinction between the moral and the non-moral virtues, the moral and the prudential virtues, if it can be made at all, is of little moment: what is crucial is that qualities of character merit approbation as virtues by conforming to the various criteria of virtue. Nor is there any suggestion that the evaluative is understood wholly in terms of value, or that value is *analyzed* in terms of reasons to feel and so forth.

As we shall explore in Chapter 5, some types of virtuous response for Hume, such as expressions of tenderness, grief, joyous appreciation of a scenic wonder, are not responses for or to reasons, but are expressive of for example bonds of affection.[50] This is not to say that there are no norms for the felicity of the expressive reactions; for Hume there are, but these are provided by norms of virtue. Given that he does not *analyze* the evaluative in terms of reasons his view is not then subject to a particular difficulty which allegedly besets fitting attitude theories of value, notably the "wrong kind of reason" problem.[51] For example the fact that one will be killed if one does not admire an evil person may arguably provide one with sufficient reason to admire that person but does not make him fitting for admiration, that is, admirable. The threat to one's well-being is the "wrong kind of reason" to admire in the sense that that reason has no bearing on his fittingness to be admired.

In summary, Hume and Nietzsche are both interpreted as a certain kind of response dependence theorist. For them virtue properties are intelligible as virtue properties only through relevant sensibilities (emotions and emotionally laden conative states, particularly as construed through the thick concepts). Their response dependence accounts of ethical properties are accounts of those properties via accounts of our unmediated openness to them. As John McDowell puts it, "We are rational animals whose minds are directly open to a world 'permeated with rationality.'"[52] When this openness is at its best the thick concepts through which we construe the ethical domain are sufficiently sophisticated, undistorted, and informed. It is this kind of emotional rationality which constitutes our intentional relation to the world of ethics – there is no "*factum brutum*" accessible by a "pure beholding" independent of human modes of making the world significant for us.[53] We could have no intentional relation to such a "reality": it would not be "open" to us. Such a view makes no metaphysical sense for Hume, Nietzsche, or for McDowell.[54]

This openness, constituted by (for Hume) the sensibilities of humanity/love/benevolence, permits the construal of states of affairs such as "my daughter is badly cut" as a reason which favors my bandaging her or taking her to the emergency department, so that damage and pain are avoided. A person totally devoid of a moral sense will not construe these facts as reasons for actions of the appropriate type, but may for example simply admire the color of the blood, or just be totally indifferent. For Nietzsche, a person completely devoid of a creative productive will not construe the facts of her talents as a reason to do anything at all with them. Ethical kinds of construal are made possible through the emotional orientations of benevolence and love; and creative drives.

Furthermore these basic emotional orientations, inherent in our frame and constitution as Hume puts it, are developed through induction into competence with the thick concepts, a process which is developmental.[55] Before we conclude that on the contrary for Hume, for example, the basic response of approval of a trait is pre-conceptual and merely causal since it is "faint" and "imperceptible" *love*, we should distinguish between the following three types of case. My grandson Sam, six weeks old, is on my knees having a mutual mirroring exchange. In response to my smiling and talking he smiles in different ways more or less broadly making appropriate noises. Delighted by this I smile and talk more and so it goes on until he gets tired. Here the baby shows empathic delight, even love, but in no way could he be said to be *approving*, in Hume's sense, of my virtue as a grandmother. His response may be a preconceptual form of love for a virtue expressed but it is not approval of my virtue. Beside me, observing this exchange, my daughter-in-law feels faint and impercep-tible love at/of my (undoubted) grandparental virtue, thereby approving of it in Hume's sense. She has mastered relevant concepts (desirable and admirable traits, vices, that these are possessed or otherwise by agents and so on). Third, the "love" constituting approval of traits must not be confused with love of individuals, although love of a person's virtue may *cause* love of its possessor, for Hume. My daughter-in-law may approve of my grandparental virtue without loving *me*, for example.

It is also clear that Hume would think that though moral expertise or coping is not of a kind rationalized by the understanding alone, our ethical behavior is mindful in Hume's sense of being "judicious." For example unless I have serious attachment difficulties with my baby causing severe neglect (in which case I am incompetent to an extreme degree), I am mindful of what solid foods to give her – what kind, when, how often, and so on – especially when I am still relatively inexpert. If I am really at sea, barely able to cope, my mindfulness will take on the full panoply of traditionally conceived moral reasoning. I will rush to principles to be found in expert books on babies (which hopefully do not all disagree) and seek general reasons for doing or not doing thus and so, reasons which seriously abstract from my current situation. If I am insensitive in the application of these principles to *my* baby here and now, I am liable to make mistakes; indeed it is likely that such principles cannot be fully and accurately applied to my case. The way in which reason and rationality feature in Hume's response dependence view of ethics, is the basic topic of the next chapter.

Finally Hume's and Nietzsche's views are "results continuous" with science but are neither forms of scientific naturalism, nor a mere subjectivism where virtue is understood as whatever properties excite our moral sense of love (as a mere feeling or passion) or (in the case of Nietzsche) our will to power understood in a non-normative way. What makes traits virtues are properties that constitute the fittingness of objects to be admired or loved, say, and whose fittingness to be so admired can be warranted by appeal to both the *Naturwissenschaften* and the *Geisteswissenschaften*, including history, literature, and psychology. Both Hume and Nietzsche were fond of appealing to such bodies of knowledge to provide the background knowledge requisite for judging genuine fittingnesses.

Notes

1 Oxford: Oxford University Press, 2003, 5. For more on my views about the nature of virtue ethics see my "Virtue Ethics," in *The Continuum Companion to Ethics*, ed. Christian Miller (London: Continuum, 2011), 190–214.
2 If Michael Slote is right in his views that perfection is impossible in his *The Impossibility of Perfection: Aristotle, Feminism, and the Complexities of Ethics* (Oxford: Oxford University Press, 2011), virtue ethics as such is not impugned, for it is not part of the definition of virtue ethics that virtue, even at its best, is an ideal of perfection.
3 *The Gay Science*, trans. Walter Kaufmann (New York: Vintage Books, 1974), Book 1, sect. 7, 81.
4 *Gay Science*, Book 1, sect. 7, 82.
5 *Gay Science*, Book 4, sect. 296, 238.
6 See Lisa Tessman, *Burdened Virtue: Virtue Ethics for Liberatory Struggles* (Oxford: Oxford University Press, 2005).
7 See Julia Annas, *Intelligent Virtue* (Oxford: Oxford University Press, 2011).
8 See further on this distinction my "The Notion of the Moral: The Relation between Virtue Ethics and Virtue Epistemology," *Philosophical Studies* 171(1) (2014), 121–134.
9 Christine M. Korsgaard, "The General Point of View: Love and Moral Approval in Hume's Ethics," *Hume Studies* 25 (1999), 3–41, 10.
10 For a discussion of my own skepticism about the relation between sporting and other virtues and so called "moral" virtue see my "The Notion of the Moral."

11   I shall not in this book spend much time arguing directly against various subjectivist, non-cognitivist, projectivist interpretations of, in particular, Hume. Excellent detailed work combating these interpretations has recently been done by Rachel Cohon (*Hume's Morality: Feeling and Fabrication*, Oxford: Oxford University Press, 2008) and I agree wholeheartedly with her rebuttals of what she calls the "common reading" of Hume (12). My interest is rather in the more positive project of offering a plausible interpretation which gels with characteristic kinds of meta-ethical assumptions associated with virtue ethics.

12   Charles R. Pigden, "If Not Non-Cognitivism, Then What?," in *Hume on Motivation and Virtue*, ed. Charles R. Pigden (Basingstoke: Palgrave Macmillan, 2010), 80–104, 95. By contrast Rachel Cohon describes the "reaction dependence," "moral sensing" interpretation of Hume as anti-realist in *Hume's Morality: Feeling and Fabrication*. I think this is unfortunate since it would be odd to think of accounts of colors as secondary properties as "anti-realist." However, and in my view unfortunately, "moral realism" is often analogized to realism in science, itself conceived as a realism where scientific propositions are conceived as describing a reality "whose nature owes nothing to our natures" and is "prior to and independent of" it: Peter Railton, "Subjective and Objective," in *Truth in Ethics*, ed. Brad Hooker (Oxford: Blackwell, 1996), 51–68, 55. Even if global response dependence were false, this kind of generic description and analogizing is rightly in my view criticized by Railton.

13   "Values and Secondary Qualities," in *Mind, Value, and Reality* (Cambridge, MA: Harvard University Press, 2002), 131–150, 146.

14   RD is not intended to apply only to secondary properties as generally understood. Consider a view of secondary properties of McDowell's: the idea of a secondary property is supposed to apply to any property the concept of which is such that its "very content cannot be specified without invoking what it is for [it] to figure in appearance" by contrast with things like cubes. Thus "what it is for something to be red is for it to be such as to look red (to certain perceivers in certain circumstances)": "Response to Robert Brandom," in *Reading McDowell: On Mind and World*, ed. Nicholas H. Smith (London: Routledge, 2002), 179–181, 181.) By contrast "a blind geometer *can* count as fully understanding the concept *square* even if the geometer cannot discriminate one by looking at it": Robert Brandom, "Placing McDowell's Empiricism," in *Reading McDowell: On* Mind and World, 92–105, 101. However I reject this account in the case of virtue properties, and I do not believe Hume or Nietzsche hold such a view. One cannot just look at a person and see for example that she is constant in Jane Austen's sense. The sensibilities required to construe ethical properties are complex, arising through a process of development and induction into concepts difficult to grasp. It may be the case that by supposed contrast to the ethical case the sensibilities/*logos* required to understand *square* are shared across many rational species, those that have a grasp of our mathematics. But even here we should be careful of ascribing a *factum brutum* grasped by what Heidegger calls a "pure beholding" just because it is a mathematical notion. Integral calculus I believe is something that is useful but has controversial foundations originating in a seventeenth-century debate "that was as religious as it was scientific": Amir Alexander, "The Secret Spiritual History of Calculus," *Scientific American* 310.4 (April 2014), 68–71, 68. "For the Jesuits the purpose of mathematics was to construct the world as eternally unchanging. For Cavalieri, it was the reverse." "'Who will be the judge' of the truth of a geometric construction, Guldin [espousing Jesuit principles] mockingly asked Cavalieri, 'the hand, the eye or the intellect?'" (71). For Guldin, "the notion that you could base mathematics on a vague and paradoxical intuition was absurd" (71).

15   McDowell, "Values and Secondary Qualities," 112.

16   Michael Shermer, "The Genesis of Justice," *Scientific American* 310.5 (May 2014), 65, citing Paul Bloom, *Just Babies: The Origins of Good and Evil* (New York: Crown Publishers, 2013). For the views of other developmental psychologists along these lines see also Gustavo Carlo et al., "The Elusive Altruist: The Psychological Study of the Altruistic Personality" and Ross A. Thompson, "Early Foundations: Conscience and the Development of Moral Character," in *Personality, Identity, and Character: Explorations in Moral Psychology*, ed. Darcia Narvaez and Daniel K. Lapsley (Cambridge: Cambridge University Press, 2009), 271–294 and 159–184 respectively, and Nancy Eisenberg, Tracy L. Spinrad, and Zoe E. Taylor, "Sympathy," in *The Handbook of Virtue Ethics*, ed. Stan van Hooft (Durham: Acumen, 2014), 409–417.

17   Shermer, 65, citing Bloom.

18 See Bloom, *Just Babies*. Here Bloom claims of a psychopath that "even as a baby psychopath he might prefer an individual who helps someone over a hill over someone who pushes the character down" but as he grows up, learning the rules of society, "he doesn't feel any of the associated moral emotions" (33–34).

19 In his *Mind and World* (Cambridge, MA: Harvard University Press, 1994).

20 Shermer, 65.

21 Thus creativity is a pervasive phenomenon central to will to power: it is not limited to artistic creativity. See further Swanton, *Virtue Ethics: A Pluralistic View* (Oxford: Oxford University Press, 2003), chapter 7.

22 "On the Prejudices of Philosophers," in *Beyond Good and Evil: Prelude to a Philosophy of the Future*, trans. R.J. Hollingdale (London: Penguin, 1973), sect. 13, 44.

23 Alasdair MacIntyre, *After Virtue: A Study in Moral Theory*, 3rd edn (Notre Dame, IN: University of Notre Dame Press, 2007), 241.

24 Linda Trinkaus Zagzebski, *Divine Motivation Theory* (Cambridge: Cambridge University Press, 2004), 25ff.

25 Ibid., 78.

26 "On the Three Metamorphoses," *Thus Spoke Zarathustra, in The Portable Nietzsche*, ed, and trans. Walter Kaufmann (New York: Penguin, 1976), 138–139.

27 *Gay Science*, Book 4, sect. 301, 241–242.

28 See McDowell, "Values and Secondary Qualities," 143.

29 *Gay Science*, Book 4, sect. 301, 241.

30 I include here the non-cognitivist, projectivist reading of Maudemarie Clark and David Dudrick, "Nietzsche and Moral Objectivity: The Development of Nietzsche's Metaethics," in *Nietzsche and Morality*, ed. Brian Leiter and Neil Sinhababu (Oxford: Oxford University Press, 2007), 192–226, who also cite (205) the cognitivist "normative subjectivism" of Richardson according to which we bestow values on things through our acts of valuing, and the cognitivist but anti-realist fictionalism of Nadeem Hussain and Bernard Reginster.

31 For an excellent defense of a non-internalist reading of Hume and Hume's so-called Motivation Argument, see Norva Y.S. Lo, "Is Hume Inconsistent? – Motivation and Morals," in *Hume on Motivation and Virtue*, ed. Charles R. Pigden (Basingstoke: Palgrave Macmillan, 2010), 57–79.

32 "Values and Secondary Qualities," 133.

33 Ibid., 133, citing Locke, *An Essay Concerning Human Understanding*, 2.8.10.

34 "Values and Secondary Qualities," 133.

35 Ibid., 143. Italics in original.

36 Wiggins, "Truth, Invention and the Meaning of Life," in *Needs, Values, Truth: Essays in the Philosophy of Value* (Oxford: Blackwell, 1987), 107.

37 Blackburn, "The Absolute Conception: Putnam vs. Williams," in *Reading Bernard Williams*, ed. Daniel Callcut (London: Routledge), 9.

38 Some argue that virtue is not a monadic property where being monadic is contrasted with being relational in another sense. Mark Alfano argues that virtue should be understood not as a "monadic property of you as a person, but rather a relation between you and other people." "[S]ome of the dispositions that constitute your virtue are actually outside your skin." Mark Alfano, "Stereotype Threat and Intellectual Virtue," in *Naturalizing Epistemic Virtue*, ed. Abrol Fairweather and Owen Flanagan (Cambridge: Cambridge University Press, 2014), 155–174, 160. I do not intend to rule out this view, which I do not discuss here.

39 This is a standard objection to the thesis of the "primacy of the virtues" where the concepts of rightness and goodness are explained in terms of virtues or virtuous agents. See David Copp and David Soble, "Morality and Virtue: An Assessment of Some Recent Work in Virtue Ethics," *Ethics* 114 (2004), 514–554, 552, and Julia Driver, "Virtue Theory," in, *Contemporary Debates in Moral Theory*, ed. James Dreier (Oxford: Blackwell, 2006), 113–123, 118. Jason Kawall, "In Defense of the Primacy of the Virtues," *Journal of Ethics and Social Philosophy* 3 (2009), 1–21, attempts to rebut this objection by distinguishing between different notions of what makes something, e.g., right. He claims that in a "meta-ethical" sense the choices of a virtuous agent make actions right in the same way that (for a utilitarian) maximizing utility makes

actions right. Both would agree that in an "instantiation" sense (using Kawall's example) the suffering of the puppies would make torturing them wrong. But the cases are disanalogous. Even in the "instantiation" sense, for the utilitarian it is not strictly the suffering of the puppies in a particular case that makes torturing them *wrong*; it is the fact that the suffering does not (in this case) maximize utility, whereas in no sense do the *choices* (or *non-choices*) of a virtuous agent make torturing the puppies wrong.

40   As Hursthouse admits, practically wise agents are fallible: their knowledge is not "encyclopaedic." Rosalind Hursthouse, "Practical Wisdom: A Mundane Account," *Proceedings of the Aristotelian Society* 106 (2006), 285–309.

41   Jason Kawall offers an "idealized virtuous observer" account of right action: a form of "qualified agent account" in order to overcome objections to orthodox qualified agent accounts, such as the kind noted above. That agent is "unimpaired" and "fully informed." See his "Qualified Agent and Agent-Based Virtue Ethics," in *The Handbook of Virtue Ethics*, ed. Stan van Hooft (Durham: Acumen, 2014), 130–140, 139. In that case on my view she/he/it is not human, and it is therefore unclear what character traits would be possessed by such a paragon.

42   As we have seen though this does not imply that for them there are no standards for virtue or that one cannot be seriously wrong about what counts as virtuous. Thus virtue concepts are not for them "model" concepts such that we can calibrate a person's virtue by a model of "ideal" virtue that "sets the top end of the scale." See Daniel C. Russell, *Practical Intelligence and the Virtues* (Oxford: Clarendon Press, 2009), 121. But they do possess the other features of Russell's notion of a model concept, standards of application and the possibility of "serious error" (121). Even Cleanthes for Hume is not an ideal in the sense of "top end of the scale": he is an exemplar.

43   Nietzsche describes various so-called "ideal" types such as the sovereign individual and the noble type but as I argue in Chapter 8, for him these types are by no means either ideal or paragons.

44   Jason Kawall, "Moral Response-Dependence, Ideal Observers, and the Motive of Duty: Responding to Zangwill," *Erkenntnis*, 60(3) (2004), 357–369, 357 (Abstract).

45   See further n. 41; also nn. 39 and 40.

46   Daniel Jacobson, "Fitting Attitude Theories of Value," *The Stanford Encyclopedia of Philosophy*, ed. Edward N. Zalta (first published March 17, 2011), 1–22, 1, http://plato.stanford.edu/archives/spr2011/entries/fitting-attitude-theories/, accessed August 15, 2014.

47   Ibid., 1.

48   Ibid., 4.

49   Ibid., 4.

50   See further for this kind of view my *Virtue Ethics: A Pluralistic View* and Talbot Brewer, *The Retrieval of Ethics* (Oxford: Oxford University Press, 2009).

51   "Fitting Attitude Theories of Value."

52   Hubert Dreyfus, describing McDowell's view, in "The Return of the Myth of the Mental," *Inquiry* 50 (2007), 352–365, 353. This is part of a fascinating exchange on the topic of the conceptual nature of expertise in the same issue, see McDowell, "What Myth?," 338–351, and "Response to Dreyfus," 366–370; Dreyfus, "Response to McDowell," 371–377.

53   These apt expressions are from Heidegger's *Being and Time*. Openness is also a central concept of Heidegger's, and is also intimately connected with the nature of our intentional relation to the world. Indeed I find remarkable similarities between Heidegger's, McDowell's, and Hume's metaphysics. Hume's famed skepticism was skepticism not about an objective world of, e.g., ethics, but about the pretensions of one mode of rationality, that appropriate to science (the faculty of the understanding), to *alone* secure an intentional relation to all aspects of reality. Making the world intelligible precedes epistemology: skepticism arises from faulty notions of the former relation, as I think Hume saw. A fuller discussion of this general issue lies outside the scope of this book, but see further my "A New Metaphysics for Virtue Ethics: Hume Meets Heidegger," in *Aristotelian Ethics in Contemporary Perspective*, ed. Julia Peters (New York: Routledge, 2013), 177–194.

54   The seamlessness of the route from property to conceptualization of that property through the notion of openness is made very clear in this passage from McDowell: "In a particular experience in which one is

not misled, what one takes in is *that things are thus and so. That things are thus and so* is the content of the experience, and it can also be the content of a judgement: it becomes the content of a judgement if the subject decides to take the experience at face value. So it is conceptual content. But *that things are thus and so* is also, if one is not misled, an aspect of the layout of the world: it is how things are. Thus the idea of conceptually structured operations of receptivity puts us in a position to speak of experience as openness to the layout of reality. Experience enables the layout of reality itself to exert a rational influence on what a subject thinks." *Mind and World* (Cambridge, MA: Harvard University Press, 1994), 26: cited in Maximilian de Gaynesford, *John McDowell* (Cambridge: Polity Press, 2004), 83–84. For an excellent discussion of McDowell's naturalistic metaphysics, see de Gaynesford, especially Part III.

For Hume, too, receptivity or openness to the world of ethics is a conceptually structured but *emotional* receptivity, allowing us to see how things are unless we are misled. Furthermore, since for Hume the operations of the "understanding" are not the only form of rational access to the world, there is in the case of moral properties "no ontological gap between the sort of thing one can experience or think or mean and the sort of thing that can be the case" (de Gaynesford, 86).

55 Extended discussion of the developmental aspects of our openness to ethics lies outside the scope of this book, but see n. 16. As far as creativity is concerned see Alison Gopnik, Andrew Meltzoff, and Patricia Kuhl, *The Scientist in the Crib* (New York: William Morrow, 1999).

Part II

The Virtue Ethics of Hume

Chapter 3

Can Hume Be Both a Sentimentalist and a Virtue Ethicist?

3.1 Introduction

The *Treatise of Human Nature* has a section entitled "Moral distinctions deriv'd from a moral sense," where Hume says "since vice and virtue are not discoverable merely by reason, or the comparison of ideas, it must be by means of some impression or sentiment they occasion, that we are able to mark the difference betwixt them" (T 3.1.2.1/470). This claim is the essence of Hume's "sentimentalism." It is the task of this chapter to provide a response dependence interpretation of it, and to show that it is compatible with a virtue ethical interpretation of Hume's moral philosophy.

Because Hume says that sentiment is the essence of ethics, as well as the essence of beauty, he has been read as a subjectivist, skeptic, or non-cognitivist in both ethics and aesthetics. More specifically the infamous Motivation Argument and the idea that "reason is the slave of the passions" have driven non-cognitivist readings;[1] the famous "gilding and staining" passage has supported a projectivist reading;[2] and other passages lend credence to error theory readings. Much good work has already been done in rejecting these interpretations and I do not intend to add further to this literature. Rather I give positive justification to the response dependence interpretation while pursuing my main task of showing how it can be compatible with a virtue ethical interpretation of Hume. This chapter aims to do justice to Hume's convictions both that sentiment lies at the foundations of ethics, and that ethics is a form of reliable, objective interaction with the world, permitting critical purchase on both people's behavior and emotions through objectively and socially accessible notions of virtue and vice. To do this I need to show how two obstacles to reading Hume as a virtue ethicist, identified in the Introduction to this book, can be overcome.

The Virtue Ethics of Hume and Nietzsche, First Edition. Christine Swanton.
© 2015 John Wiley & Sons, Ltd. Published 2015 by John Wiley & Sons, Ltd.

These are reading him as a "non-sensible" subjectivist, and reading him as a philosopher for whom reason has no place in ethics.

According to Hume the "understanding" alone cannot provide the background within which ethics is or can be made intelligible. The reasoning capacities proper to the understanding[3] for Hume are not of the sort fitted to make ethics intelligible for two basic and intimately related reasons. First, it cannot provide the needed practicality of ethics, namely (as stated in Chapter 2) morality's "tendency" to regulate our conduct. Second, as I shall elaborate below, without such feelings (notably benevolence) human beings are trapped in Buridan's Ass type dilemmas, having no ability to recognize reasons for choosing between what are highly significant moral alternatives, such as suffering a scratch to my finger, or saving countless people. Enter the requisite emotional orientation, and practicality of an appropriate kind can prevail. By contrast, Hume's faculty of the understanding discloses the blood and other evidence of a killing, but is blind to the vicious quality of a murder. Once the right sentiments, the right emotional orientations, are in play, the vicious quality can be constituted as a moral property.

The distinction between a scientific constitution of properties and an ethical or aesthetic one is nicely illustrated with Hume's discussion of the beauty of a circle. A scientific outlook reveals not the beauty of the circle but only that the circle is a line "whose parts are equally distant from a common centre" (E App. 1 para. 242, 291). As Hume claims, Euclid says nothing about the beauty of the circle, but that does not mean it is not a real property, constituted (in a response dependent way) by "a peculiar fabric or structure" of our sentiments. In vain, says Hume, would you seek that property by your senses or by "mathematical reasonings." Similarly you would in vain see the vice in a murder simply by the evidence of your senses or scientific reasoning. For it is the "moral sense," which being an emotional "sense" is not reducible to the ordinary senses, that is necessary for the constitution of vice as a moral property.

To begin my argument that Hume's sentimentalism should be interpreted in the response dependent way outlined above, it is necessary to appreciate the complexity of the relation between Hume's meta-ethics and normative ethics. In order to avoid confusion, we need to distinguish between several layers in his thought. Muddle between these layers results in the kinds of interpretations to be rejected. Here are the layers.

(1)   The moral sense.
(2)   The conditions for having a moral sense.
(3)   Causes of the activation of the moral sense.
(4)   The conditions for possession of an authoritative moral sense.
(5)   Moral judgments of someone with an authoritative moral sense.
(6)   True moral judgments.
(7)   The intelligibility conditions of virtue as a kind of property.
(8)   The features which make a trait of character a virtue: the criteria of virtue.

3.2   The Moral Sense

To argue that Hume is a response dependence virtue ethicist I need to show both that for Hume virtues and vices are properties of objects (albeit of a response dependent kind), and that there are features which *merit* those properties being called virtues and vices. In more detail I shall understand Hume as espousing a response dependent view of virtue having the following form, to be explicated in this and the following sections.

(a)   A virtue or a vice is a power in an object to elicit relevant responses, notably emotional ones. These responses are necessary for the constitution of virtue and vice as moral properties.

(b)   The relevant responses, necessary for that constitution, are those of agents possessing a *moral* sense, the conditions for the possession of which notably include benevolence, a passion which for Hume is "original" in the sense of part of our very "frame and constitution."

(c)   Nonetheless, not all who have a *moral* sense have a moral sense which is authoritative. Deploying an authoritative moral sense provides warrant for the authoritative status of approvals of traits.

(d)   An authoritative moral sense does not *guarantee* the truth of judgments made on its basis, namely that traits approved as virtues actually merit that status. The cooperation of the reason of the understanding is also necessary for authoritative judgments. Even when this cooperation occurs, however, there can be mistaken views about for example "tendencies" of traits in certain kinds of conditions.

Given (d), (Q) above (Chapter 2) is not deemed part of Hume's response dependence view. As we explore further below, the deliverances of a qualified judge are not sufficient for the truth of claims about virtue and vice.

In order to set the stage for our understanding of Hume's moral sentimentalism, consider the following well-known passage from his *Treatise of Human Nature*:

> Take any action allow'd to be vicious: Wilful murder, for instance. Examine it in all lights, and see if you can find that matter of fact, or real existence, which you call *vice*. In which-ever way you take it, you find only certain passions, motives, volitions and thoughts. There is no matter of fact in the case. The vice entirely escapes you, as long as you consider the object. You never can find it, till you turn your reflexion into your own breast, and find a sentiment of disapprobation, which arises in you, towards this action. (T 3.1.1.26/468–469)

This passage has often been interpreted in the following way. Supposedly, objective moral properties can be perceived in objects, as can properties like size. But no such properties are detectable. Were we to postulate such objective properties, they would be queer, detectable only by a mysterious faculty. Since all that is really noticeable are various mental items in the observer, moral properties really are such items.

For example, Jonathan Harrison claims "It is extremely puzzling that Hume says he is going to show that morality is *not* a matter of fact, but ends up concluding that it *is a matter of fact about our sentiments*."[4] The vice for Hume, says Harrison, is *in* our sentiments.[5] There are two mistakes here. First, Hume does not say that morality is not a matter of fact: he says that it "consists not in any *matter of fact*, which can be discover'd by the understanding" (T 3.1.1.26/468). Second, morality is not a matter of fact *about* our sentiments; it is a matter of fact about virtue and vice, which are properties of objects. Specifically, a virtue is a "stable" and "enduring" quality of mind that has a power[6] to produce love or pride: "these two particulars are to be consider'd as equivalent, with regard to our mental qualities, *virtue* and the power to produce love or pride, *vice* and the power of producing humility or hatred" (T 3.3.1.4/575).

I do not take this passage to deny that virtues are monadic properties of agents. Rather Hume is making a claim about what is required for virtues to exist as virtues: once something is intelligible as a virtue it can be conceived in the normal way as a good trait of character satisfying the criteria of virtue (see Section 3.4). In short we should not confuse layer (7) above (the intelligibility condition of virtue), which is relational, with the nature of virtue itself as a monadic property understood through (8) (the criteria of virtue).

The existence of a moral sense then presupposes that there are properties which have powers to affect it. Though sentiments of approbation (a form of pleasure) constitute our *sense* of virtue, virtues themselves for Hume are properties of agents, intelligible as good, excellent, or admirable character traits in virtue of being powers in objects (to affect the moral sense). Again we must not confuse the various layers of Hume's thought: we must not confuse (7) the intelligibility condition of virtue, with (1) (an aspect of) the moral sense (the sense of virtue). This view is consistent with Jane McIntyre's account of the ontology of a character trait for Hume. According to her, for Hume, "character is the structured set of relatively stable passions that give rise to a person's actions."[7] It is not an "occult quality."[8] I concur with this view. It is consistent with the above account of virtue as a response dependent property, since a structured set of stable passions is a *virtue* (a good, excellent, or admirable character trait) only if it has the (causal) "power" to give rise to certain sentiments in suitably constituted agents.

The response dependent interpretation allows us to solve the following puzzle. How can Hume say that the direct passions are both produced by the presentation of good or evil but also are founded on pleasure and pain (T 2.3.9.1/438)? He is saying that the pleasures and pains of the moral sense constitute, in a response dependent way, goods such as tender affections and evils such as avarice and excessive anger as *goods* and *evils*. He is not saying that all goods are reducible to pleasures and all evils are reducible to pains. A good such as tender affection activates the moral sense, since through the passions of love and benevolence we tend to unite with the good, but without the pleasure constituting the moral sense (in its manifestation as the sentiment of approbation – faint or more imperceptible love (or pride)) there would be no property *intelligible* as a *good* of affection (or a *virtue* such as being affectionate). Note that the intelligibility condition of virtue as the power to produce love or pride does not itself tell us what properties in objects *merit* being called virtue and vice. That is the job of the criteria of virtue, to be discussed in section 3.4.

We turn now to the analysis of Hume's notion of the moral sense itself. In T 469 Hume claims that "Vice and virtue … may be compared to sounds, colours, heat and cold, which, according to modern philosophy, are not qualities in objects, but perceptions in the mind." This passage should not mislead. Hume is *comparing* the sense of virtue to sense perception: he is not saying it is a special form of sense perception. The claim is that just as redness is not there wholly independent of our sensibility, neither is virtue. Nonetheless Hume also makes it clear that virtue is "in" the object in the sense that it has the power to excite the requisite "percep-tions" in his very broad sense (which includes impressions (which include the passions) and ideas.) And once the intelligibility conditions for virtue are in place, virtue can be understood as "in" the object in a very straightforward way as a good, excellent, or admirable character trait; a *well*-structured set of passions, as McIntyre might say.

The aspect of the moral sense of most importance to Hume, the sense of virtue, is described by Hume as a feeling: "To have the sense of virtue, is nothing but to *feel* a satisfaction of a particular kind from the contemplation of a character" (T 471). This feeling is the sentiment of approbation: "The very *feeling* constitutes our praise or admiration" (T 471). These sentiments arise from a virtue's power to produce them in suitably constituted subjects: a virtue "gives rise" to such sentiments, which can be more precisely described as "nothing but … fainter and more imperceptible love" (T 3.3.5.1/614) or in a case where the virtue approved is our own virtue, the feeling is pride. This love and pride are forms of pleasure, while the sentiments of disapprobation arising from the power of a vice to produce humility or hatred are forms of displeasure or pain: "we … must pronounce the impression arising from virtue, to be agreeable, and that proceeding from vice to be uneasy" (T 3.1.2.1/470); "the distinguishing impressions, by which moral good or evil is known, are nothing but *particular* pains or pleasures" (T 3.1.2.3/471).

A temptation to discount the above textual evidence for the nature of the moral sense as a species of love (or pride) – in their forms as calm passions – is that Hume is clear that love and pride as passions do not motivate. According to Hume, pride and humility, love and hate are "pure emotions in the soul, unattended with any desire, and not immediately exciting us to action" (T 2.2.6.1/367). By contrast, it is thought, the moral sentiments of approbation and disapprobation do motivate.[9] In that case how can the moral sense be understood as sentiments of love or pride, hate or humility? There is indeed a *prima facie* problem here.

On my view it should be resolved by rejecting the claim that the moral sentiments themselves motivate. While it is true, as I claimed in Chapter 2, that for Hume "morality" or "morals" motivates (T 3.1.1.5–6/457), this is not to say that the moral sentiments constituting the moral sense themselves motivate. "Morality" is not wholly or even primarily constituted by the moral sentiments of approbation and disapprobation of traits, as we pointed out in Chapter 2. Rather it is primarily constituted by the full gamut of virtues, character traits at least characteristically consisting of "structured sets" of motivating passions of various sorts.[10] The "moral sentiment" itself as a "spectator" sentiment of appreciation of virtue, for example, may well not motivate, while "morality," expressed in an agent's virtue as she lives her life, does motivate. What Hume calls the sense of "morality" or duty (not to be confused with the moral sense), associated particularly with artificial virtues (notably justice), is just one of the types of motivating passion proper to the various virtues.

Secondly we should note that though Hume claims that love and hate do not themselves motivate, he also claims that "love and hatred are not compleated within themselves" and "carry the mind to something further" (T 2.2.6.1/367). In that way love and hate are characteristically conjoined with benevolence and anger which are motivating desires. While the moral sentiments do not themselves motivate then, they are characteristically conjoined with sentiments that do.

Hume's conceptual empiricism requires that the ideas of morality, that which makes morality intelligible, must be founded in experience. Since it is the moral sense which makes morality intelligible we need to ask: What kinds of experiential features activate the moral sense? The following passage makes it clear that the moral sense may be activated by two kinds of cause: first, reflections on the tendencies of traits and passions (themselves ascertained by experience), and second, the immediate pleasurable impact of traits or passions.

> Moral good and evil are certainly distinguish'd by our *sentiments*, not by *reason*: But these sentiments may arise either from the mere species or appearances of characters and passions, or from reflexions on their tendency to the happiness of mankind, and of particular persons. My opinion is, that both these causes are intermix'd in our judgments of morals; after the same manner as they are in our decisions concerning most kinds of external beauty: Tho' I am also of opinion, that reflexions on the tendencies of actions have by far the greatest influence, and determine all the great lines of our duty. There are, however, instances, in cases of less moment, wherein this immediate taste or sentiment produces our approbation. (T 3.3.1.27/589–590)

The causes of the moral sense determine the range of properties which might merit status as virtues. Given for example that putative features such as the infinity of beings or eternal immutable fitnessess cannot have causal efficacy on the moral sense for Hume, they cannot provide criteria of virtue. As Hume says in *Dialogues Concerning Natural Religion* (in the mouth of Cleanthes), attributes such as "infinite wisdom" and other infinite attributes have no influence on the sentiments, and terms such as "admirable" and "excellent" "sufficiently fill the imaginations of men."[11]

The criteria of virtue for Hume are thus dependent on the two broad kinds of responses elicited by the powers of traits to affect the moral sense. Of particular importance is that the second kind of response is not reducible to the first (as I shall argue in Chapter 4 in connection with justice and also, more generally, in Chapter 5). If the moral sense were constituted only by pleasure triggered by reflections on consequences, then given that moral properties are response dependent properties, there would be no room for the possibility that the status of some of those properties as virtues are determined by non-consequentialist criteria. As it is, I shall argue, the second feature activating the moral sense allows for such criteria.

Finally the moral sense working properly should not be seen as merely projecting something that is not really there, as some commentators claim.[12] The sensing of virtue should not be seen as analogous to the "great propensity" of the mind "to spread itself on external objects" (T 167) in ascribing to them dubious and indeed non-existent metaphysical properties (be they "eternal immutable fitnesses" or unintelligible real necessary connections between objects' "secret causes"), in a vain effort to secure knowledge in Hume's restricted sense of "knowledge." Knowledge in this restricted sense is knowledge that is certain in the manner of knowledge by intuition and demonstration of propositions which involve only relations between ideas and which cannot be false (T 1.3.1.2/70). Hume was skeptical about our ability to have knowledge in certain domains (including the "science" of morality) in this (restricted) sense:

> There has been an opinion very industrially propagated by certain philosophers, that morality is susceptible of demonstration; and tho' no one has ever been able to advance a single step in those demonstrations; yet 'tis taken for granted, that this science may be brought to an equal certainty with geometry or algebra. (T 3.1.1.18/463)

But this does not mean that we cannot have "knowledge" that is proper to morality, as we explore in section 3.5.

3.3 Conditions for the Possibility of a Moral Sense

The problem arises: What distinguishes the moral sense from for example the sense of beauty? Are not both at bottom sentiments of approbation: forms of love? Hume claims that to have the *sense* of virtue "is nothing but to *feel* a satisfaction of a *particular kind* [my italics for these two words] from the contemplation of a character" (T 3.1.2.3/471). The "*particular kind*" of satisfaction is one distinguishable from satisfaction from the contemplation of beauty and other types of satisfactions. As Hume says at T 3.1.2.4/472 the pleasures of approval of characters is of a "*peculiar*" kind distinct from the approval of musical compositions or of a good wine. What makes the pleasures of the moral sense "particular" or "peculiar" to it? The answer lies in the nature of the conditions necessary for a sentiment of approbation to be a *moral* sense. The moral sense, as an appreciation of virtue, involves sensitivities due to the excitement of "sympathy" but a sympathy driven by or operating within the background of desires for the good of others. That is not necessary for or distinctive of the appreciation of wine or music. The desire for the good of another is benevolence, but the benevolence must be capable of being transferred through sympathy sufficiently extensively if we are to have a moral sense. The capacity for empathy (what Hume calls in the *Treatise* "sympathy") necessary for a *moral* sense is fundamentally empathic benevolence.

Recognition of the conditions of possibility for a moral sense solves another problem. A difficulty apparently besetting Hume's response dependence is this. In some possible worlds the pleasures of "fainter and more imperceptible love" constituting the pleasures of approval, may constitute a society-wide fixation on entirely the wrong properties: cruelty might be approved. What if we love vice and hate virtue? This problem has been expressed as "The Twin Earth Problem" according to which response dependence views of ethics are vulnerable to an unfortunate kind of moral relativism.[13] Consider a world in which beings have "the sort of deliberative and motivating response we [have] when we approve of things in our actual world."[14] These beings have "the same attitude toward cruelty or animal mistreatment that we do towards kindness or integrity."[15] So, it is thought, cruelty would be a virtue on Twin Earth while a vice in ours. Surely, it will be claimed, a response dependence view having this implication is not a possible option for any virtue ethics, for such a consequence would be unacceptable.

The problem is resolved in relation to Hume, I shall argue, if we distinguish the moral sense itself from its conditions of possibility. The conditions of possibility for the moral sense are the existence of certain passions, notably benevolence. These conditions, which make agents *receptive* to the powers of virtues to excite the pleasures constitutive of the moral sense, make that sense "peculiar" or "particular." In "The Sceptic" Hume describes the conditions of the possibility of a moral sense in terms of disqualifying conditions:

> … where one is born of so perverse a frame of mind, of so callous and insensible a disposition, as to have no relish for virtue and humanity, no sympathy with his fellow-creatures, no desire of esteem or applause; such a one must be allowed entirely incurable, nor is there any remedy in philosophy. (Miller 169)

The basic point is this. If the conditions for the possibility of a moral sense are not satisfied, a supposed moral sense (such as the pleasures of approval) does not count as a genuine *moral* sense. Approvals of the congenitally irredeemable "perverse" or "callous" person do not count as moral approvals, for such a person is not merely unqualified to make correct or authoritative judgments of virtue or vice (because naïve, inexperienced, excessively partial or impartial, for example), but is literally blind to the ethical realm. What makes a judge have a moral sense, for Hume, whether in our world or on Twin Earth, is neither mere deliberative capacity, nor mere ability to be motivated by what he or she takes to be a virtue or a vice. What enables a judge to have that sense is the possession of certain *emotional* and empathic capacities, notably benevolence and extensive sympathy. Such judges could not endorse cruelty as a virtue. The mistake would be to think that mere deliberative and motivational capacities of the kind necessary to *approve* of something are sufficient for *moral* response on any response dependent view. For Hume what constitutes the world of ethics through the moral sense are not mere conative and deliberative dispositions but emotional ones, namely at heart, benevolence, which enables us to love the *right sort* of qualities as virtues. Hume's view can thus preserve the intuition that cruelty is a vice in all possible worlds.[16] The moral sense, that which makes ethics intelligible as *ethics*, is not merely the capacity to approve or disapprove, or even love or hate, traits of character. The love of virtue and hatred of vice constituting the moral sense is not just bare love or hatred but love and hatred within a sensibility that is fundamentally humane.

It is a consequence of Hume's emotional response dependent conception of the intelligibility of ethics that pure emotionless reason is blind to ethics, and thus cannot provide a moral sense or moral cognition. For Hume those "who affirm that virtue is nothing but a conformity to reason; that there are eternal fitnesses and unfitnesses of things, which are the same for every rational being that considers them; that the immutable measures of right or wrong impose an obligation not only on human creatures but also on the deity himself" (T 3.1.1.4/456) cannot make morality intelligible as something that has "an influence on human passions and actions" (T 3.1.1.5/457). Thus such reason, as Hume points out, cannot be the *only* form of rationality or fittingness to apply to the world. Let us call reason in this rationalistic sense "Reason" with a capital R. Reason in this sense "of itself is utterly impotent in this particular" (T 3.1.1.6/457), for if it were "potent" then the obligations of Reason would be the same for all rational beings regardless of the kinds of sentiments (if any) that form their constitution.

For Hume there are no such eternal fitnesses in the moral, prudential, or aesthetic domains, let alone ones discoverable by moral, prudential, or aesthetic cognition. The following claims are a *reductio* of any rationalistic position that purports to establish that Reason alone ("of itself") can discriminate such properties: "Tis not contrary to reason to prefer the destruction of the whole world to the scratching of my finger" and "Tis not contrary to reason for me to chuse my total ruin, to prevent the least uneasiness of an *Indian* or person totally unknown to me" (T 2.3.3.6/416).

Here Hume means by "reason" pure emotionless Reason of the kind possessed by all rational beings regardless of their emotional constitutions. Human beings do possess such reason, provided we understand it as the operations of the *understanding*, a faculty "*considered apart from any passions or any feelings of pleasure and pain.*"[17] According to Hume, where the following is true such Reason cannot criticize desires or other passions: "Where a passion is neither founded on false suppositions, nor chuses means insufficient for the end, the understanding can neither justify nor condemn it" (T 2.3.3.7/416).

However, it does not follow that desires of the above sort are not criticizable at all for Hume.[18] Although it is not "contrary to reason" (the Reason of the understanding) to prefer the destruction of the world to the scratching of my finger, a person possessing such preferences is of a piece with the "fancied monster" of the *Enquiries* (cited in Chapter 1). His emotions are so monstrous that the emotional rationality of a person who is part of the common and usual ranks of mankind is closed to him. His "Reason" is the reason of extreme psychopathy.[19] Such a being is entirely devoid of compassion: the "core deficit" of the psychopath is "indifference toward the suffering of other people."[20]

In claiming that the emotionless person is indifferent or paralyzed in the practical domain (so that "preferences" are arbitrary) Hume anticipates the findings of those working on emotional intelligence, such as Antonio Damasio. Damasio's study of Elliot was a study of a man whose paralysis in the practical domain, due to his being oblivious to his feelings, was not solved by his evident competence in what Hume would call the faculty of the understanding: "nothing was wrong with his logic, memory, attention or any other cognitive ability."[21] Once the practical world including that of ethics is opened up, practical rationality can get a grip. Instead of practical paralysis or arbitrary "preferences" we can appreciate that "there are certain qualities in objects that are fitted by nature to produce ... particular feelings" ("Of the Standard of Taste," Miller 235) and we can be motivated accordingly. In another passage in this essay reminiscent of Aristotle, Hume claims that a "man in a fever would not insist on his palate as able to decide concerning flavours" (Miller 233).

Once benevolence operates, for example, we can appreciate that being indifferent between the ruin of the world or the sufferings of millions and the scratching of one's finger, or preferring the former to the latter, is callous and egocentric to a degree which is monstrous and unthinkable.[22] It is an attitude completely unfitting to the way the world is. The moral sense, once operational, and if sufficiently qualified, enables us to "feel" the "natural fittingness" of ends, as well as of means, and in partnership with the reason of the understanding, enables us to form warranted judgments about that fittingness.[23]

We have seen that at the foundation of a "moral sense" is benevolence: for Hume the desire for another's good. What in more detail is the nature of the benevolent sensibility that conditions the moral sense? For Hume benevolence is a distinct and "original" passion, by which he means it is part of a normal person's constitution without it having to be inculcated, even if benevolence as a *virtue* needs cultivation and refinement. As he puts it in "On Self Love," "from the original frame of our temper we may feel a desire for another's happiness or good" (E para. 254, 302). At T 2.3.3.8/417 Hume claims that benevolence and what he calls there "love of life" are "instincts originally implanted in our nature." They are distinguished from those "direct passions" which arise from a fundamental desire to "unite" with the good and avoid evil. In other words the "original instincts" would remain even if they did not fall under the rubric of pursuing the good and avoiding the bad. For Hume, then, these "instincts," basic to the moral sense, are as fundamental to the framework of our human constitution as are the appetites, the five senses, and the capacity to feel pleasure and pain.

The sensibility which conditions the moral sense is not mere benevolence. Also required for a moral sense is empathic and sympathetic capacity founded on benevolence. Empathic capacity is the engine by which another's good has sufficiently vivid reality for a person's benevolent desires to have some force, and for them to be operational on those to whom she is not in various ways partial. However, without benevolence, such a capacity may be driven by a fundamental hostility or generalized malevolence (desire for another's harm).

Empathy is described by Hume as a "contagion" or "infusion" of sentiments where we literally feel the pain or pleasure of another, for example, or aspects of these.[24] For example: "A chearful countenance infuses a sensible complacency and serenity into my mind; as an angry or sorrowful one throws a sudden damp upon me" (T 2.1.11.2/ 317). Where extensive empathy is impossible or undesirable, the mechanisms of sympathy in a modern sense may take over: here we may sympathize (imaginatively identify with) the suffering (for example) of another, and feel concern for that person, without feeling that person's pain. Empathy and sympathy are thus capacities enabling us "to receive by communication [others'] inclinations and sentiments however different from or even contrary to our own," capacities "conspicuous in children" (T 2.1.11.1/316), but empathy is more direct than sympathy. Where extensive empathy would be crippling, extensive sympathy in this sense may not be. Indeed research has shown that those measuring high on empathy can be most distressed on seeing the pain and misery of another and thus avoid them.[25]

Finally, the benevolence within which the moral sense operates is constrained by self-love. Self-love (a desire for one's own good) is also a condition of the moral sense, for without self-love, a crucial feature of the moral world (namely that we operate in it as individual agents with a sense of the worth of our *own* lives), would not be available to us. We would merely be cogs in the "ethical" machinery of the world, mere knots in the biospheric net, as it has been put in environmental ethics, mere instruments for the promotion of good as Bernard Williams might say. The moral sense in *humans* is a sense where we see ourselves as separate (though also social and relational): we do not have the hive mentality of bees. Self-love too is an original propensity and part of the internal frame and constitution of the mind to desire and seek our own good. As a motive however it may be for good or for ill: "self love, when it acts at its liberty ... is the source of all injustice and violence" (T 3.2.1.10/480). In a person of virtue, another's happiness can become part of our own good and such a person can operate with the "combined motives" of benevolence and self-love or "self-enjoyment" (E App. II, para. 254, 302).

Hume then is adamant that benevolence is a passion distinct from self-love, and that altruistic motivation is not reducible to a motive of self-interest. For it is sourced in the independent passion of benevolence.[26] Nonetheless for him there are a number of self-regarding virtues whose point or primary point is to benefit their possessors: those "serviceable to themselves" and which "enable them to promote their own interest," for example, "*prudence, temperance, frugality, industry, assiduity, enterprise, dexterity*" (T 3.3.1.24/587).

We may summarize the relation between the various conditions of a *moral* sense as follows. While some self-love is necessary for a moral sense, benevolence ensures that self-love does not "act at its liberty" and morality goes beyond narrow self-interest. However the moral sense also needs a sufficiently extensive sympathy. That require-ment ensures that benevolence extends beyond the partialistic affections.[27] Indeed Rico Vitz argues that for Hume "the scope of benevolent motivation is very broad such that it includes any creature that is conscious and capable of thought." He notes though that while the degree of benevolent motivation is extensive it is also "limited."[28]

Not only is benevolence limited in extent, it is also constrained by partial affec-tions. Mere benevolence with extensive sympathy constrained by self-love is not sufficient for a moral sense since such a sense must include some partial natural affection for one's children, for example. This requirement for a moral sense is more controversial. I attribute it to Hume because I believe that for him a person with no such partial affections *at all* is highly defective morally speaking: indeed one might say another kind of moral monster. Indeed in "On Refinement in the Arts" he claims that confining one's expense to the gratifications afforded by luxury "without regard to friends or family, is an indication of a heart destitute of humanity or benevolence" whereas to be "entirely occupied" with luxury "without any relish for the pleasures of ambition, study, or conversation is a mark of stupidity" (Miller 269). A person incapable of partialistic affection is incapable of the various kinds of relationships essential to virtue for Hume, some of which are described in his description of the highly virtuous Cleanthes (E 270). As we explore in Chapter 5, this requirement on the moral sense is served by a capacity for love, which for Hume is a passion distinct from though related to, benevolence.[29]

The above described complex of passions and psychological mechanisms consti-tutes the conditions of possibility for the "moral sense" for Hume, and thereby the conditions of intelligibility of properties as virtues and vices. It is a matter of debate how and to what degree such sentiments and capacities are to be manifested in someone with virtue. The moral sense and its conditions do not yield an account of what merits status as a virtue. To provide that account we need to discuss what for Hume constitute the criteria of virtue.

3.4   The Criteria of Virtue

The account given above of the intelligibility conditions of virtue does not yield the *criteria* of virtue: that is, a general account of those properties which make traits of character virtues. Nor does it yield an account of what makes us justified in calling a trait a virtue. The first of these issues is addressed in this section and the second in section 3.5.

If we just think of a virtue as a power, we may think of it simply as a causal power, in which case the rational aspect of ethics has not been secured. However for Hume what makes a trait a virtue at the thinnest level of description is that through properties possessed it is *naturally fitted* to be a virtue, and thus naturally fitted to "produce particular feelings" in those with a moral sense. What makes a trait "naturally fitted" to be a virtue? Answering this question requires an account of the criteria of virtue for Hume. But there is a prior problem. According to David Wiggins, the following suggestion of Hume's "has no clear place in his official theory": "It must be allowed that there are certain qualities in objects that are fitted by nature to produce particular ... feelings."[30] In my view, this claim does have a clear place in Hume's theory in general, for it is asserted not merely of vice and virtue but of a range of qualities. For example he claims: "For we reap a pleasure from the view of a character, which is naturally fitted to be useful to others, or to the person himself, or which is agreeable to others or to the person himself" (T 591).

Hume's denial that there are "eternal" and "immutable" fitnesses proper to ethics, aesthetics, and prudence is perfectly consistent with his affirmations (in, e.g., "Of the Standard of Taste") that properties may be *naturally* fitted to produce approbation in suitable observers: "A clear and distinct sentiment attends him through the whole survey of the objects; and he discerns that very degree and kind of approbation or displeasure, which each part is naturally fitted to produce" (Miller 237).

For the quoted claims are simply examples of the following thesis, which is compatible with Hume's attack on the doctrine of eternal fitnesses, namely that such properties as virtues and beauty are qualities in objects which are *powers* naturally fitted to produce certain sentiments in creatures constituted as we are constituted. In a nutshell, people endowed with a moral sense debate issues of "natural fitnesses" and make warranted or non-warranted claims about them. It is true that Hume says in the *Enquiries* that a virtue is a quality of the mind agreeable or approved by everyone, who considers or contemplates it, but the satisfaction of epistemic norms appropriate to authoritative judges is implicit in this passage. The views of, for example, a "hair-brained enthusiast" (E para. 219, 270), the self-interested, the overly partial, and so forth are discounted or given less weight.

However, it may be thought that the claims about *natural* fitnesses are merely causal claims. If we think that virtues are powers in objects which cause certain responses, and that this is a brute though natural fact, the only way we can secure any normativity in our judgments of virtue is to claim of certain responders that they have some kind of privileged undistorted causal access to relevant properties. In such a way we can discount the responses of the color-blind in judgments of color.

In the case of virtue however, we want to approve of persons of virtue, and back our approvals with *good* reasons. As Cohon points out, Hume's account of virtue and vice is "both causal and normative at once."[31] For Hume we can give reasons for our sentiments of pleasure and pain when responding to traits of character: "In giving a reason ... for the pleasure or uneasiness, we sufficiently explain the vice or virtue" (T 3.1.2.3/471). Of (particularly) companionate friendship (in marriage) Hume claims:

> But *friendship* is a calm and sedate affection, conducted by reason and cemented by habit; springing from long acquaintance and mutual obligations; without jealousies or fears, and without those feverish fits of heat and cold, which cause such an agreeable torment in the amorous passion. ("Of Polygamy and Divorces," Miller 189)

"Reason" works here in two ways. Not only does Hume have a remarkably Aristotelian conception of virtue as a reasoned state in this passage, but as the applied ethics of his *Essays* particularly illustrate, science and the social sciences (especially the *Geisteswissenschaften* such as history) are for Hume the "hand-maiden" of ethics in allowing a reasoned conception of the nature of various virtues. Such reasoning explains the fittingness of the sentiments, for they speak to the various criteria of virtue. If this is so, Philippa Foot's view that Hume's theory about moral sentiment "commits him to a subjectivist theory of ethics" and that for him there is no "method of deciding, in the case of disagreement, whether one man's opinion or another's was correct"[32] will be shown to be false. The space provided by Hume for reasoned justification of claims about virtue is not in "tension with the explicit normative sentimentalism of the *Treatise*"[33] since that sentimentalism is not normative but meta-ethical; it is the essence of his response dependent view of the ontological status of moral properties. It is indeed true that "What makes a trait ... a virtue" could be understood in terms of the "emotional impact on the observer"[34] but in that sense we are talking about the intelligibility of virtue as a normative property. In another sense, the normative sense, what makes a trait a virtue is specified by the criteria of virtue, for example its systematic consequences for mankind. The normative question asks what makes a trait of character merit its emotional impact on the observer.

It is important to note that Hume's claim that we "sense" a moral virtue because it pleases does not imply that "that it pleases" is what *makes* a trait of character a virtue. We are operating there with the intelligibility condition of virtue in terms of Hume's sentimentalist (meta-ethical or metaphysical) theory, and not with the criteria of virtue which come into play at the level of propositional judgment and justification. The criteria of virtue – specifying what makes a trait a virtue – are appealed to when we justify our claims that a trait has the status of a virtue as opposed to a vice.

We have seen that the moral sense may be activated by two kinds of cause: reflections on the tendencies of traits and passions, and the immediate pleasurable impact of traits or passions. We must distinguish however the *causes* of the activation of the moral sense both from the moral sense itself and the *criteria* of virtue, for it is the criteria of virtue which enable us to justify our claims about virtue and vice. Nonetheless, as claimed above, given Hume's conceptual empiricism, the causes of the moral sense determine the range of possibility for the criteria of virtue. Such properties are dependent on the kinds of responses elicited by the two broad kinds of powers of traits (to give pleasure or pain from reflections on consequences and also from the immediate impact of species or appearance).

Given the nature of the moral sense and its foundations in benevolent empathy, these causes of the activation of the moral sense suggest two general criteria of virtue:

(C1)   A trait is a virtue if it tends to the happiness of mankind.

(C2)   A trait is a virtue if it has properties, not reducible to consequences for happiness, which make it appropriate or "fitting" that what Hume calls its "species" or "appearance" causes "this immediate taste or sentiment" giving rise to approbation.

(C2) unlike (C1) does not specify what makes traits virtues or vices, what counts as appropriateness of immediate sentiment, since these features are so varied. (C2) accordingly may be subdivisible into several criteria given that several types of feature, not reducible to consequences for the happiness of mankind, make it appropriate that "immediate taste or sentiment" be produced. These features are discussed in Chapter 5.

It is important to note that the fitness to be approved as a virtue should not be confused with another type of fitness: namely that all virtues track natural fitnesses between objects and persons. That kind of fitness is expressly claimed by Hume not to obtain in the case of justice: "Justice, in her decisions, never regards the fitness or unfitness of objects to particular persons, but conducts herself by more extensive views. Whether a man be generous or a miser he is equally well receiv'd by her" (T 3.2.3.2/502).

The question arises: what is the relation between (C1) and (C2) as criteria of virtue and the apparently official account of virtue found in both the *Treatise* and the *Enquiries*? This account is:

(A)   Virtues are "useful" or "immediately agreeable" to oneself or to others.

According to (A), if V is a virtue it must belong to one of the four categories specified in (A). However, the individual features specified in (A) are not separately sufficient for virtue, for some immediately agreeable traits are surely not virtues. This point is made by Rosalind Hursthouse.[35] She takes Hume to propose (A) as a disjunctive criterion (as he appears to do at E para. 219, 270: "as every quality which is useful or agreeable to others is, in common life, allowed to be a part of personal merit"), and objects to that criterion on the grounds that it would count a disturbing number of vices as virtues. However the passage at E 219 is stronger than the more cautious and sensible T 3.3.1.28/590, which presents (A) as a taxonomy of virtue rather than a disjunctive criterion, claiming that "some qualities acquire their merit from their being *immediately agreeable* to others, without any tendency to public interest; ... some are denominated virtuous from their being *immediately agreeable* to the person himself, who possesses them." This formulation allows for the possibility that some "immediately agreeable" properties are not virtues, namely those that are not naturally fitted for approval, and would not be approved by a qualified judge in normal circumstances (e.g., when not drunk).

Let us then stick to T 590, which merely offers a taxonomy of virtue. We then read (A) as a taxonomy rather than a (disjunctive) criterion, and (C1) and (C2) as genuine criteria.

Consider now (C1). What for Hume constitutes a human being's happiness or good? For Hume, happiness is not constituted by pleasure alone. In "Of Refinement in the Arts" he makes this clear:

> Human happiness, according to the most received notions, seems to consist in three ingredients; action, pleasure and indolence: And though these ingredients ought to be mixed in different proportions, according to the particular disposition of the person; yet no one ingredient can be entirely wanting, without destroying in some measure, the relish of the whole composition. (Miller 269–270. See also E para. 4, 7–9)

A life of activity with no regard for pleasure is an incomplete life, for as Aristotle claims, pleasure is a good for us. Nonetheless, for Aristotle, it is not good "without qualification" unless embedded in a life of virtuous activity. Hume recognizes this point in his distinction between pleasure and activity as parts of human good. Accordingly, given that for Hume activity is part of human good, a life of hedonism where we are seen as mere receptacles for pleasure is not good for us either. Notwithstanding this point, Hume also recognizes that indolence is a necessary indulgence to the "weakness of human nature" (our need for rest, from both activity and pleasure). A similar point is made by Aristotle. Note however that "indolence" is also the name of a vice: "a fault, and a very great one, if extreme" (T 3.3.1.24/587).

The virtues speak to all three of the ingredients of happiness: for example, justice, benevolence, and courage relate to excellence in activity; temperance, charm, appreciation of beauty and the arts, are concerned with pleasure; industriousness and lack of self-indulgence correct our tendencies to excessive indolence (by for example avoiding excessive devotion to luxury). At the same time however, as we saw in Chapter 2, correct attitude to luxury permits for Hume "innocent" luxury, on the grounds that the virtue, understood in that way, is useful to society. According to Hume then, we cannot claim that any luxury exhibits the vices of self-indulgence or greed. Pleasure, activity, and "indolence" need therefore to be integrated, by the operation of virtue, in the well lived, happy life. In this regard, Hume is completely Aristotelian, and does not have a hedonistic view of human good.

When attention is turned to (C2) we need to ask: What features of traits make it naturally fitting that their species or appearance causes "this immediate taste or sentiment" (itself causing approbation), as opposed to those traits which tend to *promote* human happiness? In particular how can it be the case that the former features are able to be understood as "naturally fitting"? An answer to these questions deserves a whole chapter. Chapter 5 considers a wide variety of traits satisfying a range of non-consequentialist criteria of virtue. However, one virtue in this broad class, justice, deserves a chapter of its own. It is the special problems presented by Hume's conception of justice that form the topic of the next chapter.

3.5   The Authoritative Moral Sense

In his essay "Of the Delicacy of Taste and Passion" Hume makes an interesting distinction between "delicacy of passion" which is distorting of both the moral sense and sense of beauty, and "delicacy of taste" which enhances those senses. The former consists of overheated passion which exaggerates the "lively enjoyments" as well as the "pungent sorrows" (Miller 4), while the latter sharpens our critical faculties. Both enable us to become "sensible to pains as well as pleasures, which escape the rest of mankind" (Miller 5). Much to be preferred for Hume however is cool and sedate temper, which as we have already seen, is for him an aspect of friendship as virtue. Delicacy of passion is to be "lamented" and remedied if possible. By contrast delicacy of taste is a "higher and more refined taste, which enables us to judge the characters of men, of compositions of genius, and of the productions of the nobler arts" (Miller 6). Delicacy (of taste) is just one feature which makes a moral sense (and other sensibilities) authoritative.

Now subjectivist interpretations of Hume are not fully combated until one has made room for the idea that the operation of our sense of virtue can result in merited or warranted judgments about virtue and vice. Not all moral senses are equally authoritative for Hume. Though the world of ethics is closed off to the completely emotionally bereft, those for example with limited benevolence see the ethical world dimly or in a distorted way, and may not be justified about claims concerning "natural fittingness." If one is selfish, miserly, unable to see certain strangers as having needs because one lacks sufficiently extensive sympathy, one is not fully socially competent; for money, one's own desires, or a confining of one's emotional response only to a limited circle, block off a full emotional engagement with important aspects of the world. What features constitute an authoritative or "qualified judge": she with an authoritative moral sense?

To defend a claim that Hume can account for the reason-giving force of ethics, we must not confuse layer (2) as listed earlier (conditions for the possibility of a moral sense) with layer (4) (conditions for possession of an authoritative moral sense). Similarly, to have some taste, a conception of beauty for example, does not make one a connoisseur. An *authoritative* moral sense consists in features other than those identified in sections 3.2 and 3.3. They include certain sorts of impartiality, experience (allowing for comparison and practice), and the capacity for fine discrimination (delicacy of taste), elaborated below.

A difficulty in understanding the operations of the moral sense as rational or reasonable has been the idea that just as the sensation of red is a brute sensation – we do not infer that things are red – so for Hume the *sensing* of moral properties is non-inferential: "We do not infer a character to be virtuous, because it pleases: But in feeling that it pleases after such a particular manner, we in effect feel that it is virtuous", analogously to "all kinds" of "sensations" (T 3.1.2.3/471). This claim raises the issue of what is the place of reason or rationality in the moral sentiment itself?

First we should note that for Hume moral sentiments are revisable as a result of reflection, involving changes of perspective, and inferences (about for example consequences). But we should distinguish (a) revision resulting in revised *judgment* and (b) the "correction" of sentiments themselves as a result of the operations of the imagination. In the former case, as Rachel Cohon claims,[36] the moral sentiments are "copied" into "ideas" and thereby become truth apt. However this sense of revisability as a result of reflection must not be confused with the idea that for Hume moral sentiments are impressions of "reflection" which merely means that they are *caused* by other impressions or ideas.[37] As Cohon puts it:

> One consequence of the status of moral sentiments as impressions of reflection is that, in order for them to occur, and so for us to feel someone's virtuousness or viciousness, we need far more than to look at the person or touch her, or see her action. We need the right triggering ideas or impressions. What we need in fact proves to be a whole set of beliefs about the surrounding "circumstances" and "relations."[38]

Indeed for Hume, as Cohon notes, we can "suspend for a time all moral decision or sentiment" (E App. 1, para. 240, 290). However the capacity to suspend must not be confused with the idea that moral sentiments *themselves* are inferential. "Decision," inasmuch as it is or involves judgment, is another matter.

We turn now to (b): correctability of sentiment itself as a result of the operations of the imagination. It is this kind of correctability that is most relevant to the idea of an authoritative moral *sense*. For Hume, a "corrected" sentiment is still a sentiment and not a judgment (in the sense of being truth apt), for the correction is achieved by the faculty of imagination which "has a set of passions belonging to it" and which "are mov'd by degrees of liveliness and strength, which are inferior to *belief*" (T 3.3.1.20/585). These passions can be excited by the ideas of the imagination without the presence, or even the existence of, the object normally producing the moral sentiment. The imagination allows us to see for example that "virtue in rags" is still virtue. Thus "[w]here a character is, in every respect fitted to be beneficial to society, the imagination passes easily from cause to effect": so we can recognize it as virtue in a person even where the virtue "can no longer be exerted in action and is lost to all the world" (T 3.3.1.19/584).

A person with an authoritative moral sense then has a properly operating imagi-nation; indeed it may be so well tuned that it would be odd to describe her moral sentiment as "corrected" in any sense. In such a person the sentiments of "morals" and "interest" remain "distinct." In less authoritative individuals however, these sentiments "naturally run into one another" (T 3.1.2.4/472) so that it often requires a "straining of the imagination" (T 1.4.1.11/185) to not "confound" them. This straining "always hinders the regular flowing of the passions and sentiments" (T 185), but a person of "temper and judgment" (T 472) is able to "preserve himself from [the] illusions" (T 472) caused by the running together of sentiments of interest and morals without such "straining." In general, beliefs and passions are mutually reinforcing, and ideas of the imagination reinforce both (T 1.3.10.4/120; T 1.3.13.10/148–149): "a person of a sorrowful or melancholy disposition is very credulous of every thing that nourishes his prevailing passion" (T 120).

Although, then, the moral sense is not isolated from belief and passions affecting the imagination, features forming part of an authoritative moral *sense* are characteristically constituted by the non-inferential, and also unhindered, sentiments of moral expertise. That is, what was described above as the appropriate complex of "triggering ideas and impressions" would be present as part of that expertise. In hard cases however even an authoritative individual is capable of reasoning inferentially about relevant factors. Even her normally authoritative moral sense will be suspended or will remain in abeyance.

We have seen that although the moral sense itself does not operate through inferential reason, that sense (at least as it operates at the level of approving of virtue and disapproving of vice) is not or need not be preconceptual. It can be corrected by the operation of the imagination, and it can be suspended in an appropriate, often complex, context. These particular obstacles to thinking that Hume's theory of the moral sentiments is irrationalist have been removed.

The person with an authoritative moral sense has further features. Besides possessing the emotional conditions for having a moral sense, she has the capacity for "*steady* and *general* points of view" (T 3.3.1.15/581–582) where the sentiments are corrected for biases of distance and partiality. When Hume claims in the *Treatise* that the perspective of the person judged and his circle "are alone admitted in speculation as the standard of virtue and morality" (T 3.3.1.30/591), that standard is specified contrastively with the potentially distorted perspective of him whose sympathies are touched more vividly by proximity and partiality, and the standard is specified in the limited context of that particular problem.

The authoritative approver also possesses the *moral* point of view: that is, has the capacity for (benevolent) "extensive sympathy" (T 3.3.1.23/586) to a *sufficient* extent.[39] She is not however an idealized impartial observer, and accordingly she is not wedded to impartial maximization of utility. The corrections for bias of the immediate sympathetic judgment do not yield "impartial moral judgments as seen from the viewpoint of an impartial spectator"[40] but as Hume claims at T 3.3.1.15/581 constitute "approbation[s] … of a judicious spectator." The sentiments of a judicious[41] spectator are corrected for bias in the manner specified above, but that is a far cry from the "impartial point of view" in the modern sense. Rather, such a spectator is part of the "usual and natural" class of human being, and will hence approve reasonable favoring of near and dear:

> ...we always consider the *natural* and *usual* force of the passions, when we determine concerning vice and virtue; and if the passions depart very much from the common measures on either side, they are always disapproved of as vicious. A man naturally loves his children better than his nephews, his nephews better than his cousins, his cousins better than strangers, where everything else is equal. Hence arise the common measures of duty, in preferring the one to the other. Our sense of duty always follows the common and natural course of our passions. (T 3.2.1.18/483–484).

Correction by the imagination for biases of distance and partiality is not sufficient for an authoritative moral sense. Such a sense has been honed by the cooperation of the understanding. The authoritative approver must have paved the way for authoritative sentiments by an understanding of certain facts, and importantly the general tendencies of traits.[42]

> But in order to pave the way for such a sentiment, and give a proper discernment of its object, it is often necessary, we find, that much reasoning should precede, that nice distinctions be made, just conclusions drawn, distant comparisons formed, complicated relations examined, and general facts fixed and ascertained. (E para. 137, 173)

All this requires doxastic virtue such as absence of prejudice, credulity, and obstinate incredulity. As Baier points out, "ignorant or silly persons, who do not discern these tendencies [of superstition for example] ... are disqualified as moral judges."[43] Similarly Tom Beauchamp claims that Hume in Book I of the *Treatise* appeals to the authority of "the man of best sense and longest experience"[44] reminiscent of Aristotelian *phronesis*. Furthermore, since as Hume points out in "A Dialogue," the tendencies of traits can vary quite markedly in different social and cultural contexts, knowledge of facts cannot just be based on a general knowledge of human nature: we need also knowledge of *where* we live, and varying social customs.

The authoritative moral sense is also "fine," that is, discriminating. A qualified moral judge can attain knowledge of virtues only by a "finer internal sense"; unlike our knowledge of those sorts of facts which are discoverable by methods common to "every rational intelligible being" (E para. 134, 170). For only finely tuned and properly honed *emotion* allows one to distinguish for example genuine tenderness from phony or affected tenderness, and what is genuinely dazzling from what is dazzling to a person whose mind is "disordered by excessive enthusiasms." In his well-known essay "Of the Standard of Taste" Hume supplements his discussion of "delicacy" in "Of the Delicacy of Taste and Passion" (discussed above) with further standards of taste, claiming that "the true standard of taste and beauty" is the joint verdict of "true judges," namely those who have "strong sense, united to delicate sentiment, improved by practice, perfected by comparison, and cleared of all prejudice" (Miller 241). Given such a standard, whoever "would assert an equality of genius and elegance between OGILVY and Milton ... would be thought to defend no less an extravagance, than if he had maintained a mole-hill to be as high as TENERIFFE" (Miller 230–231).

Finally, from the perspective of a virtue ethical interpretation of Hume, it is interesting that the moral sense of a qualified judge seems to be one possessed by a sufficiently virtuous agent, otherwise her discriminations will be distorted. It is not enough that she have some sympathy: it must not for example be "narrow and ungenerous": "A griping miser, for instance, praises extremely *industry* and *frugality* even in others, and sets them, in his estimation, above all other virtues. He knows the good that results from them" (E 234 n. 1).

Even though he knows the good that results from those virtues, and therefore praises them, he has a distorted view of their importance, relative to other virtues, and a distorted view of the requirements of those virtues. Baier notes that "splenetic misanthropes who do not care ... or hidebound traditionalists who are unwilling to do any adjusting ... a creature absolutely malicious and spiteful" are also disqualified as authoritative. So there is "a virtuous circle in recognition of the components of true merit."[45]

Nonetheless there is room for variation in authoritative judgments. Authoritative discrimination may yield differing but legitimate judgments, since different qualified judges can have different "humours" depending on whether for example they are young or old. Different customs too can be a source of different but legitimate weightings of the sources of virtue:

> ... different customs have also some influences as well as different utilities; and by giving an early bias to the mind, may produce a superior propensity, either to the useful or the agreeable qualities; to those which regard self, or to those which extend to society. (E 336; Miller 38)

As a result of all these complexities and legitimate variation, we should not expect that qualified judges rely on decisive moral principles for their determinations: "It is allowed on all hands, that beauty as well as virtue, always lies in a medium; but where this medium is placed is the great question, and can never be sufficiently explained by general reasonings" ("On Simplicity and Refinement in Writing," Miller 194).

Depending on the virtue in question the "medium" may admit of more or less latitude; it does not necessarily consist in a "point" (Miller 193). For example in his discussion of luxury, Hume claims that "the bounds between the virtue and the vice cannot here be exactly fixed, more than in other moral subjects" (Miller 268).[46] Indeed in "The Sceptic" Hume says flatly that one mistake that philosophers make "without exception" is to "confine too much to principles, and make no account of that vast variety, which nature has so much affected in all her operations," even though generalities (not tantamount to principles) about the virtues needed for happiness occupy much of the subject of the essay.

A judge with an authoritative moral sense is in a position to make warranted judgments. But such judgments are not necessarily correct. Just as Aristotle states that the virtuous person is the rule and the measure of the right because only she has practical wisdom, a view that I take to be epistemological, so the qualified are the best judges of virtue. But even the best judges can get it wrong, for even they may make mistakes about the tendencies of traits in very complex worlds. In fact given Hume's view that "in moral decisions all the circumstances and relations must be previously known" (E App. 1, para. 240, 290); hence "reason must enter for a considerable share in all decisions of this kind" (E para. 234, 285), notably "a very accurate reason or judgement is often requisite, to give the true determination, amidst such intricate doubts arising from obscure or opposite utilities" (E para. 234, 286), warranted judgments may fail to be true. Status as a virtue or a vice depends on facts, potentially discoverable by the faculty of understanding, which may not be picked up, even by wise and sensitive judges.[47] In this eventuality truth as "agreement" with "*real* existence and matters of fact" (T 3.1.1.9/458) has not been attained, for our ideas of virtue do not match relevant matters of fact about what *makes* traits virtues. We are therefore wrong about a "natural fitness." In short, layer (5) (judgments of someone with an authoritative moral sense) must not be confused with layer (6) (true moral judgments). Since truth may outrun the knowledge that can be provided by the understanding, moral truth itself may not be attained via the reasoning of wise and virtuous individuals, or even by society as a whole and our best currently available science.[48]

Notes

1   For an excellent account of the motivation argument demonstrating that it should not be given a non-cognitivist interpretation, see Charles R. Pigden, "If Not Non-Cognitivism, Then What?," in *Hume on Motivation and Virtue*, ed. Charles R. Pigden (Basingstoke: Macmillan, 2010), 80–104.
2   But see Rachel Cohon, *Hume's Morality: Feeling and Fabrication* (Oxford: Oxford University Press, 2008), for a rejection of this reading.
3   "Reason" is here used in its "narrow" sense and includes demonstration (which itself includes (a) *intuition* not relying on sense impressions, and (b) *deduction*), and (c) *causal reasoning*. Through demonstration we know of relations between ideas, and through causal reasoning we acquire beliefs about "matters of fact." This is the reason proper to the "understanding."
4   *Hume's Moral Epistemology* (Oxford: Clarendon Press, 1976), 62.
5   Ibid., 62.
6   I do not intend to discuss what Hume could mean by "power" in this context. I think that serious discussion of what is meant here involves discussion of representational metaphysics, an issue beyond the scope of this book. For elaboration of Hume's use of the term "power" see Jacqueline Taylor, "Hume on Beauty and Virtue," in *A Companion to Hume*, ed. Elizabeth Radcliffe (Oxford: Blackwell), 273–292.
7   Jane L. McIntyre, "Character: A Humean Account," in *Hume: Moral and Political Philosophy*, ed. Rachel Cohon (Aldershot: Ashgate Dartmouth, 2001), 449–462, 457. Note that arguably for Hume not all structured sets of passions have motivational force, such as forms of love as character traits. It might be replied that even for Hume love as a *character trait* characteristically has a complex structure which includes some motivational passions, such as a desire to unite, or a desire to promote the good of the beloved. But for Hume these are not *part* of the passion of love proper, but are merely "conjoin'd" with that passion.

8   Ibid., 456.

9   See Elizabeth Radcliffe, "How Does the Humean Sense of Duty Motivate," in *Hume: Moral and Political Philosophy*, ed. Rachel Cohon, 383–387, 378. Radcliffe claims that T 418 "confirms that the moral sentiments [of 'approbation and disapprobation'] are among the motivating passions" but T 418 merely confirms that calm passions can motivate through the virtue of strength of will. This may well be true of the sense of morality or duty, but is not necessarily true of the moral sentiments of approbation and disapprobation.

10 McIntyre, 457.

11 *Dialogues Concerning Natural Religion*, ed. Henry D. Aiken (New York: Hafner Publishing Co., 1957), 71.

12 See, e.g., Barry Stroud, *Hume* (London: Routledge and Kegan Paul, 1977), who says: "Although there is no such characteristic [as virtue or vice] in actions or characters, the feelings we get on contemplating them inevitably lead us to ascribe it to them … Our moral judgments, like our causal judgments, are 'projections'" (185). He does not take seriously Hume's claims that impressions may "arise from virtue" or that a virtue is "whatever mental action or quality gives to the spectator the pleasing sentiment of approbation" (182; E 289), despite the fact that Hume entitles an entire section of the *Treatise* "Moral Distinctions Deriv'd from a Moral Sense."

13 See S. Holland, "Dispositional Theories of Value Meet Moral Twin Earth," *American Philosophical Quarterly* 38 (2001), 177–195; T. Horgan and M. Timmons, "New Wave Moral Realism Meets Moral Twin Earth," *Journal of Philosophical Research* 16 (1991), 447–465: D. Merli, "Return to Moral Twin Earth," *Canadian Journal of Philosophy* 32 (2002), 207–240.

14 Mark LeBar, "Three Dogmas of Response Dependence," *Philosophical Studies* 123 (2005), 175–211, 188.

15 Ibid., 188.

16 According to Michael Slote, *Moral Sentimentalism* (Oxford: Oxford University Press, 2010), chapter 4, any plausible sentimentalist view of ethics must preserve this truth.

17 See Rachel Cohon and David Owen, "Hume on Representation, Reason and Motivation," *Manuscrito* 20 (1997), 47–76, 69.

18 Herlinde Pauer-Studer, "Humean Sources of Normativity," in *Hume on Motivation and Virtue*, ed. Charles R. Pigden, 186–207, distinguishes (following John Broome) between the "normativity of rational requirements" and the "normativity of reasons," where the former corresponds to the rationality of means-end reasoning and the latter is concerned with weight of reasons. It is the latter which is at issue in the "scratching finger" passages cited.

19 See Chapter 2 n. 18.

20 Paul Bloom, *Just Babies: The Origins of Good and Evil* (New York: Crown Publishers, 2013), 39.

21 See Daniel Goleman, *Emotional Intelligence: Why It Can Matter More Than IQ* (London: Bloomsbury, 1996), 52, and Antonio Damasio, *Descartes' Error: Emotion, Reason, and the Human Brain* (New York: Avon Books, 1994).

22 See Michael Stocker, "How Emotions Reveal Value and Help Cure the Schizophrenia of Modern Ethical Theories," in *How Should One Live? Essays on the Virtues*, ed. Roger Crisp (Oxford: Oxford University Press, 2003), 173–190, 183, who cites Guntrip's schizoid (in *Schizoid Phenomena, Object Relations, and the Self*, London, The Hogarth Press, 1968): an individual "who feels no interest in objects either in consciousness or in the outer world."

23 The famous "No Ought from Is" passage (T 469–470) should be seen as making the same point. Here Hume criticizes moralists who move from statements about the existence of God or the nature of human affairs to moral facts without any decent explanation, claiming that "the distinction between virtue and vice" "is not founded merely" on that form of reason proper to the faculty of the understanding. The kind of cognitive apparatus available to Elliot is impotent in the moral or practical domain generally without the input of sentiment. You cannot move from facts about God or human affairs to facts about virtue and vice using only those resources.

24 The relation between empathy and altruism or morality has been the subject of psychological study. M.L. Hoffman defines empathy in a somewhat weaker way as an "affective response more appropriate to someone else's situation than to one's own" in "The Contribution of Empathy to Justice and Moral Judgment," in *Empathy and Its Development*, ed. N. Eisenberg and J. Strayer (Cambridge: Cambridge

University Press, 1987), 47–80, 48. See also M.L. Hoffman, "Interaction of Affect and Cognition in Empathy," in *Emotions, Cognition, and Behavior*, ed. C.E. Izard, J. Kagan, and R.B. Zajonc (Cambridge: Cambridge University Press, 1984), 103–131, and Martin Hoffman, *Empathy and Moral Development: Implications for Caring and Justice* (Cambridge: Cambridge University Press, 2000).

25 See Maia Szalavitz and Bruce D. Perry, *Born for Love: Why Empathy is Essential – and Endangered* (New York: Harper Collins, 2010), 43–44.

26 See especially E sect. 178, 218ff, and Appendix II "Of Self Love."

27 Although benevolence is particular for Hume, in the sense that it is directed at particular individuals and not at humanity in general, it is not necessarily partial. In Appendix II of the *Enquiries* Hume notes that there are two "kinds" of benevolence: "particular" and "general." The first includes the partial, being founded on "an opinion of virtue, on services done us, or on some particular connexions" such as friendship. The second "general" form of benevolence, also owed to particular individuals, is not based on such features as esteem or affection but rather on "general sympathy": a "compassion for his pains" or a "congratulation with his pleasures." General benevolence Hume also calls "humanity" or "sympathy" (E 298 n. 1; Miller App. 2.6). Extensive sympathy allows for the possibility of general benevolence.

28 "Hume and the Limits of Benevolence," *Hume Studies* 28(2) (2002), 271–295. In this paper Vitz argues persuasively against commentators such as Nicholas Capaldi, *Hume's Place in Moral Philosophy* (New York: Peter Lang, 1989), 204–205, who claims that for Hume benevolence is "restricted to family and friends."

29 Note that in the *Enquiries* Hume offers a rather simplified account of what Annette Baier, "*Enquiry Concerning the Principles of Morals*: Incomparably the Best?," in *A Companion to Hume*, ed. Elizabeth S. Radcliffe (Oxford: Blackwell, 2008), 293–320, 307, calls "the virtue recognizing moral sentiment." This is the "sentiment of humanity," a sentiment "common to all mankind," by which he means characteristic members of mankind as opposed to moral "monsters." Here the moral sense and its conditions are rolled into one: the "sentiment of humanity."

30 David Wiggins, "A Sensible Subjectivism?," in *Needs, Values, Truth: Essays in the Philosophy of Value*, ed. David Wiggins (Oxford: Oxford University Press, 1987), 184–214, 194.

31 Rachel Cohon, "Hume's Natural and Artificial Virtues," in *The Blackwell Guide to Hume's Treatise*, ed. Saul Traiger (Oxford: Blackwell, 2006), 256–275, 256.

32 Philippa Foot, "Hume on Moral Judgement," in *Virtues and Vices and Other Essays in Moral Philosophy* (Oxford: Basil Blackwell, 1978), 74–80, 76–77.

33 Cohon, "Hume's Natural and Artificial Virtues," 273.

34 Ibid., 273.

35 "Virtue Ethics and Human Nature," *Hume Studies* 25 (1999), 67–82.

36 *Hume's Morality*, 106.

37 However, according to Elizabeth S. Radcliffe, *On Hume* (Belmont, CA: Wadsworth, 2000), 47, "impressions of reflection are experiences which result from reflecting on the sources of our pleasures and pains." Hume though claims that, although impressions of reflection "are derived in great measure from our ideas" (T 7), they "*arise*" from ideas of pleasure and pain copied from impressions of pleasure or pain associated with certain events. These ideas "return upon the soul" and "*produce*" the passions of reflection themselves (T 8). Active reflection on the original sources of, e.g., envy is not necessary to produce such passions, or even characteristic. Associative mechanisms are in general sufficient.

38 *Hume's Morality*, 104.

39 See further Kate Abramson, "Correcting Our Sentiments About Hume's Moral Point of View," *The Southern Journal of Philosophy* 37(3) (1999), 333–361. Abramson distinguishes between the moral point of view and the general point of view.

40 An interpretation of T 581 by Walter Brand, *Hume's Theory of Moral Judgment* (Dordrecht: Kluwer Academic, 1992), 7.

41 The notion of judicious is an entirely non-technical term in Hume, ascribable to many things. For example conversation can be judicious (T 147).

42 See, e.g., E App. 1, 234; Miller App. 1.1).

Can Hume Be Both a Sentimentalist and a Virtue Ethicist? 69

43 Baier, "*Enquiry Concerning the Principles of Morals*," 308.

44 Tom L. Beauchamp, "The Sources of Normativity in Hume's Moral Theory," in *A Companion to Hume*, ed. Elizabeth S. Radcliffe, 493–512. In this article, Beauchamp identifies several epistemic norms, many of which are essential to his "normative virtue theory" by which moral beliefs are justified.

45 Baier, "*Enquiry Concerning the Principles of Morals*," 309. To the objection that this makes the idea of a qualified judge circular, it may be replied that her judgments are not determinative of truth, and that debate about what counts as qualified and what should be esteemed as virtues can proceed in a back and forth manner on the basis of argument involving appeals to a wide range of facts.

46 The notion of the "medium" should not be understood in terms of moderation. Avoidance of excess and deficiency is one feature, but by no means the only one. Similar issues attend Aristotle's notion of the mean.

47 See Beauchamp, "The Sources of Normativity in Hume's Moral Theory," 495.

48 I think but am not absolutely certain that this is the view of W.D. Falk, "Hume on Practical Reason," in *Ought, Reasons, and Morality: The Collected Papers of W.D. Falk* (Ithaca, NY: Cornell University Press, 1986), 143–159. According to him, for Hume, "there are factual truths and merit truths supervening on them" (150). "Merit is discerned by sentiment, but only by a "proper sentiment" and not a "false relish," one which can still be "corrected by argument and reflection" (146). To me even a "proper sentiment" – an authoritative moral sense susceptible to the cooperation of reason – could be unfitting for Hume.

Chapter 4

Hume and the Problem of Justice as a Virtue

4.1 Introduction

When Hume talks of morality as something not founded in reason he means by "reason" the operation of the understanding. That faculty, recall, is understood as existing "apart from any passions and any feelings of pleasure and pain." Indeed not even justice, an "artificial" virtue, is founded on reason or understanding in that sense:

> … the sense of justice is not founded on reason, or on the discovery of certain connexions and relations of ideas, which are eternal, immutable, and universally obligatory … [for] an alteration … in the temper and circumstances of mankind, wou'd entirely alter our duties and obligations. (T 3.2.2.20/496)

In particular, there would be no sense of justice and no justice, if there were "extensive generosity" and "perfect abundance of every thing" (T 3.2.2.20/496).

In this regard, justice is no different from other virtues. For a trait to be properly regarded as a virtue we must take into account both *who* we are and *where* we are.[1] The latter constitutes the "circumstances" of the virtue. It is still possible to speak of universal virtues as virtues whose *general* circumstances obtain throughout human society but the *particular* form of that universal virtue may vary from society to society. This is certainly true of what Hume calls the artificial virtues, such as justice and honesty. For what makes a virtue artificial is that its field (domain of concern) is constituted by "artifices": conventions of property (in the case of justice) or promise keeping (in the case of honesty), and these artifices will differ in different societies.

It is the "artificial" nature of these virtues which gives rise to "the" problem of justice. From the perspective of virtue ethics, the problem is really two related

The Virtue Ethics of Hume and Nietzsche, First Edition. Christine Swanton.
© 2015 John Wiley & Sons, Ltd. Published 2015 by John Wiley & Sons, Ltd.

problems, both concerning the issue of how justice can be regarded as a virtue on Hume's account. The problems are:

> Problem A As a virtue of character, justice seems deontological on Hume's view. How can this be so, given that Hume claims that (a) the original motive for the establishment of justice is self-interest, and (b) the rationale for the "artifices" of justice is social utility?

> Problem B How can justice be considered a virtue on Hume's account given that justice is an artificial virtue, and accordingly for Hume, there is no "natural motive" of justice? For it seems that, according to Hume, virtue proper requires a natural motive.

Problem A is the topic of the next section; the remaining sections are concerned with Problem B.

4.2 The Motive of Justice

What is the motive of justice for Hume? I shall argue that Hume's view of justice *as a personal virtue* conforms to what I call "the standard conception of justice." On this conception the just person is characteristically moved by motives we might call deontological. By this I mean that the characteristic motive of the just person when acting justly is what Hume calls the sense of justice, the sense of duty or obligation to be just independent of consequences or self-interest. I shall argue that the view that Hume does not have the standard conception of justice rests on a failure to distinguish between different categories of motive of justice, and different categories of the point and function (rationale) of justice in a generic sense. Specifically the rationale of the virtue of justice may differ from the rationale of the rules of justice. Consider now "the motive of justice."

The "motive of justice" is ambiguous between three quite different categories of motivation. These are: (a) the motive to perform a particular just act; (b) the motive to set up institutions of justice, most particularly the conventions or "artifices" which regulate and establish property; (c) a motivational disposition, or essential part of a complex of motivational dispositions, that is characteristic of a person with the *virtue* of justice.

Let us focus first on the motive of just acts. For Hume the motive to establish institutions of justice is self-interest: "Thus *self-interest* is the original motive to the *establishment* of justice" (T 3.2.2.24/499). However it seems clear that for him self-interest is not the motive for just acts. A chief reason for this is that just acts need not serve an agent's self-interest:

> ... single acts of justice may be contrary, either to public or private interest ... 'tis easily conceiv'd how a man may impoverish himself by a signal instance of integrity, and

have reason to wish, that with regard to that single act, the laws of justice were for a moment suspended in the universe. (T 3.2.2.22 /497)

The same issue arises for the motive of honesty; another "artificial" virtue:

For shou'd we say, that a concern for our private interest or reputation is the legitimate motive to all honest actions; it wou'd follow, that wherever that concern ceases, honesty can no longer have place. (T 3.2.1.10/480)

Despite these passages, some commentators believe that "the textual evidence that Hume holds that every individual act of justice yields a net advantage to the agent ... is equivocal."[2] Cohon claims, for example, that T 497 can be read as both supporting and denying this view. I do not see this. At T 497 Hume makes three claims concerning this issue:

(1)   Single acts of justice may be "contrary, either to public or private interest."
(2)   The scheme of justice is requisite to the well-being of every individual.
(3)   It is true of *every* individual that it is in her *net* interest to be a member of a society in which there is a scheme of justice rather than a member of a society in which there is no such scheme, for without such a scheme "everyone [even the strongest] must fall into that savage and solitary condition, which is infinitely worse than the worst situation that can possibly be suppos'd in society."

Nothing in T 497 suggests that Hume believes that each just *act* may be in an agent's net self-interest. Rather each of us has an interest in "*establishing* justice" (T 499); that is, in establishing rules which serve the end of social utility. When Hume claims that self-interest is the original motive for the *establishment* of justice, he means that all of us have an interest in "maintaining order" and having security of possession. Unfortunately in complex societies such as "tribes" and "nations" "we may frequently lose sight of that interest" and "may follow a lesser and present interest" in being unjust. Hume does not mean here that our net present interest is always to be just; rather our interest in stable society where property rights are respected is a greater interest than a particular act of injustice, even where *that act* serves our net interest.

However, is the motivation for performing just acts the *expectation* that such acts redound to one's self-interest? Though noting Hume's claim that "Taking any single act, my justice may be pernicious in every single respect" (T 3.2.2.22/498), David Gauthier nonetheless claims that:

Each person must expect that every choice that he makes between conforming to and violating the rules of justice to have an effect on the behaviour of others with consequences for his own advantage sufficient to afford him with a normally adequate motive for conformity.[3]

Gauthier also notes the difficulty this reading poses for Hume: Hume's discussion (in the *Enquiries*) of the "sensible knave" (someone who violates rules of justice when it suits him, and when he thinks he can get away with it) questions the plausibility of this expectation. Nor does it explain the motive to be just in a particular case when it is clear that such an act is seriously against one's interest.

Appreciating the centrality of virtue to Hume's philosophy allows us to resolve this problem. To show this we need to investigate the characteristic motivations of a person with the virtue of justice and Hume's account of the interest we have in educating people into such virtue. Given the tendency of people to inflict injustice in complex societies (like the "sensible knave" of the *Enquiries*) and given both that we "never fail to observe the prejudice we receive from the injustice of others" and that we are displeased by "distant" injustices (through sympathy), we desire to educate people to have just motivations adhering to "principles of probity" as a stable motivational set. That is we desire to educate people into the virtue of justice. As Hume claims, the demands of that virtue "have greater force when custom and education assist interest and reflexion":

> For these reasons they are induc'd to inculcate on their children, from their earliest infancy, the principles of probity ... By this means, the sentiments of honour may take root in their tender minds, and acquire such firmness and solidity, that they may fall little short of those principles, which are the most essential to our natures, and the most deeply radicated in our internal constitution. (T 3.2.2.26/500–501)

As a result of this inculcation people internalize principles of probity so that they act on them even at the expense of self-interest. As we saw above, Hume claims at T 497 that a man of integrity may knowingly impoverish himself performing a just act having reason to wish that the laws of justice were temporarily suspended.

Our approval of those with the virtue of justice is based on our approving those who respect principles of probity habitually; those who respect them are "worthy and honourable" while those who transgress are "base and infamous" (T 3.2.2.26/ 500–501). We approve of those with the virtue of justice insofar as they see themselves as having a sufficient reason to be just in particular cases, namely "regard to justice, and abhorrence of villainy and knavery" and "sense of duty and obligation" (T 3.2.1.9/479). In complex societies, where "sensible knavery" may become more likely, we want people to desist from unjust acts *because* (they believe that) such acts are in their nature base and dishonorable *qua* acts of violation of entitlements. We do not want them to desist simply because they have made calculations about utility, let alone personal utility.

Reflection on base motives for unjust acts raises the question of those who are unjust from motives that are not base, for example, motives of beneficence or compassion. Such acts of injustice presumably would not be registered by an authoritative judge as "base and infamous," but the lack of respect for rules of justice displayed would normally be disapproved. For such acts would be seen as a "sure symptom and characteristic" of arrogance, immaturity, or even worse, callousness toward individuals at the receiving end of injustice. They would be seen as callous if their acts displayed no sympathy for the harms incurred by their riding roughshod over individual entitlements. To prevent this particular form of lack of respect, education must begin early; otherwise calculating dispositions about tendencies will begin to corrupt the moral sentiments. Indeed according to Jennifer Welchman, such cases, illustrated by the "young and inexperienced" "benevolent rule breaker" Cyrus who reflected only on the "limited fitness" of the case before him rather than on the necessity of respecting the "general inflexible rules" of justice, constitute a serious (though neglected) problem.[4]

The motive of him who possesses justice as a virtue is therefore respect for the "inflexible" rules of justice and the "inviolable" system of justice, and that motive is internalized as honorable. This does not imply that we, as mature virtuous agents, when acting justly are characteristically motivated by a desire to be personally deemed honorable. Rather we are motivated, if we are just, by a concern to protect and not violate another's entitlements, motivations which we also deem to be honorable.

It is true that the process of education develops our conception of what is in our interest: it is a commonplace of virtue ethics that the acquisition of virtue alters or redirects people's conceptions of benefit, harm, and loss. For example once honesty and the virtue of friendship is inculcated in me, I do not regard it as against my interests not to obtain a beautiful vase belonging to my friend by getting someone to steal it for me just before I leave permanently for the other side of the world. However, this does not imply that for Hume an unjust act performed by her is *never* in a virtuous agent's overall best interest, for on Hume's view a virtue is not an idealized state but is a state consistent with common and usual human nature. I have already noted that for Hume an act of integrity can be against one's interests. Also, even where a just act is in an agent's interests, the motive of being in one's interests (redirected or otherwise) is not a motive for a just act in a virtuous agent, at least not characteristically.

An alternative account of the characteristic motives of those with the virtue of justice is to see them as sympathy for the public interest. This is certainly the "*source*" of the "moral approbation" which "*attends that virtue*" (T 3.2.2.24/500) in the sense that this is a necessary sentiment for the efficacious instilling of concepts of "honourable" and "dishonourable" (T 3.2.2.25/500). However, to see this as a motive for just acts is to confuse the characteristic motive of just persons in being just with the necessary materials for having that motive. For Hume: "The utmost politicians can perform, is, to extend the natural sentiments beyond their original bounds; but still nature must furnish the materials, and give us some notion of moral distinctions" (T 3.2.2.25/500). The natural sentiments are extended through education into "habits" such as the various virtues, and in the case of justice into what is deemed honorable. The claim that the characteristic deontological motivations of those with the virtue of justice would not exist if we lacked sympathy for the public interest is not to be confused with a claim that the motives which express the point of justice as a virtue, and which are characteristic of that virtue, *is* such sympathy.

If sympathy with public interest were the characteristic motive of justice as a virtue, we would be faced with the problem that where a just act is not in the public interest then justice would not require it. However as we have seen, Hume makes it clear at T 3.2.1.13/482 in his discussion of for example the "profligate debauchee," and in Appendix III of *The Principles of Morals*, that justice may require non-beneficent acts. Neither public nor private benevolence can be the "original motive" of justice (T 3.2.1.13/482). If sympathy for the public interest is the interest that provides the real point of the virtue of justice then benevolent rule breakers such as Cyrus can always appeal to that point in breaking the collectively determined rules. A stronger deontological motivation relying on a concept of respect for the rules themselves, a respect that provides the very point of the (personal) virtue of justice, seems required.

This observation raises the question then of the point or rationale of the virtue of justice. Maybe the motive of those with the virtue of justice is one thing but what makes justice a virtue, its rationale as a virtue, is different. To avoid what Stocker calls moral schizophrenia[5] one would want the justification of a trait as a virtue to be aligned with its characteristic motive. A reason for the failure to read Hume as possessing the standard conception of justice as a virtue (in respect of both motive and justification) is that the "rationale of justice" is ambiguous between two different kinds of rationale. These are: (a) the rationale of the virtue of justice itself, that is, its point or function as a personal virtue, and (b) the rationale of the "artifices" of justice, notably the rules which regulate property. These artifices constitute the field or domain of concern of the virtue of justice, whereas the virtue itself is a character trait: the trait of being well disposed in relation to that field.

The rationale of justice as a personal virtue must be distinguished from that of the rules of justice, otherwise puzzling and unattractive positions will be attributed to Hume. Stroud claims for example that "we regard justice as a virtue [but] Hume thinks he can explain what recommends it to our avidity or self-interest alone."[6] This claim confuses the point of setting up just institutions with the rationale of the virtue of justice.

Nor should we confuse the rationale or point of the rules of justice, which ultimately depends on consequences – they must serve long-term good – with the rationale of the virtue itself, which is to solidify in individual persons dispositions of non-violation and protection of people's entitlements on a case by case basis. If we do not make this distinction the deontological nature of the virtue may be thought puzzling, and justifiable only by a "noble lie." According to Marcia Baron, for example, when children are taught that injustice is "base and infamous" the "implication seems to be that it is base and infamous because injustice weakens the fabric of society, and therefore the deontological claim is not easy to disentangle from the claim that every unjust act does weaken the fabric of society."[7] Since this last claim is false (and seen by Hume himself to be false), Baron concludes that justice is not a genuine virtue for Hume, for "one ought always to be artificially virtuous" is for Hume "a noble lie, essential to our well-being as a society."[8]

This claim is based on the assumption that for Hume (C1) (see Chapter 3 section 3.4) is the only fundamental criterion of virtue: Hume is seen as a "teleologist."[9] It may be true that, as Annette Baier claims, a virtue such as justice and fidelity to promises "may be first valued for its usefulness to society."[10] It may therefore be thought that (C1) rather than (C2) rationalizes justice as a virtue. However it does not follow from Baier's claim that the point or function of justice as a personal virtue, as it operates in a virtuous agent as a personal merit, is its promotion of the general good. The baseness and infamy of unjust acts expressive of the vice of injustice is not reducible to the claim, however true, that injustice in general weakens the fabric of society.

To see this, we need to focus on (C2), Hume's second criterion of virtue discussed in Chapter 3. It is the "species" of unjust act which gives rise to the immediate sentiment of disapprobation, rather than reflection on its (usual) consequences. This is because he who has the virtue of justice has "fix[ed] an inviolable law to himself" (T 3.2.2.27/501). The actions of the "sensible knave" are immediately registered as base. Why? We regard as base those individuals who selfishly act as free riders, and acts of injustice are expressive of those "disgustful" characters. This sentiment is not washed away by reflections on consequences; if the base act turns out to be beneficial our disapprobation is not removed. Free riders in turn are base because they lack respect for rules of justice, which are conducive to social good, and they act from motives which are base and dishonorable.

We have explained the characteristic deontological motivations of someone possessing the virtue of justice and the deontological rationale of the virtue of justice, for Hume. There is no "moral schizophrenia." The rationale of protecting property rights as determined by rules of justice provides the point of the *virtue* of justice, namely a disposition to respect property through respecting those "inflexible" rules. The rationale for specific rules of justice is to set up property rights for the purposes of the protection of property, and the rationale for the system as a whole is long-term public interest. If the rules as a whole did not over the long term serve public interest they should over time be changed. Those with the *virtue* of justice respect the rules as they are. What virtuous agents do when the rules are manifestly and seriously unjust in the light of the rationale of the rules as a whole is another issue which I do not deal with here.

4.3   Can Justice Have a Natural Motive?

This section is concerned with Problem B for Hume's notion of justice as a virtue; its alleged lack of a *natural* motive. Why does justice not have a natural motive for Hume and why is that a problem for him? First, the motive characterizing justice as a virtue is as we have seen "the regard for justice and abhorrence of villainy and knavery." Similarly, Hume claims "we have no real or universal motive for observing the laws of equity, but the very equity and merit of that observance" (T 3.2.1.17/483). This cannot be a natural motive for Hume, for the regard for justice as a supposed natural motive could only be regard for justice *as a virtue*, and we "can never have a regard to the virtue of an action, unless the action be antecedently virtuous" (T 3.2.1.9/480). We could not thereby explain what *makes* justice a virtue. To suppose that mere regard for justice and equity were a natural motive would thus be "unintelligible and sophistical" (T 3.2.1.9/480). Unless "nature has establish'd a sophistry" "we must allow, that the sense of justice and injustice is not deriv'd from nature, but arises artificially, tho' necessarily from education, and human conventions" (T 3.2.2.17/483).

Why is the lack of a natural motive of justice a problem?[11] According to Hume, to be a virtue properly so called, a character trait must be constituted by a certain motivational disposition. This is a "natural" motive which is distinct from a mere sense of duty or moral obligation to perform an action. For "*no action can be virtuous, or morally good, unless there be in human nature some motive to produce it, distinct from the sense of its morality*" (T 3.2.1.7/479). For example, for friendship to be a genuine virtue in us, our habitual motivation must be expressive of friendship. This does not mean that our motive must be a desire to manifest the virtue: rather we must act *out of* friendship when we perform a friendly act. Hume's example concerns parental affection:

> We blame a parent for neglecting his child. Why? because it shows a want of natural affection, which is the duty of every parent. Were not natural affection a duty, the care of children cou'd not be a duty; and 'twere impossible we cou'd have the duty in our eye in the attention we give to our offspring. In this case, therefore, all men suppose a motive to the action distinct from a sense of duty. (T 3.2.1.5/478)

Hume concedes that like Stocker's moralistic "friend"[12] one can perform actions out of a sense of duty alone, without the natural motive proper to the virtue, but a person "who feels his heart devoid of that motive, may hate himself upon that account" (T 3.2.1.8/479).

The want of a natural motive of justice gives rise to another problem, according to Gauthier. Since there is no natural motive of justice, "under pressure of the sensible knave, Hume's account of the artificial virtues becomes an error theory."[13] Why is this? "Only by feigning a natural motive to the performance of just acts, do we develop the disposition to be just."[14] Mere words of making promises, mere rules of justice, cannot provide the "natural materials" which educators and politicians can work on to develop a virtue of justice. For Hume education "extends" our "natural sympathies" and we do have a natural sympathy for the public interest, but that does not provide materials for the peculiarly deontological motive of justice. In the words of Gauthier:

> As Hume insists "publick praise and blame" as well as "private education and instruction" cannot create the distinction between justice and injustice (T 500). Only

the peculiar working of the affections, in which the want of the imaginary motive proves to be the ground of a real one, can provide the materials needed for indoctrination to motivate us to be just.[15]

It is sometimes suggested that a natural motive of justice (that is a motive other than a sense of duty or moral obligation inculcated by education) is not necessary for a motive of justice. According to Margaret Watkins Tate, "A Humean agent tempted to injustice has various resources to appeal to: she might remind herself of the importance of smooth property transactions, honor, or the significance of a good reputation."[16] Unfortunately these "resources" are mere moonshine if the agent lacks some kind of natural humane motive; she is happy to be a free rider, she believes that honor, like phlogiston, should be consigned to the graveyard of outmoded concepts of false theories, and she only cares about her reputation with fellow rogues.

I shall argue in the remaining sections that these problems concerning the apparent lack of a natural motive of justice can be solved, while accepting Hume's view that the mere regard for justice is not itself a natural motive. I argue that Hume could admit a connection between the "mere regard" for justice and a natural passion which together comprise what we might think of as the *sense* of justice. The sense of justice could be understood as a richer notion than the mere regard for justice which is the proximate motive of those with the virtue of justice in acting justly. On this view the sense of justice possessed by a person with the virtue of justice comprises a natural *humane* motive which is not reducible to a mere regard for justice. That motive, as I shall argue in section 4.4, is the natural motive of compassion or what Hume also calls pity: a concern for the misery of others (T 369). For that passion is causally linked to the regard for justice by causing a basic desire not to violate, and thereby avoid causing misery to others.

This view has one very important qualification. The causal relation is, I shall argue, indirect. It is important to note that compassion as a natural motive of the virtue of justice is not the characteristic immediate or proximate motive of each just act. The argument will depend on the distinction between senses (a) and (c) of motive (section 4.2), that is, between the characteristic immediate motive of a just act, and an essential part of a complex of motivational dispositions (the sense of justice) characteristic of a person with the virtue of justice. Compassion could be a natural motive of justice in this latter sense. On this view our natural passions provide the basis and support for the deontological sentiments.

Could this view be Humean? On my view, Hume failed to see the resources from within his own theory of the passions for discovering a natural motive of justice in the relevant sense. This failure may be due to a mistaken inference. The error takes its starkest form when he claims that fidelity is an artificial virtue. According to T 3.2.5.6/519, "as there is naturally no inclination to observe promises, distinct from a sense of their obligation, it follows that fidelity is no natural virtue, and that promises have no force antecedent to human conventions."

Hume is right to say that there is naturally no inclination to observe promises, for they "have no force antecedent to human conventions," but wrong to claim that it *follows* that fidelity is not a natural virtue. For there is a distinction between fidelity as a basic, general universal virtue, and the particular, differentiated forms it takes in particular social institutions (e.g., promise keeping in one or other of its various forms). The "artifices" which provide the materials for the operation of the general virtue will vary, but the basic quality of the virtue is the same. There may well be a natural motive to fidelity as a basic virtue, but this natural motive must be appropriately differentiated to take account of culturally based conventional forms, for example the "artificial" nature of the institution of promise keeping. We must distinguish then between the abstractly specified "basic" virtue of fidelity and its differentiated forms in different societies with different conventions. To possess the full differentiated virtue requires facility with the relevant artifices, but this is compatible with the idea that possession of that virtue also requires a natural motive that is common to the various differentiated forms of fidelity. The basic sense of honesty may well be a natural virtue but the full virtue comprises its artificial form. On the other hand, I will argue, the full virtue requires the emotional base of the natural basic virtue: to master the artifices alone without the relevant passional base is to fail to possess the full virtue.

Hume makes the same mistaken inference in his argument for the artificial nature of the sense of justice. At T 3.2.2.21/496 he claims that "*those impressions which give rise to this sense of justice are not natural to the mind of man, but arise from artifice and human conventions.*" His argument for this claim is that given variation in and alterability of "temper and circumstance" which would change both our own and public interest, the establishment of particular rules of justice would depend on what those interests actually are. Thus Hume infers from the conventional and variable nature of the social rules of justice that the sentiments giving rise to the sense of justice are also "artificial."

Again we need to distinguish between justice as a basic virtue, and differentiated forms of that virtue. In its fullest manifestation, the sense of justice possessed by those having the virtue of justice must include awareness of and respect for relevant conventions, for the motive of justice to be successfully expressed in action. We need in short to possess the requisite differentiated form of the virtue. But this fact is quite consistent with the claim that a natural motive is an essential part of a complex of motivational dispositions characteristic of a person with the sense of justice and thus the basic virtue of justice.

4.4   Compassion as the Natural Motive of Justice

The question now arises: Can justice as a basic virtue be understood as having at its core a natural motive which is expressed in its various differentiated forms? More particularly, could Hume find such a motive? I shall argue that compassion can be seen as just that natural motive.[17]

Recall that to say that compassion is "the natural motive of justice" in the relevant sense (sense (c) above, section 4.2) is not to say that every just act is motivated by compassion. It is not to say that we should be moved by compassion for the rich bigot when we repay our debt to him.[18] Indeed when Hume says that "*no action can be virtuous, or morally good, unless there be in human nature some motive to produce it, distinct from the sense of its morality*" (T 3.2.1.7/479), he is claiming that the motive must exist in human nature and be suitably connected to the relevant virtue. This does not imply that it is the motive of *each act* which manifests the virtue in question.

Indeed even in Hume's paradigm case of a virtue having a natural motive, the parental virtue of parental love, that natural motive (affection) need not be the immediate motive of each act manifesting the virtue. Consider a parent punishing her child. Virtuous punishment of children manifesting parental love requires that the parent have knowledge of and respect for relevant laws. In New Zealand, for example, there exists the so-called "Anti-Smacking" legislation whose scope in relation to legal intent and enforcement is not entirely clear to a large number of people at least. Hence parents often consider whether a light smack is effectively illegal when considering the way they should punish their child. Furthermore the immediate motive of punishment is inflicting unpleasant consequences on the child for its transgression, with the further aim of inhibiting those actions in the future. In short the immediate motive is to punish effectively in a lawful humane way. Affection is not the motive of punishment, which administered appropriately is itself part of loving parental virtue. That natural affection is the natural motive of parental virtue does not imply that affection is (or should be) my motive for punishing my child now. Hume's point is that natural affection is the natural characteristic material for parental virtue; if a person "feels in his heart" (i.e., generally) devoid of that passion, he hates himself. Likewise, if one's heart is devoid of compassion, one might argue, the materials for inculcating deontological motivations, or the right kind of deontological motivations (for example motivations which do not express punitive rigorism and are entirely lacking in mercy), will be absent.

It may be replied that though affection is a characteristic but not invariant motive of actions manifesting parental virtue, compassion is not even a characteristic motive of just acts. As Hume says, a characteristic motive of specific just acts is the regard for justice. This problem can be addressed by distinguishing between two readings of sense (c) above, in relation to compassion as a natural motive of justice.

(ci)   Compassion is the natural motivational disposition characteristic of those who have the virtue of justice, and it is a disposition which constitutes the *characteristic* motive of just acts.

(cii)   Compassion is an essential natural part of a complex motivational disposition characterizing those with the virtue of justice (and which together comprise what I have called the sense of justice).

On the view to be explicated, (ci) is allowed to be too strong; compassion does not characteristically motivate just acts but the just motivations are leavened by compassion or constrained by compassion. Compassion is deemed to be an essential component of a motivational complex of someone who has the virtue of justice in its full or genuine form as an excellence of character. As I shall argue, a certain kind of compassion is at the emotional core of justice – a concern not to cause misery or harm by violating entitlements. Furthermore, in the absence of such a motivational core, the deontological motivations will not be leavened by humanity; they will not be of the right kind. One's "virtue" of justice, as Nietzsche puts it, will not manifest a *mild* "penetrating eye." It will be (as we shall explore further when we discuss Nietzsche) a "cold demon of knowledge"; it will be excessively punitive and rigoristic; it will lack grace, and so on. In other words, even for justice, Hume's problem of the need for natural motives if a "virtue" is to be a genuine virtue, remains a genuine problem.

We now show that for Hume compassion could be seen as a natural motive of justice in the relevant sense. In order to show this we need first to distinguish compassion from benevolence, with which it might easily be confused. This is particularly important, since we have already seen that Hume argues against benevolence as the motive of justice. Benevolence is a direct passion, by which is meant that it is a passion that arises "immediately from good or evil, pain or pleasure" (T 2.1.2.4/276). Specifically, it is a desire for the happiness of another. It is also a "primary" or "original" passion, being an "original instinct implanted in our nature" (T 2.2.7.1/368).

What in more detail is compassion for Hume, and what features make it a good candidate for a natural motive of justice in sense (cii)? Compassion (often called by Hume pity), like "particular" benevolence, is a direct passion, but unlike such benevolence is a "secondary" passion (i.e., not an original instinct implanted in our nature). It arises from "original affections" (desire for happiness), through the operation of sympathy based on resemblance, rather than on such features as merits, friendship, and services rendered: "*Pity* is a concern for … the misery of others, without any friendship … to occasion this concern … We pity even strangers, and such as are perfectly indifferent to us" (T 2.2.7.1/369). This sympathy is occasioned by *resemblance*: "Twill be easy to explain the passion of *pity*, from the precedent reasoning concerning *sympathy*. We have a lively idea of everything related to us. All human creatures are related to us by resemblance" (T 2.2.7.2/369).

Before I show how compassion or pity so described can be the natural motive of justice, it must first be noted that Hume himself seems to suggest it cannot play this role. Hume claims at T 3.3.1.12/579 that "when I relieve a person in distress, my natural humanity is my motive" and argues that just acts cannot be motivated by such an unadulterated natural motive. However, recall two points made earlier. In its deployment as the natural motive of *justice* in sense (cii), humanity as concern for misery motivates us to refrain from violating (rather than relieving distress), though when leavened by grace justice may link to the former aspect of the motive of "humanity."[19] Second, recall that if that natural motive is to be part of a full *virtue* of justice, justice must be seen as a differentiated virtue sensitive to the actual (just) institutions of one's own society. Our sense of justice must be educated to form a developing conception of the field of justice. As part of such a virtue, "humanity" is not unadulterated raw concern about misery.

What features make compassion an appropriate natural motive of justice in the required sense? They are as follows.

(a) Compassion is extensive. Justice must embrace strangers. Compassion is based on resemblance and "all human creatures are related to us by resemblance."
(b) Compassion is impartial. Compassion differs from particular benevolence in that the objects of compassion are those capable of misery, and are not limited to those with whom we have partial relations such as friendship. It can also include as its objects those without merits or even enemies.
(c) Compassion involves a concern to avoid damage to individuals, rather than (merely) to promote happiness.

Feature (c) allows us to distinguish compassion from general benevolence. We have seen that compassion arises from "original affections" through the operation of sympathy based on resemblance. However Hume also admits of a passion of general benevolence. This is a concern for the happiness of others in general (not to be confused with the (for Hume) impossible passion of love of mankind), rather than particular or private benevolence based on specific admired merits or relation of friendship and so on.

The problem then arises: How can the putative natural passion of justice guard against the problems of the benevolent rule breaker discussed above? Certainly the motive of justice is a motive which protects people's entitlements, even if happiness can be diffused by violating some of those entitlements. But how does the motive of compassion allow for the overriding of the sympathies occasioned by benevolence? According to Hume, sympathy caused by resemblance has a more lively effect on our impressions of "affliction and sorrow" than on those of "pleasure and enjoyment." The interests and passions of persons resembling us

> must strike upon us in a lively manner, and produce an emotion similar to the original one; since a lively idea is easily converted into an impression. If this be true in general, it must be more so of affliction and sorrow. These have always a more lasting influence than any pleasure or enjoyment. (T 2.2.7.2/369)

Though particular benevolence, general benevolence in the form of "congratulation with a person's pleasures," and compassion (sympathy with pain) can all be understood as species of humanity, compassion, unlike forms of benevolence, does not have an inbuilt tendency to undermine justice, or at least not such a powerful one. When compassion (concern for the misery of others) in its form as a desire to avoid causing misery is sophisticated enough to embrace a desire to avoid causing "affliction and sorrow" by violating entitlements, and particularly when that desire becomes more "artificial" by being refined through education into knowledge of the socially useful artifices which create those entitlements, any tendency of benevolence to undermine justice is weakened. Thus a *natural* motive of justice, founded on the desire not to cause affliction – a desire based on sympathy with a person by virtue of the resembling feature of humanity, as opposed to esteemed qualities – is not reducible to the regard for justice itself.

4.5   Problems with Compassion as the Natural Motive of Justice

In this section, I consider two problems for the understanding of compassion as the natural motive for justice in sense (cii), in relation to Hume's theory of the passions. These are:

(1)   How is compassion even possible on Hume's system?
(2)   Given that it is possible, how can it be extensive?

We deal with each of these problems in turn.[20]

Compassion (pity) at first sight seems impossible on Hume's psychology since "There is always a mixture of love or tenderness with pity" whereas "since pity is an uneasiness … arising from the misery of others, pity should naturally … produce hatred." Thus, says Hume, "this mixture [of love and tenderness with pity] … seems at first sight to be contradictory to my system" (T 2.2.9.1/381). This apparent contradiction does not merely threaten Hume's system: it is a paradoxical fact noted and researched on by developmental psychologists. Claims Paul Bloom: "Empathetic suffering is unpleasant, and sometimes this unpleasantness is overwhelming."[21] Yet research on babies and young children shows that they "don't just turn away from the person in pain. They try to make the other person feel better. Developmental psychologists have long observed that one-year-olds will pat and stroke others in distress."[22]

For Hume the apparent contradiction is resolved by two psychological principles. First, there is the distinction between motivating and non-motivating passions, and the relations between them. Compassion (pity) as an "aversion" to the misery of another is related to benevolence (T 2.2.9.3/382). Benevolence, unlike love or hate, is not a "pure sensation … without any direction or tendency to action" (T 2.2.9.2/382). Rather the connection between pity and benevolence, and the connection between benevolence and love, allow the passion of pity to be connected with that of love (T 2.2.9.3/382). Hence Hume claims:

> When the present misery of another has any strong influence upon me, the vivacity of the conception is not confin'd merely to its immediate object, but diffuses its influence over all the related ideas, and gives me a lively notion of all the circumstances of that

> person … By means of this lively notion I am interested in them; take part with them; and feel a sympathetic motion in my breast. (T 2.2.9.14/386)

Hence pity involves the desire to "unite" as opposed to a desire to "separate" from the object suffering.

The second principle is that of the conversion of passions. Consider a person who does not desire the good of another. Given that justice requires that we respect the entitlements of all, how can Hume account for the approbation of justice toward persons to whom we are indifferent or whom we hate? According to Hume, the desires for the misery of those hated "arise only upon the ideas of the … misery of our enemy being presented by the imagination." It is not "absolutely essential" that hate involves wishing misery on someone (T 2.2.6.5/367). Further, passions of love and hate "may subsist for a considerable time without our reflecting on the happiness or misery of their objects" (T 2.2.6.5/368). Passions of hate and wishing misery are thus not inextricably linked, and the operations of the imagination may allow desire for misery to be somehow in abeyance on account of one's commitment to justice. But how? Hume elaborates a principle of the conversion of the passions. According to this principle, "The predominant passion swallows up the inferior and converts it into itself" (T 2.3.4.2/420).

One example concerns the conversion of hatreds to love:

> When a person is once heartily in love, the little faults and caprice of his mistress, the jealousies and quarrels … however unpleasant and related to anger and hatred; are yet found to give additional force to the prevailing passion. (T 2.3.4.3/420)

This psychology can be applied to the case of justice. As a result of my natural compassion, which has been reinforced and appropriately directed through the "artifices" of education, I have internalized the idea of committing injustice as thoroughly base. A person's nastiness is still related to my hatred of him, but yet "gives additional force" to the "prevailing passion" of compassion, reinforced through training. The thought of using one's hate as a motive to commit base acts can be even more "disgustful" than committing such acts on persons to whom one is indifferent. As Hume implies, the hatred does not necessarily disappear, any more than the irritations at the "little faults" of one's lover, but they are changed in their very nature by the "opposed" passions which suffuse the enmity and the anger respectively.

A similar view is expressed in "Of Tragedy":

> The impulse or vehemence, arising from sorrow, compassion, indignation, receives a new direction from the sentiments of beauty. The latter, being the predominant emotion, seize the whole mind, and convert the former into themselves, at least tincture them so strongly as totally to alter their nature. (Miller 220)[23]

Compassion then can either overwhelm the enmity or indifference, or if not, at least change its nature, "totally." Both the connection between pity, benevolence, and love, and the conversion principle appear to be working together in Hume's example of the sickly child in "Of Tragedy":

> Parents commonly love that child most, whose sickly infirm frame of body has occasioned them the greatest pains, trouble, and anxiety in rearing him. The agreeable sentiment of affection here acquires force from sentiments of uneasiness. (Miller 221)

We turn now to problem (2). This problem concerns the scope of the passion of compassion. How can compassion not be so extensive as to be debilitating? Given that pity is "a concern for … others … without any friendship … to occasion this concern" (T 369), and that this sympathy is based on resemblance rather than the particularized properties of services rendered and so forth, the extensiveness of compassion seems limitless. Again Hume's psychology of the process of empathy shows how we are not debilitated by this feature of compassion.

First, the more remote is the object of sympathy the weaker the sympathy: "Sympathy, we shall allow, is much fainter than our concern for ourselves, and sympathy with persons remote from us much fainter than with persons near and contiguous" (E para. 186, 229). Second, the degree of empathy generated by sympathy toward persons (whether "near and contiguous" or remote) depends on the nature and degree of the ground of compassion. "A certain degree of poverty produces contempt; but a degree beyond causes compassion and good will" (T 2.2.9.16/387). If sufficiently forceful, transmission of sympathy from the sight of pain will generate such overload that benevolence cannot operate, as in the case of being "overcome with horror" on witnessing "the cruel execution of the rack" (T 2.2.10.18/388). Compassion is both possible and able to be tempered.

Finally and most importantly, Hume rejects a conception of appropriate compassion that presupposes an overly demanding conception of virtue. What is expected of us is governed by what is "natural," "usual," and "common" in human nature (see T 3.2.2.18/483–484; T 3.2.2.8/488). This feature has two aspects. First Hume has a threshold conception of virtue. What is expected of us is governed by what is allowable from that perspective: "We make allowance for a certain degree of selfishness in men; because we know it to be inseparable from human nature, and inherent in our frame and constitution" (T 3.3.1.17/583). Second, selflessness as a virtue is not to be identified with certain impartial conceptions of ethics in general, at odds with common and usual human nature. Selflessness is a vice if it does not make room for or sufficient room for, self-love and love of near and dear. A much more forceful attack on the morality of self-sacrifice is to be found in Nietzsche (see Chapter 6).

We should also remember that, as a natural motive for the virtue of justice (as opposed to compassion as a virtue), compassion is not characteristically a proximate motive for just acts. In relation to justice, overload is not a problem: rather the problem for justice is how we can be just when it is against our self-interest, how can we sympathize with the unattractive and our enemies to the extent that we are motivated to be just toward them, and how is justice leavened in sentencing, interpreting law, acts of mercy. Seeing compassion as a natural motive of justice in sense (cii) helps answer those questions.

Notes

1 An important point made by Ayn Rand (in "Philosophy and Sense of Life"), cited in Allan Gotthelf, *On Ayn Rand* (Belmont, CA: Wadsworth, 2000), 36.
2 Rachel Cohon, *Hume's Morality: Feeling and Fabrication* (Oxford: Oxford University Press, 2008), 211.
3 "Artificial Virtues and the Sensible Knave," in *Hume: Moral and Political Philosophy*, ed. Rachel Cohon (Aldershot: Ashgate Dartmouth), 313–339, 319.
4 "Hume and the Prince of Thieves," *Hume Studies* 34 (2008), 3–19, 4. Cyrus, E App. III, para. 256, 304.
5 See "The Schizophrenia of Modern Ethical Theories," *Journal of Philosophy* 73 (1976), 453–466. Stocker has done much to elaborate on the importance of this Humean point about the link between what Stocker calls "value" and motive. See also his "How Emotions Reveal Value and Help Cure the Schizophrenia of Modern Ethical Theories," in *How Should One Live? Essays on the Virtues*, ed. Roger Crisp (Oxford: Clarendon Press, 1996), 173–190.
6 Barry Stroud, *Hume* (London: Routledge and Kegan Paul, 1977), 210.
7 Marcia Baron, "Hume's Noble Lie: An Account of His Artificial Virtues," *Canadian Journal of Philosophy* 12 (1982), 539–555, 549.
8 Ibid., 541.
9 Ibid., 541.
10 Annette C. Baier, "*Enquiry Concerning the Principles of Morals*: Incomparably the Best?," in *A Companion to Hume*, ed. Elizabeth Radcliffe (Oxford: Blackwell, 2008), 293–320, 306.
11 See further on the problems faced by Hume, Rachel Cohon, "Hume's Difficulty with the Virtue of Honesty," *Hume Studies* 23 (1997), 91–112.
12 See "The Schizophrenia of Modern Ethical Theories." See also his "Values and Purposes: The Limits of Teleology and the Ends of Friendship," *Journal of Philosophy* 78 (1981), 747–765, and "How Emotions Reveal Value and Help Cure the Schizophrenia of Modern Ethical Theories."
13 David Gauthier, "Artificial Virtues and the Sensible Knave," in *Hume: Moral and Political Philosophy*, ed. Rachel Cohon (Aldershot: Ashgate Dartmouth, 2001), 313–339, 334.
14 Ibid., 334.
15 Ibid., 332.
16 "Obligation, Justice and the Will in Hume's Moral Philosophy," *Hume Studies* 31(1) (2005), 93–122, 115.
17 The nearest thing in the literature to this view of which I am aware is Livia Guimaraes, "Hume and Feminism," in *The Continuum Companion to Hume*, ed. Alan Bailey and Dan O'Brien (London: Continuum, 2012), 319–331. Here she claims that Hume is often keener on resemblance (the basis of compassion) than on difference (327), and if "human nature were only tenderness and concern for others" there would be no need for the distinction between "mine and thine" (330). I do not share this utopian vision below, but simply argue that Hume has the resources to solicit the tender passions as a core component of justice as a virtue in its most humane form.
18 I thank Annette Baier for this example and for causing me to be clearer on this point.
19 The relation between justice and grace is not an issue I can pursue here.
20 A more extensive discussion, with comparisons to Nietzsche, is to be found in my "Compassion as a Virtue in Hume," in *Feminist Interpretations of Hume*, ed. Anne Jaap Jacobson (University Park: Pennsylvania State University Press, 2000), 156–173.
21 *Just Babies: The Origins of Good and Evil* (New York: Crown Publishers, 2013), 49.
22 Ibid., 48.
23 I thank Julian Young for discussion of Hume's views in "Of Tragedy."

Chapter 5

What Kind of Virtue Ethicist Is Hume?

5.1 Hume's Pluralism

This chapter argues that Hume's views on the nature and sources of virtue are pluralistic. He has a pluralistic account of the sources of the moral sentiment, the taxonomy of virtue, and most importantly, the criteria of virtue. I argue that his views are neither utilitarian in particular nor consequentialist in general, but comprise overlooked but significant non-consequentialist features, gleaned particularly from Book II of the *Treatise* (Of the Passions), and which are characteristic of virtue ethics in general. Recall the general specification of the non-consequentialist criterion of virtue given in section 3.4:

> (C2)   A trait is a virtue if it has properties, not reducible to consequences for happiness, which make it appropriate or "fitting" that what Hume calls its "species" or "appearance" causes "this immediate taste or sentiment" giving rise to approbation.

In this chapter I discuss a range of sub-types of (C2): criteria which specify the varied types of basic grounds of the fittingness of "this immediate taste or sentiment," when contemplating traits within what I have called virtue clusters. These are virtues which have at their core one or other of the passions, for example, love, pride, joy, hope. These criteria are offered at a high level of generality, for the precise features which make it fitting that a trait cause the immediately pleasurable sentiment of approving love are hugely complex, and cannot be captured in a criterion.

To understand Hume's pluralism we need first to appreciate that just as the distinction between virtue and vice in general is response dependent – dependent

The Virtue Ethics of Hume and Nietzsche, First Edition. Christine Swanton.
© 2015 John Wiley & Sons, Ltd. Published 2015 by John Wiley & Sons, Ltd.

on the moral sense in general – the individual virtues are in their own very distinctive ways response dependent. Hume claims, for example:

> If I have no vanity, I take no delight in praise: if I be void of ambition, power gives me no enjoyment: if I be not angry, the punishment of an adversary is totally indifferent to me. In all these cases there is a passion which points immediately to the object, and constitutes it our good or happiness. (E App. II, para. 253, 301).

The moral sense itself can be viewed as "a faint and more imperceptible" love of virtue, but unless we as humans have a more fine-grained emotional make-up, for example, passions of love, pride, and hope, the virtues of love, pride, and hope will not be intelligible, and will not exist as response dependent properties. We would not have a grasp of the individual virtues to approve. Certainly insofar as we are benevolent creatures (a condition of the moral sense in general) we will not prefer the destruction of all peoples to the scratching of our finger, or be the fancied monsters of the *Enquiries*, but the basic moral sense as such is insufficient for the existence of many specific virtues. To be true competent moral agents in our kind of world we need a great many passions such as those analyzed in Book 2 of the *Treatise*, passions that are not disordered or distorted. For example, the various different virtues of love cannot be understood as *virtues* and in particular virtues of *love* unless the following is true:

(a)   We are capable of a response (passion) L of love, a passion which for Hume is distinct from the passion of benevolence (desire for another's good), such that objects can be emotionally construed as lovable.
(b)   We can conceive of objects of love as *naturally fitted* for love, naturally fitted for being loved in certain ways and so on: that is, as lovable in a way that is fitting in a normative sense, as opposed to unfitting.

That is, we must be capable of loving and construing objects as lovable in the sense of being objects of love, and also of understanding objects as fitting objects of love, in fitting ways and so on.[1] Fitted for love then is a response dependent property dependent on L. Virtues of love are dispositions of excellence in relation to manner of loving what is loved, and so on. They tell us what is naturally fitting in this domain.

As another example consider virtues of hope. Again, these virtues cannot be intelligible as virtues and in particular virtues of hope unless the following is true:

(a)   We are capable of a response (passion) H of hope, a passion understood by Hume as directed at good which is uncertain, and thereby at hoped-for objects.
(b)   We can conceive of objects of hope as *naturally fitted* for hope, that is, as *to be hoped for*; to be hoped for in a certain way at certain times, and so on.

To be hoped for is a response dependent property dependent on H. Virtues of hope are dispositions of excellence in relation to manner of hoping what is to be hoped for, and so on. They tell us what is naturally fitting in this domain.

For beings who constitutionally do not love, whose good is not at all dependent on attachment and bonding, virtues of love would not exist, although they would be capable of a passion of benevolence were they to inhabit a world of morality at all. The psychology of attachment (see Chapter 9) would not apply to them. Again, for beings who at a fundamental psychological level did not need what Erik Erikson calls the basic strengths of hope and trust in the future,[2] and in other beings, virtues of hope would not exist.

To understand Hume's pluralism about the grounds of virtue we need to revisit Hume's account of the sources of the moral sentiment, which underpin his account of the nature of virtue. In Chapter 2 we saw that Hume claims that there are two sources or causes of our "judgments of morals" (specifically judgments of virtue and vice). These are reflections on the "tendency of traits to the happiness of mankind and of particular persons," and "species and appearance of characters and passions." Both reflections on tendencies and immediate impact of species and appearance may produce approbation. Recall that this view suggests two broad *criteria* of virtue which admit as virtues those traits which conform to the taxonomy (A) above (section 3.4) of traits useful or agreeable to oneself or others. These were the consequentialist criterion (C1) and the non-consequentialist criterion (C2).

Commentators often fail to take seriously (C2) as a second broad criterion of virtue in Hume despite clear non-consequentialist sentiments in Hume such as the following:

> 'Tis certain that we are infinitely touch'd with a tender sentiment, as well as with a great one. The tears naturally start in our eyes at the conception of it; nor can we forbear giving a loose to the same tenderness towards the person who exerts it. All this seems to me a proof, that our approbation has, in those cases, an origin different from the prospect of utility and advantage, either to ourselves or others. (T 3.3.3.4 / 604)

There are two main kinds of reason for this failure. First, they may have trouble seeing how criteria of virtue and vice derived from "immediate agreeability or disagreeability" can have any justificatory force. Rachel Cohon uses the example of the immediate disagreeability of homosexuality[3] in people of Hume's day, claiming that "we must grant that for Hume, as long as most people find homosexuality immediately disagreeable, and this is transmitted to the observer via sympathy, such sexual behavior is indeed a vice."[4] For the "common point of view" is assumed to have been attained;[5] and consequently Hume would have "to include homosexuality on his list of vices simply because his contemporaries found it immediately disagreeable."[6] Now as Rosalind Hursthouse points out,[7] homosexuality is a practice and not a disposition of character, so if we were to "include homosexuality on

[Hume's] list of vices" we would have to be speaking of a disposition to homosexual behavior and attitudes (at least if manifest).

However as I argued in Chapter 3, attaining the common point of view is not the sole feature of a qualified judge. The cooperation of reason must also take place in her determinations, and this certainly involves the absence of the doxastic vices so well described by Hume in Book I of the *Treatise*. Let us consider then the powerful resources Hume has at his disposal for a critique of the view of homosexuality Cohon describes. The moral sentiment of immediate distaste or disgust can be caused by ideas of the imagination. Consider a person whose disgust is founded on lively imaginative ideas of "unmentionable practices." As Hume remarks:

> When the imagination, from any extraordinary ferment of the blood or spirits, acquires such a vivacity as disorders all its powers and faculties, there is no means of distinguishing betwixt truth and falsehood … Every chimera of the brain is as vivid and intense as any of those inferences, which we formerly dignify'd with the name of conclusions concerning matters of fact. (T 1.3.10.9/123)

Such disorders of the imagination may not only result in a failure to distinguish truth and falsity but can arise from doxastic vice. Chief amongst these as Hume asserts at T 146–148 is prejudice.[8] This results from rash adherence to inaccurate general rules, inaccurate due to our tendency to make mistakes concerning relations of resemblance, "the most fertile source of error" (T 1.2.5.21/61). Other potent doxastic vices operating here are "credulity" (e.g., as a result of well-entrenched religious superstition), "carelessness" (e.g., in assessing scientific and other evidence), and "obstinate incredulity" as a result of a tendency to continue with beliefs reinforced by our passions. As we have seen, for Hume beliefs, passions, and ideas of the imagination are mutually reinforcing: "a person of a sorrowful or melancholy disposition is very credulous of every thing, that nourishes his prevailing passion" (T 1.3.10.4/120). Thus a person or group's immediate distaste of homosexuality could be criticized on the grounds of disorder in the ideas of the imagination resulting from a variety of doxastic vices which also lead to or reinforce false beliefs. Those beliefs in turn influence in a distorting way the passions, and thereby the moral sentiment. Hence Cohon's claim does not undermine (C2) as a criterion of virtue: even if people find homosexuality immediately disagreeable it does not follow on Hume's view that homosexual dispositions are fitting objects of disapprobation.

A second reason for the failure to take (C2) seriously as an independent criterion of virtue in Hume is the notion that the suggested plurality in the criteria of virtue is apparent rather than real. Roger Crisp for example believes that Hume should be read as a species of virtue or motive consequentialist, namely a utilitarian version.[9] According to virtue consequentialism, what makes a trait a virtue is its tendency to promote good consequences overall. Certainly for Crisp, Hume is not a consequentialist about the right, for "Hume's focus in ethics is not primarily upon actions at all" and at "the level of rightness of actions ... Hume is best understood as ... a virtue-centered, common-sense moralist who will praise and blame actions in accordance with his best understanding of a common-sense morality upon which there is general agreement."[10]

Why does Crisp interpret Hume as a virtue utilitarian? According to him, the pleasures derived from the impact of appearance are consequences of traits, just as are (longer term) utilities. As a result, (C2) should not be read as an independent criterion of virtue. The failure to take (C2) seriously as a criterion of virtue, closing off the possibility of readings which are not forms of virtue utilitarianism (or virtue consequentialism more generally),[11] may be the result of confusing the criteria of virtue with the pleasures of the moral sentiments. The pleasures of the moral sense (the love and pride felt on contemplation of a suitable object) and the moral sentiment of approbation itself (which is a form of pleasure – "faint" and "more imperceptible" love) should not be confused with the criteria of virtue; with what makes a trait a virtue in a substantive sense. In this sense what makes traits virtues are determined by natural fittingness: it is fitting that persons' needs are appropriately met since they have a good; it is fitting that certain things are hoped for since certain things are proper objects of hope in being *goods* that are uncertain. The pleasures produced by contemplation of traits are indeed pleasurable consequences, but the properties in virtue of which a trait is a virtue are different. These properties are those which make a trait a virtue in a normative sense as I argued in Chapter 3.

The failure to make this distinction in Hume may also be due to calling sentiments of approbation "evaluations," as does Pall Ardal.[12] According to him, moral "evaluations" are direct (calm) passions. Certainly for Hume, sentiments of approbation are passions. But an approbation is not necessarily an evaluation. I may have a sentiment of approbation of a trait on account of its impact as immediately agreeable, but this is not *ipso facto* an evaluation. The moral sense has been awakened but maybe I am not a qualified judge or am uncertain, and further thought, "strainings" of the imagination, consultation with others, and so on may be requisite for a critical perspective. Here there will be evaluation of features of the character trait to support or otherwise my sentiment of approbation.

The remainder of this chapter is devoted to investigating the status of (C2) as an independent criterion of virtue. In Book II of the *Treatise*, Hume describes in detail a broad array of passions which are associated with "virtue clusters." For example, tenderness and intimacy cluster round the passion of love; others have at their core the passions of pride, esteem, respect, joy, hope. Once these virtue clusters are explored, we will be able to see just what it is that makes these virtues immediately agreeable, and why they are naturally fitted to produce such sentiments. The analysis of the virtues clustering round distinct passions shows that for Hume, virtue is not structured by just one type of ground of virtue such as value, or what is good for a person. Virtues also speak to status properties, and the relational property of a bond. It will also be evident that virtue is not structured by just one mode of moral response either: modes other than promotion (of value) such as respect, love, appreciation, and creativity are also basic to many virtues. For example, one respects the status of a person in virtuous deference or obedience; one respects property rules by conforming to them in the virtue of justice; one appreciates valuable qualities (such as beauty and "dazzling splendour") in natural or created items in virtues of connoisseurship, or joyfulness; one expresses love appropriate to types of bond in virtues of tenderness, friendship, grief virtuously felt and expressed, and so on. Of course one also promotes the good of others in manifesting the virtue of benevolence, a trait which is a virtue by dint of satisfying criterion (C1) of virtue.[13]

It is the task of the following four sections to explore this complexity, showing how criterion (C2) of virtue, which is specified at a high level of abstraction, resolves into several more substantive criteria. These sections discuss three broad categories of "species" or "appearance" which make a trait "naturally fitted" to be regarded as a virtue. The features are:

(1)   Being expressive of our bonds with others, self, or things connected with self.
(2)   Appreciation of valuable properties and items.
(3)   Respect (of various kinds) for people in line with their status properties.

5.2   Bond-based Virtues of Love

In this section, I show how a feature of our constitution recognized by Hume, such as the fact that we are creatures who bond, explains the "natural fittingness" of certain traits to be approved as virtues. Bonds of course are of varying strength and types, ranging from those occasioned by gratitude for services rendered, to the strongest ties of blood relation. What might be called bond-based virtues are members of the virtue clusters associated with the passions of love and pride. What is notable about such a virtue, often remarked on by Hume, is that its excellence as a trait of character tracks strength and nature of bonds rather than degree or strength of the value or merits of the items in the field of the virtue.

Consider now the bond-based virtues clustering around love. We first need to understand the passion of love for Hume, and in particular how it differs from the passion of benevolence. Only if this is understood can we appreciate the virtues of love as distinct from the virtue of benevolence, which has relatively more to do with promotion of good as opposed to the expression of bonds in for example affection or intimacy.

Love for persons or "thinking beings" is a passion which for Hume does not admit of definition, but which is nonetheless "sufficiently known from our common feeling and experience" (T 2.2.1.1/329). For Hume love of persons is a very broad-ranging passion, which may range from admiration of persons caused by pleasure in their valuable qualities, to a "violent passion" where for example love is mixed with the "appetite for generation" (T 2.2.11.3/395). Aggregates of objects or peoples cannot be an object of love for Hume: as he claims at T 481, "there is no such passion in human minds as the love of mankind, merely as such, independent of personal qualities, of services, or of relation to oneself." The object of love is not as such the cause of love. The causes of love are agreeable properties such as virtue associated with the object loved. In both the *Treatise* and the *Enquiries* Hume mentions several broad categories of causes: personal qualities of the beloved, services rendered by the beloved to the lover, and other types of relation between the lover and the beloved (such as blood relation and resemblance). Each of these categories, as we shall see, is associated with distinct clusters of virtue.

Before investigating these categories and the virtues associated with them, we need to briefly describe how love works as a passion for Hume. What is the relation between cause and object of love? It is described by Hume as a double relation of cause and effect involving ideas and impressions (see T 2.2.9.12/385). To explain this relation, consider the following example: a mother's love for her baby on its birth. First love requires an agreeable property associated with the object of love. A pleasing quality of the baby, her "baby-humanity," is associated with the idea of the baby herself as instantiating the quality, causing an impression of pleasure. Witnessing the property so instantiated is pleasurable, for the property is a property of resemblance. (If the product of birth looked more like a piece of tissue than anything recognizably human it could not be loved on Hume's picture: it is assumed here there is no associated agreeable property.) The pleasure thus generated is what Hume terms an "impression." The *effect* of the impression of pleasure thus associated with the idea of the baby is an impression (in particular a passion) of love for the baby herself. This is also a pleasurable impression, but one produced by the imagination and one which is different from the pleasure gained from the pleasing qualities of the baby. Hence the object of love is the baby itself, and *not* the resembling property of humanity.

Furthermore, as the object loved is related to the mother by the strongest ties of blood relation, the love is particularly strong. Notice that in this example there are no merits to excite the love; just resemblance properties and blood relation. This is not to imply that through the biases of the imagination, the newborn could not also be thought of by the mother as beautiful (rather fancifully perhaps), further strengthening the love.

Hume describes the double relation of cause and effect involved in love thus. The ideas of the pleasing properties "may become lively and agreeable" and "the fancy will not confine itself to them, but will carry its view to the related objects; and in particular to the person who possesses them" (T 2.2.5.5/359). This "carrying of view" in turn "produces a passion towards the person" (love) on account of his being a "related object" of the pleasurable ideas of the agreeable properties associated with that object.

Hume's notion of love allows for an important distinction between love and benevolence. Benevolence is a "direct" passion, being simply the desire for the good of another. Love by contrast is an "indirect" passion, since it does not "arise immediately from good or evil, from pain or pleasure"[14] but depends for its existence on the "conjunction of other qualities" (T 2.1.2.4/276). As we have seen, for Hume love arises from the association of agreeable properties and the object of love. What then is the relation between love and benevolence? Jane L. McIntyre elaborates on the connection thus:

> Benevolent desires, which are themselves direct passions, arise in the complex causal context created by the indirect passion of love. We take pleasure, for example, in another person's witty or intelligent conversation, and, through the double association of impressions and ideas, that pleasure gives rise to a pleasurable feeling of love for that person. It is this indirect passion of love, according to Hume, that causes the desire of that person's good.[15]

Even though the desire for another's good is not essential to love, Hume does claim that we can never love any person without desiring his happiness: indeed the *connection* between love and benevolence is part of the "original constitution of our mind" (T 2.2.6.6/367). However, other emotions such as the indirect passion of envy can be mixed with love, contaminating it, as we saw in Chapter 4.

Consider now the first category of cause of love, personal qualities of the beloved, and the virtue cluster associated with that category. Properties belonging to this category may be diverse:

> If we consider the causes of love and hatred, we shall find they are very much diversify'd, and have not many things in common. The virtue, knowledge, wit, good sense, good humour of any person, produce love and esteem; as the opposite qualities, hatred and contempt. The same passions arise from bodily accomplishments, such as beauty, force, swiftness, dexterity; and from their contraries; as likewise from the external advantages and disadvantages of family, possessions, cloaths, nation and climate. (T 2.2.1.4/330)

Given that a main cause of love is the beloved's personal qualities, which also make that love intelligible, we may think that Hume is vulnerable to the Platonic problem of love, namely if we love someone by virtue of a valuable quality such as beauty we are rationally required to love anyone else with as much or more beauty, *ceteris paribus*. Similarly, if we love someone for his virtue, we should cease to love him when he becomes vicious. Hume's theory is in an excellent position to avoid these problems. Hume is not vulnerable to the first of these difficulties because for him love is not a direct passion: love is not to be understood as *simply* arising from "good or evil, pleasure or pain." It cannot arise simply from the contemplation of virtue or beauty, for example. Rather love is a passion of relation: beauty is a cause of love in virtue of it being an aspect of a *person* which is the object of love. Moreover, since it is not the property beauty which is the object of love but the person, and each person has a complexity of agreeable and disagreeable features in various kinds of combination in various kinds of circumstance, there need be no tendency for the imagination to extend its love to all persons exhibiting the agreeable feature beauty shared by the beloved, by virtue of their possessing that quality.

What about the second problem: if we love someone "for" his handsomeness how can the love not cease when he loses his looks? Hume gives a clue about how to resolve this problem in the following passage:

> ... when we either love or hate any person, the passions seldom continue within their first bounds; but extend themselves towards all the contiguous objects, and comprehend the friends and relations of him we love or hate. (T 2.2.2.18/341)

Using the same principle of passions extending themselves beyond their "first bounds" we can see how, once a passion has fixed itself upon a man, for example, it will extend itself beyond the agreeable features for which we first loved him. As a result (through contiguity in time) we can continue to love a person when the original agreeable properties causing the love have faded.[16]

What counts as reasonable or virtuous love is determined by standards of reasonableness appropriate to the imagination, and to bonds created by the imagination's "carrying over" of the pleasures associated with properties of an individual to love for the individual herself.

We can now specify virtues in the love cluster of the first category of cause of love, personal qualities of the beloved. My basic claim is this. For Hume, certain traits are immediately agreeable (at least to true judges) by the impact of "species" or "appearance," and at least in the case of virtues in the love cluster, it is naturally fitting that this should be so. As a result, we can see how (C2), as an abstract specification of the second criterion of virtue, can be resolved into a more substantive criterion which rationalizes as virtues those in the love cluster including those involving personal qualities of the beloved:

(C2a)   Traits such as dispositions of (virtuous) admiration or appreciation merit our approbation because they are modes of expression of bonds of love fitting or appropriate to the merits and valuable qualities of persons.

Of course (as is the case with all the criteria conforming to (C2) to be discussed) the complexity of considerations which make, for example, admiration of merits fitting cannot be contained in a criterion. There are numerous dimensions in this complexity: for example, in relation to (C2a), what traits are admirable or meritorious, how admiration is fittingly expressed, which objects are admirable in the relevant respects, and so on.

Virtues in the love cluster represented by (C2a) include affections of relationship triggered by merits, such as merit-based friendship; or alternatively include what can be broadly called virtues of appreciation or admiration. Vices associated with such love include grudging admiration or absence of admiration through envy, and tendencies to admire wrong objects for the wrong reasons and in the wrong way, as in the cult of celebrity, excessive hero worship, infatuation, and so on. Here Hume would say that the imagination "acquires such a vivacity as disorders all its powers and faculties" and "degenerates into madness and folly" (T 123). Another potent vice in this general category is prejudice, where the biases of the imagination downplay or fail to recognize valuable or meritorious properties in individuals belonging to disliked groups. In this kind of case appreciation is distorted or absent as a result of prejudice. Hence one might think, because of rashly formulated "general rules" arising from prejudice, that "an *Irishman* cannot have wit" or a Frenchman solidity, even where the former's conversation is "very agreeable" and the latter's "very judicious" (T 1.3.13.7/146).[17]

Consider now the second category of cause of love, relationship, and the virtues associated with that cause. Many virtues track bonds of relationship rather than merits or value, as Hume makes clear in a number of places, for example:

> Whoever is united to us by any connexion is always sure of a share of our love, proportion'd to the connexion, without enquiring into his other qualities. Thus the relation of blood produces the strongest tie the mind is capable of in the love of parents to their children, and a lesser degree of the same affection as the relation lessens. (T 2.2.4.2/352)

Hume makes a similar point in relation to friendship and acquaintance:

> When we have contracted a habitude and intimacy with any person; tho' in frequenting his company we have not been able to discover any very valuable quality, of which he is possess'd; yet we cannot forbear preferring him to strangers, of whose superior merit we are fully convinc'd. (T 2.2.4.3/352)

The point is made yet again in Hume's discussion of grief in T 3.3.3.6/605. Here Hume is claiming that "excessive" grief for a close friend, though disutile, and a "weakness," is nonetheless "amiable," being expressive of tenderness, and thereby "bestows a merit." That is it can be seen as virtuous for it is expressive of a strong bond. Of course not all excessive grief is virtuous grief: it may be pathological or not expressive of a bond of relationship as opposed to one of the first category properly soliciting admiration or appreciation only. The outpourings of grief on the death of Princess Diana may be classed in this category, but correct judgments in this area are not clear-cut, since theories of grief themselves are subject to controversy.

We can see then that when Hume states that our hearts are seized by "engaging tenderness" he is focusing on the *bonds* of love rather than the mere promotion of good (or value) by acts of tenderness. What affords pleasure is not in this instance the thought that the consequences of such tenderness are likely to be generally beneficial, a thought more appropriate to the approbation of benevolence. Rather, the pleasure is excited by the immediate, emotionally charged, perception of a bond, which can be recognized as itself a basis of a moral response.[18]

Attentiveness has the same kind of rationale for Hume:

> 'Tis remarkable, that nothing touches a man of humanity more than any instance of extraordinary delicacy in love or friendship, where a person is attentive to the smallest concerns of his friend, and is willing to sacrifice to them the most considerable interest of his own. (T 3.3.3.5/604–605).

He goes on to make it clear that the merit in such virtue is not its tendency to the good of mankind:

> Such delicacies have little influence on society: because they make us regard the greatest trifles: But they are the more engaging, the more minute the concern is, and a proof of the highest merit in any one, who is capable of them. (T 605)

We may now specify another category of virtue falling under criterion (C2):

(C2b)   Traits such as dispositions of (virtuous) tenderness merit our approbation because they are fittingly expressive of bonds of love, proper to forms of blood relationship and other partialistic relations of affection.

As Hume claims, the tenderness expressed in grief for a friend bestows "a merit as well as it does a pleasure, on his melancholy" (T 3.3.3.6/605). Virtues in this category include what we may broadly call the virtues of affection, including virtuous romantic love, friendship, filial love/piety, parental virtue, (a disposition of excellence in) intimacy. Vices include excessively cloying kinds of tenderness, phony affections, tendencies to invasive intimacy, cold affectionless parenting.

Consider now the third category of cause of love: services rendered. An obvious candidate for a virtue associated with this cause is gratitude, which Hume confusingly lists as a virtue of benevolence in the *Enquiries* (E 139). Unfortunately, in the *Enquiries*, taxonomies are simplified as a result of Hume dividing virtues into two broad classes of "social virtues," Benevolence and Justice. Under Benevolence he lists a range of virtues including being merciful, friendly, generous, and grateful. The reason for this surprising classification is that here "benevolence" has a broader meaning than that possessed by "benevolence" referring to a virtue whose passional core is the direct passion of benevolence: desire for another's good. As a category of virtue in the *Enquiries* "benevolence" basically refers to a broad disposition of humanity. Love alas has pretty much dropped out of the picture.

However, gratitude is not fundamentally a desire for another's good, but a form of acknowledgement of services rendered, whose passional base for Hume is love or esteem (a species of love). In short for Hume, a cause of love is services rendered to one, and one expression of that love or esteem is gratitude for such services. We have then a third substantive criterion of virtue conforming to (C2):

(C2c)   Traits such as dispositions of being grateful and expressing gratitude merit our approbation because they are expressive of bonds of reciprocity, appropriate to the esteem in which we hold those who have rendered services to us.

We may call such traits virtues of love of the species virtues of reciprocity. These may involve neither admiration (for personal qualities) nor affection. What is distinctive about Hume's view however is that such virtues may be (and at their best are) expressive of a kind of love and not just a sense of justice in some sense.[19]

Finally there are a group of love-based virtues which express our bonds to our fellow humans simply as humans capable of pleasing social contact: these include Aristotle's and Kant's virtues of social intercourse. Hume recognized such virtues too: virtues of cheerfulness, wit, charm, amiability fall within this category. What Aristotle would call pleasure-friendship does not necessarily come within the category of bonds of affection, but is a kind of love which is opposed to the shyness of withdrawal, or misanthropy expressed in moroseness or generalized hostility. Buffoonery and a tendency to "dissolute mirth" are also vices in this area, not necessarily because they are expressive of misanthropy, but because they are expressive of follies and defects undermining the pleasures of social intercourse. Let us remind ourselves of Hume on "excessive" cheerfulness:

> Cheerfulness could scarce admit of blame from its excess, were it not that dissolute mirth, without a proper cause or subject, is a sure symptom and characteristic of folly, and on that account disgustful. (E para. 208, 258 n. 1)

Cheerfulness expressed as dissolute mirth is a form of cheerfulness as a vice because it is *expressive* of folly, and *as such* naturally unfitting to the conversational occasion, and is registered by a qualified judge as a species of immediate disagreeability.

We propose then a fourth category of virtues of love:

(C2d)   Traits such as dispositions to be witty (in a virtuous way) merit our approbation because they are appropriately expressive of bonds of amity suitable for social intercourse.

Like Aristotle Hume distinguishes virtuous wittiness from wit as exemplifying vice: dispositions to "true" "delicate" wit are distinguished from "false" wit (T 2.1.7.7/297).

To conclude: Hume's list of some of the love-based virtues cover all four of the categories explored above, demonstrating the great variety of virtues whose passional core is the passion of love. I have called these types of traits virtues of appreciation or admiration, virtues of affection, virtues of reciprocity, and virtues of amity. It is less clear that there is in Hume himself a category of virtues of universal love (as opposed to universal benevolence) but I canvas this option in a "new direction" for a Humean virtue ethics in Part IV. I have claimed then that for Hume there is a broad group of virtues – the love-based virtues – whose status as virtues is grounded on a feature of the human constitution: our need for bonding. Hume lists some of them: "Love may shew itself in the shape of *tenderness, friendship, intimacy, esteem, goodwill,* and in many other appearances" (T 2.3.10.31/448).

The notion of proper bonding explains why approbation of love-based virtues is sourced in the immediately agreeable rather than in reflections on utility, and why they are naturally fitted to produce such a response in qualified judges.

5.3   Virtues Which Express Pride

We turn now to the indirect passion of pride. What are we to make of our finding immediately agreeable (according to Hume) traits such as "excessive" bravery? At first sight it would appear that excessive bravery, like "excessive" grief, has to be a vice. It is a virtue "in excess," and disutile. I shall argue that investigation of another indirect passion, pride, will explain how for Hume it is fitting that such a virtue is immediately agreeable, just as "excessive grief" for a dearly loved one can also be approved in this way. It is not being suggested that excessive pride as such is a virtue, but that the passion of pride, like that of love, can explain what might be regarded as "excessive" forms of pride-related or love-related virtues.

According to Hume, the "ultimate or final" object of pride is self: "Pride and humility being once rais'd, immediately turn our attention to ourself, and regard that as their ultimate and final object" (T 2.1.2.4/278). Though pride can be taken in all manner of objects, these must somehow reflect on ourselves, as Hume makes clear in this passage:

> We found a vanity upon houses, gardens, equipages, as well as upon personal merit and accomplishments; and tho' these external advantages be in themselves widely distant from thought of a person, yet they considerably influence even a passion, which is directed to that as its ultimate object. This happens when external objects acquire any particular relation to ourselves, and are associated or connected with us. A beautiful fish in the ocean, an animal in the desert, and indeed any thing that neither belongs, nor is related to us, has no manner of influence on our vanity, whatever extraordinary qualities it may be endowed with. (T 2.1.9.1/303)

So the beautiful fish spotted by me on a snorkeling trip to Vanuatu cannot be an object of pride. However, when I, a New Zealander, am affected by the dazzling splendor of the royal processions in Pall Mall, London, I am affected not simply by their "impersonal" value but by their connection with those of us who value (take pride in) our British (or perhaps English) heritage.

It is important to note that the self is not the object of pride *simpliciter* for Hume, but the "ultimate" or "final" object. We should call the items *in* which we take pride the immediate objects of pride (as opposed to the final and ultimate ones) since it would be odd to claim that I am proud of myself (as an immediate object) when I am taking pride in my grandchildren. Indeed such narcissistic pride would be a vice.

Importantly pride, like love, legitimizes for Hume a certain partialism justified by preference for the familiar kinds of objects in which pride is taken:

> The mind finds a satisfaction and ease in the view of objects to which it is accustom'd and naturally prefers them to others, which, tho', perhaps, in themselves more valuable, are less known to it. (T 2.2.4.8/355)

Such partialism can however be a source of pride-related vice, for the "satisfaction and ease" in familiar objects, and preference for them, may be a mark of complacency, prejudice, laziness, fear, and other faults. Nonetheless Hume is drawing our attention here to a feature of human nature ignored at our peril. Like Heidegger, Hume emphasizes that we are creatures who need to belong, who need a heritage, as opposed to merely needing to appreciate the value of things (from a disinterested perspective) independent of their relation to our own particular dwelling (as Heidegger would put it).[20]

This fact accounts too, I think, for (some forms of) excessive courage being immediately agreeable, and indeed a merit: we take pride in it insofar as its manifestation in others benefits the defense of our country, our homes, our children. One's nation or country is a source of pride for Hume (T 2.2.2.8/335) and war-time reinforces the sense of unity and associated partialistic perspective (T 2.2.3.2/348). Indeed for Hume some forms of "excessive" courage or resoluteness in the prosecution of war ("treachery we call policy") can be deemed admirable from a sense of national pride.[21]

A fifth substantive criterion of virtue conforming to the abstract criterion (C2) can now be provided:

(C2e)   Traits such as (virtuous) loyalty merit our approbation because they are expressive of appropriate pride in objects which are fitting for such pride.

That is, there is a virtue cluster with proper pride at its core. Thus Hume claims: "a genuine and hearty pride, or self-esteem, if well conceal'd and well founded, is essential to the character of a man with honour" (T 3.3.2.11/598).

And there are related vices, for example the vice of "abjectness" of character:

> An abjectness of character … is disgustful and contemptible in another view. Where a man has no sense of value in himself, we are not likely to have any higher esteem of him. And if the same person, who crouches to his superiors, is insolent to his inferiors (as

often happens), this contrariety of behaviour, instead of correcting the former vice, aggravates it extremely by the addition of a vice still more odious. (E para. 204, 254 n. 4)

There are also vices of excess as well as deficiency: we have already mentioned the vice of the self being the immediate object of pride where it should only be the "ultimate" object. Hume mentions too the vice of "overweening conceit." Discussion of the limits of pride would yield a rich account of virtue: for example Annette Baier draws our attention to the fact that modesty is a virtue for Hume, on account of the fact that "modesty is simply a recognition of the limits of one's grounds for pride."[22] Modesty can then be seen as a pride-based virtue, but one that recognizes its proper limits.

Pride as an indirect passion must be distinguished from self-love, a desire for one's own good: a direct passion. It is plausible to think that for Hume these are connected, as are benevolence and love, as part of the "internal frame of our constitution." Furthermore the vices of each are very closely linked. Abjectness of character can be thought of as a vice of insufficient pride, but it may be sourced in a lack of self-love. Analogously it is hard to imagine that one can have love for another if one has no benevolence. Overweening conceit too, may be rooted in lack of self-love: one has to compensate for one's sense of inadequacy by being boastful.

Why, finally, are the virtues of pride to be categorized under (C2), the immediately agreeable? Though pride itself is an indirect passion, that passion is made possible by self-love, and at a deep level we may think of it as expressive of that quality. Just as we can be disgusted by an "abjectness of character" we take delight in traits which are signs of and appropriately express what Hume calls a "genuine and hearty pride, or self-esteem." In this respect Hume has an affinity with Nietzsche who is similarly "nauseated" by persons who have a lack of a robust sense of self.

5.4 Virtues Which Express Appreciation of Value

In Book II of the *Treatise* Hume distinguishes between the direct passion of joy aroused by a good that is certain or probable (T 2.3.9.5/439) and the indirect passion of pride, using the following example:

> We may feel joy upon being present at a feast, where our senses are regal'd with delicacies of every kind: But 'tis only the master of the feast, who, beside the same joy, has the additional passion of self-applause and vanity. (T 2.1.6.2/290)

He then goes on to claim that "many things which are too foreign to produce pride, are yet able to give delight and pleasure" (T 290–291). The appreciation of valuable qualities which are not related to us, and are not therefore pride-based, is an appreciation expressed in joy. By this means one can account for virtues related to the appreciation of the beautiful fish in the ocean when the fish is not connected with me directly or indirectly.

Attention to this passion enables us to account for the appreciative environmental virtues, the virtues of connoisseurship, delight in or passion for wisdom. The "over-flowings of an elevate or humane disposition" (T 2.2.2.8 / 335) when taking pleasure in wonderful or pleasing objects, distinguished in this passage from pride, is an expression of joy, a direct passion. We have then another ground of virtue:

> (C2f)   Traits such as (virtuously) joyful dispositions, such as joyfulness not manifesting what Hume calls a "delicacy of passion" (i.e., an exaggeration of passion discussed in his essay "Of the Delicacy of Taste and Passion"), merit our approbation insofar as they are dispositions to (appropriately) express joy.

Such virtues are (virtuously expressed and felt) joyfulness, curiosity (disposition to take joy in the process of discovery), wonder (tendency to take joy in mystery or the mysterious), cheerfulness. Corresponding vices are apathy, tendency to boredom, curmudgeonliness, tendencies to exhibit joyfulness expressed in a manner that humiliates, or that exhibits a "disordered frenzy of enthusiasm," the joylessness manifested by the monkish vices, and so on.

The reason virtues of joy are immediately agreeable is evident. They are virtues concerned with the appreciation of valuable qualities and things. It is a fine thing to appreciate ancient kauri trees or magnificent works of art: no "reflections on tendencies" are required to secure approbation of persons who are spontaneously capable of such appreciation. As Hume puts it, it is a mark of an "elevate" disposition to take joy in such things, and we take pleasure in the sight and contemplation of the workings of such a disposition. The response of joy and related passions are features of our constitution which explain how we can take delight in valuable things independent of their relationship to us and consequences for utility.

Attention to (C2f) puts into proper perspective Hume's discussion of the "monkish virtues" (E para. 219, 270). On a charitable and on my view accurate understanding of Hume's placement of the "monkish virtues" into the vice column, the basic reason for this placement lies in the fact that they cluster round a passion (or absence of passion) that is disagreeable and disutile: joylessness. Note that fasting, celibacy, mortification, solitude, and other monkish "virtues" may be seen as practices rather than traits of character,[23] but if the latter they would be for Hume stable dispositions with enduring natural motivation. Hence for example if celibacy and fasting were to be seen as vices, they would be akin to Aristotle's vices of deficiency related to temperance (being well disposed toward the bodily pleasures of food, sex, and drink). On Hume's view such vices of deficiency would be rooted in a passion of joylessness in its various manifestations of "sourness," obscuring of fancy, and so on.

If we make a distinction between a character trait and a practice, then the usual counterexamples to Hume's view of the "monkish virtues" such as those proposed by William Davie will not work.[24] Fasting to lose weight is not necessarily a manifestation of vice but may be a completely blameless activity or practice; being alone to avoid smoking companions in order to help one give up smoking is to be distinguished from a disposition of solitude as a vice – for Hume a disposition sourced in a joylessness in companionship, relationships, or the presence of other people.

So far I have painted a relatively simple picture: joy is a direct passion underlying virtues of appreciating valuable qualities unconnected with us, by contrast with pride and love where appreciation can reflect the nature of bonds. However Hume's discussion in Book II of the *Treatise* in "Of Curiosity, Or the Love of Truth" complicates matters. It may be asked: Why does Hume speak of the love of truth rather than the joy in truth? For truth, like beauty and virtue, "considered in the abstract" are not related to us, and are therefore not proper objects of love. The answer lies in the fact that love of truth is complex, involving both joy, and pride in personal qualities associated with the process of discovery and creative endeavor. This complexity resolves what Hume terms a "contradiction": were philosophers convinced that "their discoveries were of no consequence" they would lose all relish for their studies, and would certainly not destroy their health and neglect their fortune. On the other hand their "conduct and behaviour" suggests that they have little "concern for the interests of mankind" while pursuing their studies (T 2.3.10.4 / 450).

According to Hume, a belief in usefulness and importance is "requisite to fix our attention" and a degree of success is necessary to continue to motivate, but the endeavor excited by "love of truth" and curiosity is by no means proportionate to the "relish" with which philosophers may pursue their studies. In other words, dispassionate interest in truth excites joy, but pride in success and the deployment of one's own capacities enhances that joy. As Hume claims, the "pleasure of study consists chiefly in the action of the mind, and the exercise of the genius and understanding in the discovery or comprehension of any truth" (T 2.3.10.6 / 450–451). In other words joy in truth, and hope for success, is *connected* with factors in which we take pride: the use of our own faculties and success, all of which are given added luster by the difficulty of the project, and the uncertainty of attaining success. Love of truth then for Hume is not reducible to a concern for the interests of mankind.

The connection between love of truth and hope for success brings us to the virtue cluster associated with the direct passion of hope.

(C2g)   Traits such as (appropriate) hopefulness and realistic optimism merit our approbation insofar as they are expressive of hope for what it is fitting to hope for.

Corresponding vices are for example a general despair, unrealistic hope associated with grandiosity, blind hopefulness. The reason virtues of hope are immediately agreeable is that for Hume they express an original (and desirable) instinct in humans: a tendency of the mind to unite itself with the good in idea (T 438), a tendency expressed in the direct passions of joy and hope.

5.5   Virtues Which Express Respect for Status

There remains for us to consider a third broad category of character trait whose status as virtues for Hume, I shall argue, is secured by their satisfying criterion (C2) rather than criterion (C1) of virtue. Items in the fields of these virtues are acknowledged in respect of their status rather than their value or good, or their relationship to us; and in the exercise of these virtues status is respected.

Hume distinguishes two types of respect for status. One concerns the authoritative rules of justice, which for Hume protect persons' entitlements to their property. The virtue of justice is a disposition to respect such rules: as I argued in the last chapter, it is a "deontological" virtue. Unlike other virtues which cluster round natural passions such as love, pride, joy, benevolence, and esteem, justice for Hume is not founded on any natural passion, as we saw above. There is for Hume no "natural motive" of justice. As we have seen, this caused problems for Hume's views on the nature of virtue, but I argued in the previous chapter that Hume could have availed himself of the view that there is a natural passion or motive of justice (in the relevant sense). This is compassion. If I am right, we can extract an eighth substantive criterion conforming to (C2):

> (C2h)   Traits such as justice merit our approbation, because they display respect for persons and their property, and the natural motivational materials for that respect is our capacity for compassion.

The remainder of this chapter discusses the second form of respect for status; a respect that is not founded on justice but rather on esteem. Both kinds of respect (justice-based and esteem-based) involve keeping a distance, but for entirely different kinds of reason.

Esteem, which Hume also calls respect, is a passion opposed to contempt. For Hume esteem and contempt are "species of love and hatred" (T 2.2.5.1/357). How then does esteem differ from other forms of love? According to Hume, esteem or respect is mixed with humility, a passion opposed to pride, as a result of a tacit comparison with ourselves. As Korsgaard notes, (deference-based) respect is a modified, blended, passion: one that "results when the pleasing qualities in a person that cause … love also at the same time cause humility and fear."[25] We esteem or respect the prince, not just by virtue of a love of him caused by his power or riches or palaces, but by an awareness of our inferior position in relation to him. Such esteem for Hume is a special kind of love, manifested by kinds of keeping at a distance marked by deference.

> A sense of superiority in another breeds in all men an inclination to keep themselves at a distance from him, and determines them to redouble the marks of respect and reverence, when they are oblig'd to approach him; and where they do not observe that conduct, 'tis a proof they are not sensible of his superiority. (T 2.2.10.10/393)

By contrast for Hume, some properties produce "pure love" and are not prone to "convert the love into respect." Such properties are "good nature, good humour, facility, generosity, beauty." The reason for this, Hume says, is that these properties have "not so great a tendency to excite pride in ourselves" (T 2.2.10.8/392). I find this claim puzzling, but Hume is right to point out that not all properties producing an awareness of our inferiority excite humility, as opposed to "pure love." The reason for the humility I suggest is that when humility is felt, the respect in which we are aware of inferiority is linked to status properties associated with keeping distance, unlike for example beauty, good nature, good humor, generosity.

It is clear that for Hume properties occasioning esteem need not in any sense be deserved. Esteem is a "species" of love, for Hume, and as we saw above, there is a rich variety of properties causing love. Thus one can be esteemed for all kinds of natural properties that are not merited, such as being born with a title, being a woman, and so on.[26] Of course being esteemed for properties that are not merited must not be confused with being esteemed for properties ill-merited such as being a "sensible knave." Objects of virtuous esteem may possess the former properties without possessing the latter.

Esteem-based respect may or may not involve hierarchy of various types. Where there is legitimate hierarchy, a virtuous esteem-based respect takes the form of appropriate sensitivity to another's superiority. Failure to do so is a mark of "ill-breeding." Consider the following example. When a Prime Minister of Australia violated rules of distance by putting his arm round the Queen's waist, that behavior provoked a reaction of extreme immediate disagreeability on the part of many (especially in the United Kingdom) which had nothing to do with beliefs about the good of mankind. For respect has to do with treatment according to status, as opposed to good.[27]

Where there is no hierarchy, differential behavior expressing esteem-based respect is still appropriate to the esteemed qualities. For example, traditionally, special behaviors marking a person's status as a woman (e.g., opening doors for her) mark an esteemed quality which is a status property, but no sense of superiority or inferiority is implied by such behavior. How then can we say that esteem-based respect implies for Hume inferiority? It is only implied in a weak sense: temporary deferential behavior is exhibited – she is temporarily placed on a pedestal as it were – even though the deference is not meant to mark a structured pervasive inferiority. Of course it is an open and debated question whether such marks of esteem-based respect are nonetheless in some way pernicious, expressing culturally sanctioned but wrong beliefs about superiority or inferiority. Answers to the question what properties should confer status are controversial; class-based status properties prevalent in Hume's day are less acceptable now.

Many cultures mark esteem for the aged, by virtue of their status as aged. Indeed in some cultures some of the aged also possess a hierarchy-based status property, for example, the kuia and kaumatua of Maori culture in New Zealand. It is an interesting question in virtue of what properties they have or should have for that status. Where high status is thought warranted by a presumption of greater wisdom, born of experience, respect will take the form of deference to their opinion. Geoffrey Cupit suggests by contrast that respect for the aged will take the form of veneration or awe[28] – the cause of such esteem being the sense that we "enlarge" with age. What occasions respect is their "size" in the sense of longevity.

We have then a virtue cluster whose core is esteem or respect, a cluster consisting of virtues of proper demeanor according to status. What counts as proper demeanor may have large cultural variability, and it is part of virtue to recognize such culturally determined variability, and to conform to what is proper. This is not to imply cultural relativism: not all hierarchies are just, and not all ways of marking hierarchy and other status features are respectful. Virtues of proper demeanor according to status, including appropriate obedience and deference, are opposed to a range of vices, including servility, blind obedience, sycophancy, authority complex (sourced in anger against those in authority), envy-based resentment (sourced in anger against those who are superior to oneself), arrogance (in respect of others' cultures), insensitivity, and humility as a vice (where one's sense of self-worth is based on comparison with others, and Hume's passion of humility dominates over pride when it should not).

Finally then we may identify a ninth substantive criterion of virtue conforming to (C2):

(C2i)   Traits such as properly deferential respect merit our approbation because they mark proper appreciation of and respect for status properties, and that respect is caused by our capacity for esteem.

To recall: what is special about respect or esteem for Hume as a passion is that it is a love mixed with 'humility," a sense of one's own inferiority (temporary or not) or lack in a certain respect. This need not be seen as failure in any sense: it is not a personal failure that one is not aged or born with a title, nor does Hume suggest that it is.

In this chapter, I have elaborated several kinds of features which show how and when it is naturally fitting that the impact of species and appearance make traits immediately agreeable to a qualified judge. Hume himself does not offer these as separate criteria, but they may be garnered from his study of the passions. Hume's own interest here is a study of the passions themselves, as they manifest in "usual" and "common" human nature, and constitute "what is inseparable from our make and constitution." However, in the interests of a map being both accurate and helpful, it is worthwhile seeing how these features of the passions explain the operation of those traits conforming to criterion (C2), and seeing how they can be justified as virtues.

Notes

1   I thank Michelle Mason for drawing my attention to the ambiguity in the notion of "lovable."

2   According to him, hope, "the enduring belief in the attainability of fervent wishes," is one of the "basic virtues" or "unifying strengths" necessary for human development which arises very early in the order of developmental appearance. Erik Erikson, "Human Strength and the Cycle of Generations," in *The Erik Erikson Reader*, ed. Robert Coles (New York: W.W. Norton & Co., 2000), 188–225, 211.

3   In *Hume's Morality: Feeling and Fabrication* (Oxford: Oxford University Press, 2008). She argues, correctly in my view, that homosexuality on Hume's view can be regarded as a character trait, being a sexual orientation or proclivity (251–252).

4   Ibid., 265.

5   Ibid., 264.

6   Ibid., 251.

7   *On Virtue Ethics* (Oxford: Oxford University Press, 1999), 214–215.

8   Yet Cohon claims that Hume "is left without grounds to criticize a list of virtues and vices that reflects some of the baseless social prejudices of a time and place" (264). On my interpretation the resources of Book I allow Hume to claim that it is possible that very few if any people of a time or place are qualified judges in certain areas. And as I argued above, qualified judges can get things wrong, even if they are not to be blamed (for their views are not the result of intellectual vice, for example).

9   "Hume on Virtue, Utility, and Morality," in *Virtue Ethics, Old and New*, ed. Stephen M. Gardiner (Ithaca, NY: Cornell University Press, 2005), 159–178. See also Rachel Cohon who claims that according to Hume "approval of fasting, penance, and mortification is not warranted because these produce no good at all." This is correct, but it does not follow that for Hume our approval of traits is "warranted … provided the disposition has some systematic causal connection to the social good, though that connection need not be a direct or simple one": "Hume's Difficulty with the Virtue of Honesty," *Hume Studies* 23 (1997), 91–112, 103. By contrast, Annette C. Baier in *A Progress of Sentiments: Reflections on Hume's Treatise* (Cambridge, MA: Harvard University Press, 1991) takes seriously immediate agreeability as an independent standard of virtue.

10   Crisp, 167.

11   Geoffrey Sayre-McCord interprets Hume as a virtue consequentialist, though not a virtue utilitarian: "Hume and the Bauhaus Theory of Ethics," *Midwest Studies in Philosophy* 20 (1996), 280–298. He proposes an interesting interpretation of Hume, which he calls the Bauhaus theory of ethics. According to this view, a trait of character "commands approbation, when it does, in virtue of its being *well suited* for the achieving of certain ends or the solving of certain problems" (282). Particular evaluations of traits, e.g., as virtues "are driven by a concern for specific problems and are determined by what is well suited to solve the problems in question." "What the theory avoids … is any commitment to there being a single overarching standard for evaluating all solutions" (287).

12   Pall S. Ardal, *Passion and Value in Hume's Treatise* (Edinburgh: Edinburgh University Press, 1966).

13   For further discussion of the plurality of virtue in these respects (though not in relation to Hume) see my *Virtue Ethics: A Pluralistic View* (Oxford: Oxford University Press, 2003).

14   Ardal in *Passion and Value in Hume's Treatise* claims that direct passions arise immediately from pleasure and pain, and then states that Hume "hardly consistently" includes among the direct passions some that do not arise from pleasure or pain, such as desire of punishment of our enemies and some bodily appetites, such as hunger (8–9). But there is no inconsistency since Hume actually says that the direct passions arise from good or evil, pleasure or pain. For Hume it is an original feature of our constitution that we are drawn to good (as well as pleasure). Yet Ardal claims that for Hume, "the general appetite to good and aversion to evil" means appetite to pleasure and aversion to pain (10). Yet these are "calm" passions, whereas appetites to, e.g., pleasures can be "violent." Hence is born a hedonistic interpretation of Hume.

15   "Hume's Passions: Direct and Indirect," *Hume Studies* 26(1) (2000), 77–86, 80. A cautionary note however: though love may cause benevolence in a particular case, it should not be thought that love rather than benevolence for Hume is an "original and primary" passion. Rather it is benevolence that occupies

this role in the moral sense. I venture to suggest that the original and primary "instinct" of benevolence on Hume's view makes love possible in us (if we had a primary instinct of malevolence only, love would not be possible).

16 It may be thought that my resolution of the "Plato problem" cannot apply to Hume since he believes in a "Principle of Self–Other Parity" described by James King in "Pride and Hume's Sensible Knave," *Hume Studies* 25 (1999), 123–137 as follows: according to this principle, a quality independently deemed of value necessarily causes love or pride as it is realized interchangeably in other or self (127). I do not believe Hume subscribes to this principle: indeed he seems explicitly to reject it at T 392, when he claims that qualities such as good nature, good humor, and generosity can excite much love when manifested in others but cause no great pride when manifested in ourselves. Whether or not Hume is right about this example the following is true. Since it is Jane and not beauty that is the object of my love, although beauty in Jane may cause my love of Jane, a similar beauty in Miranda may not have any causal efficacy. For the "carrying over of the view" of the "fancy" from valued and esteemed property to persons instantiating that property may be quite variable or indeed capricious (and quite properly so when we are speaking of love and the operations of the imagination, even though other cases of bias in the ideas of the imagination may exhibit vice as Hume notes, e.g., at T 146). Even though King is right to note that beauty for example is both a cause that produces a "separate pleasure" and has "value independently of its possessor" (126, see T 359), the Principle of Self–Other Parity is still not entailed, for the crucial role of the imagination needs to be factored in. It may be thought that unless Hume subscribes to that principle, he cannot explain the vice of the sensible knave, since he needs the principle to explain how the sensible knave should not take pride in his sensible knavery (see further, King). And if he can properly take pride in it, how can the knavery be a vice? However, as I argued in Chapter 4, for Hume not all judges of virtue and vice are qualified, and a qualified judge could not take pride in sensible knavery. The putative pride of the sensible knave is not virtuous pride. Pride is a passion, not necessarily a virtue. Furthermore not all biases of the imagination violating the Principle of Self–Other Parity are harmless and untinged with vice. We do not need the principle to argue this.

17 See however n. 14: this point does not commit me to the view that Hume subscribes to the Principle of Self–Other Parity.

18 See further my *Virtue Ethics*, esp. chapter 2.

19 For a view that reciprocity is an aspect of justice, see David Schmidtz, *Elements of Justice* (Cambridge: Cambridge University Press, 2006).

20 See Martin Heidegger, *Poetry, Language, Thought*, trans. Albert Hofstadter (New York: Harper Collins, 1971).

21 See on the virtue status of such traits as excessive courage or resolute inflexibility the literature on admirable immorality; Michael Slote, *Goods and Virtues* (Oxford: Clarendon Press, 1983), chapter 4. For a discussion of Hume's concerns about the military virtues see Annette Baier, *A Progress of Sentiments*, 210, and see T 600–601.

22 Baier, *A Progress of Sentiments*, 207.

23 For this distinction, with celibacy as an example, see Rosalind Hursthouse, *On Virtue Ethics*, 214–216.

24 "Hume on Monkish Virtues," *Hume Studies* 25 (1999), 139–153.

25 Christine Korsgaard, "The General Point of View: Love and Moral Approval in Hume's Ethics," *Hume Studies* 25 (1999), 3–41, 19.

26 The writings of John Rawls have made such a view unpopular: for a view more like Hume's see David Schmidtz's opposition to Rawls on this matter in *Elements of Justice*, chapter 6.

27 See my *Virtue Ethics*.

28 See Geoffrey Cupit, "Justice, Age, and Veneration," *Ethics* 108 (1998), 702–718.

Part III

The Virtue Ethics of Nietzsche

Chapter 6

Can Nietzsche Be Both a Virtue Ethicist and an Egoist?

6.1 Introduction

Just as perhaps the greatest obstacle to a virtue ethical reading of Hume is his sentimentalism, so the greatest obstacle to reading Nietzsche in a virtue ethical way is his
self-ascription as an egoist and his attacks on altruism. A correct understanding of
Hume's sentimentalism cleared away the alleged difficulties of his sentimentalism; I
hope to show how a correct understanding of Nietzsche's attacks on "morality" and
altruism removes the difficulties of his egoism. Understanding his egoism is one of
the most interesting aspects of his ethics, especially from the perspective of a virtue
ethical interpretation. That interpretation will hinge on understanding Nietzsche's
view as a type of "virtuous egoism" – a form of egoism that is virtuous (and therefore
not egoism at all on some conceptions of egoism). This view is opposed to both
non-virtuous altruism and non-virtuous egoism but not to all forms of altruism.[1]

This reading may seem surprising, since attacks on "altruistic" moralities is a
recurring theme in Nietzsche. Here is a typical example:

> "Not to seek one's own advantage" – that is merely the moral fig leaf for quite a differ-
> ent physiological state of affairs: "I no longer know how to *find* my own advantage."
> Disintegration of the instincts! Man is finished when he becomes altruistic.[2]

However, what Nietzsche is against, I shall argue, is a certain sort of altruism, a
non-virtuous altruism that operates in the spirit of self-sacrifice where the self "wilts
away."[3]

The above passage goes some way to revealing the sense in which Nietzsche is an
egoist. An individual who does not suffer from "disintegration of the instincts" is
one who has a strong sense of self, who knows his own advantage, and who pursues

The Virtue Ethics of Hume and Nietzsche, First Edition. Christine Swanton.
© 2015 John Wiley & Sons, Ltd. Published 2015 by John Wiley & Sons, Ltd.

it in a non-self-sacrificing manner. This is made particularly clear by Nietzsche in the following passage:

> To make of oneself a complete *person*, and in all that one does to have in view the *highest good* of this person – that gets us further than those pity filled agitations and actions for the sake of others. We all of us to be sure, still suffer from the all-too-little regard paid to the personal in us, it has been badly cultivated – let us admit to ourselves that our minds have, rather, been drawn forcibly away from it and offered as a sacrifice to the state, to science, to those in need, as though what would be sacrificed was in any case what was bad. Even now let us work for our fellow men, but only to the extent that we discover our own highest advantage in this work: no more, no less. All that remains is what it is one understands by *one's advantage*; precisely the immature, undeveloped, crude individual will understand it most crudely.[4]

Of central importance is that the "virtuous egoist" is an individual who is mature and not crude, as is indicated by the title of the section quoted above, "Morality of the mature individual." Nietzsche makes it clear that the egoism of the mature individual is not the egoism of instant gratification (whether in the pursuit of pleasure or power) nor is it an unsocialized egoism. A mature individual is one whose actions are "no longer directed to the procurement of momentary wellbeing," but who has become "attuned to utility and purpose." In a second phase of maturation, he becomes socialized, where he develops a sense of honor and "accords others respect and wants them to accord respect to him." Finally, he possesses "an ever more highly evolving conception of usefulness and honourableness" where he acts in accordance with his "*own standard* with regard to men and things" while at the same time he "lives and acts as a collective-individual"[5] in a sense to be explored in section 6.4 below.

The mature individual then is one who can work for his fellows, but not in the spirit of self-sacrifice where one's sense of self and its advantage is submerged by the needs of others. This point is further illustrated in a passage from *Daybreak*:

> Let us for the time being agree that benevolence and beneficence are constituents of the good man; only let us add: "presupposing that he is first benevolently and beneficently inclined *towards himself!*" For without this – if he flees from himself, hates himself, does harm to himself – he is certainly not a good man. For in this case all he is doing is rescuing himself from himself *in others* ... to flee from the ego, and to hate it, and to live in others and for others – that has hitherto, and with as much thoughtlessness as self confidence, been called "*unegoistic*" *and consequently "good*."[6]

An example of such "unegoistic" escape into otherness anticipates in a trenchant manner feminist writings excoriating female self-sacrifice:

> In many people I find an overwhelmingly forceful and pleasurable desire to be a function ... Examples include those women who transform themselves into some

function of a man that happens to be underdeveloped in him, and thus become his purse or his politics or his sociability. Such beings preserve themselves best when they find a fitting place in another organism; if they fail to do this, they become grumpy, irritated, and devour themselves.[7]

An altruism of self-sacrifice, dependent as it is on a morality of sacrifice, is not only psychologically unhealthy but also downright dangerous for Nietzsche:

> Supposing we acted in the sense of self-sacrifice, what would forbid us to sacrifice our neighbour as well? – just as the state and as princes have done hitherto, when they sacrificed one citizen to another "for the sake of the general interest" as they put it.[8]

The passages cited above reveal two central features of a virtue ethical map of Nietzsche's egoism, to be explored in the remaining sections of this chapter.

(1)   Acting "in the sense of self-sacrifice," that is from the spirit of self-sacrifice, is to be deplored because such action is expressive of lack of a robust sense of self, a form of escape into otherness, a fleeing from self, a form of self-contempt.

(2)   Some forms of beneficent actions, "work for our fellow men," do not express or exhibit this deplorable spirit of self-sacrifice, for in those actions we "discover our highest advantage."

The first theme occurs throughout Nietzsche: we have as another example a passage from *The Gay Science*:

> How is it at all possible to keep to one's own way? Constantly, some clamor or other calls us aside; rarely does our eye behold anything that does not require us to drop our own preoccupation instantly to help. I know, there are a hundred decent and praiseworthy ways of losing *my own way*, and they are truly highly "moral"![9]

Yet Nietzsche's attack on a "morality" of self-sacrificing altruism should not be seen as an attack on morality as such, as he makes clear in the following passage:

> *There are two kinds of deniers of morality.* – "To deny morality" – this can mean, *first*: to deny that the moral motives which men *claim* have inspired their actions really have done so … *Then* it can mean: to deny that moral judgments are based on truths. Here it is admitted that they really are motives of action, but that in this way it is *errors* which, as the basis of all moral judgment, impel men to their moral actions. This is *my* point of view … It goes without saying that I do not deny – unless I am a fool – that many actions called immoral ought to be avoided and resisted, or that many called moral ought to be done and encouraged – but I think the one should be encouraged and the other avoided *for other reasons than hitherto*. We have to *learn to think differently* – in order at last, perhaps very late on, to attain even more: *to feel differently*.[10]

Nietzsche does not recommend immoral actions as a class, or even that we are invariably wrong in what we call immoral in the way of actions. Rather, he is a revisionist about depth phenomena: what is wrong are our feelings, our motives, our general orientation toward the world. In brief, the revisionism lies in the renunciation of the following constellation of feelings and orientations: "the feelings of devotion, self-sacrifice for one's neighbour, the entire morality of self-renunciation must be taken mercilessly to task and brought to court."[11] Nietzsche is thus an egoist in the sense that he does not see the mature individual as a being whose primary purpose or function is to be a self-sacrificing being – a being that is an instrument for the greater good, the state, serving the needs of others. Rather he should "affirm" his *own* life.

According to Nietzsche, then, genuine affirmation of one's own life cannot occur in a life that is conducted in a spirit of self-sacrifice, but occurs only in a life exhibiting virtues where that spirit is absent (e.g., in a life that is independent, "hard," truthful, honest, strong, exhibits a disposition of overflowing giving.) For example in "Schopenhauer as Educator" Nietzsche describes Schopenhauer's life as a kind of virtuous egoism, a cultivation of the personal within him through a creativity marked by cheerfulness, honesty, and hardness. His philosophy exhibits an "outpouring" of "inner strength" constituted by his honesty and hardness: "He is honest because he speaks and writes to himself and for himself, cheerful because he has conquered the hardest task by thinking, and steadfast because he has to be."[12]

This chapter investigates (a) what it is to affirm one's *own* life (section 6.2), (b) what is involved in *self-sacrificing* altruism (sections 6.3 and 6.4), and (c) how affirming one's own life can be compatible with "working for one's fellow men" (sections 6.5 and 6.6).

6.2 Affirming One's Own Life

At the heart of Nietzsche's morality of virtuous egoism is the idea that the mature individual both knows his own advantage and pursues it in a manner that does not exhibit a pattern of self-sacrifice for others' purposes. Others' purposes include those which have become one's "own" through weakness: a failure to cultivate the personal in one. Nietzsche calls the life of the "mature" individual "life affirming" as opposed to "life denying." At the basis of this idea is what Nietzsche calls the "instinct of life":

> All naturalism in morality, that is, all *healthy* morality, is dominated by an instinct of life – some commandment of life is fulfilled by a determinate canon of "shall" and "shall not", some hindrance and hostile element on life's road is thereby removed.[13]

This bare statement of the 'instinct of life" is indeterminate both in regard to what the instinct is, and how it relates to Nietzsche's ethics. At bottom, the "instinct of life" at the heart of "life affirmation" is for Nietzsche incompatible with an instinct of sacrificing one's own (mature) standards and purposes for those of others. An 'instinct of life" is contrasted with a "disintegration of the instincts" where "self-interest wilts away" in accordance with an "'altruistic' morality," "the morality of decadence."[14] In this section the basic norm of life affirmation is explicated by contrasting it with other norms with which it might be confused. The following sections give it more content through an analysis of undistorted "will to power": the central concept through which life affirmation is understood, and through which Nietzsche articulates his psychology of virtue and vice.

The basic norm of virtuous egoism (VE), "life affirmation," is understood thus:

(VE)   The fundamental shape of an individual's life ought to be one where her own life is affirmed by him or her.

(VE) is contrasted with a number of other interpretations of "life affirmation" with which (VE) might be confused, and which are now listed and discussed.

(AL)   Everyone should affirm all lives.

The idea of "*self*-overcoming" prevalent in Nietzsche suggests that affirmation should be understood in terms of affirming one's own life, not uncritical acceptance of all lives. If (VE) is not distinguished from (AL), then what Michael Tanner calls a "cleavage" may be thought present in Nietzsche's work:

> ... Nietzsche is drawn to overall affirmation ... But the movement of affirmation is powerfully countered by a fastidious revulsion from almost anything he encounters ... It is amazing that, so far as I can discover, Nietzsche never noticed this rending cleavage in his work.[15]

However I do not see a cleavage, for Nietzsche is not drawn to "overall affirmation" in this sense. The reason he is not so drawn is hinted at in this passage: there is indeed a strong impetus in Nietzsche to be disgusted at the non-affirming lives of others. He speaks for example of the "disgusting sight" of the "failed, atrophied, the poisoned."[16] However, despite this, Nietzsche claims that this is an impetus that needs to be resisted, and it is the mark of the strong to resist such impulses. As Nietzsche claims in *Zarathustra*, disgust is a world-weary, enervating attitude to the world. "The great disgust with man – *this* choked me and had crawled into my throat ... A long twilight limped before me, a sadness, weary to death."[17] Disgust is something that has to be overcome; the truly strong individual, "we immoralists," "have ... made room in our hearts for every kind of understanding, comprehending, *approving*. We do not easily negate; we make it a point of honor to be affirmers."[18]

Indeed Nietzsche himself had to fight against the temptation of disgust: "*Nausea* over man, over the 'rabble', was always my greatest danger."[19] Insofar as Nietzsche counts himself as one filled with disgust, he would at the same time label himself as one of the "convalescent."

Do these passages imply (AL)? Is there after all, as Tanner suggests, a "rending cleavage" in Nietzsche's work? It may look as if these passages imply (AL), but not so. Note that Nietzsche does not say that we affirmers should affirm all lives, but only that we *do not readily deny*; that we *make room* for approval, understanding, and seek our honor in affirming. But that is not tantamount to affirming *all* lives no matter how mediocre. In short Nietzsche is opposed to negative thinking, and to a world-weary disgust: he does not support uncritical, complacent, soft, attitudes. At any rate (VE) itself is neutral about the attitude one should take to others' lives, and in particular, does not entail:

(DL)   One should be disgusted at others' mediocre non-affirming lives.

I suggest then that Nietzsche affirms (VE), denies (DL), but does not affirm (AL). There is no "rending cleavage."

(VE) should also be distinguished from what many would regard as an unpleasantly elitist doctrine:

(BL)   Everyone should affirm only the best or superior lives.

(VE) concerns a first-person perspective: the attitude one should have to one's *own* life. Kant, recall, did not regard it as a duty to promote moral perfection in others – the duty was self-regarding. Affirmation, understood as admiration, is fine for Nietzsche, but (VE) advocates dealing with one's own life rather than merely appreciating the admirable lives of others.

(VE) should also be distinguished from and does not entail the following egoist thesis:

(FE)   Each person should put her own life first in her practical reasoning and actions.

(VE) may appear to entail (FE) but not so, as we shall explore further in section 6.5. Certainly, what Nietzsche calls the mature individual as a "collective individual" cultivates the personal in him so he does not sacrifice himself to the purposes of others which are not also his. However such an individual identifies with others, such as his children, or his people, to the point where he may even, as Nietzsche puts it, "risk himself" for these wider ends.

Both (VE) and (FE) should be contrasted with a form of evaluative egoism:

(SE)   Each person should evaluate her life as having superior value or worth than anyone else's.

Seeing one's fundamental task as enhancing one's own life by living a life of self-overcoming, as Nietzsche puts it, entails nothing about whether or not one believes that one's own life is worth more than another's. Indeed, self-referential comparisons of this kind do not constitute a virtuous pride for Nietzsche.

(VE) implies nothing about the virtuous egoist's motivation, and should also be distinguished from a form of motivational egoism:

(ME)   Each person has or should have a foreground motivation, whenever she acts, that she should enhance her own life, as opposed to that of others.

(ME) does violence to motivations associated with virtues such as friendship, parental love, generosity. On the contrary, when acting out of such virtues, one's attention is focused on relevant others, and one's motives are directed at their interests. If (VE) were to entail (ME) it could not be interpreted as compatible with *virtuous* egoism, but I do not see a narcissistic reading of (VE) in Nietzsche. His view of virtuous motivation and the altruistic virtues will be explored in section 6.4.

Finally the important question arises: to whom does (VE) apply? On one reading of Nietzsche, (VE) does not apply to all, but rather only to the elite:

(HE)   Only the higher types should affirm their *own* lives.

(HE) says that (VE) applies to a select few. According to (HE) lower types such as herd types are either incapable of affirming their own lives, or for one reason or another should not do so. I shall argue however in Chapter 8 that the herd type may or may not be sick, and for the sake of higher culture at least, the "convalescent" masses should self-overcome. This must be done if their sickness is not to infect society as a whole, creating an unfavorable culture for producing higher types.

Given that (VE) applies to all, it rejects:

(PL)   Lesser human beings should promote the life affirmation of the higher types rather than affirm their own lives.

(PL) not only presupposes that (VE) does not apply to all, but gives a reason why lower types should not affirm their own lives. For on this view the point of their lives is to be instruments in the service of the goal of cultural excellence or of the production of higher types. I shall argue against that view in section 6.6.

Though (BL) and (PL) are rejected as interpretations of Nietzsche's notion of life affirmation, (VE) should not be understood as implying that all should affirm their lives in the same kind of way. In particular (VE) should not be understood as:

(RE)   Everyone should affirm his own life by directly involving himself in the highest end (the redemption of his society and culture).

I shall investigate (RE) further in section 6.5.

We have seen how (VE) is to be distinguished from a variety of positions with which it might be confused. But what more precisely is it to *affirm* one's life? At the core of affirmation, as we have seen, is a disposition not to flee from self through self-contempt, or put positively, it is an attitude of self-love. Self-love for Nietzsche, as we will explore in this and the next chapter, has two broad aspects.

(1)   Acceptance of oneself and the world, manifested in such virtues as courage, truthfulness, (strong) forgetfulness, solitude (as opposed to loneliness), the gift-giving virtues, and objectivity as a virtue.
(2)   Creativity, manifested in passion, a certain lack of caution and even wisdom, experimentation, and (virtuously) artistic deception or license.

Without acceptance, we fall into the vices of despair, resentment, self-sacrificing tendencies of escape into otherness, hopelessness, cynicism. Without creativity, we fall into vices of laziness, complacency, self-satisfaction, passivity, non-assertiveness. These vices are "life denying" because all manifest a shrinking rather than a growing process.

Life affirming acceptance must be distinguished from two other notions of acceptance. First, such acceptance is not just mere *adjustment* to reality. As the humanist psychologist Abraham Maslow recognized,[20] it also requires self-actualization or self-realization. Second, life affirming acceptance as a core of virtue must be also be distinguished from another kind of acceptance at the core of much vice – self-satisfaction, or a compliant complacency hated by Nietzsche. Paradoxically, self-love involves a dissatisfied, even contemptuous attitude toward the self as it is now. For Nietzsche, self-love is part of a dynamic psychology where the individual thinks himself worthy of further discovery and improvement while being dissatisfied with his present state. It is this which allows for affirmation as opposed to complacency (a sense that one has arrived) to be a part of self-love. Self-love as acceptance (in the required sense) receives further treatment in Chapter 7, and creativity in Chapter 10. Here we focus on the self-sacrificing manifestation of "fleeing from self" that lies at the core of non-virtuous altruism.

6.3   Nietzsche's Virtuous Egoism and Will to Power

Understanding the nature of self-sacrifice deplored by Nietzsche requires an account of the nature and moral theoretic importance of "will to power." For that is the route to the depth psychological explanation of the nature of self-sacrifice in the required sense, and the life affirmation of the virtuous egoist.

This approach to understanding the nature of Nietzsche's virtuous egoism may be thought puzzling. For it may naturally be thought that any attempt to ascribe to Nietzsche a virtuous form of egoism is derailed by his doctrine of will to power. For

SWANTON, CHRISTINE, 1947-

VIRTUE ETHICS OF HUME AND NIETZSCHE.

                                  Cloth   227 P.
CHICHESTER: WILEY-BLACKWELL, 2015
SER: NEW DIRECTIONS IN ETHICS; 3.

AUTH: UNIV. OF AUCKLAND.

LCCN 2015001519
  ISBN 1118939395   **Library PO#** SLIP ORDERS

		List	99.95 USD
6207 UNIV OF TEXAS/SAN ANTONIO		**Disc**	17.0%
App. Date 8/12/15 PHI.APR 6108-09		**Net**	82.96 USD

SUBJ: 1. HUME, DAVID, 1711-1776. 2. ETHICS. 3.
VIRTUE.

CLASS B1499   DEWEY# 171.30922   LEVEL ADV-AC

YBP Library Services

SWANTON, CHRISTINE, 1947-

VIRTUE ETHICS OF HUME AND NIETZSCHE.

                                  Cloth   227 P.
CHICHESTER: WILEY-BLACKWELL, 2015
SER: NEW DIRECTIONS IN ETHICS; 3.

AUTH: UNIV. OF AUCKLAND.

LCCN 2015001519
  ISBN 1118939395   **Library PO#** SLIP ORDERS

		List	99.95 USD
6207 UNIV OF TEXAS/SAN ANTONIO		**Disc**	17.0%
App. Date 8/12/15 PHI.APR 6108-09		**Net**	82.96 USD

SUBJ: 1. HUME, DAVID, 1711-1776. 2. ETHICS. 3.
VIRTUE.

CLASS B1499   DEWEY# 171.30922   LEVEL ADV-AC

those who think Nietzsche is not an immoralist, there are two moves in this debate. Some, who think of Nietzsche as a species of virtue ethicist (such as Robert Solomon) or others who think he has something to offer normative ethics at least (such as Julian Young) think the notion of will to power plays but a limited role in an understanding of Nietzsche's ethics. Solomon relegates the notion of will to power to the status of serving as a reminder that we are not motivated solely by pleasure, but also by desires for status, for control, and so on.[21] I do not fall into this camp. I by contrast think the notion is central to understanding the difference between virtue and vice for Nietzsche, for it plays a powerful theoretical explanatory role in that understanding.

A huge amount of Nietzsche's philosophy gives an account of the varieties of distorted "will to power" which underlie various vices. It plays a central role in his view that psychology should be reinstated as the "queen of the sciences,"[22] for it alone can uncover the "depths" of our being, unlike traditional moral philosophy which he regards as superficial. Without this uncovering, we will not gain a correct understanding of the nature of self-sacrifice which he believes is at the core of altruistic moralities. But what is meant by will to power?

Will to power as a genus must be distinguished from various of its species. As a genus, it is a highly general idea, applicable to all life forms:

A living thing desires above all to vent its strength – life as such is will to power …

… it will want to grow, expand, draw to itself, gain ascendancy – not out of any morality or immorality but because it *lives*, and because life *is* will to power.[23]

As applied to humans, the need to "vent one's strength," expand, is connected essentially with their nature as active, growing, developing beings, rather than mere receptacles of pleasure or welfare. This notion is contrasted with a mere instinct for self-preservation which Nietzsche denies is the "cardinal drive" as opposed to "one of the indirect and most frequent consequences" of "will to power."[24] I take the above formulations to be the most general specification of will to power, a specification which admits of a variety of broad categorizations. At a fundamental level, we may distinguish between the following types or modes of venting strength:

(1) Actions versus modes of being such as "severity."[25]
(2) Expressive action versus action which manifests an intention with which it is done. The former category includes some kinds of "overflowing" acts of giving, some acts of violence, expressions of joy, creative zeal. The latter include intentional exercises of power such as the general kinds itemized by Nietzsche in *Beyond Good and Evil*, 259: intentional "appropriating," intentional "imposition of one's own forms," exploiting, (intentional) injuring.
(3) The expression of power or strength, or use of power or strength, in the pursuit of goals other than power (such as the "will to truth," the "will to knowledge"),[26] versus the pursuit of power itself.

Central to Nietzsche's view of all these forms is that the will to power displayed may be distorted or undistorted. Distorted forms come in two general types.

(A) *Forms which are distorted but quantitatively powerful.* These forms come in two broad types:
  (i) Unsublimated will to power, such as the lack of self-sufficiency in the "master" type who sees social restraints as fetters, to be escaped through an orgy of cruelty to relieve his boredom. In this state the master or noble types "regress" to the predatory animal instincts deep within, where they are no better than "predators on the rampage." Civilized instincts of fidelity, tenderness, friendship, consideration, manifested in their social peaceable lives, are ruthlessly repressed.[27]
  (ii) Will to power which is neurotically repressed in various ways, as in the "Christian neurosis." Here, will to power is expressive of powerful spiritualization, and deep-seated resentment as a solution to the unconscious conflict between desire for power or potency, and a sense of impotence.
(B) *Forms which are distorted but not quantitatively powerful.* This may manifest as:
  (i) A venting of strength which is enfeebled: such as is manifested in the passive, complacent, decadent, or unhealthy herd type. At the limit, such enfeeblement amounts to:
  (ii) An absence of "will to power" altogether as in the extreme decadent type of *Twilight of the Idols*, and the will-less Last Man of *Zarathustra* (Part I, 5), for whom everything requires too much exertion and who is a mere receptacle for "happiness."

Examples and accounts of distorted and undistorted will to power underlying respectively vice and virtue will occur throughout this and the following chapters. One should note here the following general point: though Nietzsche's rejection of Hedonism (the idea that only pleasure is intrinsically good) in his mature works is well known, what is less clearly appreciated is that for Nietzsche, power, one's own power, or one's will to power is not intrinsically good or valuable either. Rather what is good or valuable is will to power exercised well or excellently.[28] That is not to say that distorted will to power (as expressed in slave morality for example) may not have some value in its role of momentous vehicle for change in the genealogy of morals.

As I have indicated, distorted will to power, underlying vice, is compatible with a quantitatively powerful "will to power." The "domineering spiritualization" of the ascetic type, cruelty, the relentless independence of the "sovereign individual" of the *Genealogy of Morals*, the power of the slave types, may exhibit such "will to power," but I shall argue in later chapters that at a depth level it is for Nietzsche expressive of weakness. In that sense, "strong" will to power is fundamentally weak. (VE) then should not be read as a form of egoism where power as opposed to say pleasure is pursued:

(PE)   Each individual should aim to maximize his or her own power.

To understand the difference between (VE) and (PE) we need to understand in more detail the relation between the broad characterization of will to power and its specific instances.

How do we give the basic idea of will to power more determinate content? It is natural to think of will to power as consisting of something called the will, and that this will is a will to a single thing, power. However this understanding flies in the face of Nietzsche's frequent attacks on free will as a metaphysical entity. These attacks in turn have been thought puzzling to say the very least, since how can Nietzsche's emphasis on self-creation and self-overcoming be consistent with a supposed denial of free will? The clue to resolving the puzzle is to understand the nature of this denial. That understanding in turn sheds light on the nature of "will to power."

A well-known passage suggests that we are at the mercy of unalterable states, of which actions are mere expressions. In short, it appears, we do not have "free will" at all. Here is the passage:

> To demand of strength that it should *not* express itself as strength … makes as little sense as to demand of weakness that it should express itself as strength … Just as the common people distinguish lightning from the flash of light and takes the latter as *doing*, as the effect of a subject which is called lightning, just so popular morality distinguishes strength from expressions of strength, as if behind the strong individual there were an indifferent substratum which was at liberty to express or not express strength. But no such substratum exists; there is no "being" behind doing, acting becoming … the doing itself is everything.[29]

What Nietzsche is doing here however is denying a certain metaphysical understanding of human behavior which posits an entity, such as "free will" which is the operation of an "indifferent substratum," which can either switch on its "will" (conceived as a mental entity) or not (as it wishes?).[30] At one stroke he is debunking certain metaphysical postulates: the self as an indifferent substance ("substrate") and a peculiar metaphysical entity called free will, which is something that exists "behind" the action. When Nietzsche says the deed or the "doing" is all there is he does not mean to separate the physical behavior from the mental event, claiming only that the physical, understood problematically as something separable from the mental, exists. Such separations are the prerogative of the dualist metaphysics he is debunking. What he means is that the deed should be understood richly, as having both "surface" and "depths": there is no *indifferent* substratum from which it springs as effect. In particular he is asserting a standard doctrine of virtue ethics: the one thing, the deed, the "doing," cannot be understood properly unless we know the motivations and nature of the person who has performed it. For Nietzsche that includes his "depths" (his depth motivations). Given that we are not now strong, says Nietzsche in the quoted passage, it is absurd to think that our actions now can be understood and interpreted as expressing strength.

If the will is not to be understood as a single metaphysical entity belonging to an "indifferent substratum" which, via the operation of the will produces bits of behavior as effects, then a will *to power* cannot be understood as a property of such a will. There is no will which is driving to a single thing power, but rather agents who are weak or strong and who "vent their strength" (or relative lack of strength) accordingly. As Nietzsche puts it, both free and "unfree will is mythology; in real life it is only a matter of *strong* and *weak* wills."[31]

Once it is understood that "will to power" is not a type of act or motive that presupposes the fiction of free (or unfree) will, we can solve another puzzle. If everything is "will to power" why does Nietzsche speak so often of other apparent "wills," such as the will to memory of the sovereign individual, and the will to truth of the ascetic philosopher?[32] Well, they too can be seen as various kinds of or expressions of "ventings" of strength (will to power): the will to truth of the ascetic philosopher is an expression of a "domineering spirtualization," the will to memory of the sovereign individual is "protracted" and relentless, expressive of a distorted drive to autonomy and independence.[33] These as we shall see (especially in Chapters 7 and 8) are distorted forms of will to power, but the point here is that there is no single thing "power" which Nietzsche's various types seek. Rather they more or less powerfully develop, grow, expand, and vent their strength. Some of these ways of expressing strength, even if powerful, are distorted, and are thus not genuinely "strong" in a normative sense.

It remains to be seen how the notion of will to power, so understood, can have explanatory power. It can play an explanatory role only if the disparate forms of distorted will to power can be seen as related in a theoretically interesting way. For this to occur, the notion must be fleshed out within a psychological framework of the development or self-realization of human beings which gives substantive content to normative features of our lives, and in particular the various virtues and vices. As Richard D. White puts it:

> ... we should say that the will to power is Nietzsche's most basic principle of interpretation, which is justified in terms of its explanatory power. It is not a metaphysical substratum but the final instance of interpretation "beyond which we cannot go."[34]

Accordingly, psychology has to be recognized as the "queen of the sciences" once again, and be regarded as "once again the road to fundamental problems."[35] In Nietzsche's words:

> All psychology has hitherto remained anchored to moral prejudices and timidities: it has not ventured into the depths. To conceive it as morphology and the *development-theory of the will to power*, as I conceive it – has never yet so much as entered the mind of anyone else.[36]

Such a "development-theory" was provided by later depth psychologists influenced by Nietzsche, notably Alfred Adler and subsequent theorists and practitioners, such as Erich Fromm, who contrasts "malignant" and "benign" forms of aggression.[37] Not only do they theorize Nietzsche's key motif of self-contempt, a fundamental expression of distorted will to power, but they do this, as Nietzsche insists is necessary, by "venturing into the depths."

Moral philosophizing ventures into the depths in three stages according to Nietzsche's "genealogy" of the process. First, when the imperative "know thyself" "was still unknown," "the value or non-value of an action was derived from its consequences."[38] Subsequently (presumably with Kant) we have a "great event," an "inversion of perspectives": we take the origin as opposed to the consequences of an action as significant.[39] However the origin was taken to lie in the action's *intention*, and the value of the action accordingly was thought to lie in the value of its intention. But Nietzsche claims, "thanks to another self-examination and deepening on the part of man" we reject that idea as superficial:

> … the decisive value of an action resides in precisely that which is *not intentional* in it, and that all that in it is intentional, all of it that can be seen, known, "conscious", still belongs to its surface and skin – which, like every skin, betrays something but *conceals* still more?[40]

6.4   Pity and the "Gift-Giving" Virtues

We turn now to the ethical dimensions of will to power. How do actions have "value," and in particular how can we make sense of claims that "egoistic" actions may be virtuous? How can some forms of self-sacrifice be seen as a distorted form of will to power, and non-virtuous? The expressive character of our actions as strong or weak in a depth psychological sense makes intelligible a claim that some actions labeled by Nietzsche "egoistic" can be valuable, and express what we would normally call altruistic sentiments, such as love. Consider for example the following puzzling passage in *Daybreak*:

> "Unegoistic!" – this one is hollow and wants to be full, that one is overfull and wants to be emptied – both go in search of an individual who will serve their purpose. And this process, understood in its highest sense, is in both cases called by the same word: love – what? is love supposed to be something unegoistic?[41]

Nietzsche's claim here is that love is expressive of neediness, and is thereby "egoistic": the only issue is whether the neediness is healthy or strong, or weak; whether the loving behavior expresses valuable or disvaluable states in the individual. The notion of strong and weak wills gives us a clue about the source of this value, namely the character, or deeper "drives" or motives of which actions are expressions. The "intention" to act for the sake of another is as we have seen for Nietzsche, superficial. If that intention is expressive of being "overfull" and a need to bestow, then it is "egoistic" in a valuable sense. Such a person gives from a position of psychological strength as opposed to a self-sacrificial giving born of inner weakness. The latter giver, who is empty and needs to be filled, is not affirming or enhancing her own life, but is rather externalizing self-contempt by loving for and through others. Such "love" is altruistic in a non-virtuous way. So for Nietzsche both forms of love are "egoistic" in the sense of being expressive of kinds of neediness, but differ in that one is healthy and virtuous while the other is not.

One form of unhealthy neediness is manifested in what Nietzsche regards as the "altruistic" vice of pity. For Nietzsche, pity expresses distorted will to power, for it is an externalized form of self-hate – an escape from a sense of vulnerability. This sense, though repressed in one's escape through others, is still a disguised, subtle form of revenge – a repressed anger at one's own susceptibility to the fate that has befallen the one pitied. Hence the manner in which the supposed altruistic "virtues" are expressed is one of repressed hostility, as is highlighted in Nietzsche's discussion of pity in *Daybreak*:

> An accident that happens to another offends us: it would make us aware of our impotence, and perhaps of our cowardice, if we did not go to assist him. Or it brings with it in itself a diminution of our honour in the eyes of others or in our own eyes. Or an accident and suffering incurred by another constitutes a signpost to some danger to us; and it can have a painful effect upon us simply as a token of human vulnerability and fragility in general. We repel this kind of pain and offence and requite it through an act of pity; it may contain a subtle self-defence or even a piece of revenge. That at bottom we are thinking very strongly of ourselves can be divined from the decision we arrive at in every case in which we *can* avoid the sight of the person suffering, perishing or complaining: we decide *not* to do so if we can present ourselves as the more powerful and as a helper, if we are certain of applause, if we want to feel how fortunate we are in contrast, or hope that the sight will relieve our boredom.[42]

In another passage Nietzsche emphasizes the quality of pity as a form of losing oneself through suffering:

> Pity (*Mitleiden*), insofar as it really causes suffering (*Leiden*) … is a weakness, like every losing of oneself through a *harmful* affect. It *increases* the amount of suffering in the world … Supposing it was dominant even for a single day, mankind would immediately perish of it.[43]

Interestingly, in both these passages, Nietzsche echoes the sentiments of Kant:

> … when another suffers and, although I cannot help him, I let myself be infected by his pain (through my imagination), then two of us suffer, though the trouble really (in nature) affects only *one*. But there cannot possibly be a duty to increase the ills in the world and so to do good *from compassion*. This would be an insulting kind of

beneficence, since it expresses the kind of benevolence one has towards someone unworthy called *pity*; and this has no place in people's relations with one another, since they are not to make a display of their worthiness to be happy.[44]

An expression of non-virtuous altruism – pity – is characterized by self-referential comparisons which are symptoms of one's sense of vulnerability and impotence. Since the sight of someone who provokes pity triggers such unpleasant comparisons, pity more or less successfully masks externalized hostility.

Note then that for Nietzsche egocentricity is not confined to the immature egoist: it is a property also of the self-sacrificing weak altruist. The distinction between egocentricity and egoism as more superficially and commonly understood is explicit in Karen Horney:

> … the pride system removes the neurotic from others by making him egocentric. To avoid misunderstandings: by egocentricity I do not mean selfishness or egotism in the sense of considering merely one's advantage. The neurotic may be callously selfish or too unselfish … But he is always egocentric in the sense of being wrapped up in himself.[45]

For Nietzsche too, a need to escape oneself is the other side of the coin of not being able to get away from oneself: a tendency to be thinking of one's vulnerabilities and impotence for example. The pitying individual is oversensitive to his own vulnerability – he stands accused by Nietzsche of "at bottom" thinking strongly of himself, while rescuing himself from himself through others.

In *Ecce Homo* Nietzsche describes other manifestations of the phenomenon: "You [the sick person] … cannot get rid of anything, you cannot cope with anything, you cannot fend anything off – everything hurts you. People and things get intrusively close, experiences affect you too deeply, memory is a festering wound."[46] Nietzsche makes penetrating comments not only about the "subtle" revenge of the pitying, but also about the revenge of the complainer and the spiritualized revenge of the moralist:

> there is a small dose of *revenge* in every complaint … Complaining is never of any use: it comes from weakness.[47]

> Moral judgment and condemnation is the favorite form of revenge of the spiritually limited on those who are less so, likewise a form of compensation for their having been neglected by nature, finally an occasion for acquiring spirit and *becoming* refined – malice spiritualizes.[48]

By contrast, in genuine virtuous altruism the distorted will to power of pity is absent. The directing of the self to others is not an escape from self; rather it is a self-love which overflows to others with whom one has a bond. In this form of beneficence, there is an "overflowing" embracing of life and the world expressed in the "gift-giving" virtues, joyfulness, cheerfulness, to be contrasted (in an echo of Hume) with the resignatory gloomy vices characteristic of forms of Christianity: "The reverse side of Christian compassion for the suffering of one's neighbour is a profound suspicion of all the joy of one's neighbour, of his joy in all that he wants to do and can."[49]

The contrast between pity and virtuous "overflowing" altruism is made clear in the following passage: "In the foreground stands the feeling of plenitude, of power which seeks to overflow, the happiness of high tension, the consciousness of wealth which would like to give away and bestow."[50] This sentiment, even the language, is echoed by Erich Fromm:

> For the productive character, giving has an entirely different meaning. Giving is the highest expression of potency. In the very act of giving, I experience my strength, my wealth, my power. This experience of heightened vitality and potency fills me with joy. I experience myself as overflowing, spending, alive, hence, as joyous.[51]

The foregoing understanding of a distinction between altruism as a vice, weakness, or sickness, and altruism as a virtue, or strength, enables us to make sense of an otherwise puzzling distinction between sick and healthy selfishness in Zarathustra:

> This is your thirst: to become sacrifices and gifts yourselves: and that is why you thirst to pile up all the riches in your soul. Insatiably your soul strives for treasures and gems, because your virtue is insatiable in wanting to give. You force all things to and into yourself that they may flow back out of your well as the gifts of your love ... whole and holy I call this selfishness.
>
> There is also another selfishness, an all-too-poor and hungry one that always wants to steal – the selfishness of the sick: sick selfishness. With the eyes of the thief it looks at everything splendid; with the greed of hunger it sizes up those who have much to eat; and always it sneaks around the table of those who give.[52]

Healthy selfishness is not an escape from self for it is selfish only in the sense of expressing a desire to receive, absorb, appreciate the world hungrily and with passion, for the world is seen as splendid. Then, as part of that receptive absorption, one bestows, also insatiably. There is no sense here of ensuring that one does not give away more "value" than one retains for oneself. Rather, as Robert Solomon suggests, for Nietzsche, at least for the "heroic" types, "there is no meaningful distinction to be made between their personal self-satisfying desires and the larger ideals and values for which they stand."[53]

The virtue in Nietzsche's egoism can be summed up as follows. Altruism, as commonly understood in the morality which Nietzsche rejects, is for Nietzsche a form of escape from self into otherness. One abases oneself before, renders oneself insignificant in the face of, the neediness and importance of the world at large, and one derives one's self-esteem from the regard and thankfulness of that world. Nietzsche's philosophy of affirming one's own life rejects such self-abasement, but does not preclude even "insatiable" "gift-giving."

6.5   Nietzsche's Virtuous Egoism
and the "Collective-Individual"

We are now in a position to understand how Nietzsche's rejection of altruism and embracing of egoism in works such as *Daybreak* should be seen as a rejection only of a certain notion of altruism, and an embracing only of a certain form of egoism. It is the common conception of a moral or "moralistic" altruism which is rejected, and because of the close association between that form of altruism and "morality" as commonly conceived, he rejects altruism as commonly conceived. That conception of the relationship between morality and altruism is expressed thus:

(M)   "Moral" actions are ones which are done for the sake of the other and only for the sake of the other, and which arise from "freedom of the will."[54]

His rejection of (M) does not however commit him to the following form of egoism:

(E)   Valuable actions are ones which are done for the sake of the self and only for the sake of the self, and which arise from "freedom of the will."

He is not committed to (E) for two basic reasons. First, the "intention" to act for the sake of another is for Nietzsche superficial. Not only does an intention to act for the sake of another mask a neediness at a depth psychological level, so that it is misleading to say that one *only* acts for the sake of another (or *only* for the sake of oneself for that matter), but the value of an action does not lie in that intention. For the neediness which the intention expresses may be strong or weak. Second, the value of an action cannot be said to lie in the fact that it is sourced in an intention which is the product of the metaphysical fiction of free will. Thus (E) makes the same metaphysical and psychological errors as the rejected altruism (M), failing to recognize that intentions as such are superficial, and that free will in a certain metaphysical sense is a fiction.

However if we reject as superficial appeal to intentions to act only for the sake of oneself or only for the sake of another, in what sense does the virtuous egoist not act solely for the sake of himself? In the foregoing, much has been said about Nietzsche's opposition to immature unhealthy altruism, but little about his (much less salient) opposition to immature egoism. As we saw in section 6.1, for Nietzsche the egoism of the immature is characterized by instant gratification and a lack of social feeling: such immature egoism is contrasted with the "morality of the mature individual." That morality permits, indeed requires, the cultivation of what is personal, but in a manner presupposing the individual has social feeling which allows for a sense of honor and giving and expecting respect. The mature individual is in short what Nietzsche describes as a "collective-individual." This section is concerned to explicate that notion, showing how such an individual can be for Nietzsche a "virtuous egoist."

It is not surprising that Nietzsche's discussion of immature egoism is much less prominent than his attack on (self-sacrificing) altruism, for the latter constitutes his war on morality as traditionally understood. However, to complete the discussion of virtuous egoism we need to contrast it with immature egoism. We have seen that virtuous egoism is consistent with "overflowing" "gift-giving" but the overflowing nature of giving is not sufficient for virtuous egoism. Full virtue requires the social feeling of the "collective-individual." To show this we begin with a sketch of the immature badly socialized egoist. Unlike the self-sacrificing altruist who flees from self by "rescuing himself from himself in others" the immature egoist is too attached to his (relatively unsocialized) self. As Alfred Adler was later to put it, such a person who through his insecurity is "asocial" or "anti-social" "is always more concerned with himself than with others. As in other forms of ego-centricity he cannot get away from himself."[55] Such a being is in a condition well described by Karen Horney. She contrasts solid self-confidence with a "neurotic pride" whose superficial features look like virtues: "A capacity to assert egocentric claims appears as strength, vindictiveness as justice, frustrating techniques as a most intelligent weapon, aversion to work as "successfully resisting the deadly habit of work" and so on.[56]

Not only should the egoism of the mature individual be distinguished from the self-centered aggressive pride of the immature egoist, but the solitude of the socialized individual is contrasted by Nietzsche with the withdrawing tendencies of the insecure egocentric individual. The mature individual needs solitude in order to cultivate what is personal in him; his solitude is escape *from* the sick as opposed to escape *of* the sick.[57] As Nietzsche claims:

> Every superior human being will instinctively aspire after a secret citadel where he is set free from the crowd, the many, the majority, where, as its exception, he may forget the rule "man" … all company is bad company except the company of one's equals.[58]

In what way, then, is the *mature* egoist socialized? Such an individual identifies with, has a stake in, his society and individuals other than himself. Through such a social identity, Nelson Mandela had a stake in the interests of black South Africans during his struggles on their behalf, by virtue of the fact that they were *his* people. However here is a problem. From the perspective of virtue, an individual affirming her own life is criticizable if she has an overly narrow conception of those in whose interests she has a stake. One may agree that the point of our lives is not that of "the sacrificial animal," but if virtues such as "overflowing" generosity are confined to a very narrow circle through bonds of love or identification, then "virtuous egoism" may be seen as problematic. Nonetheless one thing is clear in Nietzsche. It is the destiny of the talented few to be directly involved in the flourishing of society as a whole: "the third *Meditation* is addressed … to a 'small band' who, 'through continual purification and mutual support … help prepare within themselves and around them' for the redemption of culture (UM iii 6)."[59]

At the extreme such an interest may impel cultural leaders to extreme "gift-giving." Consider the following passages from Zarathustra.

I love him whose soul squanders itself, who wants no thanks and returns none: for he always gives away and does not want to preserve himself.

I love him whose soul is overfull, so that he forgets himself, and all things are in him: thus all things spell his going under.[60]

At first sight, these passages seem incompatible with a reading of Nietzsche as an egoist, for surely, such a "going under" is the ultimate in personal sacrifice? But is it? For Nietzsche, the highest type of human being can be understood as not only having a *stake* in the flourishing of society as a whole, but that action in the service of this goal at great personal cost is not to be seen as a genuine personal sacrifice where the self "wilts away." It is no different in kind from the "overflowing" "superabundant" form of "sacrifice" of parents for their children, forms of sacrifice to be distinguished from the weak forms so deplored by both Nietzsche and for example Jean Hampton.[61]

In what sense, then, is the mature egoist who is not directly involved in the redemption of society a "collective-individual"? For Nietzsche all have, or should have, a social identity where this is interpreted as having a stake in the interests of one's society, and in its cultural health as a society with a heritage, but needing to progress. Even for the average person, on Nietzsche's view, life affirmation does not occur in isolation from the "Volk": the culture, heritage, and roles which constitute the social identity of the individual. What Julian Young calls "Volkish" thinking,[62] a tradition to which Nietzsche was heir, affirms that everyone, even those not directly involved in the redemption of culture, has a social identity. These social elements in Nietzsche's thought thus leave room for a critique of those "individualists" who have an excessively narrow conception of those in whose interests they have a stake. However we cannot provide a formula in advance for just how broadly based or extensive are those others in whose interests one has or should have a stake. For recall the mature "virtuous egoist" "cultivates what is personal," and just what that is will vary greatly from individual to individual, and in differing circumstances.

I have suggested that social identification in the sense compatible with a plausible reading of Nietzsche should be distinguished from social submersion. To read Nietzsche as recommending social identification as social submersion is to ignore one of the most powerful themes in Nietzsche's writings, to be explored in the next chapter. This is the existentialist individualist theme of avoiding the basic weakness, the basic distortion of will to power: escape from self.

6.6   Nietzsche's Virtuous Egoism and Elitism

In this section we discuss the following problem. To whom does (VE) (section 6.2) apply? Is it only the higher types who are to affirm their own lives, whereas the lower types' role is simply to be instruments for their flourishing? Is (VE) constrained by (HE) and even worse, (PL) above? Many commentators have indeed understood Nietzsche as a particularly nasty exemplar of "elitism," a species of what James Conant calls "excellence-consequentialism."[63] Excellence-consequentialism itself is a species of perfectionism, the view that goodness or value is to be understood as "what Rawls calls [in *A Theory of Justice*, 325] 'the realization of human excellence in the various forms of culture.'"[64]

Excellence-consequentialism may be more or less benign. Consider the form described by Conant thus:

> (1) ... the perfectionist is concerned with optimizing the conditions which promote the achievement of excellence in the arts and sciences, and (2) ... the goodness of an action is to be assessed in accordance with the degree to which it maximises such forms of excellence.[65]

On a benign reading, excellence-consequentialism is compatible with (VE) applying to all. For on that reading, in order to optimize the conditions for the achievement of excellence in culture, everyone must affirm their own lives in accordance with virtue, otherwise the entire culture will become corrupted. In fact this is exactly what Nietzsche is advocating, with passion, in section 1 of "Schopenhauer as Educator." He deplores the timidity and laziness of the mass of people: it "is on account of their laziness that men seem like factory products" and they have a tendency to "hide themselves behind customs and opinions."[66] In contrast Nietzsche implores us to find the genius within us; there "exists no more repulsive and desolate creature in the world than the man who has evaded his own genius."[67]

A less benign excellence-perfectionism where the bulk of society is seen as mere "scaffolding" for the production of higher beings appears to be advocated in *Beyond Good and Evil*:

> The essential thing in a good and healthy aristocracy is, however, that it does *not* feel itself to be a function (of the monarchy or of the commonwealth) but as their *meaning* and supreme justification – that it therefore accepts with a good conscience the sacrifice of innumerable men who *for its sake* have to be suppressed and reduced to imperfect men, to slaves and instruments. Its fundamental faith must be that society should *not* exist for the sake of society but only as foundation and scaffolding upon which a select species of being is able to raise itself to its higher task.[68]

However the interpretation of this passage as advocating a "nasty" elitist form of excellence-consequentialism is the result of taking the passage out of context.

Confusion may arise on two fronts. First, there may be confusion between attributive and predicative goodness. Where Nietzsche speaks of types of morality, he uses "good" or "healthy" in an attributive sense, so that he speaks of "good" or "healthy" aristocracy, meaning "good *qua* aristocracy." Thus Nietzsche speaks of "moralities" of types of human, such as herd, slave, noble, master, which can be ranked as higher or lower. In this section of *Beyond Good and Evil* ("What is Noble?") and indeed in this passage, Nietzsche portrays a type of morality, "noble" morality, and what it is to be good *qua* aristocracy in that morality. In short, Nietzsche does not mean that noble or aristocratic morality is good *simpliciter* (the predicative sense of goodness).

In this passage, too, potential for a second confusion exists. In his genealogical mode, Nietzsche frequently claims that harsh moralities are necessary for the development of more civilized higher moralities. In the first sentence of the section "What is Noble?" he says that "every elevation of the type 'man' has hitherto been the work of an aristocratic society."[69] However this idea is compatible with a claim that aristocratic, noble morality is not the highest morality to which we can aspire. Indeed I shall argue in the next chapter (section 7.3) that this is indeed Nietzsche's view.

The question arises: even if excellence-consequentialism can be applicable to all, is it compatible with (VE)? In particular, is Nietzsche an excellence-*consequentialist*? That is, does he assess the goodness or rightness of actions solely in terms of their consequences for cultural or societal flourishing, or for the flourishing of higher types? It may appear that at least in "Schopenhauer as Educator" this is so. Consider the following passage:

> … the goal of its [the species human being] evolution lies, not in the mass of its exemplars who happen to come last in point of time, but rather in those apparently scattered and chance existences which favourable conditions have here and there produced.[70]

Note however that Nietzsche is not speaking of the need for actions intentionally designed to produce the highest exemplars – how could they be so designed, for these exemplars are what he describes in *The Genealogy of Morals* as "man's lucky hits"? Rather he speaks of the need to create "favourable conditions" where they might be "here and there produced." That view is admittedly compatible with the idea that the *goodness or rightness* of actions is assessed solely in terms of their efficacy for the production of those "lucky hits," but this kind of indirect consequentialism is not implied by the above passage.

First, Nietzsche at this point of time is in his "Darwinian phase" and is speaking not of the goodness and rightness of actions or policies but of the "goal" of evolutionary processes.[71] Second, even if the highest value for Nietzsche is the absence of mediocrity in culture, or the existence of higher men, it does not follow that what makes traits virtues for Nietzsche is *simply* their conduciveness to those ends. What Nietzsche continually finds deplorable is the manifestation of a range of vices which are expressive of decline and life denial: laziness, pity, envy, belief in equality "as a certain factual increase in similarity" which is "an essential feature of decline,"[72] complacency, to name but a few. These disgust him simply as *expressions* of deplorable psychological states marking a "decadent" type of individual, even though, as he also recognizes, these states are vices for another reason: they have seriously harmful consequences. Pity for example is a vice because it is expressive of a resentment-based, self-sacrificing form of "selflessness," but it is also deplorable because of its characteristic consequences.

Finally, we should recall that as we noted in section 6.3, consequentialism for Nietzsche is the most shallow and "immature" of all the major types of moral theory, simply because it assesses states and actions solely in terms of their consequences, rather than in terms of the depth psychological states of individuals.

Notes

1   Tara Smith, *Ayn Rand's Normative Ethics: The Virtuous Egoist* (Cambridge: Cambridge University Press, 2006) introduces the notion of virtuous egoism in her work on Ayn Rand. Of course, just as there can be many types of virtue ethics, there can be more than one version of virtuous egoism. I shall argue that Nietzsche can be read as a type of virtuous egoist.
2   *Twilight of the Idols*, in *The Portable Nietzsche*, ed. and trans. Walter Kaufmann (New York: Penguin, 1976), "Skirmishes of an Untimely Man," sect. 35, 535–536.
3   Ibid.
4   *Human, All Too Human: A Book for Free Spirits*, trans. R.J. Hollingdale (Cambridge: Cambridge University Press, 1986), "On the History of the Moral Sensations," "Morality of the mature individual," sect. 95, 50–51.
5   Ibid., "On the History of the Moral Sensations," "The three phases of morality hitherto," sect. 94, 50.
6   *Daybreak: Thoughts on the Prejudices of Morality*, trans. R.J. Hollingdale (Cambridge: Cambridge University Press, 1982), Book 5, sect. 516, 518.
7   *The Gay Science*, trans. Walter Kaufmann (New York: Vintage Books, 1974), Book 3, sect. 119, 176.
8   *Daybreak*, Book 2, sect. 146, 92.
9   *The Gay Science*, Book 4, sect. 338, 270.
10 *Daybreak*, Book 2, sect. 103, 103.
11 *Beyond Good and Evil: Prelude to a Philosophy of the Future*, trans. R.J. Hollingdale (London: Penguin, 1973), "The Free Spirit," sect. 33, 64.
12 *Untimely Meditations*, trans. R.J. Hollingdale (Cambridge: Cambridge University Press, 1983), sect. 2, 136.
13 *Twilight of the Idols and The Anti-Christ*, trans. R.J. Hollingdale (Harmondsworth: Penguin, 1968), "Morality as Anti-Nature," sect. 4, 45.
14 *Twilight of the Idols*, "Skirmishes of an Untimely Man," sect. 35.
15 Michael Tanner, *Nietzsche* (Oxford: Oxford University Press, 1994), 66.
16 *On the Genealogy of Morals*, trans. Douglas Smith (Oxford: Oxford University Press, 1996), First Essay, sect. 11, 27.
17 *Thus Spoke Zarathustra*, in *The Portable Nietzsche*, ed. and trans. Walter Kaufmann (New York: Penguin, 1976), Third Part, "The Convalescent," sect. 2, 331.
18 *Twilight of the Idols*, "Morality as Anti-Nature," sect. 6, 491.
19 *Ecce Homo: How to Become What You Are*, trans. Duncan Large (Oxford: Oxford University Press, 2007), "Why I Am So Wise," 8.
20 See, e.g., Maslow, *Toward a Psychology of Being*, 2nd edn. (New York: Van Nostrand Reinhold Co., 1968).

21   Solomon, *Living With Nietzsche: What the Great "Immoralist" Has to Teach Us* (Oxford: Oxford University Press, 2003), 85.

22   *Beyond Good and Evil*, "Introduction," 23.

23   Ibid., "On the Prejudices of Philosophers," sect. 13, 44, and "What is Noble?," sect. 259, 194.

24   Ibid., 194.

25   Ibid., 194.

26   On this type or notion of will to power see John Richardson, *Nietzsche's System* (Oxford: Oxford University Press, 1996).

27   *Genealogy of Morals*, I, esp. section 11. A much more detailed account of this form of will to power occurs in Chapter 9 (section 9.4) below.

28   As a result, I reject Lester C. Hunt's view in *Nietzsche and the Origin of Virtue* (London: Routledge, 1991) that Nietzsche "evaluates the worth of persons on the basis of a single standard: the degree to which they have attained what he calls power" on two main grounds. Power is not the only goal of "will to power" and attaining power where it occurs may manifest or express a distorted, weak, or unhealthy form.

29   *Genealogy of Morals*, I, 13, 29.

30   In this respect, Nietzsche is like Hume, who rejected "free will" as an illusion of metaphysics, but in a commonsense way was a compatibilist.

31   *Beyond Good and Evil*, "On the Prejudices of Philosophers," sect. 21, 51.

32   I thank Rosalind Hursthouse for expressing this worry to me.

33   I discuss these forms of distorted will to power in Chapter 7.

34   White, *Nietzsche and the Problem of Sovereignty* (Urbana: University of Illinois Press, 1997), 128.

35   *Beyond Good and Evil*, "On the Prejudices of Philosophers," sect. 23, 54.

36   Ibid., 53.

37   Fromm, *The Anatomy of Human Destructiveness* (New York: Holt, Rinehart and Winston, 1973).

38   *Beyond Good and Evil*, "The Free Spirit," sect. 32, 62.

39   Ibid., 63.

40   Ibid., 63.

41   *Daybreak*, Book 2, sect. 145, 91–92.

42   Ibid., sect. 133, 84.

43   Ibid., sect. 134, 85.

44   Immanuel Kant, *The Metaphysics of Morals*, trans. and ed. Mary Gregor (Cambridge: Cambridge University Press, 1996), "The Doctrine of Virtue," para. 34, 205.

45   Horney, *Neurosis and Human Growth: The Struggle Toward Self-Realization* (New York: Norton, 1970), 292.

46   *Ecce Homo*, "Why I Am So Wise," sect. 6, 13.

47   *Twilight of the Idols*, "Expeditions of an Untimely Man," sect. 34, 86.

48   *Beyond Good and Evil*, "Our Virtues," sect. 219, 149.

49   *Daybreak*, Book 1, sect. 80, 48.

50   *Beyond Good and Evil*, "What is Noble?," sect. 260, 205.

51   Erich Fromm, *The Art of Loving* (London: Unwin Paperbacks, 1975), 26.

52   *Thus Spoke Zarathustra*, First Part, "On the Gift-Giving Virtue," 186–187.

53   Solomon, *Living with Nietzsche*, 172.

54   See *Daybreak*, Book 2, sect. 148.

55   "The Structure of Neurosis," in *Alfred Adler, Superiority and Social Interest: A Collection of Later Writings*, ed. Heinz L. Ansbacher and Rowena R. Ansbacher (Evanston, IL: Northwestern University Press, 1964), 90.

56   *Neurosis and Human Growth*, 97. The confusion between egocentric "neurotic" pride and solid self-confidence (self-esteem or self-love proper) receives an excellent modern discussion in Roy F. Baumeister, "Violent Pride," *Scientific American* 284(4) (2001), 96–101, 82–87. For further discussion of this distinction see my *Virtue Ethics: A Pluralistic View* (Oxford: Oxford University Press, 2003), 191–192.

57   *Thus Spoke Zarathustra*, Third Part, "Upon the Mount of Olives," 287.

58 *Beyond Good and Evil*, "The Free Spirit," sect. 26, 57.
59 Julian Young, *Nietzsche's Philosophy of Religion* (Cambridge: Cambridge University Press, 2006), 46.
60 *Thus Spoke Zarathustra*, First Part, sect. 4, 127–128.
61 Hampton, "Selflessness and Loss of Self," *Social Philosophy and Policy* 10 (1993), 135–165.
62 *Nietzsche's Philosophy of Religion*, 4 ff.
63 Conant, "Nietzsche's Perfectionism: A Reading of *Schopenhauer as Educator*," in *Nietzsche's Postmoralism: Essays on Nietzsche's Prelude to Philosophy's Future*, ed. Richard Schacht (Cambridge: Cambridge University Press, 2001), 181–257, 187.
64 Ibid., 187.
65 Ibid., 187.
66 "Schopenhauer as Educator," in *Untimely Meditations*, trans. R.J. Hollingdale (Cambridge: Cambridge University Press, 1983), sect. 1, 127.
67 Ibid., 128.
68 *Beyond Good and Evil*, "What is Noble?," sect. 258, 193.
69 Ibid., sect. 257, 192.
70 "Schopenhauer as Educator," sect. 6, 162.
71 As argued by Conant, "Nietzsche's Perfectionism." In support of this argument, Conant cites the following passage: "It is a task of history to be the mediator between these [great] individuals and thus again and again to inspire and lend the strength for the production of the greater human being. No, *the goal of humanity* cannot lie in its end, but only *in its highest exemplars*." ("On the Uses and Disadvantages of History for Life," in *Untimely Meditations*, 111, translation amended by Conant.)

According to this passage, as Conant argues, evolution – history – has as its end the improvement of the type man. However it is not the task of any set of individuals in power to usurp the "function" of history or evolution, *itself* deciding who the splendid types are or might be, or even how they are to be understood. For there lies the path of ossifying ideology, stagnation, or worse. In particular such a splendid type is not to be produced by "breeding," to which as we shall see in Chapter 8 (section 8.3) Nietzsche is vehemently opposed.
72 *Twilight of the Idols*, "Skirmishes of an Untimely Man," sect. 37, 540.

Chapter 7

Can Nietzsche Be Both a Virtue Ethicist and an Existentialist?

7.1 Existentialism and Virtue Ethics

Nietzsche is reasonably seen as an important figure in the continental Existentialist tradition. This fact, it seems, poses large problems for mapping his thought in a virtue ethical way. I shall argue that the existentialist and virtue theoretic strands of Nietzsche's thought can be reconciled by showing that Nietzsche's allusions to virtue and vice have a common theme, later built on by existentialist writers, and the post-Freudian psychoanalytic dissection of the inferiority complex and other forms of neurosis and perversion. The theme is escape from self – from its uniqueness, its freedom, its "genius" (potential for creativity), its suffering, its separateness, its memories, its impotence, its boredom, its vulnerability. We have already seen this theme illustrated in what Nietzsche called rescuing oneself from oneself in others – a symptom of escape from self – through the morality of self-sacrifice. However, throughout his writings, Nietzsche is concerned about escape from self as a quite general psychological phenomenon: "One must learn to love oneself – thus I teach – with a wholesome and healthy love, so that one can bear to be with oneself and need not roam."[1]

As a general phenomenon, escape from self manifests itself in a wide range of circumstances, for example: "Haste is universal because everyone is in flight from himself … [we] live in fear of memory and of turning inward."[2] One kind of understanding of Nietzsche's existentialist thought certainly creates insuperable problems for a virtue ethical reading of him. Julian Young describes it thus: "[Nietzsche] nonetheless retains the Cartesian view of the self as a disconnected, self-sufficient, atomic individual: an individual … with 'free' 'horizons' (GS 343), a blank sheet characterized by nothing but the power of free choice."[3]

The Virtue Ethics of Hume and Nietzsche, First Edition. Christine Swanton.
© 2015 John Wiley & Sons, Ltd. Published 2015 by John Wiley & Sons, Ltd.

Free (in a sense), disconnected and self-sufficient (to an extent) human beings may be, but a blank sheet? Not on Nietzsche's view. The "sheet" can hardly be blank when Nietzsche repeatedly emphasizes the self's hidden depths. We need to take seriously Nietzsche's view of himself as a psychologist (see Chapter 1) and his claim that value resides in the depths and not on surfaces, discussed in Chapter 6. The depth analysis of value, for example his analysis of resentment (to be discussed in section 7.5) is pivotal to a virtue ethical reading of him. For a virtue is not a surface phenomenon – not a surface intention let alone a mere action or choice, but a disposition of character embracing at least motivational and affective states, including those not transparent. Nietzsche quite routinely and generally characterizes our behavior in virtue and vice terms, embracing a much broader range of phenomena than the self-sacrifice of altruism, and the "overflowing" other-regarding virtues. The depth psychological analysis of virtue will be here applied more generally.

Before I undertake this task, I need to show how Nietzsche's existentialist strands provide ethical insights compatible with virtue ethics, for existentialism itself is standardly thought to be rather devoid of moral content. Though existentialism does not necessarily provide a complete ethics, its central focus or question is nonetheless the same as Aristotle's: what are the fundamental flaws to which humans are subject, inhibiting their prospects of living a good or meaningful life? And how should those flaws be remedied or avoided?

For Aristotle, a fundamental problem of the human condition is our tendencies to hedonism: so temperance is an important virtue. Without temperance, according to Aristotle, we go wrong in our handling of all the "external goods": money, power, honors, friends. In much existentialist thought, integrity and moral/intellectual courage are fundamental, for these correct our variously expressed tendencies to escape the self by living the inauthentic, comfortable, cowardly life of the "they," the herd, within the conventions and ceremonies of religion or social roles. The concerns of existentialists – despair, the sense of absurdity or pointlessness, fear of freedom – were not the concerns of Aristotle.

Existentialist thought, then, like Aristotelian thought, is targeted on central tendencies and failings in human beings for which the cultivation of certain attitudes is a corrective.[4] The central common thread is the emphasis on the individual: the profound sense in which she is not just a mere part of a comforting and comfortable whole, the responsibility that this entails, and the anxiety and fear that is its concomitant. For Kierkegaard, the religious commitment is not just a matter of being part of a tradition, but involves "fear and trembling" in one's passionate and personal commitment to faith. For Heidegger, the individual's greatest task and fear is facing her own death, which essentially has to be done on her own. For Sartre, the real terror is freedom, and personal responsibility for one's own choices, as opposed to passive acquiescence in role duties and expectations. For Camus, the problem is the ultimate absurdity and meaninglessness of one's life, and the individual's personal task is to face this fact, and take a suitable fearless approach to it.

Nietzsche is squarely within this tradition. The comforting and comfortable whole from which the individual must extricate herself is the mediocre herd into which the "last man" sinks without trace into a quagmire of passivity and will-lessness. Creativity is the energizer which allows the individual to escape from hedonism, comfort, and mediocrity. Expressed thus, is the existentialist tradition in general at odds with virtue ethics? My answer is: No. In fact I will go further. Virtue ethics in the analytic tradition would do well to supplement itself with a discussion of many of the insights of continental thought. For its own distinctive take on human problems considerably enriches the discussion of virtues needed as "correctives" to characteristic human weaknesses. Let me provide some illustrations.

Both Kierkegaard and Camus focus on a proper attitude towards the features of individual lives which make us, as individuals, seem absurd, worthless, insignificant. Kierkegaard's answer is to have a proper attitude to the subjective, through commitment and involvement in the "warp and woof"[5] of life, and to avoid the perspective of what I have called hyperobjective vice – the disposition to see the world, intellectually and emotionally, from the perspective of the Cosmos, the world-historical, of one detached from all personal features, including her bonds and commitments.[6] A master of portraying hyperobjective vice is Camus. One's work is seen as meaningless since it cannot be differentiated from the meaningless activity of Sisyphus. From the perspective of the Cosmos all is equally meaningless or insignificant. One's friends are seen as not really friends because they are just, fundamentally, undifferentiated persons:

> I say "my friends" moreover as a convention. I have no more friends; I have nothing but accomplices. To make up for this their number has increased; they are the whole human race. And within the human race, you first of all. Whoever is at hand is always the first.[7]

Camus attempts to portray a proper disposition towards the temptations described. The perspective of the Cosmos – the "point of view of Sirius"[8] as he puts it – is the intellectually correct perspective. The vice consists in taking this perspective seriously at an emotional level, falling into despair as a consequence. Virtue consists in laying "one's heart open to the benign indifference of the universe,"[9] in fully embracing the absurd by rebelling randomly against all and sundry, in realizing that life will be "lived all the better if it has no meaning." For him, "Living is keeping the absurd alive."[10] Hope is not a virtue, for this attitude has to "involve the certainty of a crushing fate, without the resignation that ought to accompany it."[11]

Kierkegaard's solution is superior in my view, because Camus's insistence that the hyperobjective perspective of Sirius is the correct objective perspective leads him to embrace an *emotional-practical* solution to potential despair that I have called hypersubjectivity[12] – an endorsement of the lifestyles of the absurd in which resignation gives license to self-indulgence and lack of restraint. Kierkegaard contrasts the life of commitment, the properly objective life, to the aimless "aesthetic" lifestyle of hypersubjectivity, and the hyperobjective stance of the world-historical.

Heidegger's discussion of being-toward-death also concerns the proper attitude to a fundamental problem of the human condition. If, in the contemplation of one's death, one immerses oneself in the "they" (*das Man*, Heidegger's term for the collectivity of which one is a member, under an aspect where individuals are relatively undifferentiated), one also manifests a form of hyperobjective vice – "indifferent tranquility as to the 'fact' that one dies."[13] "The 'they' does not permit us the courage of anxiety in the face of death" but rather a "constant tranqillization" because one experiences dying as "in no case is it I myself," and death "belongs to nobody in particular." Fleeing in this way needs to be replaced by the "courage of anxiety," which is distinguished from its perverted form, "cowardly fear."[14] The courage of anxiety is occasioned by the realization that our being is essentially one for which we have a "concern." To flee from this concern is to have the wrong perspective on our nature: it is to think of ourselves wrongly as beings which simply occur. Heidegger's discussion thus highlights an important virtue – intellectual and moral courage.

Sartre's emphasis on freedom and personal responsibility for choice also highlights the virtues of moral courage and integrity. In his famous discussion of the waiter, Sartre illustrates the latter virtue. The discussion does not advocate a lack of commitment to being in a role: on the contrary, the authentic waiter of integrity is one who does not see the role as a game in which one "plays" at being a waiter. One should not see one's job through the eyes merely of convention, or ceremony, which are demanded by, as Heidegger would put it, *das Man*. There is nothing wrong with fulfilling the function of a waiter, there is something wrong with doing so mechanically, for then one infects one's being a waiter with "nothingness," in the way that a pupil who "exhausts himself in playing the attentive role"[15] "ends up by no longer hearing anything."[16] As Sartre puts it, I would then be a waiter "in the mode of *being what I am not.*"[17] Sartre is not advocating a light-minded or irresponsible desertion of others or dereliction of role duties. Suddenly abandoning one's employer on the grounds of existential insight is not a mark of courage or integrity, but is narcissistic. An opposed role-related vice, also at odds with authenticity and integrity as an individual, is to allow a role to take over one's life, as is brilliantly portrayed in *The Remains of the Day.*[18]

Integrity, then, is the expression of practical choice as opposed to a drifting into modes of behavior and comportment which deny, or are an escape from, self. Like Aristotle's practical wisdom, integrity is the precondition or core of virtue, though not necessarily the whole of virtue.[19]

7.2   The Motif of Escape from Self and the World

As we have seen, a core motif in Nietzsche's depth psychology is escape from self and the world, a motif that is central to existential thought. I have suggested then that the individualism of existentialism in Nietzsche's incarnation is compatible with a virtue ethics having as a central focus virtues of strength so one can "bear to be with oneself" and not "roam." In this chapter, escape from self and world will be explored as a distortion of will to power, which as we have seen is for Nietzsche at the heart of a "developmental psychology" exploring the human need to expand, grow, and develop into a mature state. As we saw in the last chapter, mature development of the individual, with her "morality of the mature individual," is contrasted by Nietzsche both with immature forms of egoism and an immature form of failure to "cultivate the personal" in one. Mature development is associated with forms of strength, health, life affirmation, and virtue.

Although there are many forms of escape from self and the world I shall focus in subsequent sections on four major types of distortion which provide the main themes of the *Genealogy of Morals*. These are the perversion of cruelty, the neurosis of cruel punitivism, the neurosis of resentment, and the resignatory neurosis of the ascetic ideal.[20] In all four areas, virtue can be understood as having at its core self-affirmation or self-love, and vice self-hate and escape from self. That is, at a depth psychological level, virtue can be seen as expressive of a self-loving attitude and vice the reverse.[21] It is not suggested that all virtue for Nietzsche is reducible to self-love, and vice to self-hate. Still less is it suggested that the *targets* of all these virtues are self-love, self-improvement, or self-overcoming. That is not the target of "overflowing" generosity for example. The field of that virtue is not the self but others, and its target is often for Nietzsche *others'* improvement. Rather the strengths of self-affirmation or self-love are at the core of virtue: they underpin a wide range of virtues having a wide range of targets or aims.

For example, as we explore further in the next chapter, the strong forgetfulness of the person of grace and "mild" justice is distinguished from that kind of forgetfulness which is an opiate designed to repress the past. Again strong forgetfulness (of slights and harms) is contrasted with the wounding of an egocentric narcissism, expressed in, for example, rage and vengefulness. Envy with its self-referential comparisons, prominent even in pity, undermines the creative spirit. Cleverness, a self-effacing, manipulative, secretive, and even self-deceptive form of "wisdom,"[22] is distinguished from the wisdom of the strong, described thus: "Even the bravest of us rarely has the courage for what he really *knows*."[23] "*Measure of wisdom*. – Growth in wisdom can be measured precisely by decline in bile."[24] The self-effacing clever, the "men of resentment," are full of bile; as one gains in strength, the "poisonous eye" of resentment diminishes, allowing for a cleaner lens with which to view the world.

There are a great variety of virtues discussed by Nietzsche that are expressive of the strength of self-love, but easily confused with correlative vices. As we have seen, the gift-giving virtues are contrasted with pity, where the self "*languishes*"[25] (through escape into otherness). The "loneliness" of solitude (escape from the sick)[26] is not to be confused with the loneliness of resignation and withdrawal (escape of the sick). (Limited) friendship is distinguished from an inability to be alone, manifested in excessive sociability: "We are afraid that when we are alone and quiet something will be whispered into our ear, and so we hate quietness and deafen ourselves with sociability."[27] Hastiness – a form of escape from self – is not to be confused with the overflowing urgent passion of creativity. Discipline is to be distinguished from self-flagellating asceticism (escape from the flesh), and from laziness and pleasure-seeking (escape from one's potential "for genius," for creativity).

Virtues of integrity and joyfulness displayed towards the world in all its particularity, messiness, and commonplace features, are opposed to the "resignatory" vices, including the philosopher's vice of escape into a world of purity, simplification, abstraction, and systematicity: "I mistrust all systematizers and I avoid them. The will to a system is a lack of integrity."[28]

Let us now investigate in a more detailed way the psychology that provides what Nietzsche in *Beyond Good and Evil*, section 23 calls "*the development-theory of the will to power*" and through which he theorizes the nature of virtue. Several key ideas are at the heart of will to power as a *developmental* theory, ideas that will be further elucidated in this section with the help of later psychologists influenced by Nietzsche, notably Erich Fromm[29] and Alfred Adler.[30] These are:

(1) The key psychological concept of Nietzsche's developmental psychology is "will to power" as opposed to the Pleasure Principle or the libido.
(2) Distortions of will to power are understood as forms of escape from the self and the world in "life thwarting" or "life denying" ways.
(3) These distortions can be seen in characterological terms.

These basic Nietzschean ideas are further developed by psychologists such as Fromm, Horney, and Adler, who will be used to clarify Nietzsche's own psychology. In a way reminiscent of Nietzsche, Erich Fromm distinguishes between "life-furthering syndrome" and "life-thwarting syndrome."[31] As with Nietzsche, for Fromm alienation from self is destructive of life affirmation. Fromm provides a deep existentialist explanation of our tendencies to escape from self. A human's distinctive capacity of self-awareness creates for him a problem. A human being is "the only animal for whom his own existence is a problem that he has to solve and which he cannot escape."[32] "He is set apart while being apart; he is homeless, yet chained to the home he shares with all creatures ... Being aware of himself, he realizes his powerlessness and the limitations of his existence."[33]

Nietzsche himself frequently emphasizes the loneliness and apartness of the "higher man," but rather than burying himself in the comforting embrace of the herd, for him living with that apartness is a way of solving the problem of existence in a productive way.

Adler, as well as Fromm, understands development through an interpretation of Nietzsche's "will to power." As Madelaine Ganz points out, as is "well known," "far from setting up sexuality as the main principle of interpretation, as Freud had done, Adler relegated it to an importance secondary to that of will to power (Machtstreben)."[34] Taking his cue from Nietzsche's understanding of the will to power as the "will" or striving to grow and vent strength, Adler understands it variously as "a striving, an urge, a developing"; "It is always a matter of overcoming."[35] He also calls it a "striving for perfection," an "upward striving."[36] At the heart of this idea is the notion of "striving" for development: "to live means to develop."[37]

As we have seen, according to Adler's use of Nietzsche's notion of will to power the strivings associated with development are more importantly associated with feelings of power (and powerlessness) than sexual instincts. For Adler the basic notion of power has two poles: the "inferiority feeling" inevitably caused by the powerlessness of the infant, and the striving for development manifested in the striving for power broadly understood. The basic facts of the infant's powerlessness combined with the strength of his desires, which outrun his own capacity to satisfy, as well as the environmental and physical vicissitudes which beset him, are the background conditions of psychic conflict. However the driver of psychic conflict is the *incompatibility* of instincts, strivings, or impulses[38] which may or may not be overcome. The actual inferiority of the child is not itself the problem: "The actual inferiority of the child, important as it is for his psychic economy, is no criterion of the weight of his feeling of insecurity and inferiority, since these depend largely on his interpretation of them."[39]

Psychic conflict becomes problematic through interpretations which form a "crystallized" or characterological orientation to the world. Interpretations become "consolidated" forming a "crystallized norm or 'constant of self-estimation'"[40] and may or may not be error-ridden and problematic. If the child's goals are expressed through error-ridden interpretation and compensating strategies of various kinds, psychological problems occur.[41] Such consolidation is the "inferiority complex" in its various forms. In one general manifestation of the complex, however, "the danger arises that in his strivings for compensation, he will be satisfied not with a simple restoration of the balance of power; he will demand an over-compensation."[42] In this case, the "striving for power and dominance may become so exaggerated and intensified that it must be called pathological."[43] If psychic conflict is not a force for further development, it can resolve itself into the "inferiority complex" and its "sister" phenomenon, the superiority complex.

I have shown in very general terms how Nietzsche's existentialist theme of the strength not to escape from self and the world (self-love), encapsulated in his notion of will to power and its distortions, can be understood in virtue theoretic, characterological terms. Let us now fill out this picture by discussing the four types of distorted will to power identified above.

7.3   The Perversion of Cruelty

We consider now a type of immature egoism identified by Nietzsche in *Human, All Too Human*,[44] namely an unsocialized type of egoism where others in a very basic way are not treated with respect. This is the "perversion" of cruelty.

Many writing on Nietzsche think that for Nietzsche (a) we have a "basic instinct" for cruelty and (b) that it is healthy for this instinct to be manifested. This view is at the heart of immoralist interpretations of Nietzsche. I shall argue on the contrary that for Nietzsche we have a basic instinct not for cruelty but for aggression, which, in the words of Erich Fromm,[45] can be manifested in benign or malignant ways. How does this relate to Nietzsche's discussion of, in particular, noble morality in Essay I of the *Genealogy of Morals*?

According to a standard view, represented by Brian Leiter, for Nietzsche, "the instinct for cruelty is … a fundamental human instinct";[46] "humans are naturally cruel."[47] Along with this reading goes the natural assumption that the expression of fundamental instincts is for Nietzsche healthy, whereas their repression naturally unhealthy. But what is this fundamental instinct that can be healthily expressed? Both Freud and Fromm refer to this instinct as aggressiveness, which can have distorted forms. If the "fundamental instinct" is not cruelty but aggression, it is left open that cruelty may be a distorted form of will to power, specifically that fundamental form of venting strength, aggression. Along these lines, Fromm distinguishes between defensive "benign aggression" which operates "in the service of the survival of the individual and the species"[48] and "malignant aggression" "i.e. *destructiveness and cruelty*," which has no purpose and whose satisfaction is lustful and pleasurable.[49] Fromm denies that "defensive aggression" is an "'innate' instinct" though he claims it is part of human nature.

Can this reading be applied to Nietzsche? I believe it can. First it should be noted that when Nietzsche says that cruelty is natural and indeed pleasurable he means that it is usual and common, even if distorted or at least not something "natural" to the mature, "higher" individual. Recall after all that for Nietzsche we are "the most chronically and deeply sick of all the sick animals."[50] Undistorted will to power is not a "natural" condition given the vicissitudes humans face in their development, particularly for Nietzsche the internalization of the attitudes and values of a sick culture, suffered by the "Europeans" and Germans. Fromm calls such sickness "a shared pathology – the 'pathology of normalcy.'"[51]

On Nietzsche's account of the cruelty of the nobles in the *Genealogy of Morals* cruelty is a form of regression. They [the nobles] "*regress* to the innocence of the predator's conscience," engaging without qualm in a "horrific succession of murder, arson, violence, and torture, as if it were nothing more than a student prank."[52] In short the cruelty of the nobles is for Nietzsche a form of malignant aggression as Fromm describes it – lustful, pleasurable, and having no purpose. The perpetrators experience a "horrific serenity and deep pleasure in all destruction."[53] The root cause of this regression is the unbearable frustration caused by the social constraints; those of "custom, respect, usage, gratitude … consideration, self control, tenderness, fidelity, pride, and friendship."[54] The "tension" produced by these social constraints, and the need for freedom from them, require the invention of a category of the outside world: foreigners toward whom the nobles can behave as "predators on the rampage."[55] They leave "the concept 'barbarian' in their wake."[56]

It is puzzling that the social constraints should be seen as fetters. Nietzsche does not tarry over the issue, though he does speak of "the tension built up over a long period of confinement and enclosure."[57] But why should there be tension? Fromm proposes a deep-seated boredom as an explanation: "The motive for these killings [just described] does not seem to be hate, but ... an unbearable sense of boredom and impotence." The escape from self in cruelty on this view is an escape from boredom. What Fromm calls "psychic scarcity," where there is no or inadequate stimulation, generates (given other conditions) the manifestation of "vital power-lessness" constituting boredom.[58] The connection between boredom and impotence results in a particular kind of solution to psychic conflict: on an Adlerian will to power explanation there has been overcompensation for a sense of impotence and a consequent expansive drive for superiority. Note that neither for Fromm nor for Nietzsche is cruelty (of the kind exhibited by the "nobles") sourced in hate; that is the emotional orientation of the men of resentment; the priests, "the very greatest haters of world history."[59]

Whatever is the deeper cause of cruelty, it is a form of regression to immature states. Regression is a concept later employed in psychoanalytic writings to connote a reverting to and a fixation on immature or infantile modes, which block progress to maturity. Such regression is a result of psychic conflict generated by the vicissitudes of stress in the external world, or in Freud's view, sexual problems.[60] Nietzsche's portrayal of the cruelty of the nobles conforms quite remarkably to Freud's account of regression, and the aetiology of "perversion" and "neurosis" which we might sketch as follows.

For the kinds of reasons proposed above, the noble individuals are subject to frustration in the external world; the social constraints are experienced as fetters. The ensuing psychic conflict can be resolved in several ways, comprising endurance, sublimation, perversion, or neurosis. These methods of resolving conflict are elucidated by Wollheim.[61] The individual can "endure frustration"; he can "divert his desires into a social form genetically connected with their existing form, that is, he can sublimate them"; or he can "regress" or "move backwards down the path of ... development"[62] (for Freud, libidinal development). At the "fixation" point to which the individual has regressed, there are further psychic alternatives, "perversion" or "neurosis." If the individual gains satisfaction "in the more primitive mode" then what we have is a "perversion" and not yet a "neurosis." In this technical sense the cruelty of the nobles is a "perverted" form of distorted will to power rather than a neurotic one; indeed for Nietzsche, the nobles are described as "rejoicing monsters."[63] Their cruelty is thus seen as a "perversion" of aggression. Anticipating Freudian dynamic psychology, Nietzsche claims that "the energy of this hidden core [the predatory animal instincts] needs to be discharged from time to time, the animal must emerge again."[64]

A potential problem arises as a result of Nietzsche reserving the term "sick" for neurosis rather than perversion. He even describes men such as Caesar Borgia as "tropical monsters and growths"; as beasts of prey and as such "healthy."[65] In this description Nietzsche is clearly distinguishing the true account of the cruel nature of men such as Caesar Borgia from those mistaken views that their cruelty is a form of "inborn 'hell' in them." In other words he is denying that it is a neurosis in the sense described above, but is rather an uninhibited, pleasurable, discharge of "instincts" expressive of a need to "vent one's strength." However we must recognize that on this usage, "healthy" (non-neurotic) will to power can be a form of perverted distorted will to power.[66]

I have argued that for Nietzsche the cruelty of the "nobles" is a distorted, regressive, but non-neurotic form of one aspect of "will to power," aggression. By contrast with cruelty, aggression is necessary if life as development is to proceed, for as Nietzsche claims, the world lacks any benign order congenial to our interests. Recall Fromm's notion of "benign aggression," necessary for self-preservation and continuance of the species. However it is a confusion to think that for Nietzsche, just as the world is harsh and cruel, so individuals have license to be harsh and cruel by virtue of the fact that a correct response to a harsh world must be radically individualistic, egoistic, even capricious and arbitrary. Rather we are fated to develop and mature in an environment full of vicissitudes, as Adler would put it. Maturation in that environment requires endurance and overcoming, not a kind of "imitation" of harshness.

7.4   The Neurosis of Cruel Punitivism

Supporting his view that for Nietzsche, "the instinct for cruelty is ... a fundamental human instinct," Leiter cites Freud's views of the "tension between the harsh superego and the ego that is subjected to it, often called the sense of guilt"[67] expressed in the claim that "[man's] aggressiveness is introjected, internalized; it is, in point of fact, sent back to where it came from – that is, it is directed towards his own ego."[68] I argue here that in similar vein Nietzsche describes another form of distortion of aggression in his account of the origins of bad conscience; cruelty turned inwards.[69]

I argued above that perverted cruelty is for Nietzsche a non-neurotic form of will to power. As a form of regression however it is distorted, involving an escape from self, in particular the frustrations of social constraint and the boredom that these bring. It is thus an immature form of egoism in the form of pleasure-seeking instant gratification, though not of the comfort-seeking kind characterizing the "herd."

By contrast, a neurotic regression to cruelty would occur only if the individual forbids himself the untrammeled satisfaction of the primitive desires.[70] Nietzsche saves his account of neurotic manifestations of the cruel impulse for Essay II, where he describes the turning inward of "hostility, cruelty, pleasure in persecution, in assault, in change, in destruction"[71] as a form of mistreating the self. Here we are not describing perverted cruelty, but neurotic "symptoms." In neurotic manifestations, cruelty transforms into what Freud calls symptoms, something other than cruelty itself as normally understood. Here, there is no free, non-forbidden venting of "instincts," specifically that particular "instinct of freedom" ("in my terminology: the will to power")[72] to dominate through cruelty. Rather there is a turning of that instinct against the individual himself. "Every instinct that does not vent itself externally *turns inwards*."[73] Essay II is devoted to an account and aetiology of a prime symptom of that turning inwards: the "illness,"[74] the "deep sickness"[75] of bad conscience:

> This instinct of freedom made latent through force – as we have already understood – this instinct of freedom, forced back, trodden down, incarcerated within and ultimately still venting and discharging itself only upon itself: such is bad conscience at its origin, that and nothing more.[76]

The internalization of cruelty into what Nietzsche calls "psychic cruelty" is for him the most "fearful sickness which up to now has raged in man" namely "the *will* of man to find himself guilty and reprehensible to a point beyond the possibility of atonement, his *will* to think himself punished without the punishment ever being commensurate with his guilt, his *will* to infect and poison things to their very depths with the problem of punishment and guilt."[77]

However the internalized cruelty of bad conscience is but the first stage to its externalized form in cruel punitivism, a legitimized form of cruelty. Just as resentment grounded in a form of self-hate as a sense of impotence is manifested in externalized hostility, natural to that sense (see section 7.5), so the desire to punish grounded in a form of self-hate as a sense of guilt or reprehensibility "beyond the possibility of atonement" is manifested in externalized hostility natural to that bad conscience. In this case hostility takes the form of a rigorous punitivism, which is basically a compensatory pleasure, and severe to the point of extreme cruelty:

> It is in *this* sphere, in legal obligations, then, that the moral conceptual world of "guilt", "conscience", "duty", "sacred duty" originates – its beginning, like the beginning of everything great on earth, has long been steeped in blood.[78]

This legitimized "blood-letting" occurs because punishment is not basically a rational response of holding the culprit responsible for his crimes, but is sourced in anger:

> Throughout the longest period of human history, punishment was not exacted *because* the trouble-maker was held responsible for his action, that is, it was *not* exacted on the assumption that only the guilty man was to be punished, but rather, just as nowadays parents still punish their children, out of anger at harm done, anger which is then taken out on the person who causes it – albeit held in check and modified by the idea that any damage somehow has an *equivalent* and really can be paid off, even if this is through the *pain* of the culprit.[79]

However, this idea of "equivalence" is a myth, since it can never justify the cruelty of much punishment sourced in vengeful pleasure. Hence this compensation is really just cruelty, albeit cruelty sanitized through moral and legal legitimation:

> ... to what extent can suffering compensate for "debt"? To the extent that *inflicting* pain occasions the greatest pleasure, to the extent that the injured party exchanges for the damage done, together with the displeasure it causes, an extraordinary pleasure which offsets it.[80]

So this compensation consists in an entitlement and right to cruelty.[81]

Both perverted cruelty and the neurotic symptoms of repressed cruel impulses turned inwards and externalized as cruel punishment, need to be distinguished from sublimated tendencies or potential tendencies to cruelty, in Wollheim's sense. In this kind of sublimation there is no regression to actual cruelty in either a neurotic or perverted form, but there is rather a "transformation" of aggressive instincts or desires "into something ever more spiritual and 'divine', a process which runs through the whole history of higher culture."[82] For example in civilizing processes, the need for cruelty to vitalize festivals and entertainments, and to make a festivity of punishment, has gradually abated. In former times, Nietzsche claims, it was impossible to conceive of a noble household "without a creature upon whom one could vent one's malice and cruel teasing."[83] There used to be "no festivity without cruelty" and "even in relatively recent times" important festivities "were inconceivable without executions, torture."[84] The frustrations which might lead to forms of cruelty are transformed and civilized. As Wollheim puts it, desires are "diverted" into a "social form genetically connected with their existing form."

It may be thought that my understanding of Nietzsche's view of the cruelty of the nobles and the different form of cruelty in punishment just described, as forms of *distorted* will to power, contrasted with sublimated aggression as described above, founders on Nietzsche's claim that higher moralities or culture have been founded on cruelty, albeit in "sublimated" form. In *Beyond Good and Evil* Nietzsche claims that what we call "higher culture" is "based on the spiritualization and intensification of *cruelty*."[85] Two things should however be noted. The "higher culture" described is hardly admirable; it is *what we call* higher culture. Second, the cruelty referred to is not a non-neurotic *sublimated* tendency or potential tendency to cruelty in Wollheim's sense but a neurotic "*spiritualized*" cruelty against the self manifested in "desensualization, decarnalization, contrition" and "puritanical spasms of repentance."[86] This form of asceticism is discussed in section 7.6. Suffice to say here that that particular distorted form is not sublimation where aggression and frustrated desire is transformed into something valuable. Recall that in the above analysis, one option for dealing with frustration is not to turn "instincts" of aggression into regressive cruelty but either to endure that frustration or to sublimate it in a healthy way, allowing a person to proceed with her creative, productive life in a mature manner.[87] As we shall see below when we discuss asceticism, both healthy sublimation and neurotic "spiritualization" share the feature that desires are transformed into something putatively "higher" but only the latter kind is a distortion of will to power. Indeed, the capacity to endure or sublimate healthily is precisely one of the hallmarks of the higher individual.

7.5   The Neurosis of Resentment

Section 7.3 described the cruelty of the "nobles" as a form of what Adler would call a superiority complex. By contrast, in resentment, the other pole of the will to power – a feeling of inferiority – is dominant. This is made clear at the beginning of the *Genealogy of Morals* where Nietzsche describes the cultural and individual aetiology of resentment as a reaction of those who are powerless in the situation in which they find themselves. Nietzsche's account of a culture based on resentment takes the form of a "genealogy" having several stages. The *dramatis personae* are the "priests" of "slave" morality, and the "knightly-aristocratic" types of "noble" morality.

(1) According to Nietzsche's genealogy of resentment, "good" originally meant "having a refined soul," "'noble' in the sense of 'superior in soul," "privileged in soul."[88]

(2) The "noble" in this sense of "good" "felt themselves to be men of higher rank."[89]

(3) Those of higher rank thought of themselves as powerful, "the masters": "the most frequent practice is perhaps for those of higher rank to name themselves according to their superiority in matters of power ... or according to the most visible sign of this superiority, as, for example, 'the wealthy' 'the owners' ..."[90]

(4) Such a person labels himself as one who is truthful, who has reality, who is true or genuine (compare "true courage" with "true gold").

(5) By contrast we have the "forgery and self-deception of the impotence" of the priests: those of "slave morality."[91]

(6) This powerlessness of self-hate is externalized: "Priests are the most powerless, from powerlessness their hatred grows to take on a monstrous and sinister shape."[92]

(7) The "shape" is "sinister" because the externalized self-hate takes the form of resentment where the inferiority pole of will to power becomes dominant, manifesting in secretive and untruthful ways:

> [The man of resentment] is neither upright nor naïve in his dealings with others, nor is he open and honest with himself.
>
> His soul *squints*; his mind loves bolt-holes, secret paths, back doors, he regards all hidden things as *his* world, *his* security, *his* refreshment; he has a perfect understanding of how to keep silent, how not to forget, how to wait, how to make himself provisionally small and submissive.[93]

Emotionally such a person is characterized by "the downtrodden and surreptitiously smouldering emotions of revenge and hatred."[94]

(8) The moral/cultural manifestation of this externalized self-hate of impotence is the "reversal of the aristocratic value equation (good = noble = powerful = beautiful = happy = blessed)"[95] constituting the "slave revolt in morals" which "begins when resentment itself becomes creative and ordains values: the resentment of creatures to whom the real reaction, that of deed is denied."[96] Here, "impotent failure to retaliate is to be transformed into 'goodness.'"[97] The weak for whom it is good if they refrain from doing anything for which they lack sufficient strength interpret their weakness, "the way they simply are as merit."[98] In general terms the reversal of values has the following form: "the miserable alone are the good; the poor, the powerless, the low alone are the good. The suffering, the deprived, the sick, the ugly are the only pious ones."[99]

(9) Finally and crucially for the moral revolution there is a reversal or change in the understanding of the "thick" concepts and even the nature of psychological and other conditions of persons. For example not only are patience, chastity, cowardly fear, submissiveness elevated into virtues, but the understanding of their nature as virtues is also thoroughly transformed. Thus not only is cowardly fear transformed into the virtue of humility, the understanding of humility as a virtue is itself skewed. It is now a form of self-abasement as opposed to a sense of one's place in the world that is not tainted by forms of overweening pride. Nietzsche cites the following examples: fear (cowardice) is transformed into humility; "submission to those one hates into 'obedience'"; "the inevitability of his being made to wait" is understood as "'patience', that is as virtue *as such*"; "the inability to take revenge is called the refusal to take revenge, perhaps even forgiveness";[100] conditions of poverty, chastity, and lowliness are dignified by their association with virtues of abstemiousness and self-abnegation: the virtuous maintenance of a poverty-stricken state, chastity as a form of self-denial, humility as self-abasement.[101]

Resentment is understood by Nietzsche as an individual neurosis that is reinforced by the rise of Christian ethics in its cultural manifestation (whether or not this cultural manifestation expresses a proper understanding of that ethics). This rise in turn reinforces resentment at an individual level. How is it a neurosis? It is essentially a form of repression manifesting as externalized self-hate, where a fundamental desire to be "good" in the "aristocratic" sense is repressed because one's manifest impotence is too painful. It is thus one of the several forms of fleeing from self – in this case an escape from one's sense of impotence. As Bernard Reginster[102] puts it, the person of resentment on Nietzsche's understanding becomes inhibited by a feeling of incurable impotence, while retaining his "pride" or "arrogance" and a desire at some level to lead a life of nobility and strength.[103] This constitutes a dynamic conflict between two incompatible desires: a desire at some level to lead a life of strength, nobility, or achievement, and a sense of oneself as impotent and inferior. The psychic conflict created by the gap between one's "ego ideal" and one's sense of impotence creates a need for resolution. The resolution of resentment is an *escape* from one's sense of impotence in the sense that the conflict between that sense and expansive strivings is not resolved by a full (self-loving) acceptance of one's objectively-based weakness, which can then be worked on in processes of self-overcoming within a framework of acceptance of what cannot be changed. Rather the "solution" of resentment valorizes the weak reversal of value and understanding of virtue, but at the same time fails to overcome one's sense of oneself as impotent. Resentment is thus an expressive phenomenon; it expresses a psychological state of conflict.[104] At a cultural level we get "the slave revolt in morals."

The self-hate of resentment, as Nietzsche discusses it, then, has two main features:

(1) It is externalized in a hostile way, for it is manifested in forms of bringing others down, which may be subtle (as in pity), or more overt: undermining of others' achievements or ability to take pride in them (the so-called "tall poppy syndrome").[105]

(2) It is self-effacing (as opposed to expansive, to use Karen Horney's terms),[106] since the forms of bringing down are not through cruelty, overt aggression, or conquering.

As Horney puts it, we can distinguish between two forms of externalization as an expression of self-hate: passive, which can be understood as "I am not hostile to others; they are doing things to me" and active, "I am not doing anything to myself but to others and rightly so."[107] Nietzsche makes the same distinction between the reactive man of resentment and the active encroaching individual of cruelty.

7.6   The Resignatory Neurosis of the Ascetic Ideal

Essay III of the *Genealogy of Morals* is devoted to the discussion of a fourth major type of distortion of will to power, that constituted by resignatory forms of escape from self and the world manifested in attraction to the ascetic ideal. This form of neurosis Horney describes as "the appeal of freedom" and that too is how Nietzsche describes it.[108] Those attracted to the "ascetic ideal" are thinking of what is the "'saint' to them ... what is most indispensable to *them*: freedom from compulsion, disturbance, noise, business, duties, worries."[109] This "freedom from," this desire to escape, is spiritualized into a "freedom to": the attainment of an "unnatural ascetic ideal," for example "the highest artistic freedom, artistic transcendence."[110]

What is the ascetic ideal, and what kind of freedom is sought in it? As Nietzsche claims, "the ascetic ideal has meant many things to man."[111] For example he describes Schopenhauer's escape from the world of sensuality as an escape from torture: "he wishes to be *freed from a form of torture*."[112] There are three prime variants of the ascetic ideal; the artistic, the intellectual, and the priestly. Common to all forms however is something fundamental – a need for a certain sort of goal which Nietzsche calls the "preconditions favourable to higher spirituality."[113] In the ascetic ideal however this goal assumes a distorted form. For it involves in this case not an active participation in living where one strives for genuinely higher states of wisdom or aesthetic experience, but an *escape* from the world expressing an "attempt to imagine oneself 'too good' for this world."[114]

Insight into Nietzsche's notion of freedom from psychic conflicts in the form of "spiritualized escape" is gained through Horney's account of a specific kind of neurotic solution to those conflicts: "the solution of resignation." Horney, like Adler and Fromm, espouses a self-realizationist psychology where self-realization is thwarted by "alienation" from self due to an unresolved gap between the "idealized self" and a despised self. The resignatory solution of the intra-psychic conflict "consists essentially in the neurotic's withdrawing from the inner battlefield and declaring himself uninterested."[115]

What are the psychological processes of resignation? For Nietzsche, as we have seen, it involves a quest for a higher spirituality (or its conditions), but confusion may arise because for Nietzsche (and indeed Horney) such a quest has both healthy and unhealthy forms. We need then to contrast a healthy quest for the "preconditions favourable to higher spirituality" from an unhealthy one. As both Horney and Nietzsche describe it there is a distinction between a healthy form of setting higher, more "spiritual" goals and a neurotic "*restriction of wishes*":[116] a process of "shrinking, of restricting, of curtailing life and growth."[117] For Nietzsche, the ascetic ideal (the goal of an *unhealthy* quest for higher spirituality) "*is derived from the protective and healing instincts of a degenerating life.*"[118] Common to different forms of this unhealthy quest are two features: escape, and escape in what Nietzsche calls a "spiritualized" form. As part of a withdrawal from living, the resigned individual becomes detached, and views his life from the "point of view of the 'spectator'"[119] as in the asceticization of aesthetics criticized by Nietzsche.

However "spiritualization" itself is not necessarily associated with an unhealthy escape. Spiritualization as such consists essentially in the refinement and transformation of "lower" desires and instincts into higher more spiritual forms, whether aesthetic, religious, moral, or intellectual, and this may be healthy. Indeed for Nietzsche, the "aesthetic condition" is the "*highest spiritualization and sensualization*"[120] constituted by "a peculiar sweetness and plenitude."[121] In other words "sensualization" is here a form of sensuality refined and made more spiritual: the goal of higher spirituality need not take the form of a "denial of self" or a "crossing out"[122] of the sensual aspect of the self.

In the case of the intellectual person, distorted ascetic "spiritualization" takes the form of hyperobjectivity: seeking freedom from perspective in a quest for pure knowledge. Here the emulation of the "scientific conscience" and the "will to absolute truth" characterize all intellectual endeavors. Science, for Nietzsche, in its absolutist "unconditional" will to preeminence in every enquiry, "rests on the same foundation as the ascetic ideal ... a certain *impoverishment of life* – a cooling of the feelings,"[123] where even the moral and religious sensitivities have been "sublimated" into scientific models of "intellectual hygiene at all costs."[124]

What of the spiritual goals of the ascetic priest? Since resentment is the cardinal mode of distorted will to power of the slave type, it is natural to think that the ascetic priest exemplifies resentment. But the priest is also portrayed as the prime exemplar of what we have called the resignatory neurosis. He manifests "three dangerous dietary prescriptions" of the "religious neurosis": "solitude, fasting and sexual abstinence."[125] As an exemplar of the ascetic ideal the ascetic priest not only instantiates to some extent the ascetic ideals of "poverty, humility, chastity"[126] but with his "domineering spirituality" asserts his powerful will to spiritualization through escape to the desert,[127] an endless search for the thin rarefied air of "purity," both intellectually and physically.

However, resentment and resignation are not the only manifestations of distorted spirituality in the priest. Another is to turn himself into an instrument of protectiveness for and in others. Though the ascetic priest "embodies the desire for another existence, somewhere else" (an aspect of the resignatory neurosis) "the very *power* of this desire is the chain which binds him to this life; this very power transforms him into an instrument, obliged to work to create more favourable conditions for human life as it exists here."[128] He is thus, paradoxically, both an exemplar of slave morality and a leader. However, as leaders, the priests exemplify a form of superiority compensation strategy: a form characterizing the weak. The priests manifest righteous indignation as a chief weapon of the "will of the sick to display *any* form of superiority" – labeled as "this will to power of the weakest" – displaying their "instinct for secret paths which lead to a tyranny over the healthy."[129] In their role as leaders they infect others with their own distortions. For example in combating suffering, "the priest *changes the direction of ressentiment*" of those to whom he ministers, anaesthetizing it rather than allowing the natural tendency of the sick to seek relief in blaming others. Their resentment is thus turned inwards: "*you alone are to blame for yourself!*"[130] As part of the *this*-worldly manifestation of the underlying resignatory neurosis, the priests' mode of power is distorted by resentment: they "wander around among us as living reproaches and warnings – as if health, good constitution, strength, pride, the sense of power were in themselves marks of depravity ... they are all men of *ressentiment*"[131] who "enjoy being suspicious, grumbling over misdeeds and apparent insults."[132] Nor is the priest's medication apt: he combats only suffering itself, and not its cause.[133]

In short the priests manifest several major types of distorted will to power: the self-effacing but externalized hostile form of self-contempt – the solution of resentment (they are slave types); forms of "superiority complex" in their role as cultural leaders; and the resignatory "religious neurosis."

7.7 Conclusion

I have elaborated the psychology of Nietzsche's motif of escape from self with the help of the views of Adler, Fromm, and Horney. On this Nietzschean psychology we can summarize the root cause of failure of self-love as follows.

(1) It is part of the human condition to experience oneself as separate, beset by "the limitations of [one's] existence" and thus impotent.

(2)   At the same time there is a fundamental striving for development, what Nietzsche calls "will to power."

(3)   There is a "gap" at an unconscious level between what Adler calls an ego-ideal and Horney an "idealized self," reflecting a need to grow and be powerful in some way, and a sense of oneself as impotent and falling short of that ideal.

(4)   However, instead of healthy "self-overcoming" where the gap between the self as we are (as relatively limited) and a higher incarnation of ourselves[134] is a positive force for development, various distortions may occur.

(5)   At the heart of these distortions is this: the two poles of a sense of impotence and the "ego-ideal" create an incompatibility between fundamental psychic strivings. Horney, like Adler, makes this clear: "conflict is bound to arise because the neurotic identifies himself *in toto* with his superior proud self, and with his despised self."[135]

(6)   Due to the prevalence and variety of "vicissitudes" that face us, whether congenital or environmental, this psychic conflict is all too common, and is not easy to resolve in a healthy way. Hence we are the "sickest of all sick animals."

(7)   In distorted "will to power" the resolutions of the conflict are in various ways "sick" or otherwise distorted, manifesting the various forms of escape from self of repression and regression.

(8)   As Fromm, Adler, and Horney emphasize, the real problems occur when inappropriate solutions to psychic conflict are expressed in character, for then one's whole orientation to the world, or significant aspects of it, expresses a pattern of distortion.

We have described four major types of distortion of will to power. These underlie a range of vices which are easily confused with virtue if we do not take account of depth psychological springs. The existentialist motif of escape from self has in Nietzsche's hands been transformed into a characterological psychology at home in virtue ethics. We turn next to a discussion of some of the problems of Nietzsche's account of virtue in relation to orthodox Aristotelian accounts.

Notes

1   *Thus Spoke Zarathustra*, in *The Portable Nietzsche*, ed. and trans. Walter Kaufmann (New York: Penguin, 1976), Third Part, "On the Spirit of Gravity," sect. 2, 305.

2   "Schopenhauer as Educator," in *Untimely Meditations*, trans. R.J. Hollingdale (Cambridge: Cambridge University Press, 1983), 158.

3   Young, *The Death of God and the Meaning of Life* (London: Routledge, 2003), 96.

4   I borrow from an extremely useful insight of Philippa Foot's. I am not committed to the details of her analysis, nor to the idea that all virtues should be understood in this way, or that this is all there is to the understanding of virtue. See her "Virtues and Vices," in *Virtues and Vices and Other Essays in Moral Philosophy* (Oxford: Blackwell, 1978), 1–18.

5   *Concluding Unscientific Postscript*, trans. D.F. Swenson and W. Lowrie (Princeton, NJ: Princeton University Press, 1941).

6 See my *Virtue Ethics: A Pluralistic View* (Oxford: Oxford University Press, 1993), chapter 8.

7 From *The Fall*, in *Existentialism*, ed. Robert Solomon (New York: Random House, 1974), 189.

8 Camus, *The Myth of Sisyphus and Other Essays*, trans. Justin O'Brien (New York: Vintage Books, 1955), 58.

9 From *The Stranger*, in *Existentialism*, 177.

10 From *The Myth of Sisyphus*, in *Existentialism*, 183.

11 Ibid., 183.

12 In *Virtue Ethics: A Pluralistic View*.

13 From *Being and Time*, in *Existentialism*, 111.

14 Ibid., 116.

15 From *Being and Nothingness*, in *Existentialism*, 214.

16 Ibid., 214.

17 Ibid., 214.

18 Kazuo Ishiguro (New York: Random House, 1989).

19 For an advocate of this view, see Robert C. Solomon, "Corporate Roles, Personal Virtues: An Aristotelian Approach to Business Ethics," in *Virtue Ethics: A Critical Reader*, ed. Daniel Statman (Edinburgh: Edinburgh University Press, 1997), 205–226. Solomon claims that integrity is the "linchpin of all the virtues" (215).

20 Specific vices associated with these conditions, and associated virtues, are treated in my "Nietzsche and the Virtues of Mature Egoism," in *Nietzsche's* On the Genealogy of Morality: *A Critical Guide*, ed. Simon May (Cambridge: Cambridge University Press, 2011), 285–308.

21 I elaborate the notion of virtue as an expressive phenomenon in my *Virtue Ethics: A Pluralistic View*, chapter 6.

22 See *On the Genealogy of Morals*, trans. Douglas Smith (Oxford: Oxford University Press, 1996), First Essay, sect. 10, 24.

23 *Twilight of the Idols*, in *Twilight of the Idols and The Anti-Christ*, trans. R.J. Hollingdale (Harmondsworth: Penguin, 1986), "Maxims and Arrows," sect. 2, 33.

24 *Human, All Too Human: A Book for Free Spirits*, trans. R.J. Hollingdale (Cambridge: Cambridge University Press, 1986), II, "The Wanderer and His Shadow," sect. 348, 393.

25 *Twilight of the Idols*, "Expeditions of an Untimely Man," sect. 35, 87.

26 *Thus Spoke Zarathustra*, Third Part, "Upon the Mount of Olives," 267.

27 "Schopenhauer as Educator," 158.

28 *Twilight of the Idols*, "Maxims and Arrows," 36.

29 See Fromm, *The Art of Loving* (London: Unwin Paperbacks, 1975), and *The Anatomy of Human Destructiveness* (New York: Holt, Rinehart and Winston, 1973).

30 See Adler, *The Neurotic Constitution: Outlines of a Comparative Individualistic Psychology and Psychotherapy*, trans. B. Glueck and J.E. Lind (London: Kegan Paul, Trench, Trübner & Co., 1918), and *Understanding Human Nature*, trans. W.B. Wolfe (London: Allen & Unwin, 1932).

31 See *The Anatomy of Human Destructiveness*.

32 Ibid., 225.

33 Ibid., 225.

34 Ganz, *The Psychology of Alfred Adler and the Development of the Child* (London: Routledge and Kegan Paul, 1953), 2.

35 "On the Origin of the Striving for Superiority and of Social Interest," in *Alfred Adler, Superiority and Social Interest: A Collection of Later Writings*, ed. Heinz L. Ansbacher and Rowena R. Ansbacher (Evanston, IL: Northwestern University Press, 1964), 29–40, 31–32.

36 Ibid., 31.

37 Ibid., 31.

38 See Richard Wollheim, *Freud* (London: Fontana, 1971), 175.

39 Adler, *Understanding Human Nature*, 74.

40 Ibid., 75.

41   Fromm too emphasizes the "need for the development of a character structure" (whose development of course may go wrong). Character "*is the relatively permanent system of all non-instinctual strivings through which man relates himself to the human and natural world*. One may understand character as the human substitute for the missing animal instincts; it is man's second nature" (*The Anatomy of Human Destructiveness*, 226–227).

42   Adler, *Understanding Human Nature*, 75.

43   Ibid., 75.

44   See discussion in Chapter 6.

45   *The Anatomy of Human Destructiveness*.

46   *Nietzsche on Morality* (London: Routledge, 2002), 231.

47   Ibid., 232.

48   Note however that for Fromm benign aggression which characteristically "serves life" can also be distorted. For Fromm an important source of defensive aggression is the "wounding of *narcissism*," and as noted above, such wounding can lead to excessive aggressive reactions to, e.g., slights, defeats, criticism, exposure to mistake, and so on (*The Anatomy of Human Destructiveness*, 200–202).

49   *The Anatomy of Human Destructiveness*, 4. Fromm denies that "defensive aggression" is an "'innate' instinct" though he claims it is part of human nature (4). The issue of whether aggression or cruelty is an instinct is not at issue here.

50   *Genealogy of Morals*, Third Essay, sect. 13, 100.

51   *The Anatomy of Human Destructiveness*, 243.

52   *Genealogy of Morals*, First Essay, sect. 11, 26.

53   Ibid., sect. 11, 26.

54   Ibid., sect. 11, 25.

55   Ibid., sect. 11, 25.

56   Ibid., sect. 11, 26.

57   Ibid., sect. 11, 26.

58   *The Anatomy of Human Destructiveness*, 4 and 298.

59   *Genealogy of Morals*, First Essay, sect. 7, 19.

60   See Sigmund Freud, *An Outline of Psycho-Analysis*, ed. and trans. James Strachey (New York: W.W. Norton & Co., 1949), 27.

61   See Wollheim, *Freud*, 140.

62   Ibid., 140.

63   *Genealogy of Morals*, First Essay, sect. 11, 26.

64   Ibid., sect. 11, 26.

65   *Beyond Good and Evil: Prelude to a Philosophy of the Future*, trans. R.J. Hollingdale (London: Penguin, 1973), "On the Natural History of Morals," sect. 197, 118.

66   Given Nietzsche's apparent concept of health as a condition opposed to neurosis rather than (inter alia) perverted forms of regression, then as Richard Schacht points out, citing a passage from *The Gay Science*, we "would do well to consider whether [for Nietzsche] 'the will to health alone is not a prejudice, cowardice, and perhaps a bit of very subtle barbarism and backwardness'. GS 120": *Making Sense of Nietzsche: Reflections on Timely and Untimely Meditations* (Urbana: University of Illinois Press, 1995), 219.

67   Leiter, *Nietzsche On Morality*, 233 n. 13.

68   Sigmund Freud, *Civilization and Its Discontents*, ed. and trans. J. Strachey (New York: W.W. Norton & Co., 1961), 78–79, cited by Leiter.

69   I am here describing Nietzsche's view of the origins of bad conscience as a culturally prevalent and reinforced neurosis; I am not claiming that for Nietzsche (or in reality) all punishment is in fact retributive, manifests this neurosis, or is in general wrong.

70   Wollheim, *Freud*, 140.

71   *Genealogy of Morals*, Second Essay, sect. 16, 65.

72   Ibid., sect. 18, 67.

73   Ibid., sect. 16, 65.

74 Ibid., sect. 19, 68: "Bad conscience is an illness, there is no doubt about it."
75 Ibid., sect. 16, 64.
76 Ibid., sect. 17, 67.
77 Ibid., sect. 22, 73.
78 Ibid, sect. 6, 46.
79 Ibid., sect. 4, 45.
80 Ibid., sect. 6, 47.
81 Ibid., sect. 6, 46.
82 Ibid., sect. 6, 47.
83 Ibid., sect. 6, 47–48.
84 Ibid., sect. 6, 47.
85 "Our Virtues," sect. 229, 159.
86 Ibid., 160.
87 Indeed in arguing against frustration-aggression theory Fromm claims that frustration is a basic fact of life, necessary for development. He argues that frustration as such does not cause aggression, and that "the most important factor in determining one's reaction to frustration is the character of a person" (*The Anatomy of Human Destructiveness*, 68). On Aristotle's view of virtue as a *perfection*, frustration no longer occurs, but the precise nature and plausibility of this view is a topic beyond the scope of this book.
88 *Genealogy of Morals*, First Essay, sect. 4, 14.
89 Ibid., sect. 5, 15.
90 Ibid., sect. 5, 15.
91 Ibid., sect. 13, 30.
92 Ibid., sect. 7, 19.
93 Ibid., sect. 10, 24.
94 Ibid., sect. 13, 30.
95 Ibid., sect. 7, 19.
96 There is an issue about whether this "revaluation" is creative or merely a set of beliefs that grow on one. See Rüdiger Bittner, "Ressentiment," in *Nietzsche, Genealogy, Morality: Essays on Nietzsche's* Genealogy of Morals, ed. Richard Schacht (Berkeley: University of California Press, 1994), 127–138. Bittner argues that Nietzsche is wrong to think of it as creative. I claim it is creative for Nietzsche, but only in the following sense: it is a "poisonous eye" which gives values "a new colour, interpretation and aspect." Given Nietzsche's depth psychological view of phenomena, he would be generally skeptical of fully intentional rational creativity – it is rather more or less an expression of sick or healthy natures.
97 *Genealogy of Morals*, First Essay, sect. 14, 31.
98 Ibid., sect. 13, 30.
99 Ibid., sect. 7, 19.
100 Ibid., sect. 14, 31.
101 *Genealogy of Morals*, Third Essay, sect. 8, 88.
102 Reginster, "*Ressentiment*, Evaluation and Integrity," *International Studies in Philosophy* 27 (1995), 117–124.
103 Ibid., 118.
104 I discuss the phenomenon of expression, applying it to Nietzsche's discussion of resentment in my *Virtue Ethics: A Pluralistic View*, chapter 6.
105 This phrase is a New Zealand expression connoting the "cutting down of the tall poppy," and I believe unknown in the United States. This is no accident: the phenomenon is extremely prevalent in New Zealand.
106 Karen Horney has a taxonomy of three basic forms of neurotic solution to psychic conflict, all of which are well illustrated in Nietzsche's writings: (1) The "self-effacing solution." Here, the idealized self is repressed, and the sense of oneself as inferior or impotent is dominant. Resentment is an externalized form of this type of escape. (2) The "expansive solutions" of mastery. In these "solutions" the sense of oneself as inferior or impotent is repressed. (3) The solution of "resignation." This "third major solution

of the intra-psychic conflicts consists essentially in the neurotic's withdrawing from the inner battlefield and declaring himself uninterested." *Neurosis and Human Growth: The Struggle Toward Self-Realization* (New York: Norton, 1970), 259.

107   Ibid., 179.
108   Ibid., chapter 11.
109   *Genealogy of Morals*, Third Essay, sect. 8, 87.
110   Ibid., sect. 3, 79.
111   Ibid., sect. 1, 77.
112   Ibid., sect. 6, 85.
113   Ibid., sect. 1, 77.
114   Ibid., sect. 1, 77.
115   Horney, *Neurosis and Human Growth*, 259.
116   Ibid., 263.
117   Ibid., 260.
118   *Genealogy of Morals*, Third Essay, sect. 13, 99.
119   Ibid., 83. See also Horney, *Neurosis and Human Growth*, 260–261.
120   *Genealogy of Morals*, Third Essay, sect. 3, 79–80.
121   Ibid., sect. 8, 91.
122   Ibid., sect. 3, 79.
123   Ibid., sect. 25, 129.
124   Ibid., sect. 27, 134.
125   *Beyond Good and Evil*, "The Religious Nature," sect. 47, 76.
126   *Genealogy of Morals*, Third Essay, sect. 8, 88.
127   Ibid., sect. 8, 88.
128   Ibid., sect. 13, 99.
129   Ibid., sect. 14, 102.
130   Ibid., sect. 15, 106.
131   Ibid., sect. 14, 102–103.
132   Ibid., sect. 15, 106.
133   Ibid., sect. 17, 108.
134   It is not clear that this notion should be rendered as "the self we would like to become" since in a famous passage Nietzsche claims in *Ecce Homo* that becoming what you are presupposes that you do not know what you are: *Ecce Homo: How to Become What You Are*, trans. Duncan Large (Oxford: Oxford University Press, 2007), "Why I Am So Clever," sect. 9, 31. For further discussion see Chapter 10, section 10.4 below.
135   *Neurosis and Human Growth*, 189.

Chapter 8

What Kind of Virtue Ethicist Is Nietzsche?

8.1 Introduction: Nietzsche and Aristotle

It may be claimed that Nietzsche's "virtue ethics" is so far removed from that of Aristotle (the main progenitor of orthodox contemporary virtue ethics) that any claim to place Nietzsche in the virtue ethics tradition is compromised. I argue in this chapter that the differences between Nietzsche and Aristotle are easily exaggerated. There are three major points of apparent difference.

(1) Aristotle's ethics is objectivist, whereas Nietzsche's is perspectival.
(2) Whereas Aristotle argues for universal virtues proper to humans as such, Nietzsche denies all claims to universality. This claim has two aspects:
    2(i) Nietzsche rejects central universal virtues as conceived by Aristotle and standard moral theories, notably justice.
    2(ii) There is in Nietzsche a relativization of virtue to types of being or even individuals: a pluralism which is incompatible with belief in universal virtue.
(3) Aristotle claims that there is a progression in a person's life to a *telos* or terminus, whereas Nietzsche can plausibly be interpreted as espousing a philosophy of "becoming" which denies this.

Section 8.2 discusses Nietzsche's "perspectivism." I argue that for him, it is not only compatible with objectivity but is required for objectivity. Investigating claim (2), namely that Nietzsche denies the existence of universal virtue, is the task of subsequent sections of this chapter. I argue against 2(i) and 2(ii), claiming both that there are universal virtues in Nietzsche, including justice, and that this is not incompatible with Nietzsche's view that virtues are "differentiated" in being (*inter alia*)

The Virtue Ethics of Hume and Nietzsche, First Edition. Christine Swanton.
© 2015 John Wiley & Sons, Ltd. Published 2015 by John Wiley & Sons, Ltd.

relativized to types. Discussion of claim (3), that Nietzsche denies teleology, is reserved for Chapter 10.

As we saw in the Introduction there is certainly support for an "Aristotelian Nietzsche." Robert Solomon[1] classes both Nietzsche and Aristotle as advancing an ethics of "self realization" – a conception of human excellence. Nietzsche, like Aristotle, posits a basic biological conception of humanity as the starting point of his conception of health or excellence. For both thinkers that starting point is constituted by a thin rather than a thick conception of human nature. The lynchpin of Aristotle's conception – delivered by the *ergon* argument – is the idea of distinctively human rationality. This thin conception of the human *ergon* is thickened throughout the *Nicomachean Ethics* by substantive normative conceptions of various emotions, conceptions of fine or noble human ends, accounts of *phronesis* (practical wisdom), and *prohaeresis* (deliberative desire). In Nietzsche, the basic starting point is "will to power." The thin conception offered in *Beyond Good and Evil* ("A living thing desires above all to vent its strength – life as such is will to power")[2] is likewise fleshed out throughout his writings by substantive accounts of and examples of (primarily) distorted or sick manifestations of "will to power," as we saw in Chapters 6 and 7. As in Aristotle, the transformation of the thin account of human nature into the thick is irreducibly normative. In Aristotle, rational activity as characteristic human activity is transformed into substantive conceptions of the fine and the noble. In Nietzsche, will to power as a venting of strength and energy, expansion, and growth, is transformed into substantive conceptions of life affirming or healthy expressions via contrasts with a variety of "neuroses" or "perversions" – the sick or life denying forms. In both Nietzsche and Aristotle these normative transformations are the basis of accounts of virtue and vice.

Showing that Nietzsche and Aristotle are alike in basing accounts of virtue in normative conceptions of human nature is not to show that for Nietzsche there are universal virtues, let alone the standard ones. Indeed since Nietzsche frequently relativizes virtues to types of human beings and even individuals it may seem obvious that he does not believe in universal virtue. Before we leap to this conclusion however we should remind ourselves that Aristotle too relativizes some virtues to type of human being, notably *megalopsychia* ("great-souledness") and magnificence. These virtues are, as we may put it, "differentiated" forms of universal virtue for Aristotle. Let us call virtues so described "differentiated virtues." What is differentiated is virtue described at a basic level: that is, virtue described at a relatively abstract and general level. Virtue described at that level I call "basic virtue." Great-souledness then is a differentiated virtue; that is, a differentiated form of the universal virtue of excellence in respect of attitude to honors and praise. Likewise magnificence is a differentiated form of the universal virtue of excellence in dispositions to spend resources. Only those possessing great resources should be magnificent; those of more modest means should be merely liberal. The universal virtues are described at a high level of generality and abstraction and as such are basic virtues. Magnificence is of course not a universal virtue but a differentiated form of a universal virtue, described at a lower level of generality and abstraction.

To make sense of the claim that for Nietzsche virtues are differentiated we should conceive of virtue in Nietzsche as differentiable basic virtue. This presupposes that for all virtues, it can be described at a basic level by a thick concept such as justice, patience, generosity, compassion, and so forth. These concepts are throughout Nietzsche's writings. Notice what this claim does not imply:

(a)   There are universal virtues, that is, virtues that are appropriate for all.
(b)   A virtue picked out by thick concept V remains a virtue in all forms of differentiation. This claim is false if for example a virtue in role R is a vice in role S, a virtue in the "higher man" is a vice in the "herd." (See further below.)
(c)   An honorific thick concept, such as patience and justice, always picks out a virtue on current understandings. As we have seen Nietzsche is at pains to show that in the "slave revolt" the understandings of virtue concepts are distorted and have remained so.

Whereas most virtue theorists seem interested only in accounts of basic virtue, Nietzsche is particularly concerned with how virtues should be differentiated according to such factors as strength, roles such as leadership, and even the narrative particularities of individuals' lives. In sections 8.3–8.5 I discuss Nietzsche's conceptions of three important virtues, forgetfulness, justice, and wisdom, which I take to be universal for him. These are described as basic virtues: the issue of their differentiation is discussed in section 8.6.

8.2   Nietzsche's Perspectivism

Consider now (1) above. In a well-known passage in *Genealogy of Morals*, Nietzsche makes the following claim:

> Perspectival seeing is the only kind of seeing there is, perspectival knowing the *only* kind of knowing and the *more* feelings about a matter which we allow to come to expression, the *more* eyes, different eyes through which we are able to view this same matter, the more complete our "conception" of it, our "objectivity" will be.[3]

Nietzsche's points are first, we necessarily see things from within a perspective, second, that perspective is limited, and third, greater objectivity is attained if we bring multiple perspectives to bear on an issue. Seeing something from one perspective only is to lack objectivity, even if we are virtuous "life affirming" strong individuals. The mistake is to think that this position (call it Nietzsche's perspectivism) implies relativism. His position is compatible not only with the view that perspectives can be integrated or at least compared to create greater objectivity, but also with the view that some perspectives (e.g., those of "life affirming" strong individuals) are better than others.

Though seeing things through multiple perspectives is necessary for objectivity, Nietzsche does not imply that it is sufficient. As we see below, for Nietzsche further epistemic virtues are required for objectivity such as open-mindedness, deploying a critical perspective, and knowledge of facts. Given that considering and integrating the strengths of multiple perspectives are generally social phenomena, we need also the dialogical virtues.

We might call such a position, augmenting the bare statement above of Nietzsche's perspectivism, virtue perspectivism. Unfortunately Nietzsche does not say much if anything about the dialogical virtues necessary for virtue perspectivism, so I shall not investigate them here. However, an important virtue, open-mindedness, which Nietzsche describes in *Daybreak* as leaving doors open[4] warrants discussion, since it is confusion between that virtue and closely related epistemic vices which leads to understanding perspectivism as either relativism or skepticism. A crucial virtue of virtue perspectivism, open-mindedness, is contrasted with two vices, closed-mindedness and excessive open-mindedness.[5] It is forms of excessive open-mindedness which I shall argue lead to misunderstandings about the nature of Nietzsche's perspectivism. We focus first on the epistemic vice of thinking that any perspective is as good as another, or that we have no right or ability to criticize perspectives. Call this vice excessive epistemic humility.

Failure to recognize the vice of excessive epistemic humility may cause confusion between Nietzsche's perspectivism and relativism. Such a mistake is frequently made by the open-minded according to research by Joshua Knobe. Knobe reports a study designed to explore the psychological roots of those who believe in relativism and those who believe in objective moral truths. Reports Knobe, the experimenters "gave each participant a standard measure of the personality trait 'openness to experience'" with results "showing a significant correlation: the higher a participant was in openness to experience, the more likely that participant was to endorse the relativist answer."[6] Knobe concludes that when "confronted with other perspectives and other ways of life, [the open-minded] feel drawn to relativism."[7] They do not realize that rather than implying or suggesting relativism, the norm of openness to other perspectives is one which, if followed in a virtuous manner, makes our conceptions "more complete" and objective.

Excessive open-mindedness has another form which has become important in understanding Nietzsche's perspectivism. I shall call this vice epistemic cowardice to distinguish it from excessive epistemic humility as defined above. In a recent book, Jessica Berry[8] argues persuasively that Nietzsche's perspectivism is not a theory of truth. Instead she attributes to him a skeptical reading, arguing that his perspectivism is the view that we should suspend judgment for Pyrrhonian reasons, basically that one should not hold convictions since beliefs are perspectival, limited, and open to competing opinion. On my view the disposition to suspend judgment for the reason that all knowledge is perspectival is to manifest a further vice of excessive open-mindedness, which I believe Nietzsche would regard as a kind of intellectual cowardice. One can scarcely imagine someone more firm in his beliefs concerning sickness, the roots of vice, and the nature and evil of mediocrity. Rather than suggesting a need for a general suspension of belief, the perspectival nature of knowledge demands discipline and intellectual effort in forming belief: "To see differently, the *desire* to see differently for once in this way is no small discipline of the intellect and a preparation for its eventual 'objectivity' – this latter understood not as 'disinterested contemplation' (which is a non-concept and a nonsense), but as the capacity to have all the arguments for and against *at one's disposal*."[9]

The nature of this discipline is described further in *Daybreak*: we need to "read slowly, deeply, looking cautiously before and aft, with reservations, with doors left open, with delicate eyes and fingers."[10] Open-mindedness, combined with (appropriate) epistemic humility and intellectual discipline is not a suspension of belief. Nor does it signal a halt to enquiry. Unlike the Pyrrhonian view that "arrival at judgement calls a halt to enquiry,"[11] judgment may call for refinement, further explanation, and "leaving doors open." Epistemic humility ensures that one's confidence could be shaken with the input of further perspectives, and further facts.

8.3   Forgetfulness

We turn now to three central basic universal virtues which I argue Nietzsche both endorses and describes: forgetfulness, justice, and wisdom. We begin with forgetfulness.

One will not find forgetfulness in Aristotle's catalogue of virtues, or indeed in any orthodox catalogue. It is a peculiarly Nietzschean virtue of considerable psychological importance, and it underlies many other virtues such as justice. In this sense, the latter virtue may be thought of as a dependent virtue, a virtue which presupposes the existence of another.[12] At first sight it may seem strange to think of forgetfulness as a virtue at all since in common parlance "being forgetful" is the name of an epistemic vice. So we need to explore in just what the virtue consists, and what for Nietzsche are its correlative vices.

The field of forgetfulness as a virtue is dealing with aspects of the past, in relation to forgetting and remembering. Since memory is necessarily selective (we cannot as human beings remember everything) there is an issue of selectively forgetting in various ways, and that can be done well or badly. For Nietzsche, forgetting is thus an "*active*" process, and there is an issue of distinguishing forms of healthy, strong, virtuous forgetting from various correlative vices.

What are these forms? Forms of forgetting as a virtue, with their correlative vices, may be distinguished according to a number of what we might call sub-fields of the virtue, which may overlap. These are:

(1)   Attitudes toward one's past in relation to affirmation or non-affirmation.
(2)   Attitudes toward wrongs (broadly understood) done to others, past failings in relation to others, and past failings and weaknesses in general.

(3)   Attitudes toward harms and wrongs done by others to oneself, and even by
       oneself to oneself.

The idea of a virtue of forgetfulness in relation to the first of these fields is the aspect
of self-acceptance as loving one's past, famously outlined in Nietzsche's doctrine of
the eternal recurrence:

> How, if some day or night a demon were to sneak after you into your loneliest loneli-
> ness and say to you, "This life as you now live it and have lived it, you will have to live
> once more and innumerable times more; and there will be nothing new in it, but every
> pain and every joy and every thought … must return to you – all in the same succession
> and sequence – even this spider and this moonlight between the trees … the eternal
> hourglass of existence is turned over and over, and you with it a dust grain of dust …
> The question in each and everything, "Do you want this once more and innumerable
> times more?" would weigh upon your actions as the greatest stress. Or how well dis-
> posed would you have to become to your self and to life to *crave nothing more fervently*
> than this ultimate eternal confirmation and seal?[13]

Given this passage it may be odd to think of forgetfulness as a *virtue* concerned
with loving one's past – the psychological aspect of the "eternal recurrence." Is one on
the contrary not supposed to remember everything, and affirm it? The idea here is
forgetting in the sense of "forget it!": here one is not enjoined to belittle, deny, or repress
aspects of one's past, but to "forget" in the sense that one should not dwell on things
and live in a permanent state of self-hate, debilitating regret, or disappointment.

But does not Nietzsche enjoin a stronger form of affirmation? Indeed it seems so,
but only for the strongest. Only the strongest, only the best disposed toward life and
self, would not find reliving one's life in every detail over and over again "the greatest
stress," but would instead "*crave nothing more fervently*" than this. However there is
surely a vice of excess even here: are we to crave even serious harm to self, and harm
to others caused by oneself? "What does not destroy me, makes me stronger,"[14] even
if true, does not entail that *all* suffering is good, and is to be positively embraced as
such. To think that way is not to attain the epistemic virtue of (proper) perspective.[15]
Even if this virtue demands affirmation of one's life as a whole, that does not imply
affirmation of each detail of one's life.[16]

It would appear that a vice opposed to affirmation of one's past is disgust with one's
past, but one might ask: Is not disgust or shame an appropriate attitude toward a past
wasted or filled with wrongdoing? If one is inclined to answer this question in the
affirmative there remains the possibility that there is a virtue of forgetfulness in the
second sub-field, attitudes toward wrongs done to others. Here, a virtue of forgetfulness
is a tendency not to dwell on one's past with obsessive guilt or bitterness, leaving one
"stuck" in the past. Disgust or shame is one thing, becoming stuck is another. However,
forgetfulness as a virtue in this area must be distinguished from three related vices.

The first vice is an attitude of non-caring or insouciance about harms that one
has caused; harms to loved ones, or to self, even where the harms are serious.

The second is weak forgetfulness which is a form of escape from self. Here one's past is repressed in order to escape the pains of memory. "Moving on" has to be distinguished from the denial and self-deception of the slave type described in *Genealogy of Morals* Essay I. The third vice is a vice of excess: an inability to let go, a weak hanging onto memories, a self-lacerating guilt-ridden kind of reliving. This vice is of particular importance to Nietzsche:

> ... one may appreciate immediately that there could be no happiness, no hope, no pride, no present without forgetfulness. The man in whom this inhibitory apparatus is damaged and out of order may be compared to a dyspeptic ... he is never "through" with anything ... forgetting is a strength, a form of *robust* health.[17]

As we have seen though, forgetfulness as a virtue is not mere forgetfulness. On the contrary, as we saw above it is Nietzsche's point that forgetfulness is active, and can be done well or badly. Just as Nietzsche argues against a weak kind of failure to forget, so he also argues against escape from self via escape from memories – a part of oneself.

The third sub-field concerns forgetfulness of wrongs and harms done to one by others. Here too, forgetting is a kind of letting go, to be contrasted with an active harboring of memories of wrongs and of promises made and not fulfilled. The *virtue* of forgetfulness is a precondition of a virtue of forgiveness, a letting go of hurt and anger which may turn into bitterness, and an appropriate ignoring of insults: "Of what concern are my parasites to me?, it [a society of strong individuals] would be entitled to say. May they live and prosper: I am strong enough to allow that!"[18] Again however Nietzsche makes it clear that the strongest kind of forgetting is only appropriate for the strongest kind of individuals, as I explore further in section 8.6.

I have described Nietzsche's virtue of forgetting as a universal virtue, albeit one that is differentiated according to an agent's strength. However the claim of virtue status has been disputed. Paul S. Loeb, for example, claims "although Nietzsche does praise animal forgetting, it is clear that he does not atavistically think that humankind can somehow go back to this state."[19] He claims that the forgetting of the *Genealogy of Morals* is "pre-human." Nowhere in Nietzsche's discussion here does he describe the forgetting he praises as pre-human; on the contrary he claims that the "solving" of the "problem" of breeding an animal which is able to make promises will seem surprising to someone who "fully appreciates the countervailing force of forgetfulness,"[20] which he goes on to describe and praise. Certainly he reminds us that we are a *necessarily* forgetful *animal*: but this is a timely reminder of our human *animal* nature.

8.4   Justice

For many such as Simon May Nietzsche has an "appalling" conception of justice which is basically the might of the strong. I argue against this view in what follows. As described in *Genealogy of Morals* Essay II, justice is a virtue contrasted with two vices, rigorous punitivism and "scientific fairness." Indeed throughout his works justice as a virtue is also contrasted with a third vice: the egalitarian disposition. Unless the contrast between justice and related vices is carefully drawn one may think that justice has no place in Nietzsche's account of virtues.

To understand justice as a virtue it is necessary to understand its depth psychological aspects, and that in turn requires that one take seriously Nietzsche's claims about the "origins" of justice. Nietzsche makes it clear that the origin of justice is not resentment: "Let me say a word here by way of refutation of recent attempts to seek the origin of justice on a completely different ground – that is in *ressentiment*."[21] The origin lies rather in the active aggressive human being rather than in the reactive person of resentment:

> … where has the entire administration of law, and also the actual need of law, made its home up to now? In the sphere of the reactive man? Not at all; rather in that of the active, the strong, the spontaneous, the aggressive man.[22]

To understand the importance of this claim for Nietzsche's view of justice, it is necessary to clear away two potential confusions. First one might confuse Nietzsche's admiration of the "strong," "spontaneous," "aggressive" man with an admiration of the "nobles." But as we have seen, the nobles have perverted that strength, aggression, and spontaneity into "mad, absurd, sudden"[23] violence against "foreigners" and "barbarians." The origin of justice as a virtue thus lies in an admirable active type but because of the perversion of aggression into cruelty, the resulting "justice" may transform into punishing instincts sourced in such worlds as the "magnificent" but "equally horrific and violent" Homeric world.[24] Here we do not have that "rare virtue" justice but a perversion of it. The perversion of aggression into cruelty is at the foundations of a perversion of justice, rigorous punitivism, discussed in Chapter 7.

Of more immediate concern here is the potential for a second confusion. Though Nietzsche claims that the origin of justice does not lie in resentment, he also claims that "it is from the spirit of resentment itself" that "scientific fairness" grows, "to the advantage of hatred, envy, resentment, rancour, revenge."[25] It might thus be thought that the origin of justice for Nietzsche does after all lie in resentment. If this were so, then justice would not be for Nietzsche a genuine virtue. But it is *genuine* justice that has its origins in an admirable *strong* type and allows justice to be a virtue as I shall argue. By contrast "scientific fairness" for Nietzsche is not a property of justice, but a distorted form of "justice" grounded in slave morality. At this point we can read Nietzsche as dissecting two separate origins of two kinds of vice opposed to justice as a virtue. (a) Resentment-based vice: "scientific fairness," "bringing down" forms of equality, envy, rancor. (b) Vice sourced in cruelty (distorted aggression) turned inward and then externalized: punitive forms of "justice to excess" associated with a sense that punishment can never fit the crime; punishment can never be commensurate with guilt. Here the "penetrating eye" of justice is not "mild" as the virtue demands.[26]

In what then does justice as a genuine virtue consist? Can we provide a positive account or must we rest with the negative one? It does not exhibit the distorted will to power of resentment; nor does it exhibit an externalized form of cruelty turned inward – hostile punitivism. Perhaps a clue lies in Nietzsche's description of the "sovereign individual" of *Genealogy of Morals*, Essay II. Perhaps he is the paragon of justice. To the account of this "exemplar" we now turn.

Nietzsche delights in offering us exemplars or types which might be taken to embody ideals of life affirmation. Indeed such exemplars – the noble warrior or aristocratic type, the sovereign individual – might suggest that Nietzsche offers an example of "exemplarist" virtue ethics, a type of moral theory which explicates conceptions of goodness by reference to exemplars of good persons without going through concepts, thereby sidestepping the "problems with a purely conceptual foundation" for ethics.[27] However it is difficult to know what constitute genuine exemplars for Nietzsche, since they are generally embedded in his genealogical accounts and are not offered as genuine ideals. In particular, I shall argue, the "sovereign individual" is not to be regarded as a genuine exemplar of ideals dear to the hearts of modern moral philosophers, justice and autonomy. It may be thought that if this is so, such virtues are rejected by Nietzsche. I will argue against that view, showing how Nietzsche understands those virtues.

We have already discussed the noble (warrior) type, but an even more misunderstood supposed exemplar is the "sovereign individual" introduced in *Genealogy of Morals*, Essay II, and who resembles a paradigm of modern ethics. Here he is:

> … let us place ourselves at the other end of this enormous process, at the point where the tree finally bears its fruit, where society and custom finally reveal the end to which they were merely a means: there we find as the ripest fruit on their tree the *sovereign individual*, the individual who resembles no one but himself … the man with his own independent, enduring will, the man who is *entitled to make promises*.[28]

On my account the sovereign individual is a type described for a dramatic purpose within moral cultural critique, to provide a point of contrast with genuine universal virtue. However as Christa Davis Acampora notes,[29] the dominant view in Nietzsche interpretation is to regard this type as an ideal, whom we should try to emulate.[30] On this reading, this type is portrayed as admirably independent, autonomous, strong-willed, with a capability of making promises. He is wholly responsible for his actions, having no excuses, expecting others to be the same, and exacting debts accordingly. He is as Nietzsche would describe it, "scientifically fair." I agree he is independent, strong-willed, autonomous, and calculating, but I shall argue, he is not admirably so. Indeed he bears an uncanny resemblance to the Kantian "ideal type" described by Iris Murdoch, who "confronted even with Christ turns away to consider the judgement of his own conscience." She continues: "Stripped of the exiguous metaphysical background which Kant was prepared to allow him, this man is with us still, free, independent, lonely, powerful, rational, responsible, brave."[31] This is a type for whom conformity of action to rational law (keeping promises being the paradigm) – a law incorporated within his own conscience – is what ethics is supposedly all about.

The portrayal and discussion of the sovereign individual is for Nietzsche a way of distinguishing genuine virtue from vice masquerading as virtue exhibited by a cultural ideal. To fully understand how this is so, it is a good idea to examine what Nietzsche called in his later work, *Twilight of the Idols*, "the great and uncanny problem which I have been pursuing the longest," the "psychology of the 'improvers' of mankind."[32] Here he claims that there are two instruments to "improvement," that of "taming" and that of "breeding." These two processes have as their "supreme principle" "making morality" in a way which requires an "unconditional will to its opposite." In short *"all* the means by which one has so far attempted to make mankind moral were through and through *immoral*."[33]

In the task of "making morality" through developing bad conscience and a punitive ethics described in *Genealogy of Morals* Essay II, the process of "taming" is the "more immediate task," that of "*making* man to a certain extent necessary, uniform, an equal among equals, regular and consequently calculable."[34] The "ripest fruit" of this process is the "breeding" of a certain type of man, the "sovereign individual," the highest exemplar of a morality made through a process "which has long been steeped in blood" and "torture."[35] However, as is made clear in the description of a kind of "making morality" in *Twilight of the Idols* (the example of Mana), the highly bred individuals are contrasted with the "unbred" individuals (the "chandaras" of Mana) whom the bred individuals have a "right" to treat extremely cruelly and punitively. In the *Genealogy of Morals*, the "unbred" individuals are the "cowering dogs" "who make promises without entitlement" and lie, and for the punishment of whom the sovereign individual keeps the toe of his boot poised, and his stick at the ready.[36] As Julian Young notes, the Manu discussion generalizes to all "improvers" of mankind, including Christian and Jewish priests.[37]

However, "moralities" made by the "improvers" such as priests and instigators of draconian penal codes, are as Nietzsche claims through and through immoral. How is this shown, and in particular why is the sovereign individual not the highest exemplar or idealization of genuine morality, especially justice? The supposed "exemplar" is not the future paragon who will embody the genuine "revaluation of values," alluded to at the end of Essay II, the "man of the future" who "will redeem us as much from the previous ideal as from *what was bound to grow out of it*,"[38] but rather the completion and "perfection" of that very "previous ideal": the morality or set of customs that Nietzsche is criticizing. His properties, as I shall show, are contrasted with a genuine virtue: the "forgetfulness" of the strong. The sovereign individual is the "ripest fruit" certainly, but the ripest fruit of a sick moral system.

The metaphor of the "ripest fruit" to connote the idealized completion or terminus of a flawed process (or a flawed conception of a process) occurs also in Nietzsche's attack on the view of history as "the total surrender of personality to the world process for the sake of its goal, world redemption."[39] Here the "ripest fruit of the tree of knowledge"[40] is described as not perfecting nature but as destroying individual nature.[41]

The sovereign individual as an idealization (though not an ideal) is foreshadowed in *Untimely Meditations* II where Nietzsche speaks of the drive to justice. In this discussion, as elsewhere, we see not that Nietzsche is opposed to justice as a virtue, but that he is opposed to justice understood in the manner of moralities made through the processes of taming and breeding. If a person with the drive to justice is a "cold demon of knowledge" whose "vantage point" is here described as a "solitary height," he would "spread about him the icy atmosphere of a dreadful superhuman majesty which we would have to fear, not revere." He would be a "regulating and punishing judge."[42] As a consequence, says Nietzsche, to possess a powerful will to justice is not sufficient to possess justice as a *virtue*, "the rarest of all virtues," "an impossible virtue."[43]

> To possess only the will is absolutely not enough: and the most terrible sufferings sustained by mankind have proceeded precisely from those possessing the drive to justice but lacking the power of judgement.[44]

We need to say more about the nature of genuine justice for Nietzsche. First, for genuinely just individuals to occur, mankind must not be tamed and made calculable through a process of making them "equals amongst equals." For that is a process of destroying *individual* nature rather than perfecting human nature, and thereby "attracts everything shallow and mediocre."[45] According to Nietzsche, the "doctrine of equality" is the "termination of justice" rather than its foundation:

> The doctrine of equality! There is no more poisonous poison anywhere: for it seems to be preached by justice itself, whereas it really is the termination of justice. "Equal to the equal, unequal to the unequal" – *that* would be the true slogan of justice; and also its corollary: "Never make equal what is unequal."[46]

Rather than making equal what is unequal, a recipe not only for injustice but also for mediocrity, we should express any "thirst for equality" by raising people up:

> *Two kinds of equality.* – The thirst for equality can express itself either as a desire to draw everyone down to oneself (through diminishing them, spying on them, obstructing their progress) or to raise oneself and everyone else up (through recognising their virtues, helping them, rejoicing in their success).[47]

Once we let go the resentment-filled envy-driven obsession with uniformity, equality, and "scientific fairness" we may be on the way to being capable of a strong genuine justice, one tempered with grace, which ironically is a particularly Christian feature of justice:

> The justice which began with: "Everything can be paid off, everything must be paid off", ends with a look the other way ... This self-cancellation of justice: the beautiful

name it goes by is well enough known – *grace*; – needless to say, it remains the prerogative of the most powerful man, even better, his domain beyond the law.[48]

In order for a genuine virtue of justice to be strong and tempered by grace, a strong "forgetfulness" is necessary. Opposed to the picture of the "sovereign individual" as an individual who does not forget, is the account of what for Nietzsche is the virtue of forgetting, described above. The forgetfulness of the strong is an overcoming of the appalling systems of punishment designed to make us remember. There is nothing more frightening and more sinister, says Nietzsche, than man's technique for remembering things, where "Something is branded in, so that it stays in the memory: only that which *hurts* incessantly is remembered."[49]

Finally the just individual is a responsible individual, he takes responsibility for his own actions, not exploiting others or blaming them unfairly. In this respect, it may seem, the sovereign individual is a paragon of justice. However, is the mastery and autonomy of the sovereign individual of a virtuous kind? It would seem not. For he is portrayed as thinking of himself as a man of "extraordinary" freedom, possessing an enduring and indestructible will, who is therefore strong enough to be reliable "even against accidents, even 'against fate.'" He has "power over himself and over fate."[50] The mastery and autonomy exemplified by the ideal of the sovereign individual are thus superhuman fictions: they are examples of belief in a "*causa sui*" ridiculed in *Beyond Good and Evil* as "a desire to bear the whole and sole responsibility for one's actions and to absolve God, world, ancestors, chance, society from responsibility for them," a belief that is "the best self-contradiction hitherto imagined."[51] Unlike Richard D. White's portrayal of the sovereign individual as an *ideal* of responsibility,[52] the brand of responsibility exemplified is a vice both intellectually and emotionally. Emotionally, it expresses the harshness and excesses of the intellectual belief in complete personal responsibility, and failure to temper justice with grace. In general, vices of excess and deficiency of responsibility must be contrasted with a realistically psychological, commonsense conception of responsibility as a virtue:

> … one will at no price give up his "responsibility", his belief in *himself*, the personal right to *his* deserts … the other, on the contrary, will not be responsible for anything, to blame for anything, and out of an inner self-contempt wants to be able to *shift off* his responsibility for himself somewhere else.[53]

Let us now summarize the key features of justice as Nietzsche conceives it.

(1) In its genuinely virtuous form it is not a product of the system of morality whose genealogy Nietzsche exposes. In particular the just individual cannot be a product, let alone an idealized product, of a resentment-filled slavish morality that is obsessed with "scientific fairness," a bringing down form of egalitarianism, and is punitively rigoristic. The products of such a morality are thus incapable of grace, essential for justice as that "rarest" "impossible" virtue.

(2)   Justice is a virtue of *gentle* wisdom, or at least a wisdom whose "voice is neither harsh nor tearful."[54] Such wisdom is not a "cold demon of knowledge."

(3)   The "vantage point" of justice as a virtue should not be excessively lofty so that the humanity of the virtue is lost.

(4)   The just person possesses (strong) forgetfulness as a virtue. (Justice as a virtue is integrated with grace rather than being opposed to it. For that to be the case, all of the features of 1–4 must be possessed by the just individual.)

(5)   The just individual possesses (a sense of) responsibility as a virtue.

8.5   Wisdom

At the core of Aristotle's conception of universal virtue is wisdom. It is often thought, for example by Robert Solomon,[55] that Nietzsche differs from Aristotle in holding that passion and not wisdom is the mark of virtue. Virtues are described as "overflowing," have extreme enthusiasm and passion at their core, and practical wisdom is nowhere or hardly to be seen. What would naturally be called "virtue to excess" is genuine virtue for Nietzsche. Admittedly, as we shall see in the next section, what exactly is deemed wise will vary according to types of human being. Nonetheless wisdom on my view is a central virtue for Nietzsche, and many aspects of that virtue can be understood as universal. We have already noted some of these aspects, for example wisdom requires a reduction in "bile."

What is wisdom for Nietzsche? It has something to do with pursuing and knowing truth about oneself and the rest of the world. It is related primarily to the nature of individuals' goals of knowledge (do they exemplify the resignatory neurosis?) and the discipline involved in acquiring knowledge (does it manifest ascetic spiritualization?).

As has been argued,[56] Nietzsche does not hold the pursuit of truth and knowing the truth to be good or valuable without qualification. How are we to describe the "qualifications"? They are not to be understood in terms of exceptions to the requirement to pursue a value which itself is specifiable independently of virtue notions. Rather, the very value of the pursuit of truth itself is to be understood in terms of aretaic concepts.[57] Pursuit of truth is valuable or good at least in part by virtue of its being for example courageous, of its exhibiting "hardness," and so forth.[58] Nor can we understand these aretaic notions themselves in terms of universal principles, for this is precluded by the complexity and holistic nature of the particular situations and motives in which these aretaic notions apply. For example in artistic contexts, truthfulness is quite a different property: one is true to one's creative spirit or genius, but falsifying reality may be part of that genius.

As is common with Nietzsche, false ideals are employed contrastively to describe conceptions of genuine virtue, including wisdom. Just as the sovereign ideal is seen as a "perfection" of a flawed moral culture animated by a flawed psychology, so the ascetic ideal is the completion of a distorted mode of being, where, driven by disgust with the world and self, one embraces a false conception of virtue and notably wisdom. The structural similarity between the role played by the sovereign individual in *Genealogy of Morals* Essay II and the exemplars of the ascetic ideal in Essay III is striking. Again, the pseudo-virtues defining the "ideal" are portrayed as the final flowering of a mode of existence typical of those living the ideal: "the most authentic and most natural conditions of their *optimum* existence, their *most beautiful* fruitfulness!"[59]

As we have seen, the ascetic ideal has several types of incarnation: the ascetic priest who embodies the ethical-ascetic modes of "poverty, humility and chastity," the metaphysician whose intellectual orientation is one of hyperobjectivity, and the aesthetician whose approach to the world is not only that of a spectator (rather than a creator) but that of a disinterested (as opposed to impassioned) spectator. All of these types pursue truth, but none embody wisdom.

Wisdom is contrasted with vices whose core is the goal of the ascetic ideal: "unconditional" or "absolute" will to truth, in a "pure" or "transcendental" sense. Nietzsche's attack on the will to truth springing from a sick adherence to the ascetic ideal is not an attack on the notion of truth itself, nor an attack on a virtue of truth-seeking. Rather, Nietzsche rails against the "absolute will to truth" understood as belief in and search for such metaphysical fictions as the "*factum brutum*" and the "indifferent substratum" (as self); the "complete renunciation of all interpretation" and a desire to "stop short at the factual" understood in this absolute uninterpreted sense.[60] Hyperobjective vice is rooted in this false metaphysical ideal, which itself is founded in the ascetic ideal, in its form as resignatory neurosis. Ken Gemes describes Nietzsche's healthy will to truth as an active engagement with the world, to be contrasted with the passive "ineffectual contemplation" of the ascetic ideal, the "passive mirroring" of Schopenhauer who demanded a disinterested, emotion-free, pure "clear mirror of the world."[61]

Opposed to vices rooted in the unconditional will to (absolute) truth is the subtle virtue of truthfulness at the heart of wisdom. This virtue has a number of characteristics.

(1) Wisdom is closely connected with the courage of knowing oneself and one's relation to the world, and opposed to the escape from self and the world manifested in the resignatory vices of hyperobjectivity. As Nietzsche claims, such wisdom is a virtue of the strong:

> Something might be true although at the same time harmful and dangerous in the highest degree … the strength of a spirit could be measured by how much truth it could take, more clearly, to what degree it needed it attenuated, veiled, sweetened, blunted, and falsified.[62]

(2) Wisdom is opposed to an obsession with an unobtainable, indeed distorting precision; the more "powerful will" to "the uncertain," the "untrue" is not the

antithesis of a will to truth, but its "refinement." For it recognizes that "language cannot get over its coarseness" and that we should not continue to "speak of antitheses where there are only degrees and subtleties of gradation."[63]

(3) Wisdom requires recognition that there "are very many truths that are a matter of complete indifference; there are problems whose just solution does not demand even an effort, let alone a sacrifice."[64] "I want, once and for all, not to know many things. Wisdom sets limits on knowledge too."[65]

(4) Wisdom requires the strength to stick with decisions without the excessive open-mindedness displayed by revisiting those decisions. Hence even open-mindedness must exhibit strength if it is to be a virtue that is part of wisdom: "To close your ears to even the best counterargument once the decision has been taken: sign of a strong character. Thus an occasional will to stupidity."[66]

(5) Like forgetfulness, wisdom is something active, not a mere capacity to absorb and apply truths. It is essentially involved in giving "style to one's character" where "a large mass of second nature has been added ... a piece of original nature removed," and ugliness which "could not be removed is hidden." However such creation is restrained: only "the weak characters without power over themselves" "are always out to interpret themselves and their environment as *free* nature – wild, arbitrary, fantastic, disorderly, astonishing."[67]

(6) Having wisdom as a virtue involves recognizing that truth is not sought by a single individual as "the judgement of humanity." Like the just person whose "vantage point" is not a lofty height, the wise person does not manifest hyperobjectivity – a vice tinged with arrogance. Rather, for her the search for truth is tied to her own creative purposes and goals of discovery. It is a manifestation of "cultivating the personal" in her; a manifestation in short of virtuous egoism. It is "the prey joyfully seized by the individual huntsman"; it is an "egoistic possession."[68]

In the above sections, I have discussed some important virtues for Nietzsche which can be understood as universal. A problem remains. How does understanding Nietzsche as an advocate of universal virtues of life affirmation (to be distinguished from the counterfeit universal "virtues" expressive of life denial), square with the pluralistic elements of his thought? This problem is the topic of the next section.

8.6   Nietzsche's Pluralism

I claimed in section 8.1 that both Aristotle and Nietzsche espouse a universal framework of virtues in accordance with which individuals should live if they are to flourish or enhance their lives. However, in both Nietzsche and Aristotle, this monism is merely a framework. The universal virtues need to be "differentiated" or "contoured" according to the different circumstances of individual lives. This is not merely the position that virtue concepts have to be intelligently applied if they are to feature in a good life. Rather virtues themselves have a different profile according to such factors as individuals' roles, their types, and their historical and cultural circumstances. Furthermore there are systematic things one can say about what is important in role virtues, virtues proper to a given culture, and so on. The task of this section is to show how this relativization is consistent with the universality of (some) virtues.

The idea that virtue is in some way relative to types of human being has confusingly been called ethical relativism.[69] As a result, it may be thought that Nietzsche's views commit him to a kind of relativism described by Brian Leiter as "the view that judgments are only 'valid' relative to a 'framework' or 'perspective,' so that conflicting judgments can, in principle, both be true,"[70] as opposed to what he calls "relationalism": the idea for example that something may be good for one type of thing but bad for another. This section is concerned with the relativization (the relationality) of virtue. I shall argue that Nietzsche's relativization of virtue to, for example, types is compatible with an affirmation of the existence of universal virtue. This is achieved by mobilizing the distinction between basic and differentiated virtue outlined above. In short, I shall argue, Nietzsche can be read as both a universalist and a pluralist about virtue.

We have called virtues differentiated or contoured according to role or type of human being, for example, "differentiated virtues." Accordingly we can speak of the virtues of the herd, or the role virtues of a business person or a lawyer. For Nietzsche "the virtues of the common man would perhaps indicate vice and weakness in a philosopher."[71] Does this claim entail that there are after all no universal virtues? If pluralism is to be compatible with the existence of universal virtue, some at least of the differentiated virtues should be seen as differentiated forms of universal basic virtues, "differentiated" according to, for example, role. Hence we may talk of the specific forms of generosity proper to, or not proper to, business executives; the specific form of discipline proper to the creative talented artist, and so on.

From the perspective of virtue ethics the differentiation of wisdom is a central issue. In orthodox virtue ethics wisdom is seen as central to virtue. Indeed in a recent book, Daniel Russell distinguishes between "hard" and "soft" virtue ethics, defining "Hard Virtue Ethics" as the view that wisdom (as *phronesis*) is part of every virtue and "Soft Virtue Ethics" as the denial of this.[72] He argues persuasively for Hard Virtue Ethics and it is indeed an interesting issue whether Nietzsche would (a) include wisdom *in differentiated forms* as part of every virtue and (b) whether wisdom for him could be understood as *phronesis* in various differentiated forms. It is beyond the scope of this book to discuss the nature of *phronesis*, but it is not at all clear to me that Nietzsche should be regarded as a soft virtue theorist. He could well be included in the ranks of the "Hard" provided (a) that *phronesis* or (practical) wisdom is richly understood, (b) due attention is paid to differentiated forms of wisdom, and (c) wisdom as a basic virtue is a virtue in even highly creative individuals, military leaders, and so forth.[73]

Though Nietzsche claims that "the genuine philosopher" "lives 'unphilosophically' and 'unwisely', above all *imprudently*, and bears the burden and duty of a hundred attempts and temptations of life – he risks *himself* constantly,"[74] the imprudence and risk may manifest a differentiated form of wisdom appropriate to "higher types" occupying certain roles. This is suggested by Nietzsche himself who sneeringly suggests that wisdom as cautious prudence is a "small" virtue of small men. "Wisdom: that seems to the rabble to be a kind of flight, an artifice and means for getting oneself out of a dangerous game."[75] Indeed this herd virtue, as Nietzsche also suggests, is dangerously close to cowardly vice and a form of escape. Thus it is reasonable to read Nietzsche as arguing that the imprudence of the genuine philosopher is compatible with wisdom as a basic virtue; exhibiting emotions and behavior appropriate to role, and circumstance. Both her mode of operating and her motivation may be characteristic of the wise individual understood as possessing wisdom as a basic virtue, as opposed to those disposed to manifest excessive caution, hyperobjective vice, ascetic desire to escape from the world, and so on.

A major area of controversy, as far as the differentiation of virtue in Nietzsche is concerned, are the virtues proper to types of "man," particularly those of the herd by contrast with those of the "higher type" such as the "free spirit" or the "genuine philosopher" of *Beyond Good and Evil*. For the purposes of this discussion we need to show how Nietzsche's portrayal of such virtues is consistent with the universality of at least some virtues. Let us focus on the difficult area of the "virtues of the herd." Here is Nietzsche:

> On the other hand, the herd-man of Europe today makes himself out to be the only permissible type of man and glorifies their qualities through which he is tame, peaceable and useful to the herd as the real human virtues: namely public spirit, benevolence, consideration, industriousness, moderation, modesty, forbearance, pity.[76]

First, are the so-called herd virtues itemized here really virtues for Nietzsche? If so, can they then be thought of as differentiated forms of (universal) basic virtues? To answer the first question we need to distinguish the herd from the sick. Although Nietzsche frequently exhibits contempt for the herd, that contempt is based on the idea that they are by and large sick, as well as herd-like. Herd virtues should thus be distinguished from traits of the sick from which even the herd should free itself: "May they [the herd-like sick] become convalescents, men of overcoming, and create a higher body for themselves!"[77]

To be a "man of overcoming" is not necessarily to turn oneself into a cultural leader: one may instead become a healthy member of the herd, and thereby play one's part in halting the slide into mediocrity. This cannot be achieved if the herd is characteristically resentment-filled, undermining "man's lucky hits": the creative experimenter, the free spirit, the talented artist, who signal and promote society's progress, and higher culture. Healthy herd types would not do this, but would rather concentrate on their own roles in a well-functioning society.

Virtue for the herd then should thus be distinguished from vices, such as pity, which are standardly exhibited by the herd. Another symptom of herd-sickness is valorizing the "herd virtues" as the real virtues that *all* should aspire to. The admission that there are virtues for the (healthy) herd does not entail that the herd should universalize them *in their differentiated form*. On this reading of Nietzsche, patience, consideration, forbearance, industriousness, public spiritedness, *are* virtues for all, but will take different forms in different types of human being, including the herd. For example, consideration in the higher type will manifest as politeness toward the herd, but consideration in the herd will be the common or garden form of the virtue. Public spiritedness in the higher type will take the form of leadership, and benevolence the form of tenderness and patience toward one's inferiors: "Zarathustra is gentle with the sick. Verily, he is not angry with their kinds of comfort and ingratitude."[78]

In *Beyond Good and Evil* Nietzsche claims:

> Few are made for independence – it is a privilege of the strong. And who attempts it, having the completest right to it but without being *compelled* to, thereby proves that he is probably not only strong but also daring to the point of recklessness.[79]

Nietzsche is not claiming here that independence in some form or other is not a universal virtue. He is merely claiming that only in the strong should it take this form: "what serves the higher type as food or refreshment must to a very different and inferior type be almost poison."[80] In types who should not venture into labyrinths multiplying "by a thousand the dangers which life as such already brings with it"[81] independence (as normally understood) can still be a virtue, but it will take the form of, for example, non-parasitism. Again, to use another example of Nietzsche's, solitude as a virtue is a virtue of the strong. Otherwise it is a form of loneliness: the escape *of* the sick as opposed to escape *from* the sick.[82] "In solitude, whatever one has brought into it grows – also the inner beast. Therefore solitude is inadvisable for the many."[83] It is however by no means easy to distinguish in Nietzsche vices from genuine herd virtues. For example, he says "small people need small virtues"[84] but later claims "only a modest virtue gets along with contentment"[85] and "they [the small] try to please and gratify everybody,"[86] a disposition they *call* virtue, though as Nietzsche points out it is really a vice of cowardice, even in the small.

The point that there are genuine herd virtues is important for an understanding of the nature of virtue in Nietzsche. For many such as Solomon, as we have seen, virtue for Nietzsche is what would naturally be called "overflowing" "virtue to excess." However, such a reading, though natural, does not tell the complete story. As the above passage about independence shows, Nietzsche does not advocate independence to the point of daring and recklessness for everyone. Overflowing, "unwise" courage, creativity, generosity, is toxic to many personalities, and not only bad for them but also bad for society. The metaphor of overflowing and a denial of Aristotelian *phronesis* does not necessarily apply to all forms of courage as a virtue for Nietzsche, as Solomon thinks.[87]

Two more forms of differentiation apparently create problems for understanding Nietzsche as a virtue ethicist: his idea that virtues are "individual" and his idea that there are virtues of the "convalescent" by contrast with virtues of the strong. The virtues of the convalescent are considered more fully in Chapter 10; here we discuss "individual virtue."

In *Zarathustra*, Nietzsche claims:

> My brother, if you have a virtue and she is your virtue, then you have her in common with nobody … And behold, now you have her name in common with the people and have become one of the people and herd with your virtue.
>
> You would do better to say, "Inexpressible and nameless is that which gives my soul agony and sweetness …"
>
> May your virtue be too exalted for the familiarity of names: …[88]

In *The Antichrist*, individual virtue is even portrayed as necessary for healthy life affirmation: "A virtue must be *our own* invention, *our* most necessary self-expression and self-defence: any other kind of virtue is merely a danger."[89]

Although the idea that there are virtues which one shares with no-one else seems anathema to virtue ethics, the distinction between basic and differentiated virtue makes sense of the idea of individual virtue. Virtues such as generosity and kindness, not to mention patience and forbearance, have to be woven into the narrative fabric of our individual lives. In the process of living one's *own* life, Nietzsche claims, tensions manifest themselves as different virtues become salient in that life: "My brother, if you are fortunate you have only one virtue and no more … It is a distinction to have many virtues, but a hard lot … Each virtue is jealous of the others …"[90]

It is hard to integrate the virtues in a lived life, it is hard to "give style to one's character"[91] when the different virtues point in different directions, and all have a call on one. The norms for the differentiation of virtue as manifested in an individual life can reasonably be seen as a topic in narrative ethics: how coherent or experimental should one's life be, what are the standards for coherence, how should the virtues be integrated so that the tendency for each of one's virtues to "covet what is highest," to want "your whole spirit that it might become *her* herald"[92] is mitigated? Or should that tendency be mitigated at all, for example in those who are leaders?

There are two possible explanations for why having many virtues is a "hard lot." One is Aristotelian. In progressing to full virtue one needs to integrate them, and to do that in turn requires a developing practical wisdom including emotional maturation. Nietzsche suggests a different explanation. Why do the individual virtues covet what is highest? Why in short are there tendencies to possess virtues to excess? Solomon suggests an answer: "Nietzsche's Aristotelian virtues might seem to form a coherent set (as in Aristotle's unity thesis) but the metaphor of 'overflowing' suggests that each of these virtues may leave no room for others."[93]

However, as I suggested above, the notion of overflowing may be more applicable to leader-virtues than to herd virtues. In the latter case an Aristotelian picture of practical wisdom will be more appropriate, though this is not emphasized by Nietzsche. If this is so, there are implications for the discussion of altruism in Chapter 6. There are not just two alternatives: overflowing generosity ("to excess") and giving expressive of self-sacrificial vice. Wise generosity in more "herd"-like individuals exhibits neither the vices of escape from self nor necessarily the over-flowing character of Nietzsche's model of "altruism."

Notes

1   *Living With Nietzsche: What The Great "Immoralist" Has to Teach Us* (Oxford: Oxford University Press, 2003).
2   *Beyond Good and Evil: Prelude to a Philosophy of the Future*, trans. R.J. Hollingdale (London: Penguin, 1973), "On the Prejudices of Philosophers," sect. 13, 44.
3   *On the Genealogy of Morals*, trans. Douglas Smith (Oxford: Oxford University Press, 1996), Third Essay, sect. 12, 98.
4   *Daybreak: Thoughts on the Prejudices of Morality*, trans. R.J. Hollingdale (Cambridge: Cambridge University Press, 1982), Preface, 5.
5   The distinction between open-mindedness as a thick concept and open-mindedness as a genuine virtue concept is necessary to resolve some of the puzzles about the value of open-mindedness discussed by epistemologists, such as why should a virtuous person be open-minded, and whether open-mindedness is consistent with commitment and confident belief. I shall not discuss these issues here, but see Wayne Riggs, "Open-Mindedness," in *Virtue and Vice, Moral and Epistemic*, ed. Heather Battaly (Oxford: Wiley-Blackwell, 2010), 173–188.
6   Knobe, "Experimental Philosophy: Thoughts Become the New Lab Rats," *Scientific American* 305 (2011), 56–59, 59.
7   Ibid., 59.
8   Jessica N. Berry, *Nietzsche and the Ancient Skeptical Tradition* (Oxford: Oxford University Press, 2011).
9   *Genealogy of Morals*, Third Essay, section 12, 98.
10 *Daybreak*, Preface, 5.
11 Berry, 35.
12 See Michael Slote, "Dependent Goods and Dependent Virtues," in *Goods and Virtues* (Oxford: Clarendon Press, 1983).
13 *The Gay Science*, trans. Walter Kaufmann (New York: Vintage Books, 1974), sect. 341, 273.
14 Nietzsche, *Twilight of the Idols*, in *The Portable Nietzsche*, ed. and trans. Walter Kaufmann (New York: Penguin, 1976), "Maxims and Arrows," sect. 8, 467.
15 For an interesting discussion of this virtue, see Valerie Tiberius, "Perspective: A Prudential Virtue," *American Philosophical Quarterly* 39 (2002), 305–324.
16 Thanks to Nick Smith for this point.
17 *Genealogy of Morals*, Second Essay, sect. 1, 39–40.
18 Ibid., sect. 10, 54.
19 Loeb, "Finding the Übermensch in Nietzsche's *Genealogy of Morality*," in *Nietzsche's On the Genealogy of Morals: Critical Essays*, ed. Christa Davis Acampora (Lanham, MD: Rowman & Littlefield, 2006), 163–176, 164.
20 *Genealogy of Morals*, Second Essay, sect. 1, 39.
21 Ibid., sect. 11, 54.
22 Ibid., 55.
23 Ibid., First Essay, sect. 11, 26.
24 Ibid., 27.

25   Ibid., Second Essay, sect. 11, 54.
26   Ibid., 55.
27   See Linda Zagzebski, "The Admirable Life and the Desirable Life," in *Values and Virtues: Aristotelianism in Contemporary Ethics*, ed. Timothy Chappell (Oxford: Oxford University Press, 2006), 53–66, 56–57.
28   *Genealogy of Morals*, Second Essay, sect. 2, 41.
29   Acampora, "On Sovereignty and Overhumanity: Why It Matters How We Read Nietzsche's Genealogy," in *Nietzsche's On the Genealogy of Morals*, ed. Acampora, 147–162.
30   See, e.g., Simon May, *Nietzsche's Ethics and His War on "Morality"* (Oxford: Oxford University Press, 1999), 163; Randall Havas, "Nietzsche's Idealism," *Journal of Nietzsche Studies* 20 (2000), 90–99, 94–95.
31   Murdoch, *The Sovereignty of the Good* (London: Routledge, 1970), 80.
32   *Twilight of the Idols*, "The 'Improvers' of Mankind," sect. 5, 505.
33   Ibid., 505. It is indeed "uncanny" how Nietzsche's discussion anticipates the horrors of "making morality" by large-scale "improvers": such as the "taming," and "breeding" by extermination, of Nazism, Stalinism, Pol Pot, the Cultural Revolution.
34   *Genealogy of Morals*, Second Essay, sect. 2, 40.
35   Ibid., sect. 6, 46.
36   Ibid., sect. 2, 41.
37   Young, *Nietzsche's Philosophy of Religion* (Cambridge: Cambridge University Press, 2006), chapter 8.
38   *Genealogy of Morals*, Second Essay, sect. 24, 76.
39   Ibid., 110. I thank Julian Young for alerting me to this passage.
40   Ibid., 107.
41   Ibid., 108.
42   *Untimely Meditations*, trans. R.J. Hollingdale (Cambridge: Cambridge University Press, 1983), Essay II, "On the Uses and Disadvantages of History for Life," 59–123, 88.
43   Ibid., 88.
44   Ibid., 89.
45   *Twilight of the Idols*, "Skirmishes of an Untimely Man," sect. 48, 553.
46   Ibid., 553.
47   *Human, All Too Human: A Book for Free Spirits*, trans. R.J. Hollingdale (Cambridge: Cambridge University Press, 1986), I, 300. (Trans. amended by James Conant.)
48   *Genealogy of Morals*, Second Essay, sect. 10, 54.
49   Ibid., sect. 3, 42.
50   Ibid., sect. 2, 41.
51   *Beyond Good and Evil*, "On the Prejudices of Philosophers," sect. 21, 50–51.
52   See White, *Nietzsche and the Problem of Sovereignty* (Urbana: University of Illinois Press, 1997), 135 and 145.
53   *Beyond Good and Evil*, "On the Prejudices of Philosophers," sect. 21, 50–51.
54   *Untimely Meditations*, Essay II, "On the Uses and Disadvantages of History for Life," 88.
55   See Solomon, *Living With Nietzsche*, 149.
56   May, *Nietzsche's Ethics and His War on "Morality."*
57   Nietzsche may be understood in an "agent based" virtue ethical way (see Michael Slote, *Morals from Motives* (Oxford: Oxford University Press, 2001)) according to which the value of pursuing truth is wholly dependent on virtue, or as holding the weaker position that the value of the pursuit of truth is not wholly independent of virtue (see my *Virtue Ethics: A Pluralistic View*, chapter 2).
58   See May, *Nietzsche's Ethics and His War on "Morality,"* 188.
59   *Genealogy of Morals*, Third Essay, sect. 8, 88.
60   Ibid., sect. 24, 127. Note however that when Nietzsche claims, famously, that there are no moral facts, only moral interpretations of facts, this is the point he is making. He is giving an account of how a "fact" should properly be understood, not arguing for moral relativism. See, e.g., *Twilight of the Idols*, "The 'Improvers' of Mankind," sect. 1, 501. Note that here he says: "Morality is ... more precisely a misinterpretation [of certain phenomena]."

61   Gemes, "'We Remain of Necessity Strangers to Ourselves': The Key Message of Nietzsche's *Genealogy*", in *Nietzsche's* On the Genealogy of Morals, ed. Acampora, 191–208.

62   *Beyond Good and Evil*, "The Free Spirit," sect. 39, 68.

63   Ibid., sect. 24, 55.

64   *Untimely Meditations*, Essay II, "On the Uses and Disadvantages of History for Life," 89.

65   *Twilight of the Idols*, "Maxims and Arrows," sect. 5, 467.

66   *Beyond Good and Evil*, "Maxims and Interludes," sect. 107, 96.

67   *The Gay Science*, sect. 290, 232.

68   Ibid., 88–89.

69   See Lester H. Hunt, *Nietzsche and the Origin of Virtue* (London: Routledge, 1991): "Nietzsche is an ethical relativist" (130). Hunt goes on to say that "Ethical relativism is the idea that what counts as right or good varies from one individual to the next" (130).

70   Leiter, *Nietzsche on Morality* (London: Routledge, 2002), 44.

71   *Beyond Good and Evil*, "The Free Spirit," sect. 30, 61.

72   Daniel C. Russell, *Practical Intelligence and the Virtues* (Oxford: Clarendon Press, 2009).

73   I give an example in my *Virtue Ethics: A Pluralistic View*: a creative scientist working with colleagues had better not display "disorderly, careless, irresponsible and uncontrolled" traits (171).

74   *Beyond Good and Evil*, "We Scholars," sect. 205, 132.

75   Ibid., 132.

76   *Beyond Good and Evil*, "On the Natural History of Morals," sect. 199, 121.

77   *Thus Spoke Zarathustra*, in *The Portable Nietzsche*, First Part, "On the Afterworldly," 145.

78   Ibid., 145.

79   *Beyond Good and Evil*, "The Free Spirit," sect. 29, 60.

80   Ibid., sect. 30, 61.

81   Ibid., 61.

82   *Thus Spoke Zarathustra*, Third Part, "Upon the Mount of Olives," 287: "Loneliness can be the escape of the sick; loneliness can also be escape *from* the sick."

83   Ibid., Fourth Part, "On the Higher Man," sect. 13, 404.

84   Ibid., Third Part, "On Virtue that Makes Small," sect. 2, 280.

85   Ibid., 281.

86   Ibid., 282.

87   Solomon, *Living With Nietzsche*, 149.

88   *Thus Spoke Zarathustra*, First Part, "On Enjoying and Suffering the Passions," 148.

89   *The Antichrist*, in *The Portable Nietzsche*, sect. 11, 577.

90   *Thus Spoke Zarathustra*, First Part, "On Enjoying and Suffering the Passions," 149.

91   "To 'give style' to one's character – a great and rare art!" *The Gay Science*, sect. 290, 232.

92   *Thus Spoke Zarathustra*, First Part, "On Enjoying and Suffering the Passions," 149.

93   Solomon, *Living With Nietzsche*, 173.

Part IV

New Directions

Chapter 9

Humean Virtue Ethics:
Virtue Ethics of Love

9.1 Introduction

As is appropriate for a book within the series *New Directions in Ethics*, Part IV explores precisely this issue in relation to Hume and Nietzsche. In the Introduction to this work, I posed as a fourth question to be addressed: "Given that the virtue ethics of Hume and Nietzsche differs from that of Aristotle, what aspects of their ethical writings add to the virtue ethical tradition broadly conceived?" New directions for virtue ethics, then, are not here understood as further developments of Aristotelian species which have so far dominated the family. Nor is it here being claimed that no one has so far started on paths suggested by Hume or Nietzsche. But it is still early days.

The question of what Nietzsche and Hume have to offer has been partly answered in the body of this work. Hume was interpreted as a pluralistic virtue ethicist in Chapter 5, while Nietzsche's virtue ethics was seen as deploying depth psychology in a way foreign to the Aristotelian tradition. In this and the next chapter, I wish to gather some threads, and add further substance to claims that Hume and Nietzsche make a distinctive contribution to virtue ethics which can inspire developments in modern versions. I focus on three aspects which I briefly summarize here.

(1) As recent work by Michael Slote and neo-Confucian virtue ethics has illustrated, virtue ethics can be developed in a sentimentalist as opposed to a eudaimonistic direction.[1] An ethics of this kind may be, and has been, inspired by Hume. A novel direction in which such an ethics may develop is a focus not so much on benevolence but on love. At its heart is the idea that bonds between people – as opposed to, for example, value – is the driving force for ethics. Certainly Hume claims that love is associated with benevolence as an

The Virtue Ethics of Hume and Nietzsche, First Edition. Christine Swanton.

inherent feature of human nature, but an ethics where love is central has relationship as its focus, and will not have a consequentialist structure. In this chapter I show that rather than simply focusing on empathy and benevolence, Hume's notion of love may inspire a virtue ethics of love.

(2)   Ethics in the analytic tradition has been dominated by attention to justice and beneficence, with their attendant foci on rights as entitlements, needs, and welfare. Relatively absent is attention to creativity and productivity as central to ethics, with only occasional forays into virtues of productivity and vices of parasitism.[2] A pluralistic virtue ethics partially inspired by Nietzsche would redress this balance, without necessarily going all the way with the kind of essentialism espoused by Ayn Rand, who claims that the application of the species-relative standard of evaluation for the assessment of a life that is proper to the survival of humans *qua* human, reveals that productive work is the central purpose of any human life.[3] The next chapter discusses some of the important features of Nietzsche's "ethics of creativity."

(3)   Some of the problems of neo-Aristotelian virtue ethics center on the status of the non-virtuous, and what are appropriate standards of evaluation for their behavior, as they work toward becoming virtuous or more virtuous. As has been pointed out by Robert Johnson,[4] this problem has affected certain virtue ethical accounts of right action, which seem incapable of determining what counts as right for the self-improver.[5] Sections 10.2 and 10.3 of the next chapter explicate Nietzsche's "ethics of becoming," understood as a kind of virtue ethics, which would allow us to supply standards of evaluation for self-improvers.

9.2   Hume and General Love

A modern development of sentimentalist virtue ethics has been undertaken by Michael Slote. In his *Morals From Motives*, inspired in part at least by eighteenth-century sentimentalism,[6] Slote develops "a morality of universal benevolence" which he distinguishes from a morality of universal love.[7] Since, as we have seen, there are morally significant passions in Hume other than benevolence, notably compassion and love, a sentimentalist virtue ethics on Humean lines could go in other directions. In this chapter I outline the bare bones of a Humean virtue ethics of love, including a Humean account of general or agapeic love.

First I need to show how such a development would differ from Slote's morality of universal benevolence. The latter morality is based on an aggregative "fungible humanitarian concern for everyone"[8] balanced with "intimate caring" for near and dear.[9] A Humean virtue ethics of love would differ from this in several respects. First it should be remembered that (loving) intimate caring is only one of several types of love for Hume. There is also love as admiration for those with fine qualities or possessions, affection for friends, and esteem and gratitude for those who have rendered us service. Love can also take the form of tenderness for Hume, and we can be tender to those strangers for whom we feel compassion.

Second, Hume rejects the idea of love of humanity as such, as we have seen. Love in general, whether the tenderness felt for a stranger, or the love of an intimate, is not an emotion in which the objects of love are seen as fungible.

If there is no such thing as love of humanity as such, how can we make sense of general or agapeic love in Hume? Hume's distinction (in the *Enquiries*) between general and particular benevolence affords a clue. Particular benevolence toward another is made reasonable in virtue of her personal merits, services rendered to oneself, and her personal connection to one, such as friendship and blood relation. General benevolence is also benevolence toward particular people. It is not fungible humanitarian concern, but is fitting for a different, "general" reason, resemblance by virtue of humanity. It is manifested in sympathy with a person's pains (compassion or pity in the *Treatise*) and in a "congratulation" with his pleasures, the disposition toward which constitutes the virtue of goodwill. Such goodwill is exercised in action or wished for in relation to particular individuals, even where "particular" benevolence cannot apply. The distinction Hume makes in the *Enquiries* between general and particular benevolence is not then the same as that between Slote's caring for intimates and humanitarian concern.

How could we conceive of "general love" analogous to "general benevolence" on a Humean conception? Although Hume admits such virtues as general benevolence, goodwill, compassion, and humanity, it is not clear that he offers a conception of general love. Nonetheless, I shall argue, his theory has resources to explain both the intelligibility and the virtuousness of such a form of love. We ask then the following question: Are there, or could there be, on a Humean view, virtues conforming to the non-consequentialist criterion (C2) (Chapter 3), whose passional base is a love unassociated with any of the following: intimate affections, amity manifested in the various virtues of sociability, admiration for valuable qualities, blood relations, and services rendered to one? Is there in short, on a Humean picture, the possibility of a "general love" analogous to general compassion and general benevolence, bearing in mind that love, compassion, and benevolence are all different passions? To answer that question we need first to ask: Are people lovable in the sense required by general love?

9.3 The Possibility of General Love on a Humean Account

Notice first that "lovable" is ambiguous between "able to be loved" and "being a fitting object of love." Similarly, enviable may mean "able to be envied" and "being a fitting object of envy." Those who think envy is a vice based on a weak resentment will argue that no-one is a fitting object of envy. In Book 2 of the *Treatise* Hume has many interesting things to say about the enviable in the first sense, but although that helps us understand the intelligibility of envy it does not show that envy is fitting or can be the passional core of a virtue. Making sense of general love as a virtue or core of virtue in Humean terms requires us then to do two things: explain how general love is possible, and explain how it is fitting. This and the next section are concerned with the first of these tasks.

A difficult feature of general love is finding a cause of such love that makes it intelligible on Hume's picture. Such a cause is necessary if this form of love, like other forms made intelligible by the beloved's admirable properties or blood relation to the lover for example, is possible for Hume. I shall argue that to understand how general love under Hume's system can be intelligible, we need to understand the importance of relational properties as a cause of love for Hume. Recall that love for Hume is not just excited by non-relational properties such as beauty, virtue, or humanity. It is caused also by such factors as services rendered and blood ties. However none of these particular relational properties explains the intelligibility of general love. To see what relational property could explain such love on a Humean account we need to look again at Hume's discussion of compassion or pity.

Compassion arises through the operation of sympathy based on resemblance, rather than on such features as merits, friendship, and services rendered. Although compassion is appropriate to "all human creatures" insofar as they "are related to us by resemblance" (T 369) it is not general love, since compassion, like benevolence, is a direct passion, being a desire for others not to suffer. Love by contrast is an indirect passion, causally related to such a desire, but not identical with it. Love itself requires both pleasure in a feature of the beloved, and the operations of the imagination where that pleasure is "carried over" to an "indefinable" passion of love, distinct from the original pleasure which excited the love. Such a love need not be "violent" as in "the appetite for generation" but may be "calm."

If the model of compassion is to be deployed in the service of a Humean account of a capacity for universal love we run into an immediate problem. The suffering of another produces compassion, but a cause of general love could not be the suffering itself since suffering is not an agreeable property which excites the pleasurable sentiment of love. Rather the association of impressions and ideas would proceed as follows: just as we can take pleasure in another's witty conversation, so we can take pleasure in another's humanity, *qua* resembling property, which also causes the pleasurable sentiment of love for the bearer of that relational property of resemblance. As a result of that love we sympathize with that person's pain and desire its alleviation, even if we have no affection or admiration for that person.

We now ask: Can properties of resemblance, which occasion compassion, similarly occasion a general love of say strangers associated with goodwill? There is nothing in Hume's theory to preclude bonds of love based on resembling properties. Esteem/love of the rich and powerful for example is originally occasioned by our expectation of succor and protection from them (T 362). The esteem/love is transferred to others from whom we can expect no advantage, by the mechanism of sympathy. Let us take this idea further. Imagine I am forcibly aware of a stranger.

He is not suffering. He is much more powerful or dazzling than I, causing a kind of awe, even fear. Or he may be a member of a race against which there is much prejudice. These features do not cause love. However I am struck by a resembling property, notably his humanity. The pleasure I take in his humanity gives rise to a certain love of him, since I am devoid of envy and malice. Those devoid of envy and malice can take pleasure in the happiness of others (including those who are superior to them in riches, power, fame, ability) and thus have goodwill toward them. As Hume notes in the *Enquiries*, this feature of non-defective human beings "seems inseparable from our make and constitution" (E 191, 234 n. 1).

9.4   General Love and Bonds

We claimed above that what makes general love intelligible or possible is a sympathy based on resemblance, a pleasure which can be carried over by the imagination to the distinctive indirect passion of a general love for that individual, even a stranger. In other words the causal mechanisms of such a love are analogous to other forms of love. We need to explain just how a relational property of resemblance can play this role. As we have seen, Hume makes it clear that *ties* of blood relation can make the love of relatives intelligible and reasonable independent of the value of those persons (T 352). Given that Hume believes also that relations of resemblance can explain and make reasonable at least some of the humane passions, this view can be extended in a Humean virtue ethics of general love, and indeed love in general.

Central to this understanding of Hume's contribution to the idea of general love then is the notion of a bond: a bond which, as we shall see, can be imaginatively extended from intimates where it has its natural home, to a non-intimate form of general love. A bond is a psychological, relational property connoting an emotional tie between two or more individuals. To attain a more concrete notion of success in bonding we need to turn to psychology.

Psychologists recognize a fundamental human need for attachment and identification. The centrality of emotional bonding and love to human development and flourishing is recognized in attachment theory, first elaborated in the 1960s by the psychoanalytical psychiatrist John Bowlby.[10] As Jon Allen describes Bowlby's views,[11] they are drawn from evolutionary theory and ethology. Fundamental to secure attachment is a secure base, paradigmatically developed from infant attachment to a proximate, available caregiver. From that safe haven, infants can develop into agents that are secure in exploring, separating, and being autonomous and independent, without losing the capacity to trust, and come close in love. Further, insecure attachment not only inhibits the development of empathy and proper relationships to others, but is also at the root of low self-esteem which in turn feeds into problems of relatedness to others.[12]

Failures in attachment or defective attachment were studied in the well-established[13] experiments called the "Strange Situation Test" devised by psychologist Mary Ainsworth for the purposes of measuring secure and insecure attachment.[14] Various attachment problems are rooted in insecure or defective love, or a complete absence of love, resulting in syndromes called avoidant, resistant, or disorganized attachment. At the physiological level, our ability to resonate with positive feelings and positive expressions causes and reinforces secure attachment set up through appropriate pleasure pathways in the emotional brain. Recall that Hume's conception of love is an imaginative "carrying over" of pleasures associated with features of the beloved, such as crucially in the case of a young baby, the positively expressive face of notably the feeding mother, to pleasures (of love) associated with the person herself. This analysis anticipates remarkably recent findings in neuroscience which describe the "circuitous" routes by which "the family's doting looks are triggering off the pleasurable biochemicals that actually help the social brain to grow."[15] Through the sequencing of these pleasures, secure attachment (first to the proximate caregiver) is developed, and the individual becomes capable of love and empathy. If the face of that caregiver is depressed, flat, hostile, fearful, anxious, or alarming, then the pleasurable sequences fail to materialize sufficiently: there will be inadequate "carrying over" of pleasures, and no secure attachment.[16] Indeed Hume himself acknowledged that properties such as suffering as such and ugliness ("negative faces") cannot excite love, since they do not (at least characteristically) excite pleasure.

Research discloses the harmful effects of bonding failures, and the types of socially beneficial effects of the various "affectional systems." In his seminal work *Learning to Love*, Harry F. Harlow describes five such systems: maternal love, infant love, peer or age-mate love, heterosexual love, and paternal love. Each of these systems prepares the individual for later ones:

> … the maternal and infant affectional systems prepare the child for the perplexing problems of peer adjustment by providing him with basic feelings of security and trust. Playmates determine social and sexual destiny but without the certain knowledge of a safe haven, a potential playmate can at first sight be a frightening thing … In all primates the heterosexual affectional system is hopelessly inept and inadequate unless it has been preceded by effective peer partnerships and age-mate activities.[17]

If things go wrong in these systems to either excess or deficiency, successful coping, engagement with the world, is impeded or destroyed. For example, if the bonds of one affectional system remain too strong and enduring, they may "impede transition to the appropriate new system when [the individual] eventually matures."[18] These are affectional fixations. If there is deficiency in the bonding through violent separation for example, defects arise ranging from failure to respond to self-mutilation[19] and extreme or inappropriate aggression. As Harlow claims, "because the emotion of anger develops in all infants, and one outlet for this is aggression, the socialization of aggression is a primary concern for any social group."[20] Since such anger/

aggression can be at its most harmful when the mother–infant bonds have weakened, claims Harlow, the age-mate affectional system is vital for its control.[21] Fear can also be a result of bonding misattunement and failure. The infant–mother affectional system serves the needs of solace and security, and where this and other affectional systems fail, stranger and separation anxiety may become entrenched, developing eventually into free-floating anxiety.

How can this analysis be applied to general love? Given that a bond is a relation between individuals, paradigmatically an intimate relationship, it is often thought that a bond-based or relationship ethics has trouble with extension to contexts of general benevolence in Hume's non-fungible sense, Humean compassion, and general love. However some authors believe that such extension is possible. The concept of social interest made famous by Alfred Adler provides the basic idea. It is explained thus by Ursula E. Oberst and Alan E. Stewart:

> Having Social Interest means feeling part of a family, a group, a couple, and the human community. Some Adlerian authors have argued that it means even feeling part of the universe. It means to participate, to contribute, to share; to feel accepted, appreciated and loved, as well as to accept, appreciate and love other people. But this social embeddedness also means being able to cope with the obstacles and misfortunes of life in a socially adaptive way; not by seeking one's self interest and personal advancement, and by pursuing, at the same time, the benefit of – theoretically – the whole of humankind.[22]

How can there be a type of universal bond? Such a bond is ultimately based on what Willard Gaylin calls "proximate identification." He describes identification thus:

> The basic ingredient that defines identification is not the unconscious modeling, but the fusion of the stuff of our very self with the substance of another. Identity starts by knowing the toe we bite is part of us ... With fusion there is an erosion of the rigid boundaries of self, a blurring of the sense of the isolated "I", or ego.[23]

Three types of identification are defined: upward, downward, and proximate. In upward there is an attempt to model oneself on a person who may be idealized (the ego ideal), but much of the identification is unconscious and automatic. In downward, as in mother–infant, the identificatory process is not one of modeling though there is "fusion." Proximate identification is particularly relevant to groups. In this sense I identify with Aucklanders, New Zealanders tend to identify with Australians when they are abroad, and Nelson Mandela identified with "his people," black South Africans. Although as Gaylin claims proximal identification does not necessarily require "the physical proximity to or sight of the individual," it does require something like kinship. Now Gaylin claims that the "family of man" is a noble ideal that will never be realized: proximal identification can "never be extended to include the entire human race."[24] This would preclude the ideal of compassion toward all sentient beings, say, based on a notion of bond. However, Gaylin's argument for this claim appears to run together properties of downward identification with those associated with proximate identification. He says, "There is no psychological way to extend downward identification to all. It is too heavy a burden. Were we to grieve over the suffering of every child in the same way as we do with our own, life would be unendurable."[25]

However, attention to Hume's moral psychology sheds light on the problem of how proximate identification can make sense of such a bond without an unendurable emotional burden. His account of the psychology of sympathy based on resemblance can make intelligible the idea of general bonds based on a form of proximate identification or kinship. Proximate identification with a stranger to whom compassion is appropriate does not need to involve the intense psychological properties of downward identification. It merely requires a bond such that we do not treat her with indifference, let alone callousness and hatred, and we would respond to suffering according to the exigencies of the circumstances. Given that, as Steven Pinker claims, "*homo sapiens* is obsessed with kinship,"[26] there is no need to assume that we cannot bond in different ways with strangers as appropriate. A well-functioning imagination operating in a culture of benevolent empathy can allow an indefinite extension of this type of bond. For Hume this kind of bond is ultimately based on resemblance (as opposed to love caused by services rendered and so forth). Genuine bonds of this type would at least make cruelty and callousness impossible: a major advance, and further advances make possible the virtues of general love, a disposition to universal (non-fungible) beneficence, tenderness and loving kindness, forgiveness, grace.

Bonds of love, so crucial to human well-being and development as Hume recognized, is of a different moral significance and nature from recognition of value. Value is determined by reasoned thought about merits and worthwhileness and does not, as Hume also recognized, necessarily track the various types of bonds of love (T 352). Indeed even that form of love which is admiration for personal qualities and possessions, such as admiration for "fine equipages," may be associated with a bond of love for the owner out of proportion to the mere value, or even the mere value *to her*, of those qualities and possessions. For the imagination, indeed what Mark Johnson calls the "moral imagination,"[27] is central to forming bonds of love.

To show that general love is possible through bonds of proximate identification based on sympathy through resemblance, we need to say more about what kind of love is general love. Steven Tudor[28] cites three features of general or "agapeic" love. These are:

(1)   It is particular.
(2)   It is non-sentimental.
(3)   It is non-intimate.

We have already seen how a Humean account can explain the particularity of general love analogous to other forms of love. The problem lies in understanding how a love can be both particularized and general. Attention to the second and third features helps explain how such love is possible. According to Tudor: "Agape does not have the reassuring warmth of *philia* or the desiring hunger of *eros*. Instead it is a much more moderate, even attenuated emotion."[29]

Tudor rightly denies that agapeic love is emotionless. It involves an emotional construal in two ways. First general love, rather than being a debilitating, strong, emotional connection with indefinite numbers of individuals, is characterized by a general loving emotional orientation to the world as a whole: what Heidegger calls a *Grundstimmung* or (fundamental) emotional attunement often translated (problematically) as "mood."[30] This orientation predisposes the person capable of general love to be ready to experience such emotions as tenderness, compassion, and well-wishing when faced with a stranger in circumstances in which expressing one of the virtues of general love, such as loving kindness or forgiveness, is appropriate. Second, when those virtues (such as kindness) are expressed in relation to a particular individual who may have crossed your path (or whose path you have crossed), emotions toward that individual (to whom one is being kind, say) are felt and expressed. Nor need it be the case that at the point of contact the emotions of tenderness and so forth remain moderate. At that point the bonds of humanity may be intensely felt. Strong emotion may erupt from the background state of a loving *Grundstimmung*. Such was the case with Sister Prejean's relationship with Sonnier to whom she was spiritual advisor.[31]

Despite this, general love is not as such intimate. Though there is a "moral closeness" to the beloved "the agapeic self does not seek to be close in an intimate way to the Other, especially not exclusively so. It does not seek to make the Other it loves a 'partner', someone with whom it can become 'involved.'"[32] Again however this general claim is to be treated with caution: though this is the default position for agapeic love, for otherwise it would be too debilitating, the agapeic self (as Sister Prejean illustrates) can become very involved with a beloved with whom she has a great deal to do.

9.5   The Fittingness of General Love

If general love is not only possible but fitting, we can properly speak of general love as a virtue or at the core of diverse virtues of general love. The ability to take pleasure in a resembling property of say humanity, despite potentially distancing features (such as those causing fear, hate, malice, envy), is still immediately agreeable to a qualified judge, indeed admired as a virtue. A person capable of such goodwill based on a general love of those who all too often excite fear, envy, or hatred is admired by a qualified judge for its corruption or absence is so readily seen.

On such a view of "general" love, we would have a tenth set of virtues conforming to (C2); another kind of love-based cluster:

(C2j)   Traits merit our approbation because they are expressive of our bonds of humanity (or even wider bonds), namely our pleasure in the well-being of others, even those unconnected with us, whom we love through the pleasure we take in (say) their "resembling" properties of humanity (or their animality).

Belonging to this cluster are goodwill, the disposition to (appropriately) forgive, loving kindness, grace and general beneficence (a charitable disposition of helping strangers), and mercy.[33]

The difficulty of thinking of general love as fitting lies in justifying the properties which putatively make general love fitting, namely the proximate identification which makes possible the sympathy which can lead to bonds of say humanity. It may seem that for such love to be fitting there must be a *merit* of the beloved which rationalizes the love, but mere resemblance (in virtue of humanity, say) is not such a merit. However, as bonds with one's children show, not all love need be based on merits. As Hume recognizes, blood relation may be enough. Because it is not fungible humanitarian concern, in an important sense a general love of people is analogous to love of intimates such as one's children, by virtue of it not being "love" of people *as a whole*. In *Morals From Motives* Slote shows with a convincing example how our love of our children is not love of them as a whole, or a matter of maximizing net benefit for them taken together.[34] For this reason such love is manifested in a balancing of their interests in often very difficult exercises of equitable dealings with them, where a greater net good is not gained by sacrificing one to the needs of another.[35] One might apply this idea to general love: it is a love that is particularized, it is a love that is not based on merits, and it is a love that expresses an equitable "balance" of interests (where there is conflict of interests) rather than being susceptible to utilitarian calculus.

There are further criticisms of the fittingness of general love. Consider first a criticism of Slote's. Slote claims that such love is contrary to the spirit of love since love he suggests is limited in scope.[36] This is certainly true of some forms of love as forms of affection such as friendship, but the virtues of general love are not the virtues of affection. Goodwill for example does not require affection or even liking. Furthermore it is not true of those forms of affectionate love that are unconditional, such as love of one's children. *Pace* Slote the complaints of a child whose parents "want (yet) another child" and the complaints of a child "whose actual sibling gets a lop-sided amount of attention" are not similar, at least not inherently.[37] The children of a large family do not necessarily get the lop-sided attention that occurs when some are favored. Nor need each of them receive equally neglectful unloving treatment. If general love manifests as lop-sided beneficence, say, then the balancing of interests is not being done in an equitable way, and the love is not virtuous.

Another criticism originates with Peter Singer. Basing the intelligibility of general love on a resembling property such as humanity would not be for him a proper basis for such love, since it is "speciesist." What he calls the "Principle of Equal Consideration of Interests" should be based on answers not to the questions "Can they *reason*?, nor Can they *talk*?, but, Can they suffer?"[38] Though Singer is not talking about love, but about a principle of equality, his point may have force in relation to the reasonableness of general love when that love is restricted to humanity. What is special about humanity as a property which makes human creatures lovable?

In reply it must be emphasized that on the Humean picture outlined it is not the non-relational property of humanity which makes universal love reasonable, but the relational property of resemblance. Certainly humanity is a resembling property, but there are many others, such as capacity to suffer, and other properties of animality in general. It is precisely Hume's point that the imagination, so adept at extending love, can find and take pleasure in a wide variety of resembling properties. Appeal to the role of the imagination then allows for the possibility that universal love need not be confined to human creatures. There is no fixed or determinate resembling property such as humanity which rationalizes universal love. Virtues of goodwill and compassion, associated with general love, are arguably exhibited in a higher or superior form if the bounds of resembling properties, in which we sympathize or take pleasure, are appropriately extended. For example in a process of moral improvement we may extend our sympathies from cheerful humans to suffering ones; from attractive humans to ugly ones; from virtuous humans to vicious ones; from humans in general to cute animals and from cute animals to the not so cute such as weta, spiders, rats, snakes. On a Humean picture the powers of the imagination are progressively deployed to extend the original bounds of love. General love becomes even more general. Furthermore, although on Hume's view the pleasure we take in the resembling property need not translate into love as affection or admiration for the object of love, for Hume tenderness and other virtues more commonly associated with bonds of intimacy, may be extended to objects of general love. The imagination enables us to not only broaden but also deepen general love. Notice however that on a Humean view, sympathetic pleasure with some kind of resembling property or properties causing pleasure is necessary to make sense of lovability as a response dependent property since factors such as viciousness, suffering as such, and ugliness are not themselves (characteristically) properties which cause pleasure, and cannot of themselves (characteristically) excite love for Hume.

This reply to the "Singer problem" raises another issue. A Humean virtue ethics of love as sketched here may draw ire from feminists, as ethicists of care have already discovered. Sue Gerhardt reports that a major concern of her students is being blamed for not being perfect mothers. Misunderstandings about the demands of an ethics of love in general[39] coupled with findings about the development of the emotional brain in infancy and toddlerhood, have resulted in the observation that the responsibilities that such an ethics place on child rearing is "not popular."[40] However Jon Allen hits the nail on the head when he claims that "good mothering" does not demand perfect mothering but good enough mothering.[41] In other words the role virtue of being a good mother (or father), like all virtue concepts according to Daniel Russell, is a "satis" concept,[42] or what I have called a threshold concept.[43] The same applies to the demands of general love which may be both misconstrued and seen as excessively demanding.

Another criticism of the Humean account of the fittingness of general love is this. As is well known, bonds of proximate identification are a potent cause of "tribalist" vice as well as grounding kinship-type virtue. There are two points in reply. First, tribal identification can indeed cause hate of "outsiders" as well as love of "insiders." Obviously a virtue ethics of love would not say that tribalist-based hate is a virtue or basis of virtue.[44] And the whole point of general love is to extend the "tribe." Second, we should distinguish virtues of general love from vices of general love. Strictly speaking it is not general love as such that is fitting but virtuous general love. We have not said anything here about how virtues of general love should be distinguished from closely related vice (such as forms of pathological altruism discussed in relation to Nietzsche). All we have claimed here is that on a Humean picture resemblance in relevant respects makes general love intelligible and indeed (potentially) fitting, since the bonds of kinship of proximate identification can ground such fittingness. More needs to be said about how the virtues of general love are to be delineated.

The Humean picture as explicated here fits a common view that general love is not and cannot be premised on ideas of the worthiness, the value, or the deserts of the objects of love. Anders Nygren, discussing God's love of us as a paradigm of such love, claims that such love is "indifferent to value": "It is only when all thought of the worthiness of the object is abandoned that we can understand what Agape is."[45] However it does not follow from the claim that, where value or worth is not a cause or motive of love, love must *create* such worth or value if it is to be intelligible. For value or worth need not be what makes love reasonable or naturally fitting. Hume's account of the relational property of resemblance as a property causing sympathy does not depend at all on ideas of the objective value or excellence of the objects of love, although as we have seen value or excellence is *one* of the major types of property which for Hume makes love intelligible and reasonable. Love for Hume is a bond between individuals and he makes clear (as we have seen) that even strong bonds that are fitting, may not be grounded in the value or merits of the object of love.

Notes

1   For a summary of neo-Confucian sentimentalist as well as "flourishing-based" virtue ethics, see Philip J. Ivanhoe, "Virtue Ethics and the Chinese Confucian Tradition," in *The Cambridge Companion to Virtue Ethics*, ed. Daniel C. Russell (Cambridge: Cambridge University Press, 2013), 49–69.

2   See, e.g., Michael Slote, "Virtue Ethics and Democratic Values," *Journal of Social Philosophy* 24 (1993), 5–37.

3   Rand, "The Objectivist Ethics," in *The Virtue of Selfishness: A New Concept of Egoism* (New York: Signet/Penguin, 1964), 13–39, 27. However this view is more important than it is given credit for: see my "Virtues of Productivity versus Technicist Rationality," in *Economics and the Virtues*, ed. Mark D. White and Jennifer A. Baker (Oxford: Oxford University Press, forthcoming).

4   Robert N. Johnson, "Virtue and Right," *Ethics* 113(4) (2003), 810–834.

5   I offer a Nietzsche-inspired reply to Johnson, based on my target-centered virtue ethical account of right action in my "Virtue Ethics and the Problem of Demandingness," in *The Problem of Moral Demandingness*, ed. T. Chappell (London: Palgrave Macmillan, 2009), 104–122.

6   See Slote, *Morals From Motives* (Oxford: Oxford University Press, 2001), ix.
7   Ibid., 114.
8   Ibid., 118.
9   Ibid., 66.
10 Bowlby, *Attachment* (London: Pelican, 1969).
11 In Allen, *Coping With Trauma: Hope Through Understanding*, 2nd edn. (Washington, DC: American Psychiatric Publishing, 2005).
12 See Sue Gerhardt, *Why Love Matters: How Affection Shapes a Baby's Brain* (London: Routledge, 2004), 88.
13 As Jon Allen claims, "Thousands of Strange Situations have been created throughout the world" (*Coping With Trauma*, chapter 2).
14 M. Ainsworth, M. Blehar, E. Waters, and S. Wall, *Patterns of Attachment: A Psychological Study of the Strange Situation* (Hillsdale, NJ: Lawrence Erlbaum Associates, 1978).
15 Gerhardt, 42. The "circuitous routes" are described in Gerhardt, 41–42.
16 See Gerhardt on negative faces, 47–49, and the "power of a smile," 41–44.
17 Harlow, *Learning to Love* (New York: Jason Aronson Inc., 1974), 3.
18 Ibid., 3.
19 Harlow (ibid., 113) reports that self-aggression can be observed in Rhesus monkeys raised in social isolation.
20 Ibid., 116.
21 Ibid., 117, 127.
22 Oberst and Stewart, *Adlerian Psychotherapy: An Advanced Approach to Individual Psychology* (Hove and New York: Brunner-Routledge, 2003), 17.
23 Gaylin, *Hatred: The Psychological Descent into Violence* (New York: Public Affairs, 2003), 165.
24 Ibid., 171.
25 Ibid., 171.
26 Pinker, *How the Mind Works* (London: Penguin, 1997), 430.
27 Johnson, *Moral Imagination: Implications of Cognitive Science for Ethics* (Chicago: University of Chicago Press, 1993).
28 Tudor, *Compassion and Remorse* (Leuven: Peeters, 2001).
29 Ibid., 111.
30 For discussion of this feature of universal love see my "A Challenge to Intellectual Virtue from Moral Virtue: The Case of Universal Love," in *Virtue and Vice, Moral and Epistemic*, ed. Heather Battaly (Oxford: Wiley-Blackwell, 2010), 153–171.
31 Sister Helen Prejean, *Dead Man Walking* (New York: Vintage Books, 1993).
32 Tudor, 113.
33 Hence this view is opposed to that of Robert Merrihew Adams who thinks that love, even universal love, must be responsive to excellence in humans: see his *Finite and Infinite Goods: A Framework for Ethics* (Oxford: Oxford University Press, 2002), esp. chapter 6. Adams explicitly disagrees on this point with Anders Nygren, "Agape and Eros," in *Eros, Agape and Philia: Readings in the Philosophy of Love*, ed. A. Sobel (New York: Paragon House, 1989), 85–95.
34 Slote, *Morals From Motives*, 67.
35 For a fictional problem case of parental use of a child as (life-saving) resource for another, see Jodi Picoult, *My Sister's Keeper* (Crows Nest, NSW: Allen & Unwin, 2004).
36 Slote, *Morals from Motives*, 118.
37 Ibid., 118 n. 2.
38 Singer, "All Animals Are Equal," in *Animal Rights and Human Obligations*, ed. T. Regan and P. Singer (Englewood Cliffs, NJ: Prentice Hall, 1976), 148–162, 151.
39 For these issues see my "Virtue Ethics and the Problem of Demandingness."
40 Gerhardt, *Why Love Matters*, 21.
41 Allen, *Coping With Trauma*, chapter 2. Indeed it is still extraordinarily unclear what "perfect mothering" would demand, for there is still serious disagreement about important matters. Consider for example the

debate concerning the rearing of babies between those who advocate the "no cry solution" and those who advocate "controlled crying."

42   See Daniel C. Russell, *Practical Intelligence and the Virtues* (Oxford: Oxford University Press, 2009), 114–126.

43   In my *Virtue Ethics: A Pluralistic View* (Oxford: Oxford University Press, 2003).

44   I leave here open the question of whether hatred is ever permissible (as in the example of a parent of the child in the Dostoyevsky case of the General whose dogs tear apart the child), and whether the permissibility of such hatred, at least as initial response, could be compatible with an ethics of general (universal) love. (I thank Nick Smith for this example and discussion.)

45   Nygren, "Agape and Eros," 87.

Chapter 10

Nietzschean Virtue Ethics: Virtue Ethics of Becoming

10.1 Introduction

Part III of this work suggested that Nietzsche makes three major contributions to virtue ethics: his attention to the depth psychological quality of motivational dispositions as an aspect of virtue; the differentiation of virtue according to such features as one's role, type, strength, particularities of one's life; and his focus on affirming one's own life, understood as a norm. Perhaps the most radical aspect from the perspective of new directions for virtue ethics is the third, and I accordingly give this feature more attention here.

On a virtue ethical reading, Nietzsche accepts as a fundamental standard excellence as human being, but at the same time he is doubtful that excellence, understood broadly in terms of life affirmation, can be achieved or is even an appropriate goal for the many. Chapter 8 partially solved this problem by exploring Nietzsche's pluralism via the notion of differentiated virtue, but the problem remains of how this idea fits into a *developmental* view of will to power. How is virtue appropriately developed in the "convalescent" and to what extent if at all is virtue-development in individuals constrained by a fixed type to which they belong? An answer to these questions will suggest that Nietzsche offers a "new direction" for virtue ethics: what I call "a virtue ethics of becoming." Here he is understood as rejecting a standard teleological view, that humans should aim at an end state of perfection proper to humans in general, or proper to their "type." Nonetheless the core ideas of an ethics of self-realization, those of development, maturity, and excellence that are central to the interpretation of Nietzsche offered in Chapters 6 and 7 can be retained. The conventional teleological picture is replaced by a "virtue ethics of becoming" in which creativity, productivity, overcoming resistance, play a central role, without there being a determinate *telos* which is the end goal of such a development, and defines

The Virtue Ethics of Hume and Nietzsche, First Edition. Christine Swanton.
© 2015 John Wiley & Sons, Ltd. Published 2015 by John Wiley & Sons, Ltd.

perfection. In the analytic tradition, these features of "life affirmation" are not at the heart of ethical thought; indeed by and large they would not occupy even a fringe place. Although the reasons for this will not be discussed here[1] virtue ethics in its modern guise has been part of this tradition.

To affirm one's life in a Nietzschean sense one must "self-overcome," that is, one must overcome weaknesses in dealing with resistances and challenges of various kinds in a process of self-development. This process requires a certain hardness and severity toward oneself, and a creative and productive orientation toward the world as opposed to the "herd"-like tendency to be preoccupied with one's comfortable pleasures and welfare understood in a narrow or superficial sense. A focus on "self-overcoming" could set virtue ethics in a new direction for two basic reasons. First, insofar as virtue is intrinsically associated with "self-overcoming," the virtue ethics would be a "virtue ethics of becoming" (as opposed to a virtue ethics of perfection) in a sense to be explicated in sections 10.2 and 10.3. Second, a prime vehicle for self-overcoming for Nietzsche is creativity, so such a virtue ethics would be a virtue ethics of creativity, or one in which creativity plays a very important role. Key features of a Nietzschean virtue ethics of creativity are outlined and discussed in section 10.4.

10.2   An Ethics of Becoming

In *The Gay Science* Nietzsche claims: (1) "*What does your conscience say?* – 'You shall become the person you are'"[2] and (2) "We, however, *want to become those we are* – human beings who are new, unique, incomparable, who give themselves laws, who create themselves."[3] Finally he also claims in *Ecce Homo*: (3) "Becoming what you are presupposes that you have not the slightest inkling *what* you are."[4]

The injunction to become what (who) we are may suggest that Nietzsche is a teleologist in the sense that

(ST)   (Strong Teleology) There is an end state of perfection which is the *telos* of human beings, whether or not we are capable of attaining it (as opposed to approximating it) in a characteristic human life.

However (2) and (3) are in at least apparent tension with (ST). The claim of (2) suggests that there is no *telos* proper to human beings *qua* human – rather we create ourselves in an ongoing process as individuals. The claim of (3) also suggests that there is no *telos* proper to humans *qua* humans because if there were, how could it be desirable that we not know what this is?

However if (ST) is rejected, how could Nietzsche be interpreted as a virtue ethicist? How can we understand the idea of a virtue as a human excellence?

We need to show how a "virtue ethics of becoming" which rejects (ST) can retain the common understanding of human virtues as human excellences. First there is a prior task. We need to see how the imperative to become who you are need not presuppose (ST), but is rather part of an "an ethics of becoming" comprising (2) and (3) as central features. That prior task is undertaken in this section. The next section shows how "Become who you are," interpreted as an imperative within an ethics of becoming, can nonetheless speak of virtue as a human excellence. My ultimate aim is to show that an ethics of becoming can be a *virtue* ethics of becoming, and that Nietzsche's conception of virtue can be understood in this manner.

Many interpreters of Nietzsche take him to reject (ST). According to (ST) there is an end state of perfection proper to human beings, and one improves oneself by having in mind this end state (or suitable approximation) which allows for a rationally directed progression of one's life. However this picture is rejected as an interpretation of Nietzsche by, for example, Simon May who claims: "for Nietzsche, unlike for Aristotle, the perfect and final actualization of a clear and fixed potential is neither possible nor knowable nor should be sought."[5] As Alexander Nehemas also points out, this Aristotelian teleology is rejected by Nietzsche: for Nietzsche, "becoming does not aim at a final state."[6]

How can "becoming" not aim at a single final state? How can it be possible that, as May puts it, there is "*not even a theoretical* terminus of perfect fulfillment or maximum good"?[7] If Nietzsche rejects Aristotelian teleology, how can he enjoin us to become who we are? Does not the injunction suggest that there is after all a final state (of perhaps perfection) which is your *true* self and which you should aim to reach? The proper understanding of the idea of becoming who you are is suggested by the expanded version of the aphorism in "Schopenhauer as Educator":

> The human being who does not wish to belong to the mass needs only to cease being comfortable with himself; let him follow his conscience, which calls to him: "Be yourself! All you are now doing, thinking, desiring is not you yourself."[8]

As James Conant puts it, "All one need do is become uncomfortable with the discrepancy between oneself and one's self – between who we are at present, and the self that is somehow ours and yet presently at a distance from us."[9] This does not entail that there is an end state of "arrival" where the self, or one of the selves, presently at a distance from us, is the terminus of our endeavors. Self-improvement does not entail that we should have definite productive goals such as being a great artist which now drive all our actions. Nor is there an *end*-state (of perfection) which one can reach such that one can say on reaching it "I have arrived."

The above understanding of (1) does not imply that the individual should not have goals: rather they are relativized to more localized ends where the individual overcomes obstacles and resistances. Certainly the goals can be assessed as strong or weak; shallow, trivial, or meaningful and worthwhile; active or reactive, but they are not necessarily directed toward or rationalized by reference to a "terminus of perfect fulfillment." On Nietzsche's view, improvement is rather a continuous matter of overcoming obstacles, becoming stronger, while dealing with the world and achieving (worthwhile) goals.[10] Nietzsche applied this view particularly to himself: "the years when my vitality was at its lowest were when I *stopped* being a pessimist: the instinct of self recovery *forbade* me a philosophy of poverty and discouragement."[11]

Even if an ethics of becoming tolerates or even lauds goal setting we should not assume that it is the realization of the goals themselves that supply the norms or the major norms for improvement and development. In an ethics of becoming, the process of overcoming itself is importantly norm-governed. Having argued that "will to power," or power, is not itself an end but is constituted by improvement, growth, or development in "patterns of effort" in achieving the various internal ends of "drives," John Richardson puts the point this way:

> This makes the connection between power and a drive's internal end even less direct than we expected: not only does power not lie in this end's achievement, it doesn't even lie in progress toward it but in improving this progress. Moreover, the criteria for this "improvement" aren't set by the end – it's not just an improvement in the route's efficiency for achieving the end. Rather … it lies in an enrichment or elaboration of the drive's activity pattern.[12]

We turn now to the elaboration of "Become who you are" in terms of (2). Nietzsche's ethics of becoming has (2) as a central component. The question arises: How can one become "who one is" if one's life is as anarchic as (2) appears to suggest? More generally, if (ST) is rejected how can there be standards implicit in what Nietzsche calls the development psychology of will to power? Indeed can human beings be said to develop if there is no end state of perfection supplying such standards? The answer to these questions lies in an understanding of (2). The creativity, self-legislation, cultivation of individuality, and experimentation characterizing the process of "becoming" are not ungoverned by norms. We see in the next section how such norms are understood as virtues in a virtue ethics of becoming. Here it may be observed that the fact that there is no end state of perfection guiding one's choices does not imply that there are no norms governing the processes of dealing with situations, resistances and obstacles. In *Genealogy of Morals* for example we have the happiness of the active type contrasted unfavorably with the passivity of the reactive man of resentment:

> … as fully developed people overladen with strength, and consequently as necessarily active people, they knew better than to separate action from happiness … all this is diametrically opposed to "happiness" … of those who suppurate with poisonous and hostile feelings, those for whom happiness appears essentially as narcotic, anaesthetic, calm, peace.[13]

Overcoming well, as we might say, does not have its terminus in the calm or peace of happiness. It is certainly not escape into passivity in a search for such peace: it is an active engagement with the world. The norms of overcoming are given a more detailed specification in *The Antichrist*. Here the strongest individuals are described as finding their happiness in the "labyrinth," in "hardness against themselves and others," in assuming difficult complex tasks and responsibilities. However, because these difficulties and burdens are sought by the active type, and not felt as burdensome or forced on them, they are undertaken in a joyful, cheerful, and even kindly way.[14]

Before turning to a more specific account of the virtues of overcoming we need to consider (3). At first sight the injunction (1) to become who you are is in tension with the advice that one not know who one is. However the thought expressed in (3) has two main ideas which are congenial to the interpretation of (1) in an ethics of becoming. One should not have a rigid idea of the nature of one's talents and the path of one's life at any given time (epistemic humility concerning self-knowledge about one's nature and circumstances at a given time) and one should not have a firm long-term picture about the being you should become.[15] If one knows what one is in the above ways one limits oneself and prejudges what may change and what one can do in those changed circumstances. For one's goals may change as one becomes stronger and faces new obstacles and circumstances. As Edward Harcourt argues in "Nietzsche and Eudaemonism," these ideas are compatible with a developmental view of a worthwhile life for human beings, as we explore further below.[16] One should think of development as a step by step process of setting goals and over-coming obstacles, including one's own weaknesses. Norms govern this process, but we need to say more about how virtue fits into an ethics of becoming. That is the topic of the next section.

10.3   A Virtue Ethics of Becoming

A virtue ethics of becoming has three main ideas to be developed in this section.

(a)   The idea that virtue, in a process of self-overcoming, is differentiated according to the individual.
(b)   The idea that there is a virtue whose field is self-improvement.
(c)   The idea that in some way or ways virtue is relative to stages of life in a dynamic way, where a stage is calibrated according to the strength of the agent.

Consider now (a). A basic virtue, in a virtue ethics of becoming, is differentiated in two main ways.[17] It is differentiated according to the individual particularities of a person's life, especially her individual modes of creativity, and according to her strength. We consider now the first form of differentiation. In the well-known section 290 of *The Gay Science*, Nietzsche claims that one must "'give style' to one's character" by fitting strengths and weaknesses of one's nature "into an artistic plan." In that passage he makes it clear both that there are constraints of style, and that "'giving style' to one's character" is done "under a law of [one's] own." Constraints of style are constraints which "only the strong enjoy." The weak by contrast "*hate* the constraint of style*" for they hate to serve norms: not serving what they see as "bitter and evil" constraints is the only way they can please themselves. "Arbitrary" "disorderly" "wild" interpretation and creativity is the hallmark of the weak, and does not exemplify virtuous setting of one's own laws. All this implies that respecting constraints of style must be compatible with setting "one's own laws." In a virtue ethics of becoming, creative virtue is seen in its basic form as mandating constraints of style but is differentiated according to one's own individual style. Norms of basic virtue can be understood as compatible with the requirement (2) above to cultivate what is unique in one. It is not enough for Nietzsche that we simply cultivate virtues as basic virtues, for example by respecting constraints of style while putting nothing of ourselves into our "creative" endeavors. If virtues are to be human excellences in us as *individuals*, they need to be fitted into the fabric of our particular lives in a way which, as Nietzsche claims, is unique, creative, autonomous, and makes of our life an art-work, while at the same time satisfying norms of creativity, discipline, and hardness. Notice that the existence of constraints of style is compatible with further constraints on creativity as a virtue in Nietzsche; for example, creativity as a virtue serves goods understood objectively as what are *properly* served in human creativity (whatever these are).[18]

We turn now to feature (b) above of a virtue ethics of becoming, the virtue of self-improvement.[19] We need to know how this virtue operates before we can understand how a virtue such as generosity is differentiated according to the strength of the agent. Unlike traditional virtue ethics, a virtue ethics of becoming contains a virtue of self-improvement whose field is one aspect of the self – its strengthening, developing, maturing, improving. In Nietzsche's ethics of becoming this process involves "overcoming." The virtue applies to all: self-improvement in its basic form would be a universal virtue. It would apply even to the "best": "Even in the best there is still something that nauseates; and even the best is something that must be overcome."[20]

In its thin definition the virtue of self-improvement is being well disposed, affectively, motivationally, and intellectually with respect to its field. What it is to be well disposed is of course complex, and relative to the strength, circumstances and so forth of the individual. Importantly, excellence in striving for self-improvement needs to accommodate Nietzsche's warning not to overreach one's strength: "Do not be virtuous beyond your strength!"[21] At the same time we have to guard against the "religion of comfortableness" and not rest content with one's current level of strength. A vice of excess, grandiose striving, is opposed to a vice of deficiency, complacency. The virtue's manifestation has many facets: wishes appropriate to the formation of goals are translated into goals, goals are appropriately implemented in action, dreaming of and visualizing goals is suitably integrated with realism, and so on. An account of the virtue warns us that not all striving for excellence is virtuous, but we will need a thick account of the virtue to appreciate the complex and controversial nature of its features.

To understand how the virtue of self-improvement operates, we need to say more about Nietzsche's warning: "Do not be virtuous beyond your strength!" This injunction suggests that the "convalescent" should not necessarily directly emulate what Harold Alderman describes as "paradigmatic individuals" such as "Buddha, Christ, Socrates or some other moral exemplar."[22] Indeed isn't there something wrong with the attitude of someone who directly aims at a final state of perfection, as does the character Valade in *Human Traces*:

> "Each time I touched the canvas, a shadow fell across the purity of the idea and took it further from what I had envisaged. Every painting ended up as an advertisement of my limitations. Only I could see through it to the glorious thing it was meant to be."
> "They looked pretty good to me."
> "Pretty good is what they were … I aimed for transcendence … and I ended with some 'pretty good' paintings."[23]

Overcoming then is not a smooth process of directly seeking "transcendence" or "perfection" even if we were able to make sense of these notions. As we saw in Chapter 1, for Nietzsche "I am *that which must always overcome itself*"; "I must be struggle and a becoming and an end and an opposition of ends," where I proceed on "*crooked* paths."[24] At the same time the injunction not to be virtuous beyond your strength is not as we have seen a recipe for complacency or timidity. There is no algorithm for distinguishing between, or even a determinate balance between, risky overreaching, and complacent avoidance of challenge or timid caution. The "paths" are "crooked," for norms of self-overcoming are themselves relative to the changing strength of the agent, and his changing circumstances and goals. Indeed as Nietzsche suggests "*enduring* habits" are ossifying, though "brief habits" are necessary if we are to avoid the intolerable existence of "perpetual improvisation."[25] The nature of the crookedness of the paths varies according to strength: serious risk-taking, for Nietzsche, is the prerogative of the strong, but imprudence in lesser types.

Consider now (c) the differentiation of virtue according to strength. To find out how this is done we consider two problems. Just as it is not always easy to distinguish in Nietzsche between traits which are not virtues at all, from traits which are virtues for the herd, it is not always easy to distinguish between traits which are not virtues at all from those which are virtues in the convalescent. In that case, how can we conceive of "virtues" of the convalescent as virtues at all? Both issues are in play in the following passage. Consider the distinction made by Nietzsche between cynicism and honesty in *Beyond Good and Evil*:

> Cynicism is the only form in which common souls come close to honesty; and the higher man must prick up his ears at every cynicism, whether course or refined, and congratulate himself whenever a buffoon without shame or a scientific satyr speaks out in his presence.[26]

Is cynicism a vice whereas honesty is a virtue which only the strong can attain? Or is cynicism a virtue of the convalescent or of the herd: a form of honesty differentiated according to strength? Nietzsche's point seems to be at least compatible with the latter reading. Cynicism is at least better than the willful ignorance of him who makes "everything around us bright and free and easy and simple," of him who employs language which "cannot get over its coarseness and continues to speak of antitheses where there are only degrees and many subtleties of gradation."[27] But it is unclear whether cynicism is a virtue of the convalescent who is on his way to genuine honesty, or whether society needs the cynics, where cynicism is a genuine herd virtue. I suspect that there is a sense in which both claims are true: let he who is capable of strength overcome cynicism, but cynicism can be seen as a herd-role virtue (if not taken to excess) of, for example, journalists.

If there is such a thing as virtues calibrated according to strength, how is this conceived? Here are three options.

(i)   There are separate virtues for different stages of life, calibrated by strength. However rather than think of these virtues in terms of basic virtues which are differentiated according to stages of life, quite different virtues are in play in different stages. There are on this view no universal virtues, even conceived as basic.

(ii)   There are basic virtues common to different levels of strength, but differentiated according to level, where there are end states of perfection for each level. A natural way of conceptualizing such a level is to claim that there are types of being or types of level, for example, "herd," lower, higher.

(iii)   Basic virtues are differentiated according to strength but that differentiation is conceived in a dynamic way, to be explicated.

Option (i) was rejected in Chapter 8. Regardless of the merits of the idea of there being distinct (basic) virtues and vices of temporal stages of life,[28] Nietzsche's discussions often suggest accounts of universal virtue that is differentiated according to individual strength. Sometimes as we noted above, Nietzsche equates a virtue with its manifestation in the strong, so the universal but differentiated aspect of virtue may be masked. Consider for example "solitude." In its thin account it is being well disposed in relation to the avoidance of, or lack of, company. As we have seen, solitude for Nietzsche is "inadvisable for the many." By this is meant that the many should avoid the kind of solitude that is appropriate for the strong. That is, for those destined to remain herd-like that kind of solitude is inadvisable; nor should solitude as a virtue of the strong be sought by the convalescent, even by those capable (eventually) of becoming a higher type. The convalescent may not have the strength to endure that form of solitude; hence he should cultivate a more moderate degree of apartness that is opposed to a vice of losing himself in excessive sociability. For that vice, as well as the vice of excessive helpfulness (as we saw in Chapter 6), makes it impossible for one to "find one's way."

A tendency in the weak to seek (strong) solitude may be expressive of disgust, a disgust which can only be reinforced in such a state. By contrast solitude in the strong expresses an "instinct for cleanliness" and is an escape "from" as opposed to "of" the sick. This may seem puzzling. Should not the strong be immune from contamination by the sick? Nietzsche is aware of the corrupting influence of culture and institutions which can both prevent the formation of virtue and can undermine it when present. In *Twilight of the Idols* he says for example: "The criminal type is the type of the strong human being under unfavourable circumstances: a strong human being made sick."[29] The strong creative type needs to guard against the stifling effects of mediocrity, the "unfavourable circumstances" which undermine virtues of becoming.

Another example of virtue differentiated according to strength concerns generosity. Virtuous generosity for the self-improver may not be overflowing bounteousness, for attempts at such bounteousness in the relatively weak may constitute self-destructive, resentment-filled self-sacrifice that is ultimately harmful to others as well as to oneself. A core virtue, or core component of virtue, such as self-love, will not have the same features at different points along the self-improvement path.

Finally consider the disposition to "turn the other cheek" as a virtue. Just as a truly self-confident society will be able to dispense with punishment, according to Nietzsche, so the strongest individuals will be able to say: "Of what concern are these parasites to me?"[30] "Such a man with a *single* shrug shakes off much of that which worms and digs its way into others."[31] In other words, a disposition to turn the other cheek is a virtue of the strong. By contrast, such behavior in the weak is likely to be a sign of regressive self-abasement. Better perhaps for the weak to display assertiveness, even of a retaliatory kind, to lessen their tendencies to be wounded. We might consider the universal basic virtue to be assertiveness (in the face of harms inflicted): in the strong this takes the form of the kind of "passive" resistance of turning the other cheek, in the weak it will take other forms. Other virtues differentiated according to strength for Nietzsche are (at least) independence, courage, truthfulness and wisdom.

If many virtues can be seen as universal (as basic virtues) but differentiated according to strength, that leaves us with options (ii) or (iii). Option (iii) will be favored, but it may be thought that Nietzsche is committed to (ii). On a common reading which I have already accepted Nietzsche believes:

(R)   Virtue is relative to types of being.

One way of understanding this relativity is to think that there are different states of perfection for different types of being, and that for each individual, the state of perfection at which she aims throughout her life, is determined by the type of being to which she belongs. However this view is just a relativized view of (ST) which as we have seen Nietzsche rejects in his ethics of becoming.

How then is (R) to be understood as part of an ethics of becoming? Each individual is to become who she is in a way compatible with (2) and (3) above, but it should not be assumed that in this process each individual will become a "higher man" or even have the capacity to become a "higher man." Some are destined to remain as part of the "herd." It should not be assumed either that those of the "first rank," that is, those with the potential to become "higher men," are already strong. Indeed in *The Gay Science* (section 290) Nietzsche makes it clear that weak inability to serve constraints and exercise discipline and self-control occurs even in those of the "first rank."

Though some individuals are destined to remain part of the herd, being not of the "first rank," a person can be a herd-type individual now; complacent, lazy, resentment-filled and pleasure-seeking, but later become a productive individual using her considerable talents. She was, in short, a sick member of the herd, but in a process of self-overcoming becomes a higher individual. Another person of lesser talents was once a sick member of the herd, but in a process of self-overcoming becomes a healthy member of the herd. A herd individual too should be creative, and cultivate what is unique in her. As Nietzsche suggests, the stinginess of nature mandates that all engage in this hard work: "Why has nature been so stingy with human beings that it did not allow them to shine – one more, one less, each according to the plenitude of his own light?"[32] In short Nietzsche's anti-egalitarianism and his insistence on types of human as higher or lower is compatible with a virtue ethics of becoming applied to all.

How then do we understand virtues such as forgetfulness, creativity, and generosity in such an ethics? In particular how are these virtues differentiated according to the strength of an agent? This brings us to option (iii). On this view, a conception of a virtue such as generosity may be understood not merely as a threshold notion (such that it is possible that one is both virtuous and capable of improvement) but also as a continuum, which is affected both by where the agent is placed on the path of convalescence and whether or not she is capable of being a "higher" type, for example. In short we are to understand virtues such as generosity as differentiated in a dynamic way.

In this dynamic conception of virtue, a virtue such as generosity is integrated with self-improvement as a virtue, so that a person who has a form of generosity appropriate to her current level of strength, but who is both capable of and makes no effort to "self-overcome" to increase her level of strength, does not possess generosity as a virtue in an optimal form appropriate to her.[33] Again a person of the "first rank" who has a higher level of generosity than average in a higher form, may no longer be overcoming, being weak in that sense. She rests content with her level of virtue, because she is comparing herself favorably with others. On a virtue ethics of becoming she may be said not to possess generosity as a virtue. What one says of such a case depends entirely on whether one focuses on the virtue of self-improvement as integrated with generosity, or whether one focuses more on the targets of generosity itself. Circumstances and contexts will determine where and how one sets the thresholds of what counts as virtue, and there will be indeterminacy and room for reasonable disagreement.

We are now in a position to see how a dynamic, non-consequentialist, Nietzschean virtue ethics conceives of the virtues of the "man of overcoming." Progress is not understood simply in terms of realizing an already given end, for the end itself is recreated more or less continuously, and in a variety of ways for a variety of reasons. First, one's "pattern of activity" is enriched and modified as one reshapes one's ends in the light of circumstances and developing desires and interests. Second, improving one's strength or health is not a smooth progress, for in a sense one must be careful not to overreach one's (current) strength. Finally, virtues such as generosity or solitude are themselves shaped by and integrated with norms of self-improvement.

The features of a virtue-ethical, Nietzschean ethics of becoming are presupposed in the aphorism: "Become who you are." I have understood the injunction in the dynamic way elucidated above, and as intended to apply to all. Finally, as argued in Chapter 6, virtues are understood as expressive of an individual's living this maxim virtuously in her *own* life, the life proper to the mature egoist. They are not seen as traits whose status as virtues is *wholly* dependent on their systematically promoting a consequentialist-perfectionist goal.

10.4 Nietzsche and Creativity

The life affirming individual is an individual who self-overcomes, and a life of self-overcoming is a creative life. For Nietzsche, "In man, creature and creator are united; in man there is matter, fragment, excess, clay, mud and madness; but in man there is also creator, sculptor, the hardness of the hammer."[34] Unfortunately as Mary Midgley claims, in European philosophy, "since Nietzsche this notion [of creativity] has often been put in terms of creation through the will."[35] This idea, as Midgley points out, is particularly odd when we speak as does Nietzsche, of creating values. Such talk may make it appear that creation is something entirely independent of our culture and history, and also as something arbitrary and independent of shared standards.[36] This way of reading Nietzsche ignores the communitarian *Volkisch* aspects of his thought and the omnipresent language of virtue and vice, language at the heart of his plea to cultivate the genius within us rather than lead a life of laziness and slavish imitation. Creativity for Nietzsche should not be seen as an arbitrary act of the will, something which for Nietzsche is both ethically and metaphysically suspect.

This section explores the virtues associated with a life of creativity. First however we need to briefly discuss how Nietzsche's "ethics of creativity" challenges orthodox assumptions of ethics in general, and I would add virtue ethics in particular. In an excellent discussion, Bernard Reginster[37] itemizes several challenges posed by such an ethics. These are:

(1)   Suffering is an essential ingredient of creative activity.
(2)   The creative life necessarily involves a sense of loss.

(3)   Creative activity necessarily involves valuing impermanence.
(4)   Creativity makes failure inescapable.

All of these features are key components of an ethics of becoming, and involve a novel perspective on aretaic value, and virtue. However their nature is not entirely clear or uncontroversial, and I probe some of the issues here.

For Reginster, suffering is an essential ingredient of creative activity because (i) for Nietzsche "overcoming resistance is precisely what creative activity consists in" and (ii) resistance is (involves) a form of suffering. Reginster is right to claim that creativity should not be seen as a good that "redeems" suffering by compensating for it, or that creative goals are simply worth the suffering that the process of pursuing them may involve. Rather, on an ethics of becoming suffering is part and parcel of "becoming." As Nietzsche suggests:

> The discipline of suffering, of *great* suffering – do you not know that it is *this* discipline alone which has created every elevation of mankind hitherto? That tension of the soul in misfortune which cultivates its strength … its inventiveness and bravery in undergoing, enduring … has it not been bestowed through suffering, through the discipline of great suffering?[38]

Nonetheless, (i) and (ii) above are too strong. Overcoming resistance may be a necessary condition of genuine creativity, and overcoming resistance may often involve suffering, but I do not see that it necessarily involves suffering. Nonetheless, on this view suffering of the right kind has aretaic value, and suffering as such is not an "intrinsic disvalue" that needs to be compensated by goods such as creativity and products of creative processes.

The second feature of the creative life on Reginster's interpretation of Nietzsche is that it essentially involves a sense of loss. Here Reginster rightly rejects a perfectionist reading of Nietzsche according to which, since the goal of creativity is perfection, existing created objects "should be destroyed or left behind to make room for ones that approximate [the ideal] even more closely."[39] We should also note that often a sense of loss is compatible with the viciousness of destroying valuable created items that have been "left behind." Indeed a respectful love of genuine achievement is compatible with an "insatiable creative impulse that is valued for its own sake"[40] and a sense of moving on.

The idea of the creative life as one which values impermanence is, according to Reginster, an expression of will to power as an "indefinite, perpetually renewed striving."[41] Nonetheless in a *virtue* ethics of becoming, such valuing is constrained. Creative vice is manifested by one who perpetually strives in the wrong way. An academic who is such a perfectionist that she cannot get a book written because she is fixated on some unattainable vague goal of perfection is to be contrasted not only with a person who can finish books in a timely manner, but also with a person with another creative vice: she who cannot settle with her ideas and develop them to a suitable polish, but who constantly feels impelled to move on through a sense of boredom and impatience.

Finally, for Reginster, the inescapability of failure is driven by the creative individual's desire for greater challenges "which are bound to subject him to ever greater or newer risks, and given his limited strengths, lead him ultimately to failure and frustration."[42] This view has implications for the aretaic value of failure. Failure could be seen as what Aristotle might call an "external *bad*" (to be contrasted with an external good) but as something which can be accorded (aretaic) value if borne nobly or decently. On Nietzsche's ethics of becoming, however, it looks as if failure is an "internal good": that is, a good which is internal to a worthwhile practice (such as creative endeavor).

How are we to understand this? A creative virtue is appropriate realism in relation to creative ends. There are two related vices: setting one's goals too low (relative to one's circumstances, talents, and so forth) and setting them too high in relation to those factors. In relation to the virtue of a disposition to appropriate realism, what Reginster calls "failure" need not be seen as failure at all but as an achievement which can be "overcome" with greater achievements. On this understanding "failure" is not a good internal to creativity. *Genuine* failure such as a painting or book not worthy of the painter or author, could be a product of creative vice in which case the failure is both an external bad, and has no or little aretaic value (even if borne cheerfully or bravely).

As Chapter 6 shows, the emphasis on an "ethics of creativity" is not on my view the only great contribution Nietzsche may make to the development of virtue ethics. Of immense importance too, given contemporary emphasis on the other-regardingness of ethics, is Nietzsche's deployment of the depth psychology of self-love, and the various forms of alienation or escape from self. However, there are difficulties in rendering coherent Nietzsche's ethics of creativity and his views on self-acceptance as a core component of virtue. Let us now consider these difficulties.

I suggested in Chapter 7 that creativity is an aspect of self-love, but does not Nietzsche explicitly say that resentment is creative? The paradox is noted by Solomon: "If creativity is one of the highest virtues – and it certainly seems to be for him – then resentment would seem to be one of the most virtuous emotions, for it is certainly among the most creative, perhaps even more so than inspirational love."[43] A second problem is this. Might not creativity of the form valorized by Nietzsche be seen as a form of fleeing from self, and indeed a form of expansive grandiosity? In short creativity seems to be unequivocally associated neither with life enhancement nor with health. Resentment is supposed to be life denying, and even if life affirming in some sense, the grandiosity of the "expansive solution," being a neurosis, is not healthy. The seamlessness of the connections between health, strength, life affirmation, and creativity is apparently compromised. We might take the easy route and claim that Nietzsche's views lack coherence. I think a deeper look at the nature of creativity as an aspect of self-love and virtue resolves these problems. Take first the problem of resentment.

As suggested above, creativity *as such* is not a virtue. Think of the thin conception of creativity as a basic virtue. It is a disposition of excellent or good enough (receptive, appreciative, and creative) responsiveness to items in its field – objects of creative endeavor. Of course what counts as excellent depends on one's theory of creative virtue: for example do the created objects need to have value, and if so how much; is value to be distinguished from artistic quality, or novelty; is excellence to be understood in terms of a creative process (e.g., originality) or in terms of creative motivation? Whatever view one holds, to say that resentment is creative is not to say that it is expressive of or productive of *virtuous* creativity. It may be that the creativity and cleverness of the slave-type is akin to the courage, creativity, and cleverness of the thief. As Philippa Foot emphasizes, creativity, cleverness, and courage do not operate as virtues in this context; the courage of the thief is not a virtue *in him*.[44] Secondly Nietzsche may give positive valuations at times to slave creativity, but we need to be mindful of what is being compared. As an agent of social change, some good may come from it, for example the civilizing of the baser crueler "regressions" is a step toward a higher morality. Furthermore resentment-based creativity is praised by comparison with the "making small" of the "last man," where all creativity, virtuous or otherwise, has disappeared. Solomon is right to claim that resentment exhibits will to power in large measure, but quantity should not be confused with virtue.

Consider now our second problem; the sense that Nietzsche valorizes grandiose neurotic creativity. My reluctance to take the view that creativity of the form valorized by Nietzsche is really a form of the unhealthy expansive solution described in Chapter 7 depends on taking seriously Nietzsche's distinction between types of human being. If a member of the "herd" adopts the creative stance of a higher type and in so doing neglects his role as parent, teacher, or whatever, then indeed that person may exhibit grandiose vice. Discussion of the important issue of the differentiation of virtue according to types of being occurred in the previous chapter: here I shall concentrate briefly on the creativity of the higher type.

Central to understanding Nietzsche's account of this form of creativity is appreciating the fact that for Nietzsche the "gift-giver" has a passionate *receptivity* to the world: he needs to take in all its treasures before giving it out in productive or gifting endeavors. This receptivity accordingly is based on a passionate love or acceptance of the world: it is not a form of escape, though it is a form of "exhaustion":

> The danger that lies in great men and ages is extraordinary; exhaustion of every kind, sterility, follow in their wake … The genius, in work and deed, is necessarily a squanderer … The instinct of self-preservation is suspended.[45]

Hence it is a calamity for such a person to get married:

> … the philosopher loathes marriage … marriage as obstacle and disaster on the path to the optimum … the ascetic ideal points the way to so many bridges to independence that a philosopher cannot refrain from rejoicing inwardly … when he hears the story

of all those who have made up their minds and one day said No to all constraints on freedom and gone forth into some *desert* or other.[46]

The apparent grandiose cry of the philosopher "pereat mundus, fiat philosophia, fiat philosophus, *fiam*"[47] is a cry of affirmation of his own existence in creating: that is to say, the creative mode is not one of borrowing, or worrying about what others think, or being true to traditions or an ideology above all. It is one's own passionate engagement with the world that is expressed in one's receptivity to, appreciation of, and creative response to the world. Contrast the conventional artist:

> They have always acted as valets to some ethics or philosophy or religion; not to mention the unfortunate fact that they have often been the all-too malleable courtiers of their supporters and patrons, sycophants with a fine nose for established powers or those just newly emerging.[48]

In Part IV I have touched on new directions for virtue ethics as a family of moral theory that might be taken by a Nietzschean or Humean virtue ethics. Though my main task in this work has been to offer a virtue ethical map of the terrain of Nietzsche's and Hume's texts, further exciting developments in both the structure and content of virtue ethics, inspired by those texts, are in prospect.

Notes

1 But see my "Virtues of Creativity and Productivity, Moral Theory, and Human Nature," in *Ayn Rand Society Philosophical Studies*, vol. 3, ed. James Lennox and Greg Salmieri (Pittsburgh, PA: University of Pittsburgh Press, forthcoming).

2 *The Gay Science*, trans. Walter Kaufmann (New York: Vintage Books, 1974), Book 3, sect. 270, 219.

3 Ibid., Book 4, sect. 335, 266.

4 *Ecce Homo: How to Become What You Are*, trans. Duncan Large (Oxford: Oxford University Press, 2007), "Why I Am So Clever," sect. 9, 31.

5 May, *Nietzsche's Ethics and His War on "Morality"* (Oxford: Clarendon Press, 1999), 109.

6 Nehemas, "How One Becomes What One Is," in *Nietzsche*, ed. John Richardson and Brian Leiter (Oxford: Oxford University Press, 2001), 255–280, 261.

7 May, *Nietzsche's Ethics and His War on "Morality,"* 109.

8 Nietzsche, "Schopenhauer as Educator," *Untimely Meditations*, Third Essay, cited and trans. in James Conant, "Nietzsche's Perfectionism: A Reading of *Schopenhauer as Educator*," in *Nietzsche's Postmoralism: Essays on Nietzsche's Prelude to Philosophy's Future*, ed. Richard Schacht (Cambridge: Cambridge University Press, 2001), 181–257, 197.

9 Ibid., 197.

10 Bernard Reginster analyzes will to power itself in terms of overcoming obstacles, claiming that what is essential to will to power in humans is that it "seeks resistance" because the will to the overcoming of resistance (the hallmark of will to power) is necessarily also the will to have resistance to overcome: *The Affirmation of Life: Nietzsche on Overcoming Nihilism* (Cambridge, MA: Harvard University Press, 2006), 130–132.

Admittedly, as Nietzsche himself emphasizes, much expression of the basic need or drive to "vent strength" takes the form of a *seeking* of resistance. But why should we assume that *all* expressions of "will to power" take this form? In trying to become a more loving parent, a more collegial colleague, am I seeking resistance? On the contrary I may be seeking to rid myself of various resistances and defenses inhibiting my quest for improvement in these areas. It is true that there is resistance to overcome, but I question that will to power always consists in seeking such resistance.

11 *Ecce Homo*, "Why I Am So Wise," sect. 2, 9.

12 See Richardson, "Nietzsche's Power Ontology," in *Nietzsche*, ed. John Richardson and Brian Leiter (Oxford: Oxford University Press, 2001), 150–185, 158.

13 *On the Genealogy of Morals*, trans. Douglas Smith (Oxford: Oxford University Press, 1996), First Essay, sect. 10, 23.

14 *The Antichrist*, sect. 57.

15 For an excellent discussion of Nietzsche's idea of "becoming who you are" see May, *Nietzsche's Ethics and His War on "Morality,"* esp. 6.2, and 10.4.2.

16 In *Nietzsche and Ethics*, ed. Gudrun von Tevenar (Bern: Peter Lang, 2007), 89–118.

17 See Chapter 8 (section 8.1) for the distinction between basic and differentiated virtue.

18 May by contrast claims in *Nietzsche's Ethics and His War on "Morality,"* 84 n. 4, that "Obviously, it [the requirement to be disciplined] is a 'hypothetical' imperative in that it is conditional upon subscribing to those goods" (any good subscribed to, for the achievement of which discipline is a prerequisite).

19 See my "Cultivating Virtue: Two Problems for Virtue Ethics," in *Cultivating Virtue: Multiple Perspectives*, ed. Nancy Snow (Oxford: Oxford University Press, forthcoming), for more on self-improvement as a virtue.

20 *Thus Spoke Zarathustra*, in *The Portable Nietzsche*, ed. and trans. Walter Kaufmann (New York: Penguin, 1976), Third Part, "On Old and New Tablets," sect. 14, 317.

21 Ibid., Fourth Part, "On the Higher Man," sect. 13, 403.

22 Alderman, "By Virtue of a Virtue," in *Virtue Ethics: A Critical Reader*, ed. Daniel Statman (Edinburgh: Edinburgh University Press, 1997), 145–164, 151.

23 Sebastian Faulkes, *Human Traces* (London: Vintage, 2006), 277.

24 *Thus Spoke Zarathustra*, Second Part, "On Self-Overcoming," 227.

25 *The Gay Science*, Book 4, sect. 295, 237.

26 *Beyond Good and Evil: Prelude to a Philosophy of the Future*, trans. R.J. Hollingdale (London: Penguin, 1973), "The Free Spirit," sect. 26, 58.

27 Ibid., 55.

28 This view is canvassed by Michael Slote, "Relative Virtues," in *Goods and Virtues* (Oxford: Clarendon Press, 1983). He cites for example, as a virtue of maturity which is not a virtue in the very young, rational life-planfulness; trustingness as a childhood-relative virtue; and prudence as an "anti-virtue" in a child.

29 *Twilight of the Idols*, "Skirmishes of an Untimely Man," sect. 45.

30 *Genealogy of Morals*, Second Essay, sect. 10, 54.

31 Ibid., First Essay, sect. 10, 24.

32 *The Gay Science*, Book 4, sect. 336, 267.

33 In this way a virtue ethics of becoming subscribes to a limited unity of the virtues, but a discussion of this doctrine is beyond the scope of the book.

34 *Beyond Good and Evil*, sect. 225, 155.

35 Midgley, "Creation and Originality," in *Heart and Mind* (London: Routledge, 2003), 49–67, 49.

36 Thus Midgley claims that "in the Nietzschean tradition" the whole point of the will is its arbitrariness, its discontinuity with tradition and its "resistance to all explanation" (51). Both virtue ethical and "communitarian" readings of Nietzsche see this view as seriously distorting Nietzsche's thought.

37 See Reginster, "The Will to Power and the Ethics of Creativity," in *Nietzsche and Morality*, ed. Brian Leiter and Neil Sinhababu (Oxford: Clarendon Press, 2007), 32–56.

38 *Beyond Good and Evil*, sect. 225, 155.

39 Reginster, "The Will to Power and the Ethics of Creativity," 50.

40 Ibid., 51.

41 Ibid., 53.

42   Ibid., 53.
43   Richard Solomon, *Living with Nietzsche: What the Great "Immoralist" Has to Teach Us* (Oxford: Oxford University Press, 2003), 102–103.
44   See Foot, "Virtues and Vices," in *Virtues and Vices and Other Essays in Moral Philosophy* (Oxford: Basil Blackwell, 1978), 16.
45   *Twilight of the Idols*, "Skirmishes of an Untimely Man," sect. 44.
46   *Genealogy of Morals*, Third Essay, sect. 7, 86–87.
47   Ibid., 87.
48   Ibid., 81. See also sect. 1 of "Schopenhauer as Educator."

Bibliography

Abramson, Kate. 1999. "Correcting Our Sentiments About Hume's Moral Point of View." *The Southern Journal of Philosophy* 37(3): 333–361.

Acampora, Christa Davis, ed. 2006. *Nietzsche's* On the Genealogy of Morals: *Critical Essays*. Lanham, MD: Rowman & Littlefield.

Acampora, Christa Davis. 2006. "On Sovereignty and Overhumanity: Why It Matters How We Read Nietzsche's Genealogy." In *Nietzsche's* On the Genealogy of Morals: *Critical Essays*, ed. Christa Davis Acampora, 147–162. Lanham, MD: Rowman & Littlefield.

Adams, Robert Merrihew. 2002. *Finite and Infinite Goods: A Framework for Ethics*. Oxford: Oxford University Press.

Adler, Alfred. 1918. *The Neurotic Constitution: Outlines of a Comparative Individualistic Psychology and Psychotherapy*, trans. B. Glueck and J.E. Lind. London: Kegan Paul, Trench, Trübner & Co.

Adler, Alfred. 1932. *Understanding Human Nature*, trans. W.B. Wolfe. London: Allen & Unwin.

Adler, Alfred. 1964. "On the Origin of the Striving for Superiority and of Social Interest." In *Alfred Adler, Superiority and Social Interest: A Collection of Later Writings*, ed. Heinz L. Ansbacher and Rowena R. Ansbacher, 29–40. Evanston, IL: Northwestern University Press.

Adler, Alfred. 1964. "The Structure of Neurosis." In *Alfred Adler, Superiority and Social Interest: A Collection of Later Writings*, ed. Heinz L. Ansbacher and Rowena R. Ansbacher, 83–95. Evanston, IL: Northwestern University Press.

Ainsworth, M., M. Blehar, E. Waters, and S. Wall. 1978. *Patterns of Attachment: A Psychological Study of the Strange Situation*. Hillsdale, NJ: Lawrence Erlbaum Associates.

Alderman, Harold. 1997. "By Virtue of a Virtue." In *Virtue Ethics: A Critical Reader*, ed. Daniel Statman, 145–164. Edinburgh: Edinburgh University Press.

Alexander, Amir. 2014. "The Secret Spiritual History of Calculus." *Scientific American* 310.4: 68–71.

Alfano, Mark. 2014. "Stereotype Threat and Intellectual Virtue." In *Naturalizing Epistemic Virtue*, ed. Abrol Fairweather and Owen Flanagan, 155–174. Cambridge: Cambridge University Press.

Allen, Jon G. 2005. *Coping With Trauma: Hope Through Understanding*, 2nd edn. Washington, DC: American Psychiatric Publishing.

Annas, Julia. 2005. "Virtue Ethics: What Kind of Naturalism?" In *Virtue Ethics, Old and New*, ed. Stephen M. Gardiner, 11–29. Ithaca, NY: Cornell University Press.

Annas, Julia. 2011. *Intelligent Virtue*. Oxford: Oxford University Press.

Ardal, Pall S. 1966. *Passion and Value in Hume's Treatise*. Edinburgh: Edinburgh University Press.

Athams, J.E.J. and Ross Harrison, eds. 1995. *World, Mind and Ethics: Essays on the Ethical Philosophy of Bernard Williams*. Cambridge: Cambridge University Press.

The Virtue Ethics of Hume and Nietzsche, First Edition. Christine Swanton.
© 2015 John Wiley & Sons, Ltd. Published 2015 by John Wiley & Sons, Ltd.

Baier, Annette C. 1991. *A Progress of Sentiments: Reflections on Hume's Treatise*. Cambridge, MA: Harvard University Press.

Baier, Annette C. 2008. *Death and Character: Further Reflections on Hume*. Cambridge, MA: Harvard University Press.

Baier, Annette C. 2008. "*Enquiry Concerning the Principles of Morals*: Incomparably the Best?" In *A Companion to Hume*, ed. Elizabeth S. Radcliffe, 293–320. Oxford: Blackwell.

Bailey, Alan and Dan O'Brien, eds. 2012. *The Continuum Companion to Hume*. London: Continuum.

Barbre, Claude. 1999. "Reversing the Crease: Nietzsche's Influence on Otto Rank's Concept of Creative Will and the Birth of Individuality." In *Nietzsche and Depth Psychology*, ed. Jacob Golomb, Weaver Santaniello, and Ronald Lehrer, 247–267. Albany: State University of New York Press.

Baron, Marcia. 1982. "Hume's Noble Lie: An Account of His Artificial Virtues." *Canadian Journal of Philosophy* 12: 539–555.

Baron, Marcia. 2011. "Virtue Ethics in Relation to Kantian Ethics: An Opinionated Overview and Commentary." In *Perfecting Virtue: New Essays on Kantian Ethics and Virtue Ethics*, ed. Lawrence Jost and Julian Wuerth, 8–37. Cambridge: Cambridge University Press.

Baron, Marcia, Philip Pettit, and Michael Slote. 1997. *Three Methods of Ethics*. Oxford: Blackwell.

Battaly, Heather, ed. 2010. *Virtue and Vice, Moral and Epistemic*. Oxford: Wiley-Blackwell.

Baumeister, Roy F. 2001. "Violent Pride." *Scientific American* 284.4: 96–101.

Beauchamp, Tom L. 2008. "The Sources of Normativity in Hume's Moral Theory." In *A Companion to Hume*, ed. Elizabeth S. Radcliffe, 493–512. Oxford: Blackwell.

Berry, Jessica N. 2011. *Nietzsche and the Ancient Skeptical Tradition*. Oxford: Oxford University Press.

Bettelheim, Bruno. 1985. *Freud and Man's Soul*. London: Fontana.

Bittner, Rüdiger. 1994. "Ressentiment." In *Nietzsche, Genealogy, Morality: Essays on Nietzsche's Genealogy of Morals*, ed. Richard Schacht, 127–138. Berkeley: University of California Press.

Blackburn, Simon. 2009. "The Absolute Conception: Putnam vs. Williams." In *Reading Bernard Williams*, ed. Daniel Callcut, 9–23. London: Routledge.

Bloom, Paul. 2013. *Just Babies: The Origins of Good and Evil*. New York: Crown Publishers.

Botros, Sophie. 2006. *Hume, Reason and Morality: A Legacy of Contradiction*. Abingdon: Routledge.

Bowlby, John. 1969. *Attachment*. London: Pelican.

Brand, Walter. 1992. *Hume's Theory of Moral Judgment*. Dordrecht: Kluwer Academic.

Brandom, Robert. 2002. "Placing McDowell's Empiricism." In *Reading McDowell: On Mind and World*, ed. Nicholas H. Smith, 92–105. London: Routledge.

Brewer, Talbot. 2009. *The Retrieval of Ethics*. Oxford: Oxford University Press.

Callcut, Daniel, ed. 2009. *Reading Bernard Williams*. London: Routledge.

Camus, Albert. 1946. *The Stranger*, trans. Stuart Gilbert. New York: Vintage Books.

Camus, Albert. 1955. *The Myth of Sisyphus and Other Essays*, trans. Justin O'Brien. New York: Vintage Books.

Camus, Albert. 1964. *The Fall and Exile and the Kingdom*, trans. Justin O'Brien. New York: Modern Library.

Capaldi, Nicholas. 1989. *Hume's Place in Moral Philosophy*. New York: Peter Lang.

Carlo, Gustavo, et al. 2009. "The Elusive Altruist: The Psychological Study of the Altruistic Personality." In *Personality, Identity, and Character: Explorations in Moral Psychology*, ed. Darcia Narvaez and Daniel K. Lapsley, 271–294. Cambridge: Cambridge University Press.

Chappell, Timothy, ed. 2006. *Values and Virtues: Aristotelianism in Contemporary Ethics*. Oxford: Oxford University Press.

Chappell, Timothy, ed. 2009. *The Problem of Moral Demandingness*. London: Palgrave Macmillan.

Clark, Maudemarie and David Dudrick. 2007. "Nietzsche and Moral Objectivity: The Development of Nietzsche's Metaethics." In *Nietzsche and Morality*, ed. Brian Leiter and Neil Sinhababu, 192–226. Oxford: Oxford University Press.

Cohon, Rachel. 1997. "Hume's Difficulty with the Virtue of Honesty." *Hume Studies* 23: 91–112.

Cohon, Rachel, ed. 2001. *Hume: Moral and Political Philosophy*. Aldershot: Ashgate Dartmouth.

Cohon, Rachel. 2006. "Hume's Natural and Artificial Virtues." In *The Blackwell Guide to Hume's Treatise*, ed. Saul Traiger, 256–275. Oxford: Blackwell.

Cohon, Rachel. 2008. *Hume's Morality: Feeling and Fabrication.* Oxford: Oxford University Press.

Cohon, Rachel and David Owen. 1997. "Hume on Representation, Reason and Motivation." *Manuscrito* 20: 47–76.

Conant, James. 2001. "Nietzsche's Perfectionism: A Reading of *Schopenhauer as Educator.* In *Nietzsche's Postmoralism: Essays on Nietzsche's Prelude to Philosophy's Future*, ed. Richard Schacht, 181–257. Cambridge: Cambridge University Press.

Copp, David and David Soble. 2004. "Morality and Virtue: An Assessment of Some Recent Work in Virtue Ethics." *Ethics* 114: 514–554.

Crisp, Roger, ed. 2003. *How Should One Live? Essays on the Virtues.* Oxford: Oxford University Press.

Crisp, Roger. 2005. "Hume on Virtue, Utility, and Morality." In *Virtue Ethics, Old and New*, ed. Stephen M. Gardiner, 159–178. Ithaca, NY: Cornell University Press.

Cupit, Geoffrey. 1998. "Justice, Age, and Veneration." *Ethics* 108: 702–718.

Damasio, Antonio. 1994. *Descartes' Error: Emotion, Reason, and the Human Brain.* New York: Avon Books.

Davie, William. 1999. "Hume on Monkish Virtues." *Hume Studies* 25: 139–153.

De Caro, Mario and David MacArthur, eds. 2004. *Naturalism in Question.* Cambridge, MA: Harvard University Press.

de Gaynesford, Maximilian. 2004. *John McDowell.* Cambridge: Polity Press.

DiCenso, James J. 1990. *Hermeneutics and the Disclosure of Truth: A Study in the Work of Heidegger, Gadamer, and Ricoeur.* Charlottesville: University Press of Virginia.

Dreier, James, ed. 2006. *Contemporary Debates in Moral Theory.* Oxford: Blackwell.

Dreyfus, Hubert. 2007. "Response to McDowell." *Inquiry* 50: 371–377.

Dreyfus, Hubert. 2007. "The Return of the Myth of the Mental." *Inquiry* 50: 352–365.

Driver, Julia. 2006. "Virtue Theory." In *Contemporary Debates in Moral Theory*, ed. James Dreier, 113–123. Oxford: Blackwell.

Dupré, John. 1993. *The Disorder of Things: Metaphysical Foundations of the Disunity of Science.* Cambridge, MA: Harvard University Press.

Eisenberg, Nancy and Janet Strayer, eds. 1987. *Empathy and Its Development.* Cambridge: Cambridge University Press.

Eisenberg, Nancy, Tracy L. Spinrad, and Zoe E. Taylor. 2014. "Sympathy." In *The Handbook of Virtue Ethics*, ed. Stan van Hooft, 409–417. Durham: Acumen.

Erikson, Erik. 2000. "'Human Strength and the Cycle of Generations' from *Insight and Responsibility.*" In *The Erik Erikson Reader*, ed. Robert Coles, 188–225. New York: W.W. Norton & Co.

Fairweather, Abrol and Owen Flanagan, eds. 2014. *Naturalizing Epistemic Virtue.* Cambridge: Cambridge University Press.

Falk, W.D. 1986. "Hume on Practical Reason." In *Ought, Reasons, and Morality: The Collected Papers of W.D. Falk*, 143–159. Ithaca, NY: Cornell University Press.

Faulkes, Sebastian. 2006. *Human Traces.* London: Vintage.

Foot, Philippa. 1978. "Hume on Moral Judgement." In *Virtues and Vices and Other Essays in Moral Philosophy*, 74–80. Oxford: Basil Blackwell.

Foot, Philippa. 1978. "Virtues and Vices." In *Virtues and Vices and Other Essays in Moral Philosophy*, 1–18. Oxford: Basil Blackwell.

Freud, Sigmund. 1949. *An Outline of Psycho-Analysis*, ed. and trans. James Strachey. New York: W.W. Norton & Co.

Freud, Sigmund. 1961. *Civilization and Its Discontents*, ed. and trans. James Strachey. New York: W.W. Norton & Co.

Fromm, Erich. 1973. *The Anatomy of Human Destructiveness.* New York: Holt, Rinehart and Winston.

Fromm, Erich. 1975. *The Art of Loving.* London: Unwin Paperbacks.

Ganz, Madelaine. 1953. *The Psychology of Alfred Adler and the Development of the Child.* London: Routledge and Kegan Paul.

Gardiner, Stephen M. 2005. *Virtue Ethics, Old and New.* Ithaca, NY: Cornell University Press.

Garrett, Don. 1997. *Cognition and Commitment in Hume's Philosophy.* Oxford: Oxford University Press.

Garrett, Don and Edward Barbanell, eds. 1997. *Encyclopedia of Empiricism*. London: Fitzroy Dearborn.

Gauthier, David. 2001. "Artificial Virtues and the Sensible Knave." In *Hume: Moral and Political Philosophy*, ed. Rachel Cohon, 313–339. Aldershot: Ashgate Dartmouth.

Gaylin, Willard. 2003. *Hatred: The Psychological Descent into Violence*. New York: Public Affairs.

Gemes, Ken. 2006. "'We Remain of Necessity Strangers to Ourselves': The Key Message of Nietzsche's *Genealogy*." In *Nietzsche's On the Genealogy of Morals: Critical Essays*, ed. Christa Davis Acampora, 191–208. Lanham, MD: Rowman & Littlefield.

Gerhardt, Sue. 2004. *Why Love Matters: How Affection Shapes a Baby's Brain*. London: Routledge.

Goleman, Daniel. 1996. *Emotional Intelligence: Why It Can Matter More Than IQ*. London: Bloomsbury.

Golomb, Jacob. 1999. "Introductory Essay: Nietzsche's New Psychology." In *Nietzsche and Depth Psychology*, ed. Jacob Golomb, Weaver Santaniello, and Ronald Lehrer, 1–19. Albany: State University of New York Press.

Golomb, Jacob, Weaver Santaniello, and Ronald Lehrer, eds. 1999. *Nietzsche and Depth Psychology*. Albany: State University of New York Press.

Gopnik, Alison. 1999. *The Scientist in the Crib*. New York: William Morrow.

Gotthelf, Allan. 2000. *On Ayn Rand*. Belmont, CA: Wadsworth.

Guimaraes, Livia. 2012. "Hume and Feminism." In *The Continuum Companion to Hume*, ed. Alan Bailey and Dan O'Brien, 319–331. London: Continuum.

Guntrip, Harry. 1968. *Schizoid Phenomena, Object Relations, and the Self*. London: The Hogarth Press.

Hales, Steven D. and Rex Welshon. 2000. *Nietzsche's Perspectivism*. Urbana: University of Illinois Press.

Hampton, Jean. 1993. "Selflessness and Loss of Self." *Social Philosophy and Policy* 10: 135–165.

Harcourt, Edwin. 2007. "Nietzsche and Eudaemonism." In *Nietzsche and Ethics*, ed. Gudrun von Tevenar, 89–118. Bern: Peter Lang.

Harlow, Harry F. 1974. *Learning to Love*. New York: Jason Aronson Inc.

Harrison, Jonathan. 1976. *Hume's Moral Epistemology*. Oxford: Clarendon Press.

Havas, Randall. 2000. "Nietzsche's Idealism." *Journal of Nietzsche Studies* 20: 90–99.

Heidegger, Martin. 1962. *Being and Time*, trans. J. Macquarrie and E. Robinson. Oxford: Blackwell.

Heidegger, Martin. 1971. *Poetry, Language, Thought*, trans. Albert Hofstadter. New York: Harper Collins.

Higgins, Kathleen and David Sherman, eds. 2012. *Passion, Death, and Spirituality: The Philosophy of Robert C. Solomon*. Dordrecht: Springer.

Hoffman, Martin L. 1984. "Interaction of Affect and Cognition in Empathy." In *Emotions, Cognition, and Behavior*, ed. Carroll E. Izard, Jerome Kagan, and Robert B. Zajonc, 103–131. Cambridge: Cambridge University Press.

Hoffman, Martin L. 1987. "The Contribution of Empathy to Justice and Moral Judgment." In *Empathy and Its Development*, ed. Nancy Eisenberg and Janet Strayer, 47–80. Cambridge: Cambridge University Press.

Hoffman, Martin L. 2000. *Empathy and Moral Development: Implications for Caring and Justice*. Cambridge: Cambridge University Press.

Holland, Sean. 2001. "Dispositional Theories of Value Meet Moral Twin Earth." *American Philosophical Quarterly* 38: 177–195.

Hooker, Brad, ed. 1996. *Truth in Ethics*. Oxford: Blackwell.

Hookway, Christopher. 1995. "Fallibilism and Objectivity: Science and Ethics." In *World, Mind and Ethics: Essays on the Ethical Philosophy of Bernard Williams*, ed. J.E.J. Altham and Ross Harrison, 46–67. Cambridge: Cambridge University Press.

Horgan, Terence and Mark Timmons. 1991. "New Wave Moral Realism Meets Moral Twin Earth." *Journal of Philosophical Research* 16: 447–465.

Horney, Karen. 1970. *Neurosis and Human Growth: The Struggle Toward Self-Realization*. New York: Norton.

Hume, David. 1912. *Essays, Moral, Political, and Literary*, vol. 1, ed. T.H. Green and T.H. Grose. London: Longmans, Green, & Co.

Hume, David. 1957. *Dialogues Concerning Natural Religion*, ed. Henry D. Aiken. New York: Hafner Publishing Co.

Hume, David. 1968. *A Treatise of Human Nature*, ed. L.A. Selby-Bigge. Oxford: Clarendon Press.

Hume, David. 1975. *Enquiries Concerning Human Understanding and Concerning the Principles of Morals*, 3rd edn, ed. P.H. Nidditch. Oxford: Clarendon Press.

Hume, David. 1987. *Essays, Moral, Political, and Literary*, ed. Eugene F. Miller. Indianapolis, IN: Liberty Fund.

Hume, David. 1987. "Dignity or Meanness in Human Nature." In *Essays, Moral, Political, and Literary*, ed. Eugene F. Miller, 80–86. Indianapolis, IN: Liberty Fund.

Hume, David. 1987. "Of Polygamy and Divorces." In *Essays, Moral, Political, and Literary*, ed. Eugene F. Miller, 181–190. Indianapolis, IN: Liberty Fund.

Hume, David. 1987. "Of Refinement in the Arts." In *Essays, Moral, Political, and Literary*, ed. Eugene F. Miller, 268–280. Indianapolis, IN: Liberty Fund.

Hume, David. 1987. "Of Superstition and Enthusiasm." In *Essays, Moral, Political, and Literary*, ed. Eugene F. Miller, 73–79. Indianapolis, IN: Liberty Fund.

Hume, David. 1987. "On Simplicity and Refinement in Writing." In *Essays, Moral, Political, and Literary*, ed. Eugene F. Miller, 191–196. Indianapolis, IN: Liberty Fund.

Hume, David. 2000. *A Treatise of Human Nature*, ed. David Fate Norton and Mary J. Norton. Oxford: Oxford University Press.

Hume, David. 2006. *An Enquiry Concerning the Principles of Morals*, ed. Tom Beauchamp. Oxford: Clarendon Press.

Hunt, Lester C. 1991. *Nietzsche and the Origin of Virtue*. London: Routledge.

Hursthouse, Rosalind. 1999. *On Virtue Ethics*. Oxford: Oxford University Press.

Hursthouse, Rosalind. 1999. "Virtue Ethics and Human Nature." *Hume Studies* 25: 67–82.

Hursthouse, Rosalind. 2006. "Practical Wisdom: A Mundane Account." *Proceedings of the Aristotelian Society* 106: 285–309.

Hursthouse, Rosalind, Gavin Lawrence, and Warren Quinn, eds. 1998. *Virtues and Reasons*. Oxford: Oxford University Press.

Ishiguro, Kazuo. 1989. *The Remains of the Day*. New York: Random House.

Ivanhoe, Philip J. 2013. "Virtue Ethics and the Chinese Confucian Tradition." In *The Cambridge Companion to Virtue Ethics*, ed. Daniel C. Russell, 46–69. Cambridge: Cambridge University Press.

Izard, Carroll E., Jerome Kagan, and Robert B. Zajonc, eds. 1984. *Emotions, Cognition, and Behavior*. Cambridge: Cambridge University Press.

Jacobson, Anne Jaap, ed. 2000. *Feminist Interpretations of David Hume*. University Park: Pennsylvania State University Press.

Jacobson, Daniel. 2011. "Fitting Attitude Theories of Value." In *The Stanford Encyclopedia of Philosophy*, ed. Edward N. Zalta. Spring Edition, March 17, http://plato.stanford.edu/archives/spr2011/entries/fitting-attitude-theories/, accessed August 15, 2014.

Janaway, Christopher. 2007. *Beyond Selflessness: Reading Nietzsche's Genealogy*. Oxford: Oxford University Press.

Johnson, Mark. 1993. *Moral Imagination: Implications of Cognitive Science for Ethics*. Chicago: University of Chicago Press.

Johnson, Robert N. 2003. "Virtue and Right." *Ethics* 113(4): 810–834.

Jost, Lawrence, and Julian Wuerth, eds. 2011. *Perfecting Virtue: New Essays on Kantian Ethics and Virtue Ethics*. Cambridge: Cambridge University Press.

Kant, Immanuel. 1996. *The Metaphysics of Morals*, ed. and trans. Mary Gregor. Cambridge: Cambridge University Press.

Kawall, Jason. 2004. "Moral Response-Dependence, Ideal Observers, and the Motive of Duty: Responding to Zangwill." *Erkenntnis* 60(3): 357–369.

Kawall, Jason. 2009. "In Defense of the Primacy of the Virtues." *Journal of Ethics and Social Philosophy* 3: 1–21.

Kemp Smith, Norman. 2005. *The Philosophy of David Hume* [1941]. Basingstoke: Palgrave Macmillan.

Kierkegaard, Søren. 1941. *Concluding Unscientific Postscript*, trans. D.F. Swenson and W. Lowrie. Princeton, NJ: Princeton University Press.

King, James. 1999. "Pride and Hume's Sensible Knave." *Hume Studies* 25: 123–137.

Knobe, Joshua. 2011. "Thought Experiments." *Scientific American* 305: 56–59.

Korsgaard, Christine M. 1999. "The General Point of View: Love and Moral Approval in Hume's Ethics." *Hume Studies* 25: 3–41.

LeBar, Mark. 2005. "Three Dogmas of Response Dependence." *Philosophical Studies* 123: 175–211.

Lehrer, Ronald. 1999. "Adler and Nietzsche." In *Nietzsche and Depth Psychology*, ed. Jacob Golomb, Weaver Santaniello, and Ronald Lehrer, 229–245. Albany: State University of New York Press.

Lehrer, Ronald. 1999. "Freud and Nietzsche, 1892–1895." In *Nietzsche and Depth Psychology*, ed. Jacob Golomb, Weaver Santaniello, and Ronald Lehrer, 181–203. Albany: State University of New York Press.

Leiter, Brian. 2002. *Nietzsche on Morality*. London: Routledge.

Leiter, Brian and Neil Sinhababu, eds. 2007. *Nietzsche and Morality*. Oxford: Oxford University Press.

Lo, Norva Y.S. 2010. "Is Hume Inconsistent? – Motivation and Morals." In *Hume on Motivation and Virtue*, ed. Charles R. Pigden, 57–79. Basingstoke: Palgrave Macmillan.

Locke, John. 1975. *An Essay Concerning Human Understanding*, ed. Peter H. Nidditch. Oxford: Oxford University Press.

Loeb, Paul S. 2006. "Finding the *Übermensch* in Nietzsche's *Genealogy of Morality*." In *Nietzsche's On the Genealogy of Morals: Critical Essays*, ed. Christa Davis Acampora, 163–176. Lanham, MD: Rowman & Littlefield.

MacIntyre, Alasdair. 2007. *After Virtue: A Study in Moral Theory*, 3rd edn. Notre Dame, IN: University of Notre Dame Press.

Maslow, Abraham. 1968. *Toward a Psychology of Being*, 2nd edn. New York: Van Nostrand Reinhold Co.

May, Simon. 1999. *Nietzsche's Ethics and His War on "Morality."* Oxford: Clarendon Press.

McDowell, John. 1994. *Mind and World*. Cambridge, MA: Harvard University Press.

McDowell, John. 1998. "Two Sorts of Naturalism." In *Virtues and Reasons*, ed. Rosalind Hursthouse, Gavin Lawrence, and Warren Quinn, 149–179. Oxford: Oxford University Press.

McDowell, John. 2002. "Response to J.M. Bernstein." In *Reading McDowell: On Mind and World*, ed. Nicholas H. Smith, 297–300. London: Routledge.

McDowell, John. 2002. "Response to Robert Brandom." In *Reading McDowell: On Mind and World*, ed. Nicholas H. Smith, 179–181. London: Routledge.

McDowell, John. 2002. "Values and Secondary Qualities." In *Mind, Value, and Reality*, 131–150. Cambridge, MA: Harvard University Press.

McDowell, John. 2007. "Response to Dreyfus." *Inquiry* 50: 366–370.

McDowell, John. 2007. "What Myth?" *Inquiry* 50: 338–351.

McIntyre, Jane L. 2000. "Hume's Passions: Direct and Indirect." *Hume Studies* 26(1): 77–86.

McIntyre, Jane L. 2001. "Character: A Humean Account." In *Hume: Moral and Political Philosophy*, ed. Rachel Cohon, 449–462. Aldershot: Ashgate Dartmouth.

Merli, David. 2002. "Return to Moral Twin Earth." *Canadian Journal of Philosophy* 32: 207–240.

Midgley, Mary. 2003. "Creation and Originality." In *Heart and Mind*, 49–67. London: Routledge.

Miller, Christian, ed. 2011. *The Continuum Companion to Ethics*. London: Continuum.

Murdoch, Iris. 1970. *The Sovereignty of the Good*. London: Routledge.

Narvaez, Darcia and Daniel K. Lapsley, eds. 2009. *Personality, Identity, and Character: Explorations in Moral Psychology*. Cambridge: Cambridge University Press.

Nehemas, Alexander. 2001. "How One Becomes What One Is." In *Nietzsche*, ed. John Richardson and Brian Leiter, 255–280. Oxford: Oxford University Press.

Nietzsche, Friedrich. 1967. *The Will to Power*, trans. Walter Kaufmann. New York: Random House.

Nietzsche, Friedrich. 1968. *Twilight of the Idols and The Anti-Christ*, trans. R.J. Hollingdale. Harmondsworth: Penguin.

Nietzsche, Friedrich. 1973. *Beyond Good and Evil: Prelude to a Philosophy of the Future*, trans. R.J. Hollingdale. London: Penguin.

Nietzsche, Friedrich. 1974. *The Gay Science*, trans. Walter Kaufmann. New York: Vintage Books.

Nietzsche, Friedrich. 1976. *The Antichrist*. In *The Portable Nietzsche*, ed. and trans. Walter Kaufmann. New York: Penguin.

Nietzsche, Friedrich. 1976. *Thus Spoke Zarathustra*. In *The Portable Nietzsche*, ed. and trans. Walter Kaufmann. New York: Penguin.

Nietzsche, Friedrich. 1976. *Twilight of the Idols*. In *The Portable Nietzsche*, ed. and trans. Walter Kaufmann. New York: Penguin.

Nietzsche, Friedrich. 1982. *Daybreak: Thoughts on the Prejudices of Morality*, trans. R.J. Hollingdale. Cambridge: Cambridge University Press.

Nietzsche, Friedrich. 1983. *Untimely Meditations*, trans. R.J. Hollingdale. Cambridge: Cambridge University Press.

Nietzsche, Friedrich. 1984. *Human, All Too Human: A Book for Free Spirits*, trans. Marion Faber with Stephen Lehmann. Lincoln: University of Nebraska Press.

Nietzsche, Friedrich. 1986. *Human, All Too Human: A Book for Free Spirits*, trans. R.J. Hollingdale. Cambridge: Cambridge University Press.

Nietzsche, Friedrich. 1996. *On the Genealogy of Morals*, trans. Douglas Smith. Oxford: Oxford University Press.

Nietzsche, Friedrich. 2007. *Ecce Homo: How to Become What You Are*, trans. Duncan Large. Oxford: Oxford University Press.

Nygren, Anders. 1989. "Agape and Eros." In *Eros, Agape and Philia: Readings in the Philosophy of Love*, ed. A. Sobel, 85–95. New York: Paragon House.

Oberst, Ursula E. and Alan E. Stewart. 2003. *Adlerian Psychotherapy: An Advanced Approach to Individual Psychology*. Hove and New York: Brunner-Routledge.

Parkes, Graham. 1994. *Composing the Soul: Reaches of Nietzsche's Psychology*. Chicago: University of Chicago Press.

Pauer-Studer, Herlinde. 2009. "Humean Sources of Normativity." In *Hume on Motivation and Virtue*, ed. Charles R. Pigden, 186–207. Basingstoke: Palgrave Macmillan.

Peters, Julia, ed. 2013. *Aristotelian Ethics in Contemporary Perspective*. New York: Routledge.

Picoult, Jodi. 2004. *My Sister's Keeper*. Crows Nest, NSW: Allen & Unwin.

Pigden, Charles R., ed. 2010. *Hume on Motivation and Virtue*. Basingstoke: Palgrave Macmillan.

Pigden, Charles R. 2010. "If Not Non-Cognitivism, Then What?" In *Hume on Motivation and Virtue*, ed. Charles R. Pigden, 80–104. Basingstoke: Palgrave Macmillan.

Pinker, Steven. 1997. *How the Mind Works*. London: Penguin.

Pinker, Steven. 2002. *The Blank Slate*. Harmondsworth: Penguin Allen Lane.

Prejean, Sister Helen. 1993. *Dead Man Walking*. New York: Vintage Books.

Price, Huw. 2004. "Naturalism Without Representationalism." In *Naturalism in Question*, ed. Mario De Caro and David MacArthur, 71–88. Cambridge, MA: Harvard University Press.

Putnam, Hilary. 1992. *Renewing Philosophy*. Cambridge, MA: Harvard University Press.

Quine, W.V.O. 1981. "On the Nature of Moral Values." In *Theories and Things*, 55–66. Cambridge, MA: Harvard University Press.

Radcliffe, Elizabeth S. 2000. *On Hume*. Belmont, CA: Wadsworth.

Radcliffe, Elizabeth S. 2001. "How Does the Humean Sense of Duty Motivate?" In *Hume: Moral and Political Philosophy*, ed. Rachel Cohon, 383–387. Aldershot: Ashgate Dartmouth.

Radcliffe, Elizabeth S. 2008. *A Companion to Hume*. Oxford: Blackwell.

Raichle, Marcus E. 2010. "The Brain's Dark Energy." *Scientific American* 302.3: 44–49.

Railton, Peter. 1996. "Subjective and Objective." In *Truth in Ethics*, ed. Brad Hooker, 51–68. Oxford: Blackwell.

Rand, Ayn. 1964. "The Objectivist Ethics." In *The Virtue of Selfishness: A New Concept of Egoism*. New York: Signet/Penguin.

Rand, Ayn. 1975. "Philosophy and Sense of Life." In *The Romantic Manifesto: A Philosophy of Literature*, revised edn, 25–33. New York: Signet.

Regan, Tom and Peter Singer. 1976. *Animal Rights and Human Obligations*. Englewood Cliffs, NJ: Prentice Hall.

Reginster, Bernard. 1995. "*Ressentiment*, Evaluation and Integrity." *International Studies in Philosophy* 27: 117–124.

Reginster, Bernard. 2006. *The Affirmation of Life: Nietzsche on Overcoming Nihilism.* Cambridge, MA: Harvard University Press.

Reginster, Bernard. 2007. "The Will to Power and the Ethics of Creativity." In *Nietzsche and Morality*, ed. Brian Leiter and Neil Sinhababu, 32–56. Oxford: Clarendon Press.

Richardson, John. 1996. *Nietzsche's System.* Oxford: Oxford University Press.

Richardson, John. 2001. "Nietzsche's Power Ontology." In *Nietzsche*, ed. John Richardson and Brian Leiter, 150–185. Oxford: Oxford University Press.

Richardson, John and Brian Leiter, eds. 2001. *Nietzsche.* Oxford: Oxford University Press.

Ricoeur, Paul. 1981. *Hermeneutics and the Human Sciences*, ed. and trans. John B. Thomson. Cambridge: Cambridge University Press.

Riggs, Wayne. 2010. "Open-Mindedness." In *Virtue and Vice, Moral and Epistemic*, ed. Heather Battaly, 173–188. Oxford: Wiley-Blackwell.

Russell, Daniel C. 2009. *Practical Intelligence and the Virtues.* Oxford: Clarendon Press.

Russell, Daniel C., ed. 2013. *The Cambridge Companion to Virtue Ethics.* Cambridge: Cambridge University Press.

Russell, Paul. 2008. *The Riddle of Hume's Treatise: Skepticism, Naturalism, and Irreligion.* Oxford: Oxford University Press.

Sartre, Jean-Paul. 1992. *Being and Nothingness*, trans. Hazel E. Barnes. New York: Washington Square Press.

Sayre-McCord, Geoffrey. 1995. "Hume and the Bauhaus Theory of Ethics." *Midwest Studies in Philosophy* 20: 280–298.

Schacht, Richard, ed. 1994. *Nietzsche, Genealogy, Morality: Essays on Nietzsche's Genealogy of Morals.* Berkeley: University of California Press.

Schacht, Richard. 1995. *Making Sense of Nietzsche: Reflections on Timely and Untimely Meditations.* Urbana: University of Illinois Press.

Schacht, Richard, ed. 2001. *Nietzsche's Postmoralism: Essays on Nietzsche's Prelude to Philosophy's Future.* Cambridge: Cambridge University Press.

Schmidtz, David. 2006. *Elements of Justice.* Cambridge: Cambridge University Press.

Shermer, Michael. 2014. "The Genesis of Justice." *Scientific American* 310.5: 65.

Singer, Peter. 1976. "All Animals Are Equal." In *Animal Rights and Human Obligations*, ed. Tom Regan and Peter Singer, 148–162. Englewood Cliffs, NJ: Prentice Hall.

Slote, Michael. 1983. *Goods and Virtues.* Oxford: Clarendon Press.

Slote, Michael. 1983. "Dependent Goods and Dependent Virtues." In *Goods and Virtues.* Oxford: Clarendon Press.

Slote, Michael. 1983. "Relative Virtues." In *Goods and Virtues.* Oxford: Clarendon Press.

Slote, Michael. 1993. "Virtue Ethics and Democratic Values." *Journal of Social Philosophy* 24: 5–37.

Slote, Michael. 1995. "Agent-Based Virtue Ethics." *Midwest Studies in Philosophy* 20: 83–101.

Slote, Michael. 2001. *Morals From Motives.* Oxford: Oxford University Press.

Slote, Michael. 2010. *Moral Sentimentalism.* Oxford: Oxford University Press.

Slote, Michael. 2011. *The Impossibility of Perfection: Aristotle, Feminism, and the Complexities of Ethics.* Oxford: Oxford University Press.

Small, Robin. 2005. *Nietzsche and Ree: A Star Friendship.* Oxford: Clarendon Press.

Smith, Nicholas H., ed. 2002. *Reading McDowell: On Mind and World.* London: Routledge.

Smith, Tara. 2006. *Ayn Rand's Normative Ethics: The Virtuous Egoist.* Cambridge: Cambridge University Press.

Snow, Nancy, ed. Forthcoming. *Cultivating Virtue: Multiple Perspectives.* Oxford: Oxford University Press.

Solomon, Robert C., ed. 1974. *Existentialism.* New York: Random House.

Solomon, Robert C. 1997. "Corporate Roles, Personal Virtues: An Aristotelian Approach to Business Ethics." In *Virtue Ethics: A Critical Reader*, ed. Daniel Statman, 205–226. Edinburgh: Edinburgh University Press.

Solomon, Robert C. 2003. *Living With Nietzsche: What the Great "Immoralist" Has to Teach Us*. Oxford: Oxford University Press.

Statman, Daniel, ed. 1997. *Virtue Ethics: A Critical Reader*. Edinburgh: Edinburgh University Press.

Stocker, Michael. 1976. "The Schizophrenia of Modern Ethical Theories." *Journal of Philosophy* 73: 453–466.

Stocker, Michael. 1981. "Values and Purposes: The Limits of Teleology and the Ends of Friendship." *Journal of Philosophy* 78: 747–765.

Stocker, Michael. 2003. "How Emotions Reveal Value and Help Cure the Schizophrenia of Modern Ethical Theories." In *How Should One Live? Essays on the Virtues*, ed. Roger Crisp, 173–190. Oxford: Oxford University Press.

Stroud, Barry. 1977. *Hume*. London: Routledge and Kegan Paul.

Stroud, Barry. 2004. "The Charm of Naturalism." In *Naturalism in Question*, ed. Mario De Caro and David MacArthur, 21–35. Cambridge, MA: Harvard University Press.

Swanton, Christine. 2000. "Compassion as a Virtue in Hume." In *Feminist Interpretations of Hume*, ed. Anne Jaap Jacobson, 156–173. University Park: Pennsylvania State University Press.

Swanton, Christine. 2003. *Virtue Ethics: A Pluralistic View*. Oxford: Oxford University Press.

Swanton, Christine. 2009. "Virtue Ethics and the Problem of Demandingness." In *The Problem of Moral Demandingness*, ed. Timothy Chappell, 104–122. London: Palgrave Macmillan.

Swanton, Christine. 2010. "A Challenge to Intellectual Virtue from Moral Virtue: The Case of Universal Love." In *Virtue and Vice, Moral and Epistemic*, ed. Heather Battaly, 153–171. Oxford: Wiley-Blackwell.

Swanton, Christine. 2011. "Nietzsche and the Virtues of Mature Egoism." In *Nietzsche's On the Genealogy of Morality: A Critical Guide*, ed. Simon May, 285–308. Cambridge: Cambridge University Press.

Swanton, Christine. 2011. "Virtue Ethics." In *The Continuum Companion to Ethics*, ed. Christian Miller, 190–214. London: Continuum.

Swanton, Christine. 2012. "Robert Solomon's Aristotelian Nietzsche." In *Passion, Death, and Spirituality: The Philosophy of Robert C. Solomon*, ed. Kathleen Higgins and David Sherman, 113–126. Dordrecht: Springer.

Swanton, Christine. 2013. "The Definition of Virtue Ethics." In *The Cambridge Companion to Virtue Ethics*, ed. Daniel C. Russell, 315–338. Cambridge: Cambridge University Press.

Swanton, Christine. 2013. "A New Metaphysics for Virtue Ethics: Heidegger Meets Hume." In *Aristotelian Ethics in Contemporary Perspective*, ed. Julia Peters, 177–194. New York: Routledge.

Swanton, Christine. 2014. "The Notion of the Moral: The Relation between Virtue Ethics and Virtue Epistemology." *Philosophical Studies* 171(1): 121–134.

Swanton, Christine. 2015. "Cultivating Virtue: Two Problems for Virtue Ethics." In *Cultivating Virtue: Perspectives from Philosophy, Theology, and Philosophy*, ed. Nancy Snow, 111–134. Oxford: Oxford University Press.

Swanton, Christine. Forthcoming. "Virtues of Creativity and Productivity, Moral Theory, and Human Nature." In *Ayn Rand Society Philosophical Studies*, vol. 3, ed. James Lennox and Greg Salmieri. Pittsburgh, PA: University of Pittsburgh Press.

Swanton, Christine. Forthcoming. "Virtues of Productivity versus Technicist Rationality." In *Economics and the Virtues*, ed. Mark D. White and Jennifer A. Baker. Oxford: Oxford University Press.

Szalavitz, Maia and Bruce D. Perry. 2010. *Born for Love: Why Empathy is Essential – and Endangered*. New York: Harper Collins.

Tanner, Michael. 1994. *Nietzsche*. Oxford: Oxford University Press.

Tate, Margaret Watkins. 2005. "Obligation, Justice, and the Will in Hume's Moral Philosophy." *Hume Studies* 31(1): 93–122.

Taylor, Jacqueline. 2005. "Virtue and the Evaluation of Character." In *The Blackwell Guide to Hume's Treatise*, ed. Saul Traiger, 276–295. Oxford: Blackwell.

Taylor, Jacqueline. 2008. "Hume on Beauty and Virtue." In *A Companion to Hume*, ed. Elizabeth S. Radcliffe, 273–292. Oxford: Blackwell.

Tersman, Folke. 1998. "Quine on Ethics." *Theoria* 64: 84–98.

Tessman, Lisa. 2005. *Burdened Virtue: Virtue Ethics for Liberatory Struggles*. Oxford: Oxford University Press.

Tevenar, Gudrun von, ed. 2007. *Nietzsche and Ethics*. Bern: Peter Lang.

Thompson, Ross A. 2009. "Early Foundations: Conscience and the Development of Moral Character." In *Personality, Identity, and Character: Explorations in Moral Psychology*, ed. Darcia Narvaez and Daniel K. Lapsley, 159–184. Cambridge: Cambridge University Press.

Tiberius, Valerie. 2002. "Perspective: A Prudential Virtue." *American Philosophical Quarterly* 39: 305–324.

Traiger, Saul, ed. 2005. *The Blackwell Guide to Hume's Treatise*. Oxford: Blackwell.

Tudor, Steven. 2001. *Compassion and Remorse*. Leuven: Peeters.

van Hooft, Stan, ed. 2014. *The Handbook of Virtue Ethics*. Durham: Acumen.

Vitz, Rico. 2002. "Hume and the Limits of Benevolence." *Hume Studies* 28(2): 271–295.

Welchman, Jennifer. 2008. "Hume and the Prince of Thieves." *Hume Studies* 34: 3–19.

White, Richard J. 1997. *Nietzsche and the Problem of Sovereignty*. Urbana: University of Illinois Press.

Wiggins, David. 1987. "A Sensible Subjectivism?" In *Needs, Values, Truth: Essays in the Philosophy of Value*, 185–214. Oxford: Blackwell.

Wollheim, Richard. 1971. *Freud*. London: Fontana.

Young, Julian. 2003. *The Death of God and the Meaning of Life*. London: Routledge.

Young, Julian. 2006. *Nietzsche's Philosophy of Religion*. Cambridge: Cambridge University Press.

Zagzebski, Linda Trinkaus. 2004. *Divine Motivation Theory*. Cambridge: Cambridge University Press.

Zagzebski, Linda Trinkaus. 2006. "The Admirable Life and the Desirable Life." In *Values and Virtues: Aristotelianism in Contemporary Ethics*, ed. Timothy Chappell, 53–66. Oxford: Oxford University Press.

Index

The Virtue Ethics of Hume and Nietzsche, First Edition. Christine Swanton.
© 2015 John Wiley & Sons, Ltd. Published 2015 by John Wiley & Sons, Ltd.

gentleness, 169, 174
Gerhardt, Sue, 191
Golomb, Jacob, 13
good, human, 14, 20, 60, 112, 130–131, 136, 157, 171–2, 185, 195–8, 201–3
grace, xvi, 81, 86 n, 139, 167–9, 188, 190
gratitude, 92, 97–8, 142, 174, 182
grief, xv, xvii, 27, 35, 92, 96–7, 99
guilt, 144–5, 162–4

Hales, Steven D., 7
Hampton, Jean, 129
hardness, 114, 169, 196, 199–200, 205
harshness, 131, 144, 168–9
happiness *see* good, human
Harcourt, Edward, 199
Harlow, Harry F., 186–7
Harrison, Jonathan, 48
haste, xii, 135, 140
health, 23, 26, 28, 31, 103, 113–14, 120, 123–4, 126–7, 129–31, 133 n, 135, 139, 142–4, 146–7, 150–152, 154 n, 155 n, 158, 161, 163, 170, 173–5, 204–5, 207–8
hedonism, xiv, xvi–xvii, 13–14, 60, 107 n, 120, 136–7 *see also* pleasure
Heidegger, Martin, 38 n, 40 n, 100, 136, 138, 189
Higgins, Kathleen, ix
Hill, Thomas E., Jr., 20
homosexuality, 89–90, 107 n
honesty, xii, xv, 70, 72, 74, 79, 114, 147, 201–2 *see also* truthfulness
honor, 21, 25, 73–4, 76, 78, 112, 115–16, 127, 136, 158
hope, xvi, 13, 27, 87–9, 91, 103, 107 n, 118, 137, 163
Horney, Karen, 125, 128, 140, 149–52, 155 n
humility, 21, 48–9, 99, 104–6, 148, 160–161 *see also* epistemic humility
Hursthouse, Rosalind, 40 n, 59, 89
Hutcheson, Francis, xi, 23

identification, proximate, downward, upward, 187–8, 190, 192
imagination, 10, 62–4, 84, 90–91, 95–6, 108 n, 184–5, 188, 191
impartiality *see* partiality
impressions, 13, 31, 49, 62–3, 65 n, 67 n, 68 n, 79, 82, 93–4, 184
independence, 114, 165, 185
indolence, 60 *see also* laziness

industriousness, 23, 56, 60, 65, 173–4
intemperance, xiv
internalism (judgment), 30
intimacy, 91–2, 96–7, 99, 182–3, 185, 187–91
irresponsibility, 138, 178 n *see also* responsibility

Jacobson, Anne, ix
Janaway, Christopher, 11, 16
Johnson, Mark, 188
Johnson, Robert N., 182
joy, 101–3, 125–6
justice, xv–xvi, 25, 50–51, 55, 59–60, 70–86, 97–8, 104, 163–9

Kant, Immanuel, xii–xiii, 3, 7, 20, 98, 116, 123–4, 165
Kemp Smith, Norman, 13
Kierkegaard, Søren, 136–7
kindness, 52, 188–9, 190, 199
Knobe, Joshua, 160
Korsgaard, Christine, 20, 22, 104

laziness, xvi–xvii, 100, 118, 130–131, 140, 204–5
Leibniz, Gottfried Wilhelm, 14
Leiter, Brian, 9, 11, 16, 18 n, 34, 142, 144, 172
liberality, 158
Locke, John, 31
Loeb, Paul S., 163
logos, 12, 24–5, 33, 38 n
loneliness, 118, 139–40, 165, 174, 178 n
love, xi, 28, 36–7, 48–56, 64, 66 n, 80, 82–5, 87–9, 91–9, 101, 103–6, 107–8 n, 117–18, 123–6, 139, 151–2, 181—192 *see also* self love
    general, 182–92, 194 n
    Platonic problem, 94

MacIntyre, Alasdair, 26
magnificence, 102, 158, 164
malice, 65, 125, 146, 185, 189
map, interpretive, 3–5
Maslow, Abraham, 118
maturity, xv, 74, 112, 114–16, 127–9, 141–4 *see also* egoism, immature
May, Simon, 163, 197
McDowell, John, 8–9, 12, 23–5, 29, 31–4, 36, 38 n, 40 n
McIntyre, Jane, 48–9, 94
mediocrity, 116, 131, 137, 161, 167, 173, 203
megalopsychia (great-souledness), 158